The Best
AMERICAN
ESSAYS
College Edition

GUEST EDITORS OF

The Best American Essays

The Best
AMERICAN
ESSAYS
College Edition
Sixth Edition

Edited and with an Introduction
by ROBERT ATWAN

WADSWORTH
CENGAGE Learning

Australia • Brazil • Japan • Korea • Mexico • Singapore • Spain • United Kingdom • United States

WADSWORTH
CENGAGE Learning™

The Best American Essays College Edition, Sixth Edition
Robert Atwan

Senior Publisher: Lyn Uhl

Acquisitions Editor: Kate Derrick

Senior Assistant Editor: Kelli Strieby

Editorial Assistant: Jake Zucker

Media Editor: Amy Gibbons

Marketing Manager: Jenn Zourdos

Marketing Coordinator: Ryan Ahern

Marketing Communications Manager: Stacey Purviance

Content Project Manager: Georgia Young

Art Director: Jill Ort

Print Buyer: Marcia Locke

Permissions Editor: Katie Huha

Production Service: MPS Limited, A Macmillan Company

Photo Manager: Mandy Grozko

Cover Designer: Wing Ngan

Cover Image: Angelo Cavalli/Getty Images

Compositor: MPS Limited, A Macmillan Company

For product information and technology assistance, contact us **at Cengage Learning Customer & Sales Support, 1-800-354-9706**

For permission to use material from this text or product, submit all requests online at **cengage.com/permissions** Further permissions questions can be emailed to **permissionrequest@cengage.com**

Library of Congress Control Number: 2009936697

ISBN-13: 978-1-4390-8387-1

ISBN-10: 1-4390-8387-8

Wadsworth
20 Channel Center Street
Boston, MA 02210
USA

Cengage Learning is a leading provider of customized learning solutions with office locations around the globe, including Singapore, the United Kingdom, Australia, Mexico, Brazil, and Japan. Locate your local office at: **international.cengage.com/region**

Cengage Learning products are represented in Canada by Nelson Education, Ltd.

For your course and learning solutions, visit **www.cengage.com.**

Purchase any of our products at your local college store or at our preferred online store **www.ichapters.com.**

Printed in the United States of America
1 2 3 4 5 6 7 13 12 11 10 09

Contents

Annotated Table of Contents

"Did education mean moving from one class to the next? My grandmothers told me again and again that one could scale a mountain with a good education. But could I still talk to them, to my parents, my siblings? I would try to live in two worlds—at the very least. That was now my task."

"What terrified me that late summer day was the sudden greenness of the trees, the way their beauty insinuated itself into my vision—peripherally at first, vaguely, and without my consent. I blinked to stop what felt like tears, which I hadn't tasted for so long I'd forgotten that they were made of salt, that they were something my body was producing on its own, long after I thought I had shut down. O.K., I said to the steering wheel, the padded dashboard, the pines. If I can think of five reasons not to die, I won't."

"The tools in my workbench are a double inheritance, for each hammer and level and saw is wrapped in a cloud of knowing."

"That first day, sitting on the green lawn, watching a girl do a cartwheel and another girl mount the parallel bars, I developed an irrational fear that is still hard to explain: I became hyperaware of my own body, the swoosh of my blood and the paddling of my heart and the huh huh huhs of my breath, and it seemed amazing and tenuous to me that my body did all of this without any effort on my part."

"Like the storm-harried Crusoe, I found myself after her death mucking through strange, flickering, opposite states of mind where, at more than a few moments, a seemingly parallel grand confusion of terror and calm, desolation and thin hope, bereftness and bounty all commingled."

"Language is the tool of my trade. And I use them all—all the Englishes I grew up with."

"Years from this evening, I won't actually be sure that this boy sitting beside me is named Ben. But that doesn't matter tonight. What I know for certain right now is that I love him, and I need to tell him this fact before we turn to our separate houses, next door to each other. We are both five."

2.THE ATTENTIVE MIND: OBSERVATION, REFLECTION, INSIGHT • 152

"Nothing on earth is more gladdening than knowing we must roll up our sleeves and move back the boundaries of the humanly possible once more."

"Every creature on earth has approximately two billion heartbeats to spend in a lifetime. You can spend them slowly, like a tortoise, and live to be two hundred years old, or you can spend them fast, like a humming-bird, and live to be two years old."

"You took a sentence, threw it against the wall, picked up the pieces, and put them together again, slotting each word into its pigeonhole. When you got it right, you made order and sense out of what we used all the time and took for granted: sentences."

"'What are you *doing*?' The question pursues me still. When I go fishing and catch no fish, the idea that it's fun simply to be out on the river consoles me for not one second. I must catch fish; and if I do, I must then catch more and bigger fish."

"I took myself off to the Minneapolis Institute of Arts and plunked myself down in front of a Bonnard. I wrote the painting. Described it. I went home and looked at a teacup on my table—I wrote that too. Still life descriptions that ran on for several pages. I wrote and wrote, describing my way through art galleries and the inadvertent still lives of my house and my memory, my grandmother's garden, her Sunday dinners."

"I am not a total idiot. I always had the sense to say no wedding cake, no officiant, no first dance, no here comes the bride, no Times announcement, and absolutely no white dress. Who are we kidding? And why? We just wanted a big, awesome party where everyone could meet and go bananas."

"I waited until I held his eye. I assured him I would not tell anyone else how to get there. He looked at me with stoical despair, like a man who had been robbed twice, whose belief in human beings was offered without conviction."

"Thread holds together and restricts, while yarn stretches and gives. Thread is the overall theme that gives meaning to our words and thoughts—to lose the thread is to be incoherent or inattentive. A yarn is a long, pointless, but usually amusing story whose facts have been exaggerated. It is infinitely more relaxing to listen to a yarn than to a lecture whose thread we must follow."

"As a woman and as a writer, I have long wondered at the wellsprings of female masochism. Or what, in despair of a more subtle, less reductive phrase, we can call the congeries of predilections toward self-hurt, self-erasure, self-repudiation in women."

"It was the business of dealing with dead things, coupled with the questionable enterprise of making dead things look like live things.

In spite of its scientific value, it was usually regarded as almost a black art, a wholly owned subsidiary of witchcraft and voodoo."

"The man's eyes wandered around the parlor, and through them I saw what he did: a dirty room full of junk. It had never been anything more than that, but for some reason—the heat, maybe, or the couple's heavy, almost contagious sense of despair—every gouge and smudge jumped violently into focus. More depressing still was the thought that I belonged here, that I fit in."

"The road to Fidel Castro's Palace of the Revolution leads through a memory lane of old American automobiles chugging along at about twenty-five miles an hour—springless, pre-embargo Ford coupes and Plymouth sedans, DeSotos and LaSalles, Nashes and Studebakers, and various vehicular collages created out of Cadillac grilles and Oldsmobile axles and Buick fenders patched with pieces of oil-drum metal and powered by engines interlinked with kitchen utensils and pre-Batista lawn mowers and other gadgets that have elevated the craft of tinkering in Cuba to the status of high art."

3. THE PUBLIC SPHERE: ADVOCACY, ARGUMENT, CONTROVERSY • 288

"Justice Oliver Wendell Holmes's classic example of unprotected speech—falsely shouting 'Fire!' in a crowded theater—has been invoked so often, by so many people, in such diverse contexts, that it has become part of our national folk language."

"In October of 1998 I finally gave in and signed up for e-mail. I had resisted for a long time. My husband and I were proud of our retrograde status. Not only did we lack a modem, but we didn't have a car, a microwave, a Cuisinart, an electric can opener, a cellular phone, a CD player, or cable television."

"The tormenters are my fellow countrymen and -women. They look like people on the street, and from all reports they are ordinary citizens. But the prisoners, in their fear, anguish, and humiliation, are more immediately recognizable as human beings—even with digitally blanked-out faces."

"Animal-rights publications are illustrated largely with photographs of two kinds of animals—'Helpless Fluff' and 'Agonized Fluff,' the two conditions in which some people seem to prefer their animals, because any other version of an animal is too complicated for propaganda."

"Historians of weaponry tell us that one effect of the gun was to change the ideal of courage on the battlefield from a willingness to engage in hand-to-hand combat to an ability to stand firm under fire. At this point in our history, I'll take any form of courage I can get, but had Congress the smallest measure of the gunner's kind, the Patriot Act might still be a doodle on Dick Cheney's cocktail napkin."

"When my teacher had pinned this map up on the blackboard, she said, 'This is England'—and she said it with authority, seriousness, and adoration, and we all sat up. It was as if she had said, 'This is Jerusalem, the place you will go to when you die but only if you have been good.'"

"We've grown so used to this pervasive orange haze that the original glory of an unlit night—dark enough for the planet Venus to throw shadows on Earth—is wholly beyond our experience, beyond memory almost. And yet above the city's pale ceiling lies the rest of the universe, utterly undiminished by the light we waste—a bright shoal of stars and planets and galaxies, shining in seemingly infinite darkness."

"Americans feel a deep urge to live in houses that are bigger than they can afford. This desire cuts so cleanly through the population that it touches just about everyone. It's the acceptable lust."

"His voice was plaintive but resigned. 'Why should I live this life? I can't walk, my wife don't speak to me, I can't do nothing. What's the point?' He fixed his mournful gaze upon me. '*You* tell *me*'"

"I would suggest that it is not only permissible for those who care about animals to eat meat; they have a duty to do so. If meat eating should ever become confined to those who do not care about animal suffering, then compassionate farming would cease."

"In the world as it is now, I can see no escape from the conclusion that each one of us with wealth surplus to his or her essential needs should be giving most of it to help people suffering from poverty so dire as to be life-threatening. That's right: I'm saying that you shouldn't buy that new car, take that cruise, redecorate the house, or get that pricy new suit. After all, a thousand-dollar suit could save five children's lives."

"The defense of living nature is a universal value. It doesn't rise from, nor does it promote, any religious or ideological dogma. Rather, it serves without discrimination the interests of all humanity. Pastor, we need your help. The Creation—living nature—is in deep trouble."

Preface

What Is *The Best American Essays* Series?

Back in the 1970s Edward Hoagland wondered why no one had compiled an annual collection of the year's best essays, especially since comparable short story volumes had been around for decades. I agreed with Hoagland, and after a few false starts (I thought at first of calling the series "The E. B. White Awards" and later "The Emerson Awards"), I founded *The Best American Essays* as a companion volume to *The Best American Short Stories.* The first volume was published in 1986. Since then, the series has grown in popularity; each year more and more readers seem drawn to the vitality and versatility of the contemporary American essay.

For readers unfamiliar with the series, a brief introduction may be useful. As the series editor, I screen hundreds of essays from an enormous variety of general, specialized, and literary magazines. I then turn over roughly one hundred of these to a guest editor, a prominent American writer, who makes the final selection of approximately twenty essays. To qualify for selection, the essays must be works of high literary quality intended as fully developed, independent essays on subjects of general interest, originally written in English for first appearance in an American periodical during a calendar year. In general, selections for the book are included on the basis of literary achievement: they must be admirably written and demonstrate an awareness of craft as well as a forcefulness of thought. Since each guest editor, of course, possesses a different idea about what comprises a fine essay, each book also represents a unique literary sensibility. This variety of literary taste and opinion (which can be sampled in the prologue, "Essayists on the Essay") keeps the series healthy and diverse.

The College Edition

This version of *The Best American Essays* is designed for college students and classroom use. Essays have long been a staple of writing courses, so why not a collection of the "best" contemporary essays for today's students? I believe that many writing instructors wish to expose their students to high-quality, socially relevant, and intellectually challenging prose. With this end in mind, I selected particular essays from *The Best American Essays* series that I thought would work best for writing instructors and their students. Among the considerations for selection were length, topicality, diverse perspectives, and rhetorical and thematic variety.

Since the majority of essays we encounter today tend to fall into three general, though fairly distinct, categories—personal, informative, and argumentative—I arranged the selections accordingly. The book reflects the types of writing most often taught in introductory and even advanced composition courses. Instructors will find a generous number of selections to use if they want to teach excellent writing within the context of personal narratives, expository patterns, and persuasive strategies. In addition, I included within these three categories selections that also reflect many of the topics and issues that currently enliven discussion and debate: multiculturalism, race and gender, sexual and identity politics, popular culture, and media studies.

I've also drawn from the various "Forewords" I contribute to the annual volumes to develop an introduction to the literary and compositional features of the contemporary American essay. And, though space would not permit the inclusion of all the guest-editor introductions, I orchestrated incisive excerpts into a prologue that should stimulate critical discussion of the genre and lead to writing assignments.

In addition, to help orient student readers, the volume contains an informative "lead-in" to each essay and a brief biographical note. "Reflections and Responses," a set of questions designed to assist class discussion or to instigate ideas for papers, follows each selection. The questions range from a consideration of compositional details to broader reflections on theme and issue. Instructors who wish to delve deeper into the literary and rhetorical features of the essays should appreciate the thorough instructor's manual that readily can be found online.

For instructors who prefer to teach essays along different lines, the manual now includes three alternative arrangements: (a) a rhetorical table of contents that rearranges the essays into ten traditional modes or patterns; (b) a table of contents that focuses on salient literary and journalistic features; and (c) a thematic and topical organization that places the essays in a context of current issues.

Given its arrangement, flexibility, and emphasis on recently published essays, the college edition of *The Best American Essays* is suitable for various writing courses. It can be used in mainstream freshman composition programs with a focus on personal, expository, and argumentative essays. Instructors who want to concentrate on the contemporary essay, creative nonfiction techniques, or the essay as a literary genre will also find the collection and its instructional apparatus extremely suitable.

New to the Sixth Edition

For this sixth college edition, I updated the *Prologue: Essayists on the Essay*, a unique feature that has proved to be popular with instructors who enjoy the wide range of bite-sized comments on the art and craft of the genre from many of the nation's premier essayists. I also revised over a third of the book; of the thirty-six selections, thirteen are new. All of these new selections are drawn from the most recent volumes of *The Best American Essays*. My choices were partially guided by several useful reviews from writing instructors who shared with me some of their classroom experiences with particular selections. For their many useful suggestions for this revision I would like to thank

Andrea DeFusco, *Boston College*
Elizabeth Hutton, *University of Michigan*
Sharon Pomerantz, *University of Michigan*

I have revised the final chapter on public controversy to expand the range and variety of issues. The chapter now features a dozen different topics to invite class discussion and essay responses: free speech, technology, torture, animal rights, gun control, colonialism, the environment, the economy, medical ethics, food values, global poverty, and Creationism.

The Instructor's Resource Manual has been extensively revised. It now will include an interactive online component, offering instructors a forum in which to share lesson plans, discuss approaches to each essay, and find and distribute relevant background material. Each essay in the book will have its own page of supplementary and complementary materials.

No collection, of course, can entirely please everyone. I have listened carefully to reviewers and have relied on my own classroom and writing workshop experiences in choosing contemporary essays that—in their variety of subject, style, and structure—would best serve as an introduction to the genre. I ought to add that I based my choices on the essays themselves, considering mainly their relevance to writing courses, not the reputations of their authors. You will certainly find many well-known essayists in the collection; but you will also discover several unfamiliar writers, some of whom have rarely been anthologized. A large part of my purpose in editing *The Best American Essays* series is to introduce to the reading public young and emerging writers.

I am always interested in comments and suggestions, especially regarding the book's classroom utility, and invite responses from teachers and students. Please address responses to Robert Atwan/ Series Editor/The Best American Essays/P.O. Box 220/Readville, MA 02137.

Although anthologies such as this one may appear simple to construct, they actually involve the professional efforts of many people. I appreciate the enthusiasm for the project and the help I've received from the Cengage Learning staff: I especially appreciate the advice and support I received from my editors, Kate Derrick, Kelli Strieby, and Jake Zucker. I would also like to thank Georgia Young, who handled production; and permissions editor Katie Huha. I'm especially indebted to my son Gregory for his indispensable support and advice.

R. A.

Encountering the Essay

What Are Essays?

Like poems, plays, novels, and short stories, essays resist simple definition or classification. There are so many types of essays that any attempt to come up with a single, authoritative description of *the* essay is likely to be overly general or critically useless. A well-known handbook of literary terms, for example, doesn't even attempt to define the form: "A moderately brief prose discussion of a restricted topic," the entry begins. But it then goes on to say: "Because of the wide application of the term, no satisfactory definition can be arrived at; nor can a wholly acceptable 'classification' of essay types be made." So much writing today goes under the name of essay—celebrity profiles, interviews, political commentary, reviews, reportage, scientific papers, scholarly articles, snippets of humor, and newspaper columns—that it's virtually impossible for readers to obtain any clear and consistent impression of the form.

Though many illustrious examples of "brief prose discussion" can be found in classical Greek and Latin literature, the modern essay had its origins in the European Renaissance. At a time when writers and artists throughout Europe were exploring ways to express their personalities more freely in painting and literature, a French magistrate, Michel de Montaigne, retired to his Bordeaux estate in 1570 and began experimenting with a new kind of prose. Impatient with formal philosophy and academic disquisition, he soon found a way to create a more flexible and personal discourse.

Realizing that his efforts fit no conventional category—they could not be termed letters, or memoirs, or treatises—he simply referred to them by the French word *essais,* meaning *attempts, trials,* or *experiments.* By adopting a casual, everyday word to describe his endeavors, Montaigne called attention to the informal character of this new literary genre. His essays were personal, tentative, highly digressive, and wholly unsystematic in their approach to a topic.

Montaigne's brand of essay became for many later writers *the* genuine essay. For William Hazlitt, Virginia Woolf, and E. B. White, this was the only type of essay that could be considered a literary form. It went under different names; sometimes it was called the periodical, informal, or familiar essay. This was to differentiate it from types of prose discourse composed in a more systematic and formal fashion, writing that conformed to objective rather than subjective standards. Some examples of the formal essay are philosophical and ethical arguments, historical and scientific papers, dissertations, and critical articles. Today the informal essay is best represented by the personal essay, whereas the most popular type of formal essay is the magazine article. Although writers and editors may use the terms interchangeably, many periodicals routinely distinguish between essay and article in their tables of contents, a distinction that usually boils down to personal memoir or reflection as opposed to reportage, interviews, or feature stories.

Essays and Articles

If it's impossible to produce an airtight definition of an essay, it's equally impossible to define an article. Like "essay," this all-purpose literary label has a long, complex history. The word goes back to the Latin term for a joint (*artus*) connecting two parts of a body, and its literal use was eventually extended to include the components of writing and discourse. By the eighteenth century, "article" was used regularly for literary compositions that treated a specific topic. The first to use the term in its modern journalistic sense was one of English literature's foremost essayists, Joseph Addison.

Articles require not just a topic, but a timely topic. Unlike essays, articles are usually (a) about something specific and (b) about something of *current* interest. Essays, on the other hand, can take large liberties with subject, theme, organization, and point of view. Essayists tend to be personal, reflective, leisurely; article writers (they used to be called "articlers") usually stay close to the facts, rarely stray from "the point," and seldom interrupt the flow of information with personal opinion or reflection. The essayist will feel comfortable writing about various general topics—friendship, envy, manners, nature. The article writer is often looking for an angle, or "hook," that will directly relate the article to some current event or fashionable trend.

For example: assign the topic of "revenge" to two authors—one who prefers to write personal or familiar essays and one who specializes in journalistic articles or feature stories. Chances are the essayist will take a first-person, reflective look at the nature of revenge, blending together personal experience and literary references. The journalist will most likely conduct several interviews with psychologists and then skillfully choreograph these into an informative piece on how to deal constructively with vengeful emotions. These are, of course, extremes, but they suggest the divergent routes of the essay and article in today's literature. In general, the personal, reflective essay is often found in the literary quarterlies and periodicals; articles, like the example above, are the mainstay of popular magazines.

With a few exceptions, our major magazines print relatively few personal essays. Editors believe that their readers want news and information, not personal reminiscence or leisurely reflection. As a result, the weekly and monthly magazines depend on hard news stories, interviews, profiles, and "service articles" that offer readers practical advice on everything from child rearing to the latest diet. Few of these pieces could be called "literary"; most of them fall rapidly out of date and are not likely to be read even a few months after their appearance. If the personal essayist faces the challenge of making his or her experiences and reflections interesting and relevant, the article writer faces a different challenge: how to handle current issues and topics in such a way that people will still read the work with pleasure long after those issues and topics have vanished from public discussion.

Yet, as the selections in this volume show, most good prose is not easy to pigeonhole. At either end of the spectrum, it's fairly easy to distinguish a literary essay from a journalistic article. But as we move toward the center of the spectrum, the distinctions become less clear. We begin to find a compositional mix: personal essays that depend on research and reporting, topical articles that feature a personal voice and individual viewpoint. Such literary mixtures have become increasingly prevalent in today's magazines and literary periodicals. Note, for example, the selection by Gay Talese, the writer who was one of the founders of a literary movement known as "The New Journalism." This movement attracted many prominent authors (Joan Didion, Truman Capote, Norman Mailer, among others) who wanted to incorporate a variety of literary techniques—many borrowed from novels and essays—into the conventionally "objective" magazine article. In Talese's talented hands, the ordinary celebrity profile becomes infused with mood, atmosphere, and conflict as personalities develop within a narrative that bristles with dramatic tension. Many readers coming across "Ali in Havana" (see page 265) in *Esquire* magazine would naturally consider Talese's profile of the world's most famous athlete an article; yet a close reading will demonstrate not only Talese's meticulous skills as a journalist but also his mastery of dramatic irony and literary form. Readers will want to note, too, how Annie Dillard (see page 153) elevates a "profile" of a famous stunt pilot into an essay of astonishing lyric power. In a number of the essays collected here, the writers move between the topical requirements of an article and the literary demands of an essay, adroitly balancing fact and observation with the nuances of voice and style, irony and wit.

Essays and Fiction

What ultimately makes a piece of prose an essay is usually found in the personal quality of its writing. Many of the essays in this book are not only written in the first-person singular, but they are also *about* the first-person singular. As Montaigne proved long ago, the essay is the perfect literary vehicle for both self-disclosure and self-discovery: "The wisdom of my lesson," he wrote, "is wholly in truth, in freedom, in reality." Writers today use the essay to explore their personal relationships, their individual identities, and their ethnic or racial heritages. Personal essays like Judith Ortiz Cofer's "Silent Dancing" (see page 57) and Scott Russell Sanders's "The Inheritance of Tools" (see page 110) are intimate, candid, revealing, close to the pulse of everyday human experience.

Yet *personal* can be a tricky term. Its roots reach back to the Latin *persona,* the literal term for "mask." The word was traditionally used for a theatrical character, a *dramatis persona.* Thus, oddly enough, the word we use to convey intimacy and sincerity—we often approvingly speak of someone's *personal* touch—has hidden overtones of disguise and performance. Readers may overlook this double sense of the term, but personal essayists rarely do. They know that the first-person singular is not a simple equivalent of the self, a mere matter of slapping down the word "I" in front of every sentence. They know that the single letter "I" is one of the English language's most complex words.

Who is the "I" of the essay—a real person or a *dramatis persona?* Did Scott Russell Sanders really bang his thumb with a hammer just before learning of his father's death? Did Rebecca McLanahan actually come across the intriguing marginal comments in used books that she writes about (see "Book Marks," p. 93)? Or have these essayists contrived incidents and fabricated moods in the interests of creating a story or endorsing a position? Unless we personally know the writers, how can we verify their accounts?

When the essay is philosophical or argumentative, we can decide whether we accept an essayist's opinions or not on the basis of logic, evidence, proof, or internal consistency. For example, we would base our agreement or disagreement with George Gessert (see "An Orgy of Power," p. 308) entirely on information that has nothing to do with the author's personal life. But once essayists begin to tell stories—about sampling dog food or playing with their children—they move dangerously close to fiction, especially when they add characters, dialogue, episodes, and climaxes. When constructing personal narratives, the essayist confronts the toughest challenge of the craft: telling stories that are at once artful, true, and *believable.* One of the essayist's most frustrating moments is when he or she relates a true story with the utmost candor and discovers that nobody believes it.

The personal essayist, then, must balance craft and credibility, aesthetics and accuracy. The first-person singular is both person and *persona,* a real person and a literary construct. The "I" is both reporting a story and simultaneously *shaping* one. If essayists hope to be wholly believable, however, they need to worry about too much shaping. A true story doesn't usually come prepackaged in a compellingly dramatic shape—many elements just don't fit in. To be believable, the essayist may narrate a story that doesn't— like much of life itself—possess a satisfying narrative closure. Sometimes what one expects to happen doesn't happen. "The writer in me," wrote the novelist Frank Conroy in 1988 "is tempted to create a scene here—to invent one for dramatic purposes—but of course I can't do that." His literary impulse as a novelist is to create a scene; his honesty as an essayist won't let him. In fact, the tension between personal essays and stories recurs throughout this collection and is especially apparent in such selections as Anwar F. Accawi's "The Telephone" (see p. 40) and Edwidge Danticat's "Westbury Court" (see p. 77).

Autobiography and Truth

The boundary lines between a memoir and a novel (or a personal essay and a short story) can often be confusing. Many memoirs are written in a first-person narrative, and so are many novels. Great novels like Mark Twain's *The Adventures of Huckleberry Finn,* F. Scott Fitzgerald's *The Great Gatsby,* or J. D. Salinger's *The Catcher in the Rye* sound very much like memoirs, especially in their opening sections, though they are entirely fictional. Today, many memoirs and personal essays borrow heavily from the novelist's toolbox and seem indistinguishable from fiction. Note how the poet Yusef Komunyakaa opens his autobiographical essay (see page 86):

> "I feel like I'm part of this damn thing," Frank said. He carried himself like a large man even though he was short. A dead cigarette dangled

from his half-grin. "I've worked on this machine for twenty-odd years, and now it's almost me."

Short story writers commonly open their stories with dialogue, often introducing a character abruptly and without establishing any situational context. This is precisely the way Komunyakaa decides to start an essay that recounts his experiences one summer when he took a job as a factory worker.

Contrast Komunyakaa's opening to the way Harper Lee begins her famous novel *To Kill a Mockingbird:*

> When he was nearly thirteen, my brother Jem got his arm badly broken at the elbow. When it healed, and Jem's fears of never being able to play football were assuaged, he was seldom self-conscious about his injury. His left arm was somewhat shorter than his right; when he stood or walked, the back of his hand was at right angles to his body, his thumb parallel to his thigh. He couldn't have cared less, so long as he could pass and punt.
>
> When enough years had gone by to enable us to look back on them, we sometimes discussed the events leading to his accident. . . .

Which opening passage sounds like it belongs in a work of fiction, and which sounds closer to a memoir? With only the two passages in front of them, most people, assuming that they weren't familiar with the original works, would say the first sounded fictional and the second truthful. And yet the opposite is the case.

If its prose style is no indication of whether a piece of writing is factual or fictional, then how can we tell the difference between an essay and a short story or between a memoir and a novel? As any cautious reader can see, it's nearly impossible to establish internal characteristics—such as voice, tone, or diction—that help us to easily distinguish one genre from the other. Therefore, if we are curious about the degree of fabrication, we usually need to rely on verifiable external factors—facts, actual events, people, places and institutions, dates, and so forth. Once the writer begins to disclose concrete or factual information, then other issues come quickly into play. The reader, if so inclined, can now use those details to test the writer's veracity or can begin inferential processes that can damage authorial credibility. Records can be discovered that prove someone didn't spend nearly as much time in the Peace Corps as claimed, or was never admitted to a certain psychiatric hospital, or hadn't served as much prison time as reported. According to many accounts, the publishing sensation of 2005, James Frey's *A Million Little Pieces*, was originally widely submitted (and widely rejected) as a *novel*. It was only when resubmitted as a *memoir* that publishers jumped.

Therefore, anyone writing a memoir (or an autobiographical essay) needs to be careful when recounting verifiable details or risks being called a liar, a phony, or an opportunist. The unverifiable world is vast and accommodating. The classic memoir, in which a celebrated individual offers an account of his or her public life and adventures, along with profiles of the important people encountered along the way, usually depended upon verifiable details—at least it is possible to confirm whether Benjamin Franklin ever met the famous Methodist preacher George Whitefield or lived for a time in London. But the modern memoir is different since it so often focuses on the private life of a not well-known or perhaps even an obscure person. Who's to say if the author ever really took a life-transforming midnight swim all alone in Buzzard's Bay when she was fifteen? And unless a description is biologically or physically implausible, who would bother to question it? Perhaps a question to ask of a memoir is something the American philosopher William James might have asked: If a report of something is wholly unverifiable, should we even concern ourselves with the issue of truth?

We have thousands of critical studies dealing with the art of fiction, but very little exists on the art of the memoir aside from a growing number of "how-to" books. One reason for this situation is that despite its present popularity, the memoir has not yet become a fully accredited genre in our universities. Most educated readers are still uncertain about how best to evaluate a memoir or an autobiographical essay. What makes one memoir or essay outstanding and another forgettable? Does it largely depend on the quality of the prose? Will the particulars of an author's life bias our aesthetic responses either positively or negatively? Why is the first question that readers ask of a memoir "Is it true?" Is it a critical error to apply modern journalistic fact-checking standards to memoirs and essays intended as works of literature? If a personal essay turns out to have some fictional elements and details, does that automatically turn it into a short story—or does it become something else: a fictive essay? a fable? an outright lie? Does using the term *creative nonfiction* solve anything?

In the eighteenth and nineteenth centuries, writers like Addison and Steele, Washington Irving, and Nathaniel Hawthorne could invent characters and situations for their nonfiction works (many of these were published in the newspapers of their day), and readers found their essays and sketches delightful. As you encounter the autobiographical essays in this volume, you might ask yourself to what extent your enjoyment and appreciation of a selection depends on whether you are convinced that the writer is telling the truth. When do you think it matters, and when do you think it doesn't?

The Autobiographical "I"

In college writing courses years ago, instructors referred to a syllogism that may help explain the enormous popularity of the personal memoir. It went something like this: "You write best when you write about what you know; what you know best is yourself; therefore, you write best when you write about yourself." As a syllogism, this seemed valid: The conclusion followed logically from its premises, no? So why didn't teachers always receive better essays when they assigned personal topics?

As anyone can see, the conclusion rests on dubious assumptions. The premises sound reasonable, but they raise some fundamental questions. Do people really write best about the subjects they know best? We see evidence all the time of experts being unable to communicate the basic concepts of their professions, which explains why so many technical books are authored by both an expert and a writer. Brilliant academics so committed to their vast research that they can't bear to part with any detail thus clog up their sentences with an excess of information. If a little knowledge is a dangerous thing, too much can sometimes be an impediment to clear and robust expression. Shakespeareans do not always write the best books on Shakespeare.

Can we also safely conclude that we know ourselves best of all? If so, then why do so many of us spend so much time in psychotherapy or counseling sessions? Surely, the pursuit of the self—especially the "hidden" self—has been a major industry. Self-knowledge, of course, confronts us with another logical problem: How can the self be at the same time the knower and the known? That's why biographies can be so much more revealing than autobiographies. As Dostoyevsky said in his *Notes from Underground:* "A true autobiography is almost an impossibility . . . man is bound to lie about himself."

Yet the illusion that we do know ourselves best must serve as both comfort and inspiration to the growing wave of memoirists who seem to write with one finger glued to the shift key and another to the letter *I*, which on the keyboard looks nothing like it does on the page, thus appropriately symbolizing the relationship between that single letter and the "self" it presumes to represent. Today's writer's market is flooded with autobiography—now more likely to be labeled "memoir" in the singular, as though the more fashionable literary label promises something grander. Memoirs (the term was almost always used in the plural) were customarily written by public figures who recorded their participation in historical events and their encounters with other prominent individuals. General Ulysses S. Grant's two-volume *Personal Memoirs* (1885–86) were bestsellers. The old memoirs were penned by well-established individuals in the twilight of their careers; the new memoir is frequently the work of an emerging writer aspiring to be well established.

The memoir is easily abused by those who believe the genre automatically confers upon the author some sort of importance. It's only natural, isn't it, to be the heroes or heroines of our own lives? And as the main protagonists, how can we resist the impulse to occupy center stage and not consider ourselves gifted with greater sensitivity, finer values, higher moral authority, and especially keener powers of recollection than any member of our supporting cast of characters? The most interesting autobiography ever conceived must be Mark Twain's. Partly written, partly dictated, never published in its entirety, and never according to his intentions—in many ways a colossal failure of a book—Twain's autobiography grappled with every psychological and compositional difficulty characteristic of the genre. Twain knew how easy it was to exhibit ourselves in "creditable attitudes exclusively" and tried to display himself as honestly as he could. It was a noble experiment, but it proved impossible: "I have been dictating this autobiography of mine," he wrote, "for three months; I have thought of fifteen hundred or two thousand incidents in my life which I am ashamed of but I have not gotten one of them to consent to go on paper yet."

To say that memoir, autobiography, and the personal essay are easily abused is not to disparage these vigorous genres. Democratizing the memoir has resulted in many wonderful books, not a few crafted by young or relatively young writers who have learned to ask themselves how to prevent their personal writing from deteriorating into narcissism and self-absorption. This is a question anyone setting out to write personally must face sooner or later. The solution requires a healthy regimen of self-skepticism and a respect for uncertainty. Though the first-person singular may abound, it should be a richly complex and mutable "I," never one that designates a reliably known, wholly static entity. In some of the best memoirs and personal essays, the writers are mysteries to themselves, and the work evolves into an enactment of surprise and self-discovery. These elements keep "life writing" *live* writing, as a mysterious "I" converses with an equally mysterious "I."

Writing the "Standard" Essay

Many students who enter their first-year writing courses already know how to manufacture the "perfect paper." For some reason, they know it should begin with an introductory paragraph that contains a thesis statement and often cites an expert named Webster. It then pursues its expository path through three paragraphs that develop the main idea until it finally reaches a concluding paragraph that industriously summarizes all three previous paragraphs. The conclusion often begins, "Thus we see that. . . ." If the paper tells a personal story, it might conclude, "Suddenly I realized. . . ." Epiphanies abound.

What is especially maddening about the typical five-paragraph paper has less to do with its tedious, predictable structure than with its implicit message that writing should be the end product of thought and not the enactment of its process. Many students seem unaware® that writing can be an act of discovery, an opportunity to say something they had never before thought of saying. The worst papers instructors receive are largely the products of premature conclusions, of unearned assurances, of minds irrevocably made up. As Robert Frost once put it, for many people thinking merely means voting. Why go through the trouble of writing papers on an issue when all that's required is an opinion poll? Do you agree? Disagree? It makes sense to call such productions "papers" (or "themes" or "assignments") since what is written has almost no connection with the true sense of "essaying"—trying out ideas and positions, writing while in a state of uncertainty, of not knowing.

The five-paragraph theme is also a charade. It not only parades in lock-step toward its conclusion; it begins with its conclusion. It is all about its conclusion. Its structure permits no change of direction, no reconsideration, no wrestling with ideas. It is—and has long been—the perfect vehicle for the sort of reader who solemnly likes to ask: "And your point is . . . ?"

The most talented essayists have aims other than merely getting a point across or a position announced or an identity established. It may help to imagine an essay as a sort of Cubist rendition of an idea: the essayist would rather you consider all sides and aspects of a thought or concept, much in the same multiperspectival fashion that Picasso or Braque portrayed an ordinary table on canvas. Some essayists—Montaigne again was the first—seem literally to be turning ideas over in their minds. The intellectual essay is nothing if not ruminative; the autobiographical essay may continually lose its sense of direction. Both kinds of essays, like Samuel Johnson's eighteenth-century fable, *Rasselas*, will often reach a "conclusion in which nothing is concluded."

Evaluating the "Standard" Essay

Can a computer evaluate an essay? This question has been on people's minds since Educational Testing Service recently unveiled e-rater®, its new computer program that will grade essay questions on the Graduate Management Admissions Test. As news of e-rater spread, newspaper reports appeared across the nation nervously wondering how essays can be machine scored. Objective tests, with their multiple choices, are one thing; but aren't sentences, paragraphs, and organization quite another?

The answer is that a computer can very easily score the results of essay questions, assuming that all anyone wanted to know was whether the writing conformed to standard English usage and reflected a few other elements of style, like syntactic variety, that can be measured conveniently and objectively. Computers have been able to do this for quite some time, and most word-processing applications currently provide a few (though still rudimentary) tools to check grammar and style. But can a computer detect humor and irony (which skilled readers themselves sometimes fail to catch)? Can it evaluate the use of imagery and metaphor, or discern the nuances of a writer's tone of voice? E-rater's developer honestly admitted to the *New York Times* that it cannot: "It's not designed to score Montaigne," she said. "It's designed for a specific purpose: to score the kinds of essays we see on standardized tests." Admittedly, these would be "standard" essays.

Are these what we talk about when we talk about essays? Montaigne's term for his eccentric and digressive meditations is now employed so broadly and indiscriminately that its traditional literary meaning is all but forgotten. An essay, it seems, is anything we want it to be. Our dailies, weeklies, and monthlies are chock full of nonfiction prose, but little of it is either creative or literary. Most of it is informative, functional, or advisory, and that's as it should be. Produced with built-in obsolescence, such writing is made for the month (at best) and not for the years. E-rater may do fine evaluating standardized expression, but it is educationally unfortunate that its name and use will continue to confuse people about the true literary nature of essays.

Essays Can Be a Risky Business

"Where there's a will there's a way," an excited William Hazlitt says to himself as he hurries down Chancery Lane "about half-past six o'clock, on Monday the 10th of December, to enquire at Jack Randall's where the fight the next day was to be." The year is 1821, the city is London, and Hazlitt is pursuing his way to an out-of-town boxing match, his first fight ever. He's eager to see big Bill Neate, the raging Bristol "Bull," take on the "Gas-Man," Tom Hickman, the bravest and cruelest fighter in all of England. "I was determined to see this fight, come what would, and see it I did, in great style."

You can consult all the handbooks on literary fiction for all the elements of style, structure, and composition, but you'll rarely find mention of what Hazlitt just noted—*determination*. Yet its literary value is inestimable.

This collection is filled with determination. You can see the fight in great style. You can narrate it with equally great style. But as Hazlitt reminds us, you first have to get there. No sitting in your study with a boxing encyclopedia, no telephone interviews with experts, no electronic highway; and the travel involved takes you beyond your local library.

Such narratives can be a risky business. For one thing, the destinations are often uncertain. When Jamaica Kincaid decides to see England for the first time, or when Barry Lopez strays far from the beaten track in search of an ancient stone horse, or even when Ian Frazier journeys around his Ohio and Montana neighborhoods, they have no idea what surprising emotions or events they will encounter. But there's an additional risk. After writing "The Fight," Hazlitt was surprised to find that people considered his eyewitness report a "vulgar thing." This wasn't simply because his story took readers into an unfamiliar subculture, but because it took them into unfamiliar prose territory as well. In other words, Hazlitt risked the unliterary; he was determined to find a way to develop an essay out of "unsuitable" material. We can find a similar determination throughout this volume: Look at how such writers as Marcia Aldrich, Rebecca McClanahan, Lauren Slater, and Ryan Van Meter creatively confront ordinary, unpromising, uncomfortable, or even intractable subjects. Where there's a will, there's a way.

Risk and determination—at both a personal and creative level—will often transform a piece of nonfiction prose into a memorable literary work. Our finest essayists seek out challenges, go for the toughest questions on the board. The challenges may spring from the demands of the assignment or of the composition—or both.

These essayists resist the plodding memoir, the facile discovery of identity, the predictable opinion, or the unearned assertion. What many of the essays collected here have in common is their determination to take on the tough assignment, to raise the difficulty level of the game.

The Contemporary American Essay: A Diversity of Forms and Voices

The personal essay has long existed in a literary twilight zone. Because it presumes to tell a true story yet often employs fictional or poetic techniques, it stands awkwardly with one foot in and one foot out of "imaginative" literature. It was partially for this reason that one of America's foremost essayists, E. B. White, complained in 1977 that the essayist "unlike the novelist, the poet, and the playwright, must be content in his self-imposed role of second-class citizen." Writers who have their eyes on a Nobel Prize or "other earthly triumphs," White continued, "had best write a novel, a poem, or a play." White was responding not only to the critical reception of his own work but also to a general decline in the literary quality of the American essay. Essays struck a lot of readers as "old-fashioned." When readers thought of essays, they thought of writing that was stiff, stuffy, textbookish—things teachers forced them to read and write in school.

A century ago, however, the essay occupied a prominent position in American literature. It fell into the class of writing that critics called "polite letters." The essayists, mostly men, addressed the literate world in an urbane, congenial, comfortable manner. These gentlemen, it seemed, always possessed three names—James Russell Lowell, Oliver Wendell Holmes, Thomas Wentworth Higginson—and more often than not lived in New England. In this era, when "coming out" referred only to a young woman's debut, the typical essay was proper, genteel, and Anglophilic. Although it atrophied during the 1930s, the polite essay retained for many years an insidious power over American students, who were often forced to imitate its polished civility in that shadow genre known as the "freshman theme." The goal of English

teachers, Kurt Vonnegut recalls, was to get you "to write like culti-
vated Englishmen of a century or more ago."

Essays began to seem old-fashioned to the American reader
mainly because they were too slow in coming to terms with
twentieth-century modernism. While William Faulkner, T. S. Eliot,
and Eugene O'Neill were radically transforming fiction, poetry,
and drama, the essay retained much of its relaxed, genteel manner.
Adventurous writers considered the essay a holdover from Victorian
times. With few exceptions, the essay broke no new ground, violated no literary conventions. Instead of standing as modern works
of literature in themselves, essays simply tried to explain those
works. For the academic community as well as for many general
readers, the essay gradually grew synonymous with literary criticism.
Essays were written *about* literature, not *as* literature.

Since E. B. White issued his complaint, the literary status of the
essay has been steadily improving. As Annie Dillard says, the essay
"has joined the modern world." Essays are now written in the same
imaginative spirit as fiction and poetry. Contemporary essays can
rival the best fiction and poetry in artistic accomplishment. Far
from being hesitant about literary aims and methods, today's
essayists delight in the use of imagery, symbol, and metaphor, often
interweaving them into such complex mosaic patterns as those we
find in Kyoko Mori's "Yarn" and Joyce Carol Oates's "They All Just
Went Away." Boundary lines—between life and art, prose and
poetry, truth and fiction, the world and self—are often blurred as
essayists take greater liberties with language and form. This is now
true even of essays grounded in information and explanation.

Nor can the essay be characterized any longer by its homogene-
ity. In fact, its diversity may now be its most noticeable feature. In
light of the essay's transformation, today's poetry and fiction
appear stagnant: The essay may be our most exciting literary form.
We see narrative essays that are indistinguishable from short
stories, mosaic essays that read like prose poems. We find literary
criticism with an autobiographical spin, journalism sensitively
attuned to drama and metaphor, reflection with a heavy dose of
information. Some essayists write polemic that sounds like poetry.
Physicists, mathematicians, and philosophers are finding that complex ideas and a memorable prose style are not irreconcilable.

Even law review articles have taken a literary turn. Today's essays are incredibly difficult to categorize and pin down.

This volume collects and celebrates the contemporary American essay. Never before—except perhaps in the days of Ralph Waldo Emerson and Henry David Thoreau—have so many fine young American writers begun to explore the essay's literary possibilities. They come to the form with a renewed enthusiasm for its astonishing flexibility and versatility—the essay can incorporate an enormously wide range of subjects and styles. The personal essay has grown increasingly candid, more intimate, less polite. Essayists seem willing to take greater emotional risks. Essayists today seem less relaxed and more eager to confront urgent social questions. Journalism has contributed to this sense of risk and urgency, encouraging essayists to fuse within a single style both personal experience and public issues, dual themes that Barry Lopez brilliantly combines in "The Stone Horse."

The Essay and Public Events

As Stephen Jay Gould was making selections for the 2002 volume of *The Best American Essays,* he observed how everything seemed "shaped by 9/11," regardless of whether it was written before or after. Later, I realized how every few years some pivotal event dominates the national attention and dramatically narrows the literary scope of this series. In 1995 it seemed that half the essays published in magazines dealt either directly or tangentially with the O. J. Simpson trial. The nation couldn't stop talking about it, and many distinguished writers weighed in with insightful and sometimes brilliant commentary. In a similar occurrence toward the end of 2000, the American political process was put on hold during the most bizarre presidential election in our history. Yet coverage of these events—as influential and absorbing as they still are—did not necessarily find their way into the volumes featuring the best essays of those years.

But the terrorist attacks of 9/11 and their aftermath were altogether another story. The written response was overwhelming, and not merely because of the immediate and massive news coverage. One could expect the coverage, commentary, and reportage;

unexpected was their astonishingly high quality. Anticipating that thoughtful essays would require months of reflection and deliberation, the "literature of 9/11" was surely several years away. But essays of high literary quality began appearing within weeks of the incident.

In fact, we should have expected the abundance of fine 9/11 essays. The essay always seems to be revitalized in times of war and conflict—and usually with the return of peace and prosperity, fiction and poetry regain their literary stature. The First World War resulted in an eruption of essays and introduced the work of some of our finest nonfiction writers, many of whom, like Randolph Bourne, took up the pacifist cause. But then the postwar years saw the flourishing of some of our most celebrated poets and novelists, those members of the "lost generation." This was true, too, in the Second World War (E. B. White published his greatest essay collection in 1942) and especially true during Vietnam. It seems to me no coincidence that the Vietnam years saw the emergence of the New Journalism, an exciting and innovative brand of nonfiction pioneered (as mentioned earlier) by Gay Talese, a writer included in this volume.

This theory about essays in time of war is not easily proven, but the idea also appears in Czeslaw Milosz's brilliant long poem, A *Treatise on Poetry*, which appeared shortly before the 9/11 carnage. Though he promotes the value of poetry in difficult times, Milosz, who won the Nobel Prize in 1980, prefaces *Treatise* with the recognition that in our time, "serious combat, where life is at stake, is fought in prose." Perhaps in times of conflict and crisis, people want to be in the presence of less mediated voices; we need more debate and directives; we desire more public discourse. We instinctively turn to writing that displays a greater sense of immediacy and urgency. "These are the times that try men's souls," Tom Paine memorably wrote in 1776, in what would be the first essay of *The American Crisis*. At that moment in history, radicalism and nationalism could go hand in hand.

The Essay's Future

The year 1995 marked the 400th anniversary of the first complete edition of Montaigne's essays. As we progress into the twenty-first century, it will be natural to speculate on how the essay will change. Will essays be shaped in new, surprising ways by the digital revolution? Will cyberspace breed new essayists and new kinds of essays? Will original, literary prose works begin appearing in underground sites without benefit of agents, editors, publishers, and prestige periodicals? Will young, struggling writers find a quicker and less stressful way to break into print? As voice and video become increasingly common, will a new age of graphic/audio texts and devices such as the enormously popular Kindle dramatically alter the reading habits of a future generation? In 2020, as one commentator wondered, will book publishers as a trade be as obsolete as blacksmiths?

There's no reason to oppose technology; the digital revolution is here to stay, and one can amply enjoy its products and conveniences. A younger generation may be more comfortable reading electronic books, but if they are reading something worth reading, they will more than likely—to borrow the title of critic Ruben Brower's seminal essay—do their "reading in slow motion." Though retrieving and downloading *Walden* or *Portrait of a Lady* can be done in the blink of an eye, savoring the prose, word by word, sentence by sentence, will always take time. One danger, of course, is that as people become more accustomed to instantaneous acquisition of texts, they may simultaneously grow so impatient with the time-consuming process of reading them that reading itself will become as obsolete as Sunday family strolls down Main Street.

The issue really isn't the future of books but of reading, and since people were reading long before the paginated book was developed some five hundred years ago, chances are good that they'll be reading long after it has been radically transformed. It is hardly a coincidence that the essay was invented not long after the bound book, for we owe to the physical feature of books the personal essay's idiosyncratic and circuitous manner. Montaigne equipped his home office with one of the earliest book-lined studies, where he loved to spend his time *browsing*. His mind too mercurial to concentrate wholeheartedly on any one volume, he would "leaf through now one book now another, without order and without plan, by disconnected fragments." An idea took hold; he began to write just the way he read. His medium became his message, and the personal essay was born.

For those who enjoy leisurely reading, the essay remains the ideal form, as the selections in this volume amply demonstrate. A ruminative, unhurried style has long been part of the essay's tradition. Early in the twentieth century, literary critics were predicting that the slow-paced "old-fashioned essay" would soon disappear. It was, as William Dean Howells observed in 1902, being driven out by newsworthy articles with no interest in the "lounging gait," and the "wilding nature" that characterized what Howells called the "right" essay. His concerns about a readership so corrupted and depraved, so bereft of a lyrical sense that they preferred articles to essays, were echoed through every decade of the twentieth century. Yet somehow "right" or true essays still manage to be written, published, and admired. This volume—with its many sinuous selections that wind through time and memory, that blur the distinctions between past and present, that take us intimately into the multilayered processes of thought—attests to that fact.

Robert Atwan

Essayists on the Essay

Each edition of The Best American Essays *features a guest editor who makes the final selections and writes an introduction to the volume. The guest editors themselves are distinguished American writers, many of whom have excelled in various literary forms. In their introductions, they almost always address the question of the essay: its history, definition, style, audience, composition. Their essays on the essay would in themselves make an interesting collection. What follows are some of their most incisive remarks.*

What Is an Essay?

What *is* an essay, and what, if anything, is it about? "Formal" and "informal," "personal," "familiar," "review-essay," "article-essay," "critical essay," essays literary, biographical, polemic, and historical—the standard lit-crit lexicon and similar attempts at genre definition and subclassification in the end simply tell you how like an eel this essay creature is. It wriggles between narcissism and detachment, opinion and fact, the private party and the public meeting, omphalos and brain, analysis and polemics, confession and reportage, persuasion and provocation. All you can safely say is that it's not poetry and it's not fiction.

—Justin Kaplan

Resisting Definitions

AN ESSAY! The fixed form or the fixed category of any kind, any definition at all, fills me with such despair that I feel compelled to do or be its opposite. And if I cannot do its opposite, if I can in fact complete the task that is the fixed form, or fill the fixed category, I then deny it, I then decline to participate at all. Is this a complex view? But I believe I have stated it simply: anything that I might do, anything that I might be, I cannot bear to be enclosed by, I cannot bear to have its meaning applied to me.

The Essay: and this is not a form of literary expression unfamiliar to me. I can remember being introduced to it. It was the opinions and observations of people I did not know, and their opinions and observations bore no relationship to my life as I lived it then. But even now, especially now, I do not find anything peculiar or wrong about this; after all, the opinions and observations of people you do not know are the most interesting, and even the most important, for your own opinions and observations can only, ultimately, fix you, categorize you—the very thing that leads me to dissent or denial.

—Jamaica Kincaid

The Ideal Essay

In reading an essay, I want to feel that I'm communing with a real person, and a person who cares about what he or she's writing about. The words sound sentimental and trite, but the qualities are rare. For me, the ideal essay is not an assignment, to be dispatched efficiently and intelligently, but an exploration, a questioning, an introspection. I want to see a piece of the essayist. I want to see a mind at work, imagining, spinning, struggling to understand. If the essayist has all the answers, then he isn't struggling to grasp, and I won't either. When you care about something, you continually grapple with it, because it is alive in you. It thrashes and moves, like all living things.

When I'm reading a good essay, I feel that I'm going on a journey. The essayist is searching for something and taking me along. That something could be a particular idea, an unraveling of identity, a meaning in the wallow of observations and facts. The facts are important but never enough. An essay, for me, must go past the facts, an essay must travel and move. Even the facts of the essayist's own history, the personal memoir, are insufficient alone. The facts of personal history provide anchor, but the essayist then swings in a wide arc on his anchor line, testing and pulling hard.

—Alan Lightman

The Essay as Object

If kids still write essays in school the way people my age used to, they meet the essay first as pure object. In school, it is (or was) a written paper of a certain length, on an assigned subject, with specified margins and neatness, due on the teacher's desk at a certain date. From about fourth grade on, I wrote many essays. "An essay a week" was a philosophy lots of grammar school teachers subscribed to back then. Recently I came across an essay of mine I'd saved from the fifth grade. It's called "If I Had Three Wishes." My first wish, as I described it, was for lots of fishing equipment, my second was for a canoe in which to go fishing, and my third was for a cabin in the woods somewhere near good fishing. I have more or less gotten those wishes, writing occasional essays about fishing all the while. Even in its present state as childhood artifact, "If I Had Three Wishes" retains its purposeful object-ness: the three-ring-binder paper with regular lines and space at the top for student's name, teacher's name, and date; the slow, newly learned script, in blue ballpoint, almost without mistakes; and the circled good grade in the teacher's hand.

—Ian Frazier

The Essay as Action

Beneath the object, the physical piece of writing with its unpredictable content, is the action that produced it. The action, it seems to me, is easier to predict. The difference is like that between a golf ball in the air and the swing of the golfer that propelled it; the flight of a struck ball varies, but the swing tends always to be the same. An essay is a golf swing, an angler's cast, a tennis serve. For example, say, an experience happens to you, one that seems to have literary potential. You wait for it to grow in your mind into a short story or even just an episode of "Friends," but somehow it doesn't. Then a further experience, or an odd chance, or something a friend says, or something in the newspaper chimes with the first experience, and suddenly you understand you can write about it, and you do. You quit longing for form and write what's there, with whatever serviceable prose comes to hand, for no better reason than the fun and release of saying. That sequence—that combination of patience with sudden impatience, that eventual yielding to the simple desire to tell—identifies the essay.

—Ian Frazier

Essays and the Real World

The essay can do everything a poem can do, and everything a short story can do—everything but fake it. The elements in any nonfiction should be true not only artistically—the connections must hold at base and must be veracious, for that is the convention and the covenant between the nonfiction writer and his reader. Veracity isn't much of a drawback to the writer; there's a lot of truth out there to work with. And veracity isn't much of a drawback to the reader. The real world arguably exerts a greater fascination on people than any fictional one; many people, at least, spend their whole lives there, apparently by choice. The essayist does what we do with our lives; the essayist thinks about actual things. He can make sense of them analytically or artistically. In either case he renders the real world coherent and meaningful, even if only bits of it, and even if that coherence and meaning reside only inside small texts.

—Annie Dillard

The Essay's Subjectivity

As near as I can figure, an essay can be . . . a query, a reminiscence, a persuasive tract, an exploration; it can look inward or outward; it can crack a lot of jokes. What it need not be is objective. An essay can certainly present facts and advocate a position, but that seems quite different from objectivity, whereby a writer just delivers information, adding nothing in the process. Instead, essays take their tone and momentum from the explicit presence of the writer in them and the distinctiveness of each writer's perspective. That makes essays definitely subjective—not in the skewed, unfair sense of subjectivity, but in the sense that essays are conversations, and they should have all the nuances and attitude that any conversation has. I'm sure that's why newspapers so rarely generate great essays: even in the essay-allowed zone of a newspaper, the heavy breath of Objective Newspaper Reporting is always blowing down the writer's neck. And certainly there is no prescribed tone that is "correct" for essays. Sometimes it seems that they have a sameness of manner, a kind of earnest, hand-wringing solemnity. Is this necessary? I don't think so. Many of the essays (2005) that intrigued me this year were funny, or unusually structured, or tonally adventurous—in other words, not typical in sound or shape. What mattered was that they conveyed the writer's journey, and did it intelligently, gracefully, honestly, and with whatever voice or shape fit best.

—Susan Orlean

No Standard Essay

As there is no standard human type who writes essays, so is there no standard essay: no set style, length, or subject. But what does unite almost all successful essays, no matter how divergent the subject, is that a strong personal presence is felt behind them. This is so even if the essayist never comes out to tell you his view of the matter being discussed, never attempts directly to assert his personality, never even slips into the first-person singular. Without that strong personal presence, the essay doesn't quite exist; it becomes an article, a piece, or some other indefinable verbal construction. Even when the subject seems a distant and impersonal one, the self of the writer is in good part what the essay is about.

—Joseph Epstein

The Essay's Diversity

It is not only that the essay *could* be about anything. It usually was. The good health of essay writing depends on writers continuing to address eccentric subjects. In contrast to poetry and fiction, the nature of the essay is diversity—diversity of level, subject, tone, diction. Essays on being old and falling in love and the nature of poetry are still being written. And there are also essays on Rita Hayworth's zipper and Mickey Mouse's ears.

—Susan Sontag

The Memorable Essay

I am predisposed to the essay with knowledge to impart—but, unlike journalism, which exists primarily to present facts, the essays transcend their data, or transmute it into personal meaning. The memorable essay, unlike the article, is not place- or time-bound; it survives the occasion of its original composition. Indeed, in the most brilliant essays, language is not merely the medium of communication; it *is* communication.

—Joyce Carol Oates

The Author's Gumption

Given the confusion of genre minglings and overlaps, what finally distinguishes an essay from an article may just be the author's gumption, the extent to which personal voice, vision, and style are the prime movers and shapers, even though the authorial "I" may be only a remote energy, nowhere visible but everywhere present. ("We commonly do not remember," Thoreau wrote in the opening paragraphs of *Walden*, "that it is, after all, always the first person that is speaking.")

—Justin Kaplan

Essays and the Imagination

An essay is a thing of the imagination. If there is information in an essay, it is by-the-by, and if there is an opinion in it, you need not trust it for the long run. A genuine essay has no educational, polemical, or sociopolitical use; it is the movement of a free mind at play. Though it is written in prose, it is closer in kind to poetry than to any other form. Like a poem, a genuine essay is made out of language and character and mood and temperament and pluck and chance.

—Cynthia Ozick

Essays Versus Articles

And if I speak of a genuine essay, it is because fakes abound. Here the old-fashioned term poetaster may apply, if only obliquely. As the poetaster is to the poet—a lesser aspirant—so the article is to the essay: a look-alike knockoff guaranteed not to wear well. An article is gossip. An essay is reflection and insight. An article has the temporary advantage of social heat—what's hot out there right now. An essay's heat is interior. An article is timely, topical, engaged in the issues and personalities of the moment; it is likely to be stale within the month. In five years it will have acquired the quaint aura of a rotary phone. An article is Siamese-twinned to its date of birth. An essay defies its date of birth, and ours too.

—Cynthia Ozick

Essays Versus Stories

In some ways the essay can deal in both events and ideas better than the short story can, because the essayist—unlike the poet—may introduce the plain, unadorned thought without the contrived entrances of long-winded characters who mouth discourses. This sort of awful device killed "the novel of idea." (But eschewing it served to limit fiction's materials a little further, and likely contributed to our being left with the short story of scant idea.) The essayist may reason; he may treat of historical, cultural, or natural events, as well as personal events, for their interest and meaning alone, without resort to fabricated dramatic occasions. So the essay's materials are larger than the story's.

—Annie Dillard

Essays Versus Poems

The essay may deal in metaphor better than the poem can, in some ways, because prose may expand what the lyric poem must compress. Instead of confining a metaphor to half a line, the essayist can devote to it a narrative, descriptive, or reflective couple of pages, and bring forth vividly its meanings. Prose welcomes all sorts of figurative language, of course, as well as alliteration, and even rhyme. The range of rhythms in prose is larger and grander than that of poetry. And it can handle discursive idea, and plain fact, as well as character and story.

—Annie Dillard

Essays Versus Blogs

And while the essay may be a living form for the moment, like all living things it may be ailing even as it thrives. With the decline of places where the essay once ran into coterie political journals, or group blogs, the place for the essay proper grows smaller. The blogger, newly born, might be, should be, an essayist manqué, but the first thing about the blog form is that its units are short. It has already taken its place as part of the history of the pamphlet, the polemic, the pointed epistle—but doesn't yet build up enough acceleration to make a left turn into something else. Blogs play a terrific role as makers of solidarity, community, and network—as builders of social capital. But though I am persuaded beyond argument that there must be an Emily Dickinson or an Agnes

Repplier of the Internet out there somewhere, blogging away for her life and ours, I haven't found her, at least not yet.

—Adam Gopnik

Why Essays Can Confuse People

I picked up my pen again and began to write, began to write directly, honestly, began to converse, showing, telling, pausing, contradicting, setting the frayed contents of my mind down on plain paper to be plainly seen by anyone who cared to look. That doesn't mean there isn't art and artifice involved in the writing of an essay. But it does mean that the art is in revealing the voice of the writer, as opposed to trying to transform it to suit the requirements of a fictional character or narrator. Essay writing is not about facts, although the essay may contain facts. Essay writing is about transcribing the often convoluted process of thought, leaving your own brand of breadcrumbs in the forest so that those who want to can find their way to your door.

Essays, therefore, confuse people. They occupy a quirky place in the general genre of nonfiction, a place many people seem not to understand. It has been my experience that people not acquainted with the literary essay expect it to behave like an article or a piece of journalism. Journalism is a broad category unto itself, but it is probably finally defined by its mission to report to readers clear facts that have been thoroughly investigated and digested by the journalist. One does not expect to read a piece of journalism filled with tentative reflections or outright contradictions. However, essays thrive on these, because contradiction, paradox, and questioning best reflect the moving, morphing human mind, which is what the essayist wants to capture.

—Lauren Slater

Essays Are Not Scientific Documents

An essay is not a scientific document. It can be serendipitous or domestic, satire or testimony, tongue-in-cheek or a wail of grief. Mulched perhaps in its own contradictions, it promises no sure objectivity, just the condiment of opinion on a base of observation, and sometimes such leaps of illogic or superlogic that they may work a bit like magic realism in a novel: namely, to simulate the mind's own processes in a murky and incongruous world. More than being instructive, as a magazine article is, an essay has a slant, a seasoned personality behind it that ought to weather well. Even if we think the author is telling us the earth is flat, we might want to listen to him elaborate upon the fringes of his premise because the bristle of his narrative and what he's seen intrigues us. He has a cutting edge, yet balance too. A given body of information is going to be eclipsed, but what lives in art is spirit, not factuality, and we respond to Montaigne's human touch despite four centuries of technological and social change.

—Edward Hoagland

The Essayist's Defensiveness

No poet has a problem saying, I am a poet. No fiction writer hesitates to say, I am writing a story. "Poem" and "story" are still relatively stable, easily identified literary forms or genres. The essay is not, in that sense, a genre. Rather, "essay" is just one name, the most sonorous name, bestowed on a wide range of writings. Writers and editors usually call them "pieces." This is not just modesty or American casualness. A certain defensiveness now surrounds the notion of the essay. And many of the best essayists today are quick to declare that their best work lies elsewhere: in writing that is more "creative" (fiction, poetry) or more exacting (scholarship, theory, philosophy).

—Susan Sontag

On Being an Essayist

As someone who takes some pride in being known as "Joseph Epstein, an essayist"—or, even better, "the essayist Joseph Epstein"—who takes the term "essayist" as an honorific, I have both an interest and a stake in the form. I hate to see it put down, defamed, spat upon, even mildly slighted. The best luck that any writer can have is to find his or her form, and I feel fortunate in having found mine some twenty years ago in the familiar essay. It happened quite by luck: I was not then a frequent reader of Montaigne and Hazlitt; in those days I was even put off by Charles Lamb, who sometimes seemed to me a bit precious. For me the novel was the form of forms, and easily the one I most admired and should most have liked to master. Although I have published a dozen or

so short stories, I have not yet written a novel—nor have I one in mind
to write—and so I have to conclude that despite my enormous regard
for that form, it just isn't mine. Perhaps it is quite useless for a writer to
search for his perfect form; that form, it may well be, has to find him.

—Joseph Epstein

Essayists Must Tell the Truth

I work by Hemingway's precept that a writer's root charge is to distinguish what you really felt in the moment from the false sentiment of what
you now believe you should have felt. The personal essay, autobiography,
has been a red flag to professional classifiers and epistemologists; a critical industry has flourished for the refinement of generic protocols (many
in French, with as much fine print as an installment purchase agreement), subcontracted principally to skeptics. In the judgment of Northrop
Frye, for instance, a piece of work is shelved with autobiography or with
fiction according to whether the librarian chooses to believe it.

Well. I've written one, and I've written the other, and I'm here to tes-
tify that the issue is at once weightier and simpler: a personal essayist
means to tell the truth. The contract between a personal essayist and a
reader is absolute, an agreement about intention. Because memory is
fallible, and point of view by its nature biased, the personal essayist will
tell a slant tale, willy-nilly. But not by design.

—Geoffrey Wolff

The Essayist's Voice

The influential essayist is someone with an acute sense of what has not
been (properly) talked about, what should be talked about (but differently). But what makes essays last is less their argument than the display
of a complex mind and a distinctive prose voice.

—Susan Sontag

Voice and Personality

Writing that has a voice is writing that has something like a personality.
But whose personality is it? As with most things in art, there is no straight
road from the product back to the person who made it. There are

writers read and loved for their humor who are not especially funny people, and writers read and loved for their eloquence who, in conversation, swallow their words or can't seem to finish a sentence. Wisdom on the page correlates with wisdom in the writer about as frequently as a high batting average correlates with a high IQ: they just seem to have very little to do with one another. Charming people can produce prose of sneering sententiousness, and cranky neurotics can, to their readers, seem to be inexhaustibly delightful. Personal drabness, through some obscure neural kink, can deliver verbal blooms. Readers who meet writers whose voice they have fallen in love with usually need to make a small adjustment in order to hang on to their infatuation.

—Louis Menand

The Demands of the First Person Singular

The thoroughgoing first person is a demanding mode. It asks for the literary equivalent of perfect pitch. Even good writers occasionally lose control of their tone and let a self-congratulatory quality slip in. Eager to explain that their heart is in the right place, they baldly state that they care deeply about matters with which they appear to be only marginally acquainted. Pretending to confess to their bad behavior, they revel in their colorfulness. Insistently describing their own biases, they make it all too obvious that they wish to appear uncommonly reliable. Obviously, the first person doesn't guarantee honesty. Just because they are committing words to paper does not mean that writers stop telling themselves the lies that they've invented for getting through the night. Not everyone has Montaigne's gift for candor. Certainly some people are less likely to write honestly about themselves than about anyone else on earth.

—Tracy Kidder

The "Who Cares?" Factor

Not every voice a great soliloquy makes, a truth at odds with the education of many an American writer, with the education of *this* American writer. I remember (see how difficult, even now, to break the habit of that pronoun, that solipsistic verb), at boarding school in England, writing about Cordelia in the moment when she recognizes how mistaken is her father's measurement of affection. I spent the greater part of my allotted space telling about a tangled misunderstanding between my dad and myself: "So I understand just how Cordelia felt." Of course my teacher wrote "who cares?" Of course he was right to write that: to filter all data through the mesh of personal relevance is the voice's tyrannical sway over listener and speaker alike. Sometimes it should be okay to take facts in, quietly manipulate them behind an opaque scrim, and display them as though the arranger never arranged. It should be all right to mediate, let another voice speak through your spirit medium, pretend as a writer not to be front and center on stage.

—Geoffrey Wolff

What "Confessional Writing" Must Do

I knew that "confessional writing" now enjoys quite a vogue, but I had no idea how pervasive the practice of personal storytelling has become among our finest writers. I can't help asking myself (although all lives are, by definition, interesting, for what else do we have?): why in heaven's name should I care about the travails of X or Y unless some clear generality about human life and nature emerges thereby? I'm glad that trout fishing defined someone's boyhood, and I'm sad that parental dementia now dominates someone's midlife, but what can we do in life but play the hand we have been dealt?

—Stephen Jay Gould

Why I Distrust Memoirs

. . . I first owe some account of why certain types of essays were maybe easier for me to exclude than others. I'll try to combine candor with maximum tact. Memoirs, for example. With a few big exceptions, I don't much care for abreactive or confessional memoirs. I'm not sure how to explain this. There is probably a sound, serious argument to be made about the popularity of confessional memoirs as a symptom of something especially sick and narcissistic/voyeuristic about U.S. culture right now. About certain deep connections between narcissism and voyeurism in the mediated psyche. But this isn't it. I think the real reason is that I just don't trust them. Memoirs/confessions, I mean. Not so much their factual truth as their agenda. The sense I get from a lot of contemporary memoirs is that they have an unconscious and unacknowledged project, which is to make the memoirists seem as endlessly fascinating and important to the reader as they are to themselves. I find most of them sad in a way that I don't think their authors intend.

—David Foster Wallace

How the Essayist Acquires Authority

Essays are how we speak to one another in print—caroming thoughts not merely in order to convey a certain packet of information, but with a special edge or bounce of personal character in a kind of public letter. As a writer you multiply yourself, gaining height as though jumping on a trampoline, if you can catch the gist of what other people have also been feeling and clarify it for them. Classic essay subjects, like the flux of friendship, "On Greed," "On Religion," "On Vanity," or solitude, lying, self-sacrifice, can be major-league yet not require Bertrand Russell to handle them. A layman who has diligently looked into something, walking in the mosses of regret after the death of a parent, for instance, may acquire an intangible authority, even without being memorably angry or funny or possessing a beguiling equanimity. *He* cares; therefore, if he has tinkered enough with his words, we do too.

—Edward Hoagland

The Conversational Style

While there is no firmly set, single style for the essayist, styles varying with each particular essayist, the best general description of essayistic style was written in 1827 by William Hazlitt in his essay "Familiar Style." "To write a genuine familiar or truly English style," Hazlitt wrote, "is to write as any one would speak in common conversation who had a thorough command and choice of words, who could discourse with ease, force, and perspicuity, setting aside all pedantic and oratorical flourishes." The style of the essayist is that of an extremely intelligent, highly commonsensical person talking, without stammer and with impressive coherence, to him- or herself and to anyone else who cares to eavesdrop. This self-reflexivity, this notion of talking to oneself, has always seemed to me to mark the essay off from the lecture. The lecturer is always teaching; so, too, frequently is the critic. If the essayist does so, it is usually only indirectly.

—Joseph Epstein

The Essay as Dialogue

Human storytelling was once all breath, the sacred act of telling family stories and tribal histories around a fire. Now a writer must attempt to breathe life into the words on a page, in the hope that the reader will discover something that resonates with his or her own experience. A genuine essay feels less like a monologue than a dialogue between writer and reader. *This is a story I need*, we conclude after reading the opening paragraph. *It will tell me something about the world that I didn't know before, something I sensed but could not articulate.*

An essay that is doing its job feels right. And resonance is the key. To be resonant, the dictionary informs us, is to be "strong and deep in tone, resounding." And to resound means to be filled to the depth with a sound that is sent back to its source. An essay that works is similar; it gives back to the reader a thought, a memory, an emotion made richer by the experience of another. Such an essay may confirm the reader's sense of things, or it may contradict it. But always, and in glorious, mysterious ways that the author cannot control, it begins to belong to the reader.

—Kathleen Norris

The Attractions of Autobiography

Contemporary critical theory lends authority to the autobiographical impulse. As every graduate student knows, only a fool would try to think or bear witness to events objectively anymore, and only an intellectual crook would claim to have done so. There's a line of reasoning that goes like this: writers ought to acknowledge that they are subjective filtering agents and let themselves appear on the page; or, in greater honesty, describe themselves in detail; or, most honest of all, make themselves their main subject matter, since one's own self is the only subject one can really know. Maybe widespread psychotherapy has made literary self-revelation popular. Certainly there are economic reasons. Editors and agents seem to think that the public's hunger for intimate true-life stories has grown large enough to include the private lives of literary figures as well as those of movie stars, mass murderers, and athletes. And the invitation to write about oneself has intrinsic attractions. The subject interests most writers. The research doesn't usually require travel or phone calls or hours in a library. The enterprise *looks* easy.

—Tracy Kidder

The Essayist's Audience

Essays are addressed to a public in which some degree of equity exists between the writer and the reader. Shared knowledge is a necessity, although the information need not be concrete. Perhaps it is more to be
thought of as a sharing of the experience of reading certain kinds of
texts, texts with omissions and elisions, leaps. The essayist does not stop
to identify the common ground; he will not write, "Picasso, the great
Spanish painter who lived long in France." On the other hand, essays are
about something, something we may not have had reason to study and
master, often matters about which we are quite ignorant. Elegance of pre-
sentation, reflection made interesting and significant, easily lead us to
engage our reading minds with Zulus, herbaceous borders in the English
garden, marriage records in eighteenth-century France, Japanese scrolls.

—Elizabeth Hardwick

Essays Start Out in Magazines

Essays end up in books, but they start their lives in magazines. (It's hard
to imagine a book of recent but previously unpublished essays.) The
perennial comes now mainly in the guise of the topical and, in the short
run, no literary form has as great and immediate an impact on contemporary readers. Many essays are discussed, debated, reacted to in a way
that poets and writers of fiction can only envy.

—Susan Sontag

The Importance of Being Edited

A few years ago, the author of an autobiographical essay I was planning to
publish in *The American Scholar*—a very fine writer—died suddenly. The
writer had no immediate relatives, so I asked his longtime editor at the
New Yorker if he would read the edited piece, hoping he might be able to
guess which of my minor changes the writer would have been likely to accept and which he would have disliked. Certainly, said the editor. Two
days later, he sent the piece back to me with comments on my edits and
some additional editing of his own. "My suggestions are all small sentence
tweaks," he wrote. "I could hear——'s voice in my head as I did them

and I'm pretty sure they would have met with his approval—most of them, anyway." Some examples: "A man who looked unmusical" became "a man so seemingly unmusical." "They made a swift escape to their different homes" became "They scattered swiftly to their various homes." "I felt that that solidity had been fostered by his profession" became "That solidity, I felt, had been fostered by his profession." These were, indeed, only small tweaks, but their precision filled me with awe. Of *course* you couldn't look unmusical. Of *course* it was awkward to use "escape" (singular) with "homes" (plural). Of *course* I should have caught "that that." I faxed the piece to my entire staff because editors rarely get a chance to see the work of other editors; we see only its results. This was like having a front-row seat at the Editing Olympics.

Five days later, the editor sent the piece back to us, covered with a second round of marginalia. "No doubt this is more than you bargained for," he wrote. "It's just that when the more noticeable imperfections have been taken care of, smaller ones come into view . . . I've even edited some of my own edits—e.g., on page 25, where I've changed 'dour,' which I inserted in the last go-round, to 'glowering.' This is because 'dour' is too much like 'pinched,' which I'm also suggesting."

If you're not a writer, this sort of compulsiveness may seem well nigh pathological. You may even be thinking, "What's the difference?" But if you *are* a writer, you'll realize what a gift the editor gave his old friend. Had not a word been changed, the essay would still have been excellent. Each of these "tweaks"—there were perhaps a hundred, none more earthshaking than the ones I've quoted—made it a little better, and their aggregate effect was to transform an excellent essay into a superb one.

—Anne Fadiman

On Certain Magazine Interviews

I myself have been interviewed by writers carrying recorders, and as I sit answering their questions, I see them half-listening, nodding pleasantly, and relaxing in the knowledge that the little wheels are rolling. But what they are getting from me (and I assume from other people they talk to) is not the insight that comes from deep probing and perceptive analysis and old-fashioned legwork; it is rather the first-draft drift of my mind, a once-over-lightly dialogue that—while perhaps symptomatic of a society permeated by fast-food computerized bottom-line impersonalized workmanship—too frequently reduces the once-artful craft of magazine writing to the level of talk radio on paper.

—Gay Talese

Listening to People Think

Quoting people verbatim, to be sure, has rarely blended well with my narrative style of writing or with my wish to observe and describe people actively engaged in ordinary but revealing situations rather than to confine them to a room and present them in the passive posture of a monologist. Since my earliest days in journalism, I was far less interested in the exact words that came out of people's mouths than in the essence of their meaning. More important than what people say is what they think, even though the latter may initially be difficult for them to articulate and may require much pondering and reworking within the interviewee's mind—which is what I gently try to prod and stimulate as I query, interrelate, and identify with my subjects as I personally accompany them whenever possible, be it on their errands, their appointments, their aimless peregrinations before dinner or after work. Wherever it is, I try physically to be there in my role as a curious confidant, a trustworthy fellow traveler searching into their interior, seeking to discover, clarify, and finally to describe in words (my words) what they personify and how they think.

—Gay Talese

On the Subjects of Essays

Those with the least gift are most anxious to receive a commission. It seems to them that there lies waiting a topic, a new book, a performance, and that this is known as material. The true prose writer knows there is nothing given, no idea, no text or play seen last evening until an assault has taken place, the forced domination that we call "putting it in your own words." Talking about, thinking about a project bears little relation to the composition; enthusiasm boils down with distressing speed to a paragraph, often one of mischievous banality. To proceed from musing to writing is to feel a robbery has taken place. And certainly there has been a loss; the loss of the smiles and ramblings and discussions so much friendlier to ambition than the cold hardship of writing.

—Elizabeth Hardwick

The Essay's Unlimited Possibilities

The essay is, and has been, all over the map. There's nothing you cannot do with it; no subject matter is forbidden, no structure is proscribed.

You get to make up your own structure every time, a structure that arises from the materials and best contains them. The material is the world itself, which, so far, keeps on keeping on. The thinking mind will analyze, and the creative imagination will link instances, and time itself will churn out scenes—scenes unnoticed and lost, or scenes remembered, written, and saved.

In his essay "Home," William Kittredge remembers Jack Ray, his boyhood hero, whom he later hired as a hand on his Oregon ranch. After a bout in jail, Jack Ray would show up in the bunkhouse grinning. "Well, hell, Jack," Kittredge would say. "It's a new day."

"Kid," he would say, "she's a new world every morning."

—Annie Dillard

1

*The Personal Voice:
Identity, Diversity,
Self-Discovery*

ANWAR F. ACCAWI

The Telephone

Newspapers and popular magazines indirectly encourage readers to think essays are synonymous with opinion pieces—columns and articles in which writers speak their minds and air their views on topics in the news. But essays can be effective means of storytelling, as Anwar Accawi proves in the following account of his childhood in a tiny village in southern Lebanon. In "The Telephone," Accawi offers an unpretentious description of how the modern world began its intrusion into a timeless and insulated culture, where "there was no real need for a calendar or a watch to keep track of the hours, days, months, and years." As Accawi says of village life: "We lived and loved and toiled and died without ever needing to know what year it was, or even the time of day."

Accawi, who was born in Lebanon in 1943 and came to the United States in 1965, began writing essays as a way to preserve a disappearing culture for his young children, who knew nothing of the old country. A teacher at the English Language Institute at the University of Tennessee, Knoxville, he is the author of a memoir, The Boy from the Tower of the Moon *(1999). "The Telephone," which originally appeared in* The Sun *(1997), was one of Accawi's first publications and was selected by Cynthia Ozick for* The Best American Essays *1998.*

When I was growing up in Magdaluna, a small Lebanese village in the terraced, rocky mountains east of Sidon, time didn't mean much to anybody, except maybe to those who were dying, or those waiting to appear in court because they had tampered with the boundary markers on their land. In those days, there was no real need for a calendar or a watch to keep track of the hours, days, months, and years. We knew what to do and when to do it, just as

the Iraqi geese knew when to fly north, driven by the hot wind that
blew in from the desert, and the ewes knew when to give birth to
wet lambs that stood on long, shaky legs in the chilly March wind
and baaed hesitantly, because they were small and cold and did
not know where they were or what to do now that they were here.
The only timepiece we had need of then was the sun. It rose and
set, and the seasons rolled by, and we sowed seed and harvested
and ate and played and married our cousins and had babies who
got whooping cough and chickenpox—and those children
who survived grew up and married *their* cousins and had babies
who got whooping cough and chickenpox. We lived and loved and
toiled and died without ever needing to know what year it was, or
even the time of day.

It wasn't that we had no system for keeping track of time and of
the important events in our lives. But ours was a natural—or,
rather, a divine—calendar, because it was framed by acts of God.
Allah himself set down the milestones with earthquakes and
droughts and floods and locusts and pestilences. Simple as our calendar was, it worked just fine for us.

Take, for example, the birth date of Teta Im Khalil, the oldest
woman in Magdaluna and all the surrounding villages. When I
first met her, we had just returned home from Syria at the end of
the Big War and were living with Grandma Mariam. Im Khalil
came by to welcome my father home and to take a long, myopic
look at his foreign-born wife, my mother. Im Khalil was so old that
the skin of her cheeks looked like my father's grimy tobacco
pouch, and when I kissed her (because Grandma insisted that I
show her old friend affection), it was like kissing a soft suede glove
that had been soaked with sweat and then left in a dark closet for a
season. Im Khalil's face got me to wondering how old one had to
be to look and taste the way she did. So, as soon as she had hob-
bled off on her cane, I asked Grandma, "How old is Teta Im
Khalil?"

Grandma had to think for a moment; then she said, "I've been
told that Teta was born shortly after the big snow that caused the
roof on the mayor's house to cave in."

"And when was that?" I asked.

"Oh, about the time we had the big earthquake that cracked the
wall in the east room."

Well, that was enough for me. You couldn't be more accurate than that, now, could you? Satisfied with her answer, I went back to playing with a ball made from an old sock stuffed with other, much older socks.

And that's the way it was in our little village for as far back as anybody could remember: people were born so many years before or after an earthquake or a flood; they got married or died so many years before or after a long drought or a big snow or some other disaster. One of the most unusual of these dates was when Antoinette the seamstress and Saeed the barber (and tooth puller) got married. That was the year of the whirlwind during which fish and oranges fell from the sky. Incredible as it may sound, the story of the fish and oranges was true, because men—respectable men, like Abu George the blacksmith and Abu Asaad the mule skinner, men who would not lie even to save their own souls—told and re-told that story until it was incorporated into Magdaluna's calendar, just like the year of the black moon and the year of the locusts before it. My father, too, confirmed the story for me. He told me that he had been a small boy himself when it had rained fish and oranges from heaven. He'd gotten up one morning after a stormy night and walked out into the yard to find fish as long as his forearm still flopping here and there among the wet navel oranges.

The year of the fish-bearing twister, however, was not the last remarkable year. Many others followed in which strange and wonderful things happened: milestones added by the hand of Allah to Magdaluna's calendar. There was, for instance, the year of the drought, when the heavens were shut for months and the spring from which the entire village got its drinking water slowed to a trickle. The spring was about a mile from the village, in a ravine that opened at one end into a small, flat clearing covered with fine gray dust and hard, marble-sized goat droppings, because every afternoon the goatherds brought their flocks there to water them. In the year of the drought, that little clearing was always packed full of noisy kids with big brown eyes and sticky hands, and their mothers—sinewy, overworked young women with protruding collarbones and cracked, callused brown heels. The children ran around playing tag or hide-and-seek while the women talked, shooed flies, and awaited their turns to fill up their jars with drinking water to bring home to their napping men and wet babies.

There were days when we had to wait from sunup until late afternoon just to fill a small clay jar with precious, cool water.

Sometimes, amid the long wait and the heat and the flies and the smell of goat dung, tempers flared, and the younger women, anxious about their babies, argued over whose turn it was to fill up her jar. And sometimes the arguments escalated into full-blown, knockdown-dragout fights; the women would grab each other by the hair and curse and scream and spit and call each other names that made my ears tingle. We little brown boys who went with our mothers to fetch water loved these fights, because we got to see the women's legs and their colored panties as they grappled and rolled around in the dust. Once in a while, we got lucky and saw much more, because some of the women wore nothing at all under their long dresses. God, how I used to look forward to those fights. I remember the rush, the excitement, the sun dancing on the dust clouds as a dress ripped and a young white breast was revealed, then quickly hidden. In my calendar, that year of drought will always be one of the best years of my childhood, because it was then, in a dusty clearing by a trickling mountain spring, I got my first glimpses of the wonders, the mysteries, and the promises hidden beneath the folds of a woman's dress. Fish and oranges from heaven . . . you can get over that.

But, in another way, the year of the drought was also one of the worst of my life, because that was the year that Abu Raja, the retired cook who used to entertain us kids by cracking walnuts on his forehead, decided it was time Magdaluna got its own telephone. Every civilized village needed a telephone, he said, and Magdaluna was not going to get anywhere until it had one. A telephone would link us with the outside world. At the time, I was too young to understand the debate, but a few men—like Shukri, the retired Turkish-army drill sergeant, and Abu Hanna the vineyard keeper— did all they could to talk Abu Raja out of having a telephone brought to the village. But they were outshouted and ignored and finally shunned by the other villagers for resisting progress and trying to keep a good thing from coming to Magdaluna.

One warm day in early fall, many of the villagers were out in their fields repairing walls or gathering wood for the winter when the shout went out that the telephone-company truck had arrived at Abu Raja's *dikkan*, or country store. There were no roads in those days, only footpaths and dry streambeds, so it took the telephone-company truck almost a day to work its way up the rocky terrain from Sidon—about the same time it took to walk. When the truck came into view, Abu George, who had a huge voice and, before the telephone, was Magdaluna's only long-distance communication system, bellowed the news from his front porch. Everybody dropped what they were doing and ran to Abu Raja's house to see what was happening. Some of the more dignified villagers, however, like Abu Habeeb and Abu Nazim, who had been to big cities like Beirut and Damascus and had seen things like telephones and telegraphs, did not run the way the rest did; they walked with their canes hanging from the crooks of their arms, as if on a Sunday afternoon stroll.

It did not take long for the whole village to assemble at Abu Raja's *dikkan*. Some of the rich villagers, like the widow Farha and the gendarme Abu Nadeem, walked right into the store and stood at the elbows of the two important-looking men from the telephone company, who proceeded with utmost gravity, like priests at Communion, to wire up the telephone. The poorer villagers stood outside and listened carefully to the details relayed to them by the not-so-poor people who stood in the doorway and could see inside.

"The bald man is cutting the blue wire," someone said.

"He is sticking the wire into the hole in the bottom of the black box," someone else added.

"The telephone man with the mustache is connecting two pieces of wire. Now he is twisting the ends together," a third voice chimed in.

Because I was small and unaware that I should have stood outside with the other poor folk to give the rich people inside more room (they seemed to need more of it than poor people did), I wriggled my way through the dense forest of legs to get a firsthand look at the action. I felt like the barefoot Moses, sandals in hand, staring at the burning bush on Mount Sinai. Breathless, I watched as the men in blue, their shirt pockets adorned with fancy lettering in a foreign language, put together a black machine that supposedly would make it possible to talk with uncles, aunts, and cousins who lived more than two days' ride away.

It was shortly after sunset when the man with the mustache announced that the telephone was ready to use. He explained that all Abu Raja had to do was lift the receiver, turn the crank on the black box a few times, and wait for an operator to take his call. Abu Raja, who had once lived and worked in Sidon, was impatient with the telephone man for assuming that he was ignorant. He grabbed the receiver and turned the crank forcefully, as if trying to start a Model T Ford. Everybody was impressed that he knew what to do. He even called the operator by her first name: "Centralist." Within moments, Abu Raja was talking with his brother, a concierge in Beirut. He didn't even have to raise his voice or shout to be heard.

If I hadn't seen it with my own two eyes and heard it with my own two ears, I would not have believed it—and my friend Kameel didn't. He was away that day watching his father's goats, and when he came back to the village that evening, his cousin Habeeb and I told him about the telephone and how Abu Raja had used it to speak with his brother in Beirut. After he heard our report, Kameel made the sign of the cross, kissed his thumbnail, and warned us that lying was a bad sin and would surely land us in purgatory. Kameel believed in Jesus and Mary, and wanted to be a priest when he grew up. He always crossed himself when Habeeb, who was irreverent, and I, who was Presbyterian, were around, even when we were not bearing bad news.

And the telephone, as it turned out, was bad news. With its coming, the face of the village began to change. One of the first effects was the shifting of the village's center. Before the telephone's arrival, the men of the village used to gather regularly at the house of Im Kaleem, a short, middle-aged widow with jet-black hair and a raspy voice that could be heard all over the village, even when she was only whispering. She was a devout Catholic and also the village *shlikki*—whore. The men met at her house to argue about politics and drink coffee and play cards or backgammon. Im Kaleem was not a true prostitute, however, because she did not charge for her services—not even for the coffee and tea (and, occasionally, the strong liquor called arrack) that she served the men. She did not need the money; her son, who was overseas in Africa, sent her money regularly. (I knew this because my father used to read her son's letters to her and take down her replies, as Im Kaleem could not read and write.) Im Kaleem was no slut either—unlike some women in the village—because she loved all the men she entertained, and they loved her, every one of them. In a way, she was married to all the men in the village. Everybody knew it—the wives knew it; the itinerant Catholic priest knew it; the Presbyterian minister knew it— but nobody objected. Actually, I suspect the women (my mother included) did not mind their husbands' visits to Im Kaleem. Oh, they wrung their hands and complained to one another about their men's unfaithfulness, but secretly they were relieved, because Im Kaleem took some of the pressure off them and kept the men out of their hair while they attended to their endless chores. Im Kaleem was also a kind of confessor and troubleshooter, talking sense to those men who were having family problems, especially the younger ones.

Before the telephone came to Magdaluna, Im Kaleem's house was bustling at just about any time of day, especially at night, when its windows were brightly lit with three large oil lamps, and the loud voices of the men talking, laughing, and arguing could be heard in the street below—a reassuring, homey sound. Her house was an island of comfort, an oasis for the weary village men, exhausted from having so little to do.

But it wasn't long before many of those men—the younger ones especially—started spending more of their days and evenings at Abu Raja's *dikkan*. There, they would eat and drink and talk and play checkers and backgammon, and then lean their chairs back against the wall—the signal that they were ready to toss back and forth, like a ball, the latest rumors going around the village. And they were always looking up from their games and drinks and talk to glance at the phone in the corner, as if expecting it to ring any minute and bring news that would change their lives and deliver them from their aimless existence. In the meantime, they smoked cheap, hand-rolled cigarettes, dug dirt out from under their fingernails with big pocketknives, and drank lukewarm sodas they called Kacula, Seffen-Ub, and Bebsi. Sometimes, especially when it was hot, the days dragged on so slowly that the men turned on Abu Saeed, a confirmed bachelor who practically lived in Abu Raja's *dikkan*, and teased him for going around barefoot and unshaven since the Virgin had appeared to him behind the olive press.

The telephone was also bad news for me personally. It took away my lucrative business—a source of much-needed income. Before the telephone came to Magdaluna, I used to hang around Im

Kaleem's courtyard and play marbles with the other kids, waiting
for some man to call down from a window and ask me to run to
the store for cigarettes or arrack, or to deliver a message to his
wife, such as what he wanted for supper. There was always something in it for me: a ten- or even a twenty-five-piaster piece. On a
good day, I ran nine or ten of those errands, which assured a steady
supply of marbles that I usually lost to Sami or his cousin Hani, the
basket weaver's boy. But as the days went by, fewer and fewer men
came to Im Kaleem's, and more and more congregated at Abu
Raja's to wait by the telephone. In the evenings, no light fell from
her window onto the street below, and the laughter and noise of
the men trailed off and finally stopped. Only Shukri, the retired
Turkish-army drill sergeant, remained faithful to Im Kaleem after
all the other men had deserted her; he was still seen going into or
leaving her house from time to time. Early that winter, Im Kaleem's
hair suddenly turned gray, and she got sick and old. Her legs
started giving her trouble, making it hard for her to walk. By spring
she hardly left her house anymore.

At Abu Raja's *dikkan*, the calls did eventually come, as expected,
and men and women started leaving the village the way a hail-
storm begins: first one, then two, then bunches. The army took
them. Jobs in the cities lured them. And ships and airplanes carried them to such faraway places as Australia and Brazil and New
Zealand. My friend Kameel, his cousin Habeeb, and their cousins
and my cousins all went away to become ditch diggers and mechanics and butcher-shop boys and deli owners who wore dirty
aprons sixteen hours a day, all looking for a better life than the
one they had left behind. Within a year, only the sick, the old, and
the maimed were left in the village. Magdaluna became a skeleton
of its former self, desolate and forsaken, like the tombs, a place to
get away from.

Finally, the telephone took my family away, too. My father got a
call from an old army buddy who told him that an oil company in
southern Lebanon was hiring interpreters and instructors. My
father applied for a job and got it, and we moved to Sidon, where
I went to a Presbyterian missionary school and graduated in 1962.
Three years later, having won a scholarship, I left Lebanon for the
United States. Like the others who left Magdaluna before me, I am
still looking for that better life.

Reflections and Responses

---

1. Why do you think Accawi begins his recollections of childhood by focusing on the way the passage of time was measured by the villagers? Does Accawi see the village's attitude toward time in positive or negative ways? How do his word choices and images reflect his position?

2. Consider the way Accawi introduces the telephone into the village. How does he prepare for its appearance? From whose perspective do we view the installation? How are the class lines of the village drawn when the telephone is installed? Finally, why did the telephone turn out to be "bad news" for the village as a whole?

3. How would you assess Accawi's attitude in the final paragraph? How did the telephone personally change his life? Do you think the change was for the worse? Do you think Accawi himself believes it was for the worse? How do you interpret his final sentence?

MARCIA ALDRICH

Hair

Montaigne, the first essayist, would have enjoyed Marcia Aldrich's wonderful meditation on hairstyles and the way they reflect our personal identity. When Montaigne began writing personal essays in the 1570s, he initiated a new style of self-portrayal. He brought his whole body into his writing, inviting his readers to see his essays not simply as thoughts on a page but as an extension of his physical being. Not having (as he put it) an "imposing presence" in actual life, he tried to create one in and through his remarkable essays. A very "physical" writer, he would discuss his looks, height, voice and complexion, the way he walked, and his habit of scratching the inside of his ears. A persistent self-reviser, Montaigne would also appreciate Aldrich's resistance to a settled style ("a new hairstyle," she says, "will write over the last") and to a coherent philosophy.

Marcia Aldrich is a professor of English who specializes in twentieth-century poetry at Michigan State University. She is the author of a memoir about growing up in the '50s, Girl Rearing *(1998), and is also working on a study of the poet Louise Bogan. Her work can be found in a wide variety of literary journals, including* Fourth Genre, Brevity, Nerve, Puerto del Sol, The Pinch, *and* Seneca Review. *"Hair" originally appeared in* The Northwest Review *(1992) and was selected by Joseph Epstein for* The Best American Essays *1993.*

I've been around and seen the Taj Mahal and the Grand Canyon and Marilyn Monroe's footprints outside Grauman's Chinese Theater, but I've never seen my mother wash her own hair. After my mother married, she never washed her own hair again. As a girl and an unmarried woman—yes—but, in my lifetime, she never washed her hair with her own two hands. Upon matrimony, she began weekly treks to the beauty salon where Julie washed and styled her hair. Her appointment on Fridays at two o'clock was never cancelled or rescheduled; it was the bedrock of her week, around which she pivoted and planned. These two hours were indispensable to my mother's routine, to her sense of herself and what, as a woman, she should concern herself with—not to mention their being her primary source of information about all sorts of things she wouldn't otherwise come to know. With Julie my mother discussed momentous decisions concerning hair color and the advancement of age and what could be done about it, hair length and its effect upon maturity, when to perm and when not to perm, the need to proceed with caution when a woman desperately wanted a major change in her life like dumping her husband or sending back her newborn baby and the only change she could effect was a change in her hair. That was what Julie called a "dangerous time" in a woman's life. When my mother spoke to Julie, she spoke in conspiratorial, almost confessional, tones I had never heard before. Her voice was usually tense, on guard, the laughter forced, but with Julie it dropped much lower, the timbre darker than the upper-register shrills sounded at home. And most remarkably, she listened to everything Julie said.

As a child I was puzzled by the way my mother's sense of self-worth and mood seemed dependent upon how she thought her hair looked, how the search for the perfect hairstyle never ended. Just as Mother seemed to like her latest color and cut, she began to agitate for a new look. The cut seemed to have become a melancholy testimony, in my mother's eyes, to time's inexorable passage. Her hair never stood in and of itself; it was always moored to a complex set of needs and desires her hair couldn't in itself satisfy. She wanted her hair to illuminate the relationship between herself and the idea of motion while appearing still, for example. My mother wanted her hair to be fashioned into an event with a complicated narrative past. However, the more my mother attempted to impose a hairstyle pulled from an idealized image of herself, the more the hairstyle seemed to be at odds with my mother. The more the hairstyle became substantial, the more the woman underneath was obscured. She'd riffle through women's magazines and stare for long dreamy hours at a particular woman's coiffure. Then she'd ask my father in an artificially casual voice: "How do you think I'd look with really short hair?" or "Would blonde become me?" My father never committed himself to an opinion. He had learned from long experience that no response he made could turn out well; anything he said would be used against him, if not in the immediate circumstances, down the line, for my mother never forgot anything anyone ever said about her hair. My father's refusal to engage the "hair question" irritated her.

So too, I was puzzled to see that unmarried women washed their own hair, and married women, in my mother's circle at least, by some unwritten dictum never touched their own hair. I began studying before and after photographs of my mother's friends. These photographs were all the same. In the pre-married mode, their hair was soft and unformed. After the wedding, the women's hairstyles bore the stamp of property, looked constructed from grooming talents not their own, hairstyles I'd call produced, requiring constant upkeep and technique to sustain the considerable loft and rigidity—in short, the antithesis of anything I might naively call natural. This was hair no one touched, crushed, or ran fingers through. One poked and prodded various hair masses back into formation. This hair presented obstacles to embrace, the scent of the hair spray alone warded off man, child, and pests. I never saw my father stroke my mother's head. Children whimpered when my mother came home fresh from the salon with a potent do. Just when a woman's life was supposed to be opening out into daily affection, *the* sanctioned affection of husband and children, the women of my mother's circle encased themselves in a helmet of hair not unlike Medusa's.

In so-called middle age, my mother's hair never moved, never blew, never fell in her face: her hair became a museum piece. When she went to bed, she wore a blue net, and when she took short showers, short because, after all, she wasn't washing her hair and she was seldom dirty, she wore a blue plastic cap for the sake of preservation. From one appointment to the next, the only change her hair could be said to undergo was to become crestfallen. Taking extended vacations presented problems sufficiently troublesome to rule out countries where she feared no beauty parlors existed. In the beginning, my parents took overnighters, then week jaunts, and thereby avoided the whole hair dilemma. Extending their vacations to two weeks was eventually managed by my mother applying more hair spray and sleeping sitting up. But after the two week mark had been reached, she was forced to either return home or venture into an unfamiliar salon and subject herself to scrutiny, the kind of scrutiny that leaves no woman unscathed. Then she faced Julie's disapproval, for no matter how expensive and expert the salon, my mother's hair was to be lamented. Speaking just for myself, I had difficulty distinguishing Julie's cunning from the stranger's. In these years my mother's hair looked curled, teased, and sprayed into a waved tossed monument with holes poked through for glasses. She believed the damage done to her hair was tangible proof she had been somewhere, like stickers on her suitcases.

My older sisters have worked out their hair positions differently. My oldest sister's solution has been to fix upon one hairstyle and never change it. She wants to be thought of in a singular fashion. She may vary the length from long to longer, but that is the extent of her alteration. Once, after having her first baby, the "dangerous time" for women, she recklessly cut her hair to just below the ear. She immediately regretted the decision and began growing it back as she walked home from the salon, vowing not to repeat the mistake. Her signature is dark, straight hair pulled heavily off her face in a large silver clip, found at any Woolworth's. When one clip breaks, she buys another just like it. My mother hates the timelessness of my sister's hair. She equates it with a refusal to face growing old. My mother says, "It's immature to wear your hair the same way all your life."

My sister replies, "It's immature to never stop thinking about your hair. If this hairstyle was good enough when I was twenty, it's good enough when I'm forty, if not better."

"But what about change?" my mother asks.

"Change is overrated," my sister says flipping her long hair over her shoulder definitively. "I feel my hair."

My other sister was born with thin, lifeless, nondescript hair: a cross she has had to bear. Even in the baby pictures, the limp strands plastered on her forehead in question marks wear her down. Shame and self-effacement are especially plain in the pictures where she posed with our eldest sister, whose dark hair dominates the frame. She's spent her life attempting to disguise the real state of her hair. Some years she'd focus on style, pulling it back in ponytails so that from the front no one could see there wasn't much hair in the back. She tried artless, even messy styles—as if she had just tied it up any old way before taking a bath or bunched it to look deliberately snarled. There were the weird years punctuated by styles that looked as if she had taken sugar water and lemon juice and squeezed them onto her wet hair and then let them crystallize. The worst style was when she took her hair and piled it on the top of her head in a cone shape and then crimped the ponytail into a zigzag. Personally, I thought she had gone too far. No single approach solved the hair problem, and so now, in maturity, she combines the various phases of attack in hope something will work. She frosts both the grey strands and the pale brown, and then perms for added body and thickness. She's forced to keep her hair short because chemicals do tend to destroy. My mother admires my sister's determination to transform herself, and never more than in my sister's latest assault upon middle age. No one has known for many years nor does anyone remember what the untreated color or texture of either my mother's or my sister's hair might be.

As the youngest by twelve years, there was little to distract Mother's considerable attention from the problem of my hair. I had cowlicks, a remarkable number of them, which like little arrows shot across my scalp. They refused to be trained, to lie down quietly in the same direction as the rest of my hair. One at the front insisted on sticking straight up while two on either side of my ears jutted out seeking sun. The lack of uniformity, the fact that my hair had a mind of its own, infuriated my mother and she saw to it that Julie cut my hair as short as possible in order to curtail its wanton expression. Sitting in the swivel chair before the mirror while Julie snipped, I felt invisible, as if I was unattached to my hair.

Just when I started to menstruate, my mother decided the battle plan needed a change, and presto, the page boy replaced the pixie. Having not outgrown the thicket of cowlicks, Mother bought a spectrum of brightly colored stretch bands to hold my hair back off my face. Then she attached thin pink plastic curlers with snap on lids to the ends of my hair to make them flip up or under, depending on her mood. The stretch bands pressed my hair flat until the very bottom, at which point the ends formed a tunnel with ridges from the roller caps—a point of emphasis, she called it. Coupled with the aquamarine eyeglasses, newly acquired, I looked like an overgrown insect that had none of its kind to bond with.

However, I was not alone. Unless you were the last in a long line of sisters, chances were good that your hair would not go unnoticed by your mother. Each of my best friends was subjected to her mother's hair dictatorship, although with entirely different results. Perry Jensen's mother insisted that all five of her daughters peroxide their hair blonde and pull it back into high ponytails. All the girls' hair turned green in the summer from chlorine. Melissa Matson underwent a look-alike "home perm" with her mother, an experience she never did recover from. She developed a phobic reaction to anything synthetic, which made life very expensive. Not only did mother and daughter have identical tight curls and wear mother-daughter outfits, later they had look-alike nose jobs.

In my generation, many women who survived hair bondage to their mothers now experiment with hairstyles as one would test a new design: to see how it works, what it will withstand, and how it can be improved. Testing requires boldness, for often the style fails dramatically, as when I had my hair cut about a half inch long at the top, and it stood straight up like a tacky shag carpet. I had to live with the results, bear daily witness to the kinks in its design for nine months until strategies of damage control could be deployed. But sometimes women I know create a look that startles in its originality and suggests a future not yet realized.

The women in my family divide into two general groups: those who fasten upon one style, become identified with a look, and are impervious to change, weathering the years steadfastly, and those who, for a variety of reasons, are in the business of transforming themselves. In my sister's case, the quest for perfect hair originates in a need to mask her own appearance; in my mother's case, she wants to achieve a beauty of person unavailable in her own life story. Some women seek transformation, not out of dissatisfaction with themselves, but because hair change is a means of moving along in their lives. These women create portraits of themselves that won't last forever, a new hairstyle will write over the last.

Since my mother dictated my hair, I never took a stand on the hair issue. In maturity, I'm incapable of assuming a coherent or consistent philosophy. I have wayward hair: it's always becoming something else. The moment it arrives at a recognizable style, it begins to undo itself, it grows, the sun colors it, it waves. When one hair pin goes in, another seems to come out. Sometimes I think I should follow my oldest sister—she claims to never give more than a passing thought to her hair and can't see what all the angst is about. She asks, "Don't women have better things to think about than their hair?"

I bite back: "But don't you think hair should reflect who you are?"

"To be honest, I've never thought about it. I don't think so. Cut your hair the same way, and lose your self in something else. You're distracted from the real action."

I want to do what my sister says, but when I walk out into shop-lined streets, I automatically study women's hair and always with the same question: How did they arrive at their hair? Lately, I've been feeling more and more like my mother. I hadn't known how to resolve the dilemma until I found Rhonda. I don't know if I found Rhonda or made her up. She is not a normally trained hair-dresser: she has a different set of eyes, unaffected. One day while out driving around to no place in particular, at the bottom of a hill, I found: "Rhonda's Hair Salon—Don't Look Back" written on a life-size cardboard image of Rhonda. Her shop was on the top of this steep orchard planted hill, on a plateau with a great view that opened out and went on forever. I parked my car at the bottom and walked up. Zigzagging all the way up the hill, leaning against or sticking out from behind the apple trees were more life-sized cardboard likenesses of Rhonda. Except for the explosive sun-bursts in her hair, no two signs were the same. At the bottom, she wore long red hair falling below her knees and covering her en-tire body like a shawl. As I climbed the hill, Rhonda's hair gradu-ally became shorter and shorter, and each length was cut differently, until when I reached the top, her head was shaved and glistening in the sun. I found Rhonda herself out under one of the apple trees wearing running shoes. Her hair was long and red and looked as if it had never been cut. She told me she had no aspirations to be a hairdresser, "she just fell into it." "I see hair," she continued, "as an extension of the head and therefore I try to do hair with a lot of thought." Inside there were no mirrors, no swivel chairs, no machines of torture with their accompanying stink. She said, "Nothing is permanent, nothing is forever. Don't feel hampered or hemmed in by the shape of your face or the shape of your past. Hair is vital, sustains mistakes, can be born again. You don't have to marry it. Now tip back and put your head into my hands."

Reflections and Responses

1. Consider how Aldrich invites you to see hairstyles in terms of personal identity. Compare the different female members of her family. How does each reflect a different philosophical attitude through her hairstyle? What are they? Why do you think Aldrich left her father out of these reflections?

2. How does Aldrich establish a relationship between hairstyle and writing style? For Aldrich, what do the two have in common? In going through her essay, identify some features of her writing style that also reflect her attitude toward her hair.

3. Reread Aldrich's final paragraph carefully. It's tricky. What do you think is happening? Is "Rhonda" real or fictitious? What makes you think she is real? Alternatively, what makes you think Aldrich made her up? Why do you think Aldrich concluded her essay with this visit to Rhonda's Hair Salon?

JUDITH ORTIZ COFER

Silent Dancing

Nothing rekindles childhood memories better than old photographs or home movies. In this vivid essay, a grainy and poorly focused five-minute home movie of a New Year's Eve party helps a writer capture the spirit of a Puerto Rican community in Paterson, New Jersey. That the movie is fragmented and silent adds to its documentary value and, for a lyrical essayist, it evokes much more than it can possibly reveal. "Even the home movie," Cofer writes, "cannot fill in the sensory details such a gathering left imprinted in a child's brain." Those sensory details—"the flavor of Puerto Rico"—must be supplied through the art of writing.

A professor of English and creative writing at the University of Georgia, Judith Ortiz Cofer has published prize-winning books in a number of genres: a novel, The Line of the Sun *(1989); three poetry collections,* Reaching for the Mainland *(1986),* Terms of Survival *(1987), and* A Love Story Beginning in Spanish *(2005); two autobiographical books combining prose and poetry,* Silent Dancing *(1990) and* The Latin Deli *(1993); and* An Island Like You: Stories of the Barrio *(1995). She has recently published* The Year of Our Revolution: New and Selected Stories and Poems *(1998),* Sleeping with One Eye Open: Women Writers and the Art of Survival *(1999),* Women in Front of the Sun: On Becoming a Writer *(2000), and two novels,* The Meaning of Consuelo *(2003) and* Call Me Maria *(2004). Cofer has received many prestigious awards, including fellowships from the National Endowment for the Arts, the Witter Bynner Foundation for Poetry, and the Bread Loaf Writers' Conference. "Silent Dancing" originally appeared in* The Georgia Review *(1990) and was selected by Joyce Carol Oates for* The Best American Essays 1991. *Ms. Cofer courteously supplied the notes to this selection.*

We have a home movie of this party. Several times my mother and I have watched it together, and I have asked questions about the silent revelers coming in and out of focus. It is grainy and of short duration, but it's a great visual aid to my memory of life at that time. And it is in color—the only complete scene in color I can recall from those years.

We lived in Puerto Rico until my brother was born in 1954. Soon after, because of economic pressures on our growing family, my father joined the United States Navy. He was assigned to duty on a ship in Brooklyn Yard—a place of cement and steel that was to be his home base in the States until his retirement more than twenty years later. He left the Island first, alone, going to New York City and tracking down his uncle who lived with his family across the Hudson River in Paterson, New Jersey. There my father found a tiny apartment in a huge tenement that had once housed Jewish families but was just being taken over and transformed by Puerto Ricans, overflowing from New York City. In 1955 he sent for us. My mother was only twenty years old, I was not quite three, and my brother was a toddler when we arrived at *El Building*, as the place had been christened by its newest residents.

My memories of life in Paterson during those first few years are all in shades of gray. Maybe I was too young to absorb vivid colors and details, or to discriminate between the slate blue of the winter sky and the darker hues of the snow-bearing clouds, but that single color washes over the whole period. The building we lived in was gray, as were the streets, filled with slush the first few months of my life there. The coat my father had bought for me was similar in color and too big; it sat heavily on my thin frame.

I do remember the way the heater pipes banged and rattled, startling all of us out of sleep until we got so used to the sound that we automatically shut it out or raised our voices above the racket. The hiss from the valve punctuated my sleep (which has always been fitful) like a nonhuman presence in the room—a dragon sleeping at the entrance of my childhood. But the pipes were also a connection to all the other lives being lived around us. Having come from a house designed for a single family back in Puerto Rico—my mother's extended-family home—it was curious to know that strangers lived under our floor and above our heads, and that the heater pipe went through everyone's apartments. (My first spanking in Paterson came as a result of playing tunes on the pipes in my room to see if there would be an answer.) My mother was as new to this concept of bee-hive life as I was, but she had been given strict orders by my father to keep the doors locked, the noise down, ourselves to ourselves.

It seems that Father had learned some painful lessons about prejudice while searching for an apartment in Paterson. Not until years later did I hear how much resistance he had encountered with landlords who were panicking at the influx of Latinos into a neighborhood that had been Jewish for a couple of generations. It made no difference that it was the American phenomenon of ethnic turnover which was changing the urban core of Paterson, and that the human flood could not be held back with an accusing finger.

"You Cuban?" one man had asked my father, pointing at his name tag on the Navy uniform—even though my father had the fair skin and light-brown hair of his northern Spanish background, and the name Ortiz is as common in Puerto Rico as Johnson is in the U.S.

"No," my father had answered, looking past the finger into his adversary's angry eyes. "I'm Puerto Rican."

"Same shit." And the door closed.

My father could have passed as European, but we couldn't. My brother and I both have our mother's black hair and olive skin, and so we lived in El Building and visited our great-uncle and his fair children on the next block. It was their private joke that they were the German branch of the family. Not many years later that area too would be mainly Puerto Rican. It was as if the heart of the city map were being gradually colored brown—*café con leche* brown. Our color.

The movie opens with a sweep of the living room. It is "typical" immigrant Puerto Rican decor for the time: the sofa and chairs are square and hard-looking, upholstered in bright colors (blue and yellow in this instance), and covered with the transparent plastic that furniture salesmen then were so adept at convincing women to buy. The linoleum on the floor is light blue; if it had been subjected to spike heels (as it was in most places), there were dime-sized indentations all over it that cannot be seen in this movie. The room is full of people dressed up: dark suits for the men, red dresses for the women. When I have asked my mother why most of the women are in red that night, she has shrugged, "I don't remember. Just a coincidence." She doesn't have my obsession for assigning symbolism to everything.

The three women in red sitting on the couch are my mother, my eighteen-year-old cousin, and her brother's girlfriend. The novia *is just up from the Island, which is apparent in her body language. She sits up formally, her dress pulled over her knees. She is a pretty girl, but her posture makes her look insecure, lost in her full-skirted dress, which she has carefully tucked around her to make room for my gorgeous cousin, her future sister-in-law. My cousin has grown up in Paterson and is in her last year of high school. She doesn't have a trace of what Puerto Ricans call la* mancha *(literally, the stain: the mark of the new immigrant—something about the posture, the voice, or the humble demeanor that makes it obvious to everyone the person has just arrived on the mainland). My cousin is wearing a tight, sequined cocktail dress. Her brown hair has been lightened with peroxide around the bangs, and she is holding a cigarette expertly between her fingers, bringing it up to her mouth in a sensuous arc of her arm as she talks animatedly. My mother, who has come up to sit between the two women, both only a few years younger than herself, is somewhere between the poles they represent in our culture.*

It became my father's obsession to get out of the barrio, and thus we were never permitted to form bonds with the place or with the people who lived there. Yet El Building was a comfort to my mother, who never got over yearning for *la isla.* She felt surrounded by her language: the walls were thin, and voices speaking and arguing in Spanish could be heard all day. *Salsas* blasted out of radios, turned on early in the morning and left on for company. Women seemed to cook rice and beans perpetually—the strong aroma of boiling red kidney beans permeated the hallways.

Though Father preferred that we do our grocery shopping at the supermarket when he came home on weekend leaves, my mother insisted that she could cook only with products whose labels she could read. Consequently, during the week I accompanied her and my little brother to *La Bodega*—a hole-in-the-wall grocery store across the street from El Building. There we squeezed down three narrow aisles jammed with various products. Goya's and Libby's—those were the trademarks that were trusted by *her mamá,* so my mother bought many cans of Goya beans, soups, and condiments, as well as little cans of Libby's fruit juices for us. And she also bought Colgate toothpaste and Palmolive soap. (The final *e* is pronounced in both these products in Spanish, so for many years I believed that they were manufactured on the Island. I remember my surprise at first hearing a commercial on television in which Colgate rhymed with "ate.") We always lingered at La Bodega, for it was there that Mother breathed best, taking in the familiar aromas of the foods she knew from Mamá's kitchen. It was also there that she got to speak to the other women of El Building without violating outright Father's dictates against fraternizing with our neighbors.

Yet Father did his best to make our "assimilation" painless. I can still see him carrying a real Christmas tree up several flights of stairs to our apartment, leaving a trail of aromatic pine. He carried it formally, as if it were a flag in a parade. We were the only ones in El Building that I knew of who got presents on both Christmas day AND *día de Reyes*, the day when the Three Kings brought gifts to Christ and to Hispanic children.

Our supreme luxury in El Building was having our own television set. It must have been a result of Father's guilt feelings over the isolation he had imposed on us, but we were among the first in the barrio to have one. My brother quickly became an avid watcher of Captain Kangaroo and Jungle Jim, while I loved all the series showing families. By the time I started first grade, I could have drawn a map of Middle America as exemplified by the lives of characters in *Father Knows Best, The Donna Reed Show, Leave It to Beaver, My Three Sons,* and (my favorite) *Bachelor Father,* where John Forsythe treated his adopted teenage daughter like a princess because he was rich and had a Chinese houseboy to do everything for him. In truth, compared to our neighbors in El Building, *we* were rich. My father's Navy check provided us with financial security and a standard of life that the factory workers envied. The only thing his money could not buy us was a place to live away from the barrio—his greatest wish, Mother's greatest fear.

In the home movie the men are shown next, sitting around a card table set up in one corner of the living room, playing dominoes. The clack of the ivory pieces was a familiar sound. I heard it in many houses on the Island and in many apartments in Paterson. In Leave It to Beaver, *the Cleavers played bridge in every other episode; in my childhood, the men started every social occasion with a hotly debated round of dominoes. The women would sit around and watch, but they never participated in the games.*

Here and there you can see a small child. Children were always brought to parties and, whenever they got sleepy, were put to bed in the host's bedroom. Babysitting was a concept unrecognized by the Puerto

Rican women I knew: a responsible mother did not leave her children
with any stranger. And in a culture where children are not considered
intrusive, there was no need to leave the children at home. We went
where our mother went.

Of my preschool years I have only impressions: the sharp bite of
the wind in December as we walked with our parents towards the
brightly lit stores downtown; how I felt like a stuffed doll in my
heavy coat, boots, and mittens; how good it was to walk into the
five-and-dime and sit at the counter drinking hot chocolate. On
Saturdays our whole family would walk downtown to shop at the
big department stores on Broadway. Mother bought all our clothes
at Penney's and Sears, and she liked to buy her dresses at the wom-
en's specialty shops like Lerner's and Diana's. At some point we'd
go into Woolworth's and sit at the soda fountain to eat.

We never ran into other Latinos at these stores or when eating
out, and it became clear to me only years later that the women
from El Building shopped mainly in other places—stores owned
by other Puerto Ricans or by Jewish merchants who had philosophically accepted our presence in the city and decided to make
us their good customers, if not real neighbors and friends. These
establishments were located not downtown but in the blocks
around our street, and they were referred to generically as *La
Tienda, El Bazar, La Bodega, La Botánica*. Everyone knew what was
meant. These were the stores where your face did not turn a clerk
to stone, where your money was as green as anyone else's.

One New Year's Eve we were dressed up like child models in the
Sears catalogue: my brother in a miniature man's suit and bow tie,
and I in black patent-leather shoes and a frilly dress with several
layers of crinoline underneath. My mother wore a bright-red dress
that night, I remember, and spike heels; her long black hair hung
to her waist. Father, who usually wore his Navy uniform during his
short visits home, had put on a dark civilian suit for the occasion:
we had been invited to his uncle's house for a big celebration.
Everyone was excited because my mother's brother Hernan—a
bachelor who could indulge himself with luxuries—had bought a
home movie camera, which he would be trying out that night.

Even the home movie cannot fill in the sensory details such a
gathering left imprinted in a child's brain. The thick sweetness of

women's perfumes mixing with the ever-present smells of food cooking in the kitchen: meat and plantain *pasteles*, as well as the ubiquitous rice dish made special with pigeon peas—*gandules*—and seasoned with precious *sofrito** sent up from the Island by somebody's mother or smuggled in by a recent traveler. *Sofrito* was one of the items that women hoarded, since it was hardly ever in stock at La Bodega. It was the flavor of Puerto Rico.

The men drank Palo Viejo rum, and some of the younger ones got weepy. The first time I saw a grown man cry was at a New Year's Eve party: he had been reminded of his mother by the smells in the kitchen. But what I remember most were the boiled *pasteles*—plantain or yucca rectangles stuffed with corned beef or other meats, olives, and many other savory ingredients, all wrapped in banana leaves. Everybody had to fish one out with a fork. There was always a "trick" pastel—one without stuffing—and whoever got that one was the "New Year's Fool."

There was also the music. Long-playing albums were treated like precious china in these homes. Mexican recordings were popular, but the songs that brought tears to my mother's eyes were sung by the melancholy Daniel Santos, whose life as a drug addict was the stuff of legend. Felipe Rodríguez was a particular favorite of couples, since he sang about faithless women and brokenhearted men. There is a snatch of one lyric that has stuck in my mind like a needle on a worn groove: *De piedra ha de ser mi cama, de piedra la cabezera . . . la mujer que a mi me quiera . . . ha de quererme de veras. Ay, Ay, Ay, corazón, porque no amas.*† . . . I must have heard it a thousand times since the idea of a bed made of stone, and its connection to love, first troubled me with its disturbing images.

The five-minute home movie ends with people dancing in a circle—the creative filmmaker must have set it up, so that all of

Author's note—*****sofrito**: A cooked condiment. A sauce composed of a mixture of fatback, ham, tomatoes, and many island spices and herbs. It is added to many typical Puerto Rican dishes for a distinctive flavor.

Author's note—†**"De piedra ha de ser . . . "** Lyrics from a popular romantic ballad (called a bolero in Puerto Rico). Freely translated: "My bed will be made of stone, of stone also my headrest (or pillow), the woman who (dares to) loves me, will have to love me for real. Ay, Ay, Ay, my heart, why can't you (let me) love . . . "

them could file past him. It is both comical and sad to watch silent dancing. Since there is no justification for the absurd movements that music provides for some of us, people appear frantic, their faces embarrassingly intense. It's as if you were watching sex. Yet for years, I've had dreams in the form of this home movie. In a recurring scene, familiar faces push themselves forward into my mind's eye, plastering their features into distorted close-ups. And I'm asking them: "Who is she? Who is the old woman I don't recognize? Is she an aunt? Somebody's wife? Tell me who she is."

"See the beauty mark on her cheek as big as a hill on the lunar landscape of her face—well, that runs in the family. The women on your father's side of the family wrinkle early; it's the price they pay for that fair skin. The young girl with the green stain on her wedding dress is *La Novia*—just up from the Island. See, she lowers her eyes when she approaches the camera, as she's supposed to. Decent girls never look at you directly in the face. *Humilde*, humble, a girl should express humility in all her actions. She will make a good wife for your cousin. He should consider himself lucky to have met her only weeks after she arrived here. If he marries her quickly, she will make him a good Puerto Rican–style wife; but if he waits too long, she will be corrupted by the city—just like your cousin there."

"She means me. I do what I want. This is not some primitive island I live on. Do they expect me to wear a black mantilla on my head and go to mass every day? Not me. I'm an American woman, and I will do as I please. I can type faster than anyone in my senior class at Central High, and I'm going to be a secretary to a lawyer when I graduate. I can pass for an American girl anywhere—I've tried it. At least for Italian, anyway—I never speak Spanish in public. I hate these parties, but I wanted the dress. I look better than any of these *humildes* here. My life is going to be different. I have an American boyfriend. He is older and has a car. My parents don't know it, but I sneak out of the house late at night sometimes to be with him. If I marry him, even my name will be American. I hate rice and beans—that's what makes these women fat."

"Your *prima*[*] is pregnant by that man she's been sneaking around with. Would I lie to you? I'm your *Tiá Política,*[†] your great-uncle's

Author's note—[*]**prima**: Female cousin.

Author's note—[†]**tía política**: Aunt by marriage.

common-law wife—the one he abandoned on the Island to go marry your cousin's mother. *I* was not invited to this party, of course, but I came anyway. I came to tell you that story about your cousin that you've always wanted to hear. Do you remember the comment your mother made to a neighbor that has always haunted you? The only thing you heard was your cousin's name, and then you saw your mother pick up your doll from the couch and say: 'It was as big as this doll when they flushed it down the toilet.' This image has bothered you for years, hasn't it? You had nightmares about babies being flushed down the toilet, and you wondered why anyone would do such a horrible thing. You didn't dare ask your mother about it. She would only tell you that you had not heard her right, and yell at you for listening to adult conversations. But later, when you were old enough to know about abortions, you suspected.

I am here to tell you that you were right. Your cousin was growing an *Americanito* in her belly when this movie was made. Soon after she put something long and pointy into her pretty self, thinking maybe she could get rid of the problem before breakfast and still make it to her first class at the high school. Well, *Niña*,* her screams could be heard downtown. Your aunt, her mamá, who had been a midwife on the Island, managed to pull the little thing out. Yes, they probably flushed it down the toilet. What else could they do with it—give it a Christian burial in a little white casket with blue bows and ribbons? Nobody wanted that baby—least of all the father, a teacher at her school with a house in West Paterson that he was filling with real children, and a wife who was a natural blond.

Girl, the scandal sent your uncle back to the bottle. And guess where your cousin ended up? Irony of ironies. She was sent to a village in Puerto Rico to live with a relative on her mother's side: a place so far away from civilization that you have to ride a mule to reach it. A real change in scenery. She found a man there—women like that cannot live without male company—but believe me, the men in Puerto Rico know how to put a saddle on a woman like her. *La Gringa,*† they call her. Ha, ha, ha. *La Gringa* is what she always wanted to be . . . "

Author's note—*niña: Girl.

Author's note—†**La gringa**: Derogatory epithet used here to ridicule a Puerto Rican girl who wants to look like a blonde North American.

The old woman's mouth becomes a cavernous black hole I fall into. And as I fall, I can feel the reverberations of her laughter. I hear the echoes of her last mocking words: *La Gringa, La Gringa!* And the conga line keeps moving silently past me. There is no music in my dream for the dancers.

When Odysseus visits Hades to see the spirit of his mother, he makes an offering of sacrificial blood, but since all the souls crave an audience with the living, he has to listen to many of them before he can ask questions. I, too, have to hear the dead and the forgotten speak in my dream. Those who are still part of my life remain silent, going around and around in their dance. The others keep pressing their faces forward to say things about the past.

My father's uncle is last in line. He is dying of alcoholism, shrunken and shriveled like a monkey, his face a mass of wrinkles and broken arteries. As he comes closer I realize that in his features I can see my whole family. If you were to stretch that rubbery flesh, you could find my father's face, and deep within *that* face—my own. I don't want to look into those eyes ringed in purple. In a few years he will retreat into silence, and take a long, long time to die. *Move back, Tío,* I tell him. *I don't want to hear what you have to say. Give the dancers room to move. Soon it will be midnight. Who is the New Year's Fool this time?*

Reflections and Responses

1. Consider the idea of "silence" in the essay. Why is it significant that the home movie has no soundtrack? What does Cofer do with that missing element? How does silence contribute to the theme of the essay?

2. What connections does Cofer make between the home movie and her dreams? In what ways is the movie dreamlike? In what ways does the essay become more nightmarish as it proceeds?

3. Consider Cofer's final paragraph. How does it pull together the various strands of the essay?

RICH COHEN

Becoming Adolf

Hannah Arendt looked at a captured Nazi leader and saw what she fa-
mously called the "banality of evil." In "Becoming Adolf," Rich Cohen looks
at an apparently banal piece of facial decoration—the toothbrush mus-
tache—and examines how it became inextricably linked with the nefarious-
ness of its most famous wearer, winding up "no less a symbol of evil than the
cloven hoof." Cohen tests the association with an ingenious and quirky ex-
periment: He grows the decidedly unpopular 'stache and wears it around
New York for a week. Finally, Cohen concludes that he can't appropriate a
styling with such a checkered past: "no matter how long, or how casually, or
how sarcastically I wore the mustache, it still belonged to Hitler."

Cohen's piece originally appeared in Vanity Fair, *where he is a contrib-*
uting editor. It was selected by Adam Gopnik for The Best American Essays 2008. *Cohen is also a frequent contributor to* Rolling Stone, *and is*
the author of several books, including Tough Jews *(1999),* The Avengers
(2001), Lake Effect *(2003),* Machers and Rockers *(2004),* Sweet
and Low *(2007), and* Israel Is Real *(2009). He lives in Connecticut.*

I decided to grow a Toothbrush mustache. Well, that's not what I
called it. Until I started this story, I had only one name for the
thing in mind: a Hitler mustache. An inch of hair that speaks of
bottomless evil. A few nights earlier, I had seen Richard Dawkins,
the author of *The God Delusion*, interviewed by Bill O'Reilly, who,
citing Stalin and Hitler, said he thought atheists, because of
their lack of restraining faith, were more susceptible to evil. To
which Dawkins (in essence) replied: both Stalin and Hitler wore
mustaches—do we therefore think the mustache was the cause of
their behavior? I experienced this as an epiphany: *By Jove!* I said to

myself. *It was the mustache!* From that moment, I stopped shaving.
From that moment, I started reading. From that moment, I became wrapped up in facial hair, and the role it has played in politics. The Toothbrush mustache offered a new way to look at the
past. It was a pinprick through which I could see the old scene
from a fresh angle. It was the history of our time retold as the story
of the 'stache.

The Toothbrush mustache is the most powerful configuration
of facial hair the world has ever known. It overpowers whoever
touches it. By merely doodling a Toothbrush mustache on a poster,

you make a political statement. Actually wearing a Hitler mustache, as I planned to do—well, that is like yelling racial epithets in a crowded subway. Wasn't Hitler amazing? Whatever he touched turned to ice. His life ended the long and fabled career of the name Adolf, which had included the stories of Adolph Zukor, Adolphe Menjou, Adolph Ochs, and Adolph Coors*. Never again will a pregnant mother innocently consider the name for her son, or imagine shouting it across a teeming playground. As for the Toothbrush mustache, it did not only die with the *Führer*—it was embalmed with him. It was his essence, and so it has been relegated to the black book of history.

This is the part where I am supposed to explain just why I decided to write this story now. I might talk about the re-emergence of facial hair on the world stage, or the rise of the "new anti-Semitism," or Holocaust denial in Iran, but, the fact is, my interest in the Hitler mustache never started and never ends. It is always. If you're a Jew, the Hitler mustache exists in the eternal present. I grew it for the same reason Richard Pryor said the word "nigger." I wanted to defuse it. I wanted to own it. I wanted to reclaim it for America and for the Jews. My name is Rich Cohen, and I wear a Hitler mustache.

The Imperial, the Walrus, the Stromboli, the Handlebar, the Horseshoe, the Mustachio (also called the Nosebeard or the Fantastico), the Pencil, also called (by idiots) the Mouthbrow—the catalogue is illustrious. (The history of the razor is longer than the history of the mustache, but only by a few minutes.) Most mustaches lie waiting for some Clark Gable or Tom Selleck to fix them in the mind. The greatest are identified with a single man, a bad man, usually, who so wrapped his identity with a particular configuration of facial hair that the two became inseparable. Like the Fu Manchu, in which long tresses hang to the chin, where they can be stroked as the madman laughs. It is named for Sax Rohmer's (racist) villain from the golden age of Hollywood, the bad guy from the B movies who became a symbol for the creeping Asian menace. Or think of the long, droopy Pancho Villa. It was worn by the

---

*Adolph Zukor, Adolphe Menjou, Adolph Ochs, and Adolph Coors:** Zukor was the founder of Paramount Pictures; Menjou was an early American film actor; Ochs owned the *New York Times*; and Coors started the Coors brewing company.

pistol-flashing Mexican bandito as he chased gringos through the border towns along the Rio Grande. These days, you see it only on Halloween, or at reunion shows of Crosby, Stills & Nash.

The Toothbrush mustache was first introduced in Germany by Americans, who turned up with it at the end of the nineteenth century the way Americans would turn up with ducktails in the 1950s. It was a bit of modern efficiency, an answer to the ornate mustaches of Europe—pop effluvia that fell into the grip of a bad, bad man.[1] Before that, the most popular mustache in Germany and Austria had been the sort worn by the royals. It was called the Kaiser, and it was elaborate. It was perfumed, styled, teased and trained. It turned up at the ends. It was the old, monarchical world that was about to be crushed by the rising tide of assembly-line America. In other words, in the case of Hitler and his 'stache, America faced an extreme case of blowback.

By the beginning of the century, it had been taken up by enough Germans to draw notice in the foreign press. In 1907, *The New York Times* chronicled a growing distaste for the import under the headline "TOOTHBRUSH" MUSTACHE: GERMAN WOMEN RESENT ITS USURPATION OF THE "KAISERBART."

In the years before the First World War, the Toothbrush was taken up by a German folk hero, which is the moment it became a craze. Before that, it had been an elite fashion shared by the dandies and swells of Berlin and Vienna. After that, it was worn by every yokel who dreamed of greatness. I am imagining young Hitler poring over newspapers in search of any mention of Hans Koeppen, a Prussian lieutenant who had become a pop star in the manner of the solo aviator, the illusionist, or the tightrope walker. Here is how he was described in *The New York Times*: "Lieut. Koeppen is 31 years old and unmarried. Six feet in height, slim and athletic, with a toothbrush mustache characteristic of his class."

The moment he appeared in the press with the Toothbrush mustache is like the moment Michael Jordan appeared on the basketball court in Bermuda-length shorts, changing the look of the game forever. In early 1908, Koeppen was given leave from the Prussian Army to cover a New York–to–Paris motor race for *Zeitung am Mittag*, a German newspaper. When I think of the Hitler who must have followed this race, because it was followed by everyone,

I think of the Hitler who loved cars and built the autobahn. (As opposed to the Hitler who killed the Gypsies and the Jews.)

After a disagreement with the German drivers, Koeppen took over. By the time he left Vladivostok, he was a star. The *Times*: "When he dashes across the German frontier from Russia . . . the tall, trim young infantry officer"—with the Toothbrush mustache— "may count upon a greeting hardly less joyful than if he were returning from victorious battle."

By the end of the war, the Toothbrush mustache was being sported even by the defeated royals. A last image of the Old World is captured in pictures taken in November 1918, when William Hohenzollern Jr., the son of the Kaiser, the heir to an office that had ceased to exist, was sent into exile. He stands on the deck of an imperial steamer. He wears shiny boots, a greatcoat, a military cap, and a Toothbrush mustache. When he turns to look at the people crowding the shore, showing them only his Toothbrush mustache, he is showing them a picture of their future.

I search the photos that survive of Hitler before Hitler was famous for the moment the 'stache appears. Because that is the moment the Devil gets his horns. In early photos, he is barefaced. The first shot that captures Hitler being Hitler was taken in August 1914, at the Odeonsplatz, in Munich. It was photographed from high above the square and shows thousands of people. Hitler, who was nothing and nobody, is no bigger than a cigarette burn, yet he jumps out. Once you see him, you can't stop seeing him. He wears the sort of grand mustache you expect to see on a barkeep. His eyes glow. A speaker has just read the declaration of war. I shudder when I see this photo, and remind myself he is dead and I am alive.

Experts disagree on the exact year Hitler began wearing the Toothbrush. Ron Rosenbaum, perhaps the only historian to give the mustache its proper due, fixes its appearance with confidence. "It was Chaplin's first, before Hitler's," he writes in an essay from *The Secret Parts of Fortune*. "Chaplin adopted a little black crepe blot beneath the nose for his Mack Sennett silent comedies after 1915, Hitler didn't adopt his until late 1919, and there's no evidence (though some speculation) that Hitler modeled his 'stache on that other actor's."

But some suggest Hitler began wearing it earlier. According to a recently re-discovered essay by Alexander Moritz Frey, who served with Hitler in the First World War, Hitler wore the mustache in the trenches. Because he had been ordered to. The old bushy mustache did not fit under his equipment. In other words, the mustache that defines Hitler was cut in a shape to fit a gas mask. Which is perfect. Because Hitler was the bastard son of the Great War, conceived in the trenches, born in defeat. He inhaled mustard gas and exhaled Zyklon B*. In another memoir, dismissed by some as a fraud, Hitler's sister-in-law Bridget claims she was the cause of the mustache. Bridget Hitler was Irish and lived in Liverpool, where, according to the memoir, the young Adolf spent a lost winter. Bridget (or whoever) says she often bickered with her brother-in-law. Because he was disagreeable, but mostly because she could not stand his unruly 'stache. In one of the great inadvertent summaries of historical character, she writes that in this, as in everything, he went too far.

He was wearing the Toothbrush at the first Nazi meetings, when there were just a few people in a room full of empty chairs. One day, an early financial supporter of the Nazi Party advised Hitler to grow out his mustache. He did this delicately but firmly, in the manner of a man trying to protect an investment. The mustache made the Nazi look freakish. Hitler was advised to grow it at least "to the end of the lips." Hitler was a vain man, and you can almost feel him bristle. Here's what Hitler said: "If it is not the fashion now, it will be later because I wear it."

In the coming years, the Toothbrush mustache would belong to just two men, Chaplin and Hitler. The funniest and the scariest. The dialectic of history. For many people, the Toothbrush mustache became no less a symbol of evil than the cloven hoof.

But here's the big question: Did the mustache affect history, or was it just a matter of style? Did it attach itself to a person and drive him crazy? Was the man in charge, or was the mustache calling the shots? Ron Rosenbaum argues that the presence of Chaplin's 'stache on Hitler's face encouraged Western leaders to underestimate the *Führer*. "Chaplin's mustache became a *lens* through which to look at Hitler," he writes. "A glass in which Hitler became *merely*

---

*He inhaled mustard gas and exhaled Zyklon B**: Mustard gas, or yperite, was a chemical weapon used during World War I. Zyklon B was an insecticide gas used to kill prisoners, particularly Jews, in large numbers in Nazi concentration camps.

Chaplinesque: a figure to be mocked more than feared, a comic villain whose pretensions would collapse of his own disproportionate weight like the Little Tramp collapsing on his cane. Someone to be ridiculed rather than resisted."

In 1942, Vidkun Quisling, the premier of Norway, whose name, because of his sellout to the Nazis, became synonymous with treachery, forbade Norwegian actors from mustache wearing. Because thespians had been donning the 'stache to parody the *Führer.* "The purpose of this singular ordinance is . . . to halt 'actor-pranks' that have been 'stopping the show' by affecting a Hitler mustache," *The New York Times* reported. Note how, in this story, the Toothbrush mustache is not identified as the Toothbrush mustache but as the Hitler mustache. From then on, the Toothbrush would belong only to Adolf. Not just a symbol but a totem of the dictator. A voodoo doll. It's not hard to see how you go from here to the plan cooked up by officers of the Office of Strategic Services, the precursor to the C.I.A., to inject estrogen into Hitler's food—female hormone that would make Hitler grow weepy, make Hitler grow breasts, and, crucially, destroy his mustache. A smooth-faced Adolf would lose confidence and fall from power. I mean, without the mustache, is Hitler even Hitler?

When Hitler died, he took his mustache with him. Not even the most cutting-edge stylist can pry them apart. If you dress like Chaplin, you run the risk of being mistaken for Hitler, as, if you dress like Evel Knievel, as I do when it rains, you run the risk of being mistaken for Elvis. The Vandyke, the Goatee, the Soul Patch, these things can become the objects of nostalgia, but the Hitler mustache is never coming back.

You could not wear a Toothbrush mustache after World War II, obviously. Because if you did, you were Hitler. In fact, you could not wear any kind of mustache after the war, because, running from Hitler, you might run into Stalin. Hitler plus Stalin ended the career of the mustache in Western political life. Before the war, all kinds of American presidents wore a mustache and/or beard. You had John Quincy Adams, with his muttonchops. You had Abe Lincoln, whose facial hair, like his politics, was the opposite of Hitler's: beard full, lip bare. You had James Garfield, who had the sort of vast rabbinical beard into which whole pages of legislation could vanish. You had Rutherford B. Hayes, Grover Cleveland, and Teddy Roosevelt, whose asthma and elephant gun were just a frame for his mustache. You had William Howard Taft—*the man wore a Walrus!*

After the war, the few American politicians who still wore a mustache were those who had made their name before Hitler and so had been grandfathered in. Like Thomas Dewey. Dewey was Eliot Spitzer. He was a prosecutor in New York in the 1930s (and later governor), the only guy with the guts to take on the Mob. For Dewey, the rise of Hitler was a fashion disaster. Because Dewey wore a neat little mustache. Dewey ran for president twice—losing to F.D.R., losing to Truman. In my opinion, without the mustache, the headline in the *Chicago Daily Tribune* (DEWEY DEFEATS TRUMAN) turns true. One of the few prominent American politicians to wear facial hair in recent memory is Al Gore, who grew a Grizzly Adams beard after he lost to George Bush, in 2000. The appearance of this beard was taken to mean either (1) Gore would never again run for office, or (2) Gore had gone completely mental. The decision to grow a mustache or a beard is all by itself reason to keep a man away from the nuclear trigger.

As a player in political life, the mustache lives on only in the Third World—a conclusion drawn not from any statistical analysis but from my own travels. You see the mustache on politicians in such lands the way you see old Peugeots in the French Antilles. It is the past. It is what we left behind. In the Third World, a portion of voters still go for the sort of hair-growing display that once brought the *Volk* to Hans Koeppen. Until recent events caused me to re-assess, I even entertained a theory—my only stab at a Tom Friedman–like, one-phrase-tells-all formulation—which I call "¿Quien es mas macho?" According to this theory, a country led by a man with a mustache is more likely to start a war, and more likely to lose it.[2] Because such a country is certain to value machismo over the nerdy qualities that actually win wars. A macho leader will counter a tank division with a cavalry charge—or promise, on the eve of battle, to drive his enemies into the sea. Such a leader will make some of the same mistakes as Hitler: he will overvalue physical courage; he will call on supernatural forces; he will consider even the smallest skirmish a "test of wills"; worst of all, he will answer the question "How will we win?" with the question "¿Quien es mas macho?*"

I cut my beard on a Friday. I did what everyone who has ever cut a full beard does: I took it through every configuration. Like passing over the stages of man, or watching cultures rise and fall until the face of Hitler emerged. I went to the closet. What would the *Führer* wear on a sunny day? It does not matter, I decided. Because I am Hitler—whatever I wear, Hitler is wearing. A dozen Hitlers passed through my mind: Hitler in a sport coat; Hitler in a lab coat. Hitler in a Speedo; Hitler in a Camaro. I shook myself and said, "Get it together, Hitler—you're losing your mind!"

I went out. In the street, some people looked at me, but most looked away. A few people said things after I passed. One man gave me a kind of Heil, but it was lackadaisical, and I am fairly certain he was being ironic. (People can be so mean!) Even friends said nothing until I asked, or else acted embarrassed for me. A woman said, "I think you were more handsome *without* the mustache." I had been worried someone might try to hurt me. I imagined toughs from the Jewish Defense League attacking with throwing stars—Jewish throwing stars! But it turns out, when you shave like Hitler, you follow the same rule you follow with bees: They're more scared of you than you are of them. Because either you really are Hitler, or you're a nut. So people do with little Hitlers what people always do with lunatics in New York, the harmless or dangerous— they ignore, they avert, they move away. If you want to fly coach without being hassled, grow a Toothbrush mustache.

I wore the mustache for about a week. It preceded me into stores and hung in the air after I exited. It sat on my face as I slept. I was Hitler in my dreams. I went to the Jewish Museum. I went to Zabar's†. I went to the Met. I went to the modern wing. I said, "All of this art is decadent." I stood on the corner of 82nd and Fifth. I stared into space. When you stare into space with a Toothbrush mustache, you are glowering. You can't help it. You're looking into crowds. You're looking at the names on the census that end in

---

*Quien es mas macho?: Spanish for "Who is more macho?" or manly.

†I went to Zabars: Zabars is a Jewish deli on the Upper West Side of Manhattan

"-berg" and "-stein" while thinking, How do we get all these *Juden* onto trains? But in the end, my project, in its broader aims, was a failure. Because no matter how long, or how casually, or how sarcastically I wore the mustache, it still belonged to Hitler. You cannot claim it, or own it, or clean it as a drug lord cleans money. Because it's too dirty. Because it's soaked up too much history. It's his, and, as far as I'm concerned, he can keep it. When you wear the Toothbrush mustache, you are wearing the worst story in the world right under your nose.

Reflections and Responses

1. Why do you think the toothbrush mustache is so inextricably linked to Hitler, while other facial features don't automatically put us in mind of their famous wearers? Does Cohen offer a satisfactory answer to that question?

2. Cohen says he grew his experimental mustache because "I wanted to reclaim it for America and for the Jews. My name is Rich Cohen, and I wear a Hitler mustache." How does Cohen's Jewish identity aid or complicate his experiment? Would a non-Jew have had the same parameters? The same results? The same conclusions? What is the upshot of Cohen's wearing the mustache, according to the final paragraphs?

3. Would you classify "Becoming Adolf" as a humorous essay? Find three points in the piece where Cohen uses a joke or a humorous phrase. Why is humor necessary in an essay of this scope and genre? Does it simply provide comic relief from a topic that touches on genocide, or is it—as Cohen says he set out to do—"diffusing" the topic of Hitler himself?

EDWIDGE DANTICAT

Westbury Court

What do we remember from our childhood? And why do we remember some things vividly, some things not at all, and yet others in some fuzzy in-between? In "Westbury Court," Edwidge Danticat examines the inner workings of memory, as she describes a deadly fire that took the lives of two children who lived next door to her in a New York apartment building when she was fourteen. Though vivid in many ways, the memory still leaves her wondering if she recalls the most significant details correctly: "Even now, I question what I remember about the children. Did they really die? Or did their mother simply move away with them after the fire?" She wonders if she is really "struggling to phase them out of [her] memory altogether."

Born in Port-au-Prince, Haiti, in 1969, Edwidge Danticat settled with her family in New York at age twelve. She began writing stories as a child and at fourteen she published a short essay about her experiences as a Haitian immigrant in New York. After graduating from Barnard College in Manhattan, she went on to earn an MFA from Brown University. Her books include the novels Breath, Eyes, Memory *(1994),* The Farming of Bones *(1998), and* The Dew Breaker *(2004); a collection of short stories,* Krik? Krak! *(1995);* After the Dance *(2002), and several compilations of essays. A memoir,* Brother, I'm Dying, *won the National Book Critics Circle Award for autobiography in 2007. "Westbury Court" originally appeared in* New Letters *and was selected by Alan Lightman for* The Best American Essays 2000.

When I was fourteen years old, we lived in a six-story brick building in a cul-de-sac off of Flatbush Avenue, in Brooklyn, called Westbury Court. Beneath the building ran a subway station through which rattled the D, M, and Q trains every fifteen minutes or so.

Though there was graffiti on most of the walls of Westbury Court, and hills of trash piled up outside, and though the elevator wasn't always there when we opened the door to step inside and the heat and hot water weren't always on, I never dreamed of leaving Westbury Court until the year of the fire.

I was watching television one afternoon when the fire began. I loved television then, especially the afternoon soap operas, my favorite of which was *General Hospital.* I would bolt out of my last high school class every day, pick up my youngest brother, Karl, from day care, and watch *General Hospital* with him on my lap while doing my homework during the commercials. My other two brothers, André and Kelly, would later join us in the apartment, but they preferred to watch cartoons in the back bedroom.

One afternoon while *General Hospital* and afternoon cartoons were on, a fire started in apartment 6E, across the hall. There in that apartment lived our new neighbors, an African-American mother and her two boys. We didn't know the name of the mother, or the names and ages of her boys, but I venture to guess that they were around five and ten years old.

I didn't know a fire had started until two masked, burly firemen came knocking on our door. My brothers and I rushed out into the hallway filled with smoke and were quickly escorted down to the first floor by some other firemen already on our floor. While we ran by, the door to apartment 6E had already been knocked over by the fire squad and inside was filled with bright flames and murky smoke.

All of the tenants of the building who were home at that time were crowded on the sidewalk outside. My brothers and I, it seemed, were the last to be evacuated. Clutching my brothers' hands, I wondered if I had remembered to lock our apartment door. Was there anything valuable we could have taken?

An ambulance screeched to a stop in front of the building, and the two firemen who had knocked on our door came out carrying the pliant and lifeless bodies of the two children from across the hall. Their mother jumped out of the crowd and ran toward them, screaming, "My babies—not my babies," as the children were lowered into the back of the ambulance and transferred into the arms of the emergency medical personnel. The fire was started by the two boys, after their mother had stepped out to pick up some

groceries at the supermarket down the street. They had been playing with matches.

(Later my mother would tell us, "See, this is what happens to
children who play with matches. Sometimes it is too late to say, 'I
shouldn't have.'" My brother Kelly, who was fascinated with fire
and liked to hold up a match to the middle of his palm until the
light fizzled out, gave up this party trick after the fire.)

We were quiet that afternoon when both our parents came
home. We were the closest to the fire in the building, and the
most religious of our parents' friends saw it as a miracle that we
had escaped safe and sound. When my mother asked how come I,
the oldest one, hadn't heard the children scream or hadn't
smelled the smoke coming from across the hall, I confessed that I
had been watching *General Hospital* and was too consumed in the
intricate plot.

(After the fire, my mother had us stay with a family on the second floor for a few months, after school. I felt better not having to
be wholly responsible for myself and my brothers, in case something like that fire should ever happen again.)

The apartment across the hall stayed empty for a long time, and
whenever I walked past it, a piece of its inner skeleton would
squeak, and occasionally burnt wood that might have been hanging by a fragile singed thread would crash down and cause a dom-
ino effect of further ruptures, unleashed like those children's last
cries, which I had not heard because I had been so wrapped up in
the made-up drama of a world where, even though the adults' lives
were often in turmoil, the children came home to the welcoming
arms of waiting mommies and nannies who served them freshly
baked cookies on porcelain plates and helped them to remove
their mud-soaked boots, if it was raining, lest they soil the lily-white
carpets. But should their boots accidentally sully the carpet, or
should their bright yellow raincoats inadvertently drip on the spar-
kling linoleum, there would be a remedy for that as well. And if
their house should ever catch fire, a smart dog or a good neighbor
would rescue them just in time, and the fire trucks would come
right quick because some attentive neighbor would call them.

Through the trail of voices that came up to comfort us, I heard
that the children's mother would be prosecuted for negligence
and child abandonment. I couldn't help but wonder, would our

parents have suffered the same fate had it been my brothers and me who were killed in the fire?

When they began to repair the apartment across the hall, I would occasionally sneak out to watch the workmen. They were shelling the inside of the apartment and replacing everything from the bedroom closets to the kitchen floors. I never saw the mother of the dead boys again and never heard anything of her fate.

A year later, after the apartment was well polished and painted, two blind Haitian brothers and their sister moved in. They were all musicians and were part of a group called les Frères Parent, the Parent Brothers. Once my parents allowed my brothers and me to come home from school to our apartment, I would always listen carefully for our new tenants, so I'd be the first to know if anything went awry.

What I heard coming from the apartment soon after they moved in was music, "engagé" music, which the brothers were composing to protest against the dictatorship in Haiti, from which they had fled. The Parent Brothers and their sister, Lydie, did nothing but rehearse a cappella most days when they were not receiving religious and political leaders from Haiti and from the Haitian community in New York.

The same year after the fire, a cabdriver who lived down the hall in 6J was killed on a night shift in Manhattan; a good friend of my father's, a man who gave great Sunday afternoon parties in 6F, died of cirrhosis of the liver. One day while my brothers and I were at school and my parents were at work, someone came into our apartment through our fire escape and stole my father's expensive camera. That same year a Nigerian immigrant was shot and killed in front of the building across the street. To appease us, my mother said, "Nothing like that ever happens out of the blue. He was in a fight with someone." It was too troublesome for her to acknowledge that people could die randomly, senselessly, at Westbury Court or anywhere else.

Every day on my way back from school, I hurried past the flowers and candles piled in front of the spot where the Nigerian, whose name I didn't know, had been murdered. Still I never thought I was living in a violent place. It was an elevated castle above a clattering train tunnel, a blind alley where children from our building and the building across the street had erected a common basketball court for hot summer afternoon games, an urban yellow brick road where hopscotch squares dotted the sidewalk next to burned-out, abandoned cars. It was home.

My family and I moved out of Westbury Court three years after the fire. Every once in a while, though, the place came up in conversation, linked to either a joyous or a painful memory. One of the girls who had scalded her legs while boiling a pot of water for her bath during one of those no-heat days got married last year. After the burglar had broken into the house and taken my father's camera, my father—an amateur photography buff—never took another picture.

My family and I often reminisce about the Parent Brothers when we see them in Haitian newspapers or on television; we brag that we knew them when, before one of the brothers became a senator in Haiti and the sister, Lydie, became mayor of one of the better-off Haitian suburbs, Pétion-Ville. We never talk about the lost children.

Even now, I question what I remember about the children. Did they really die? Or did their mother simply move away with them after the fire? Maybe they were not even boys at all. Maybe they were two girls. Or one boy and one girl. Or maybe I am struggling to phase them out of my memory altogether. Not just them, but the fear that their destiny could have so easily been mine and my brothers'.

A few months ago, I asked my mother, "Do you remember the children and the fire at Westbury Court?"

Without missing a flutter of my breath, my mother replied, "Oh those children, those poor children, their poor mother. Sometimes it is too late to say, 'I shouldn't have.'"

Reflections and Responses

1. Consider the way Danticat narrates her essay. What information does she introduce that she would not have known during the incident of the fire? What other methods of telling the story might she have chosen?

2. Why does Danticat emphasize her mother's response to the fire, referring to it at the time and then repeating it later? In what

sense is her mother's comment a warning? How do you think Danticat wants us to interpret her mother's comment in the final paragraph?

3. Why do you think that after vividly describing the firefighters carrying out the "lifeless bodies of the two children," Danticat toward the end of the essay wonders whether the children actually did die? What effect does her wondering about this produce? Do you think it leaves the issue open-ended? In light of her questions, how are we to understand the final paragraph?

YUSEF KOMUNYAKAA

The Blue Machinery of Summer

The central purpose behind an autobiographical essay can sometimes remain obscure, never explicitly stated by the writer, who may be more interested in self-exploration than full disclosure, more concerned with raising questions than with answering them. Essayists are under no obligation to write only about personal experiences they fully understand. In "The Blue Machinery of Summer," an essay full of questions and "maybes," one of America's foremost poets describes his successes and failures years ago at a summer factory job that forced him to realize the difficulties his education would bring.

Yusef Komunyakaa, who has received numerous honors and awards, including a 1994 Pulitzer Prize for Neon Vernacular, *the 2001 Ruth Lilly Poetry Prize, and a Bronze Star for service as a journalist in Vietnam, was born in Bogalusa, Louisiana, in 1947. His first book of poetry,* Dedications & Other Darkhorses, *appeared in 1977, and subsequent volumes include* Copacetic *(1984);* I Apologize for the Eyes in My Head *(1986);* Dien Cai Dau *(1988);* Magic City *(1992);* Thieves of Paradise *(1998);* Talking Dirty to the Gods *(2000);* Pleasure Dome: New & Collected Poems, 1975–1999 *(2001); and* Taboo: The Wishbone Trilogy, Part I *(2004). He has written extensively on jazz and in 1999 was elected a Chancellor of the Academy of American Poets. Currently Distinguished Senior Poet in New York University's graduate creative writing program, Komunyakaa has most recently published* Gilgamesh: A Verse Play *(2006) and* Warhorses: Poems *(2008). "The Blue Machinery of Summer" first appeared in* The Washington Post Magazine *and was selected by Kathleen Norris for* The Best American Essays 2001.

"I feel like I'm part of this damn thing," Frank said. He carried himself like a large man even though he was short. A dead cigarette dangled from his half-grin. "I've worked on this machine for twenty-odd years, and now it's almost me."

It was my first day on a summer job at ITT Cannon in Phoenix in 1979. This factory manufactured parts for electronic systems—units that fit into larger, more complex ones. My job was to operate an air-powered punch press. Depending on each item formed, certain dies or templates were used to cut and shape metal plates into designs the engineers wanted.

"I know all the tricks of the trade, big and small, especially when it comes to these punch presses. It seems like I was born riding this hunk of steel."

Frank had a gift for gab, but when the foreman entered, he grew silent and meditative, bent over the machine, lost in his job. The whole day turned into one big, rambunctious dance of raw metal, hiss of steam, and sparks. Foremen strutted about like banty roosters. Women tucked falling curls back into hair nets, glancing at themselves in anything chrome.

This job reminded me of the one I'd had in 1971 at McGraw Edison, also in Phoenix, a year after I returned from Vietnam. Back then, I had said to myself, this is the right setting for a soap opera. Muscle and sex changed the rhythm of this place. We'd call the show "The Line."

I'd move up and down the line, shooting screws into metal cabinets of coolers and air conditioners—one hour for Montgomery Ward or Sears, and the next two hours for a long line of cabinets stamped McGraw Edison. The designs differed only slightly, but made a difference in the selling price later on. The days seemed endless, and it got to where I could do the job with my eyes closed.

In retrospect, I believe I was hyper from the war. I couldn't lay back; I was driven to do twice the work expected—sometimes taking on both sides of the line, giving other workers a hand. I worked overtime two hours before 7 A.M. and one hour after 4 P.M. I learned every thing about coolers and air conditioners, and rectified problem units that didn't pass inspection.

At lunch, rather than sitting among other workers, I chose a secluded spot near the mountain of boxed-up coolers to eat my homemade sandwiches and sip iced tea or lemonade. I always had a paperback book in my back pocket: Richard Wright's *Black Boy*,

Albert Camus' *The Fall*, Frantz Fanon's *The Wretched of the* Earth, or C. W. E. Bigsby's *The Black American Writer*. I wrote notes in the margins with a ballpoint. I was falling in love with language and ideas. All my attention went to reading.

When I left the gaze of Arizona's Superstition Mountain and headed for the Colorado Rockies, I wasn't thinking about higher education. Once I was in college, I vowed never to take another job like this, and yet here I was, eight years later, a first-year graduate student at the University of California at Irvine, and working another factory job in Phoenix, hypnotized by the incessant clang of machinery.

Frank schooled me in the tricks of the trade. He took pride in his job and practiced a work ethic similar to the one that had shaped my life early on even though I had wanted to rebel against it. Frank was from Little Rock: in Phoenix, everyone seemed to be from somewhere else except the indigenous Americans and Mexicans.

"If there's one thing I know, it's this damn machine," Frank said. "Sometimes it wants to act like it has a brain of its own, as if it owns me, but I know better."

"Iron can wear any man out," I said.

"Not this hunk of junk. It was new when I came here."

"But it'll still be here when you're long gone."

"Says who?"

"Says iron against flesh."

"They will scrap this big, ugly bastard when I'm gone."

"They'll bring in a new man."

"Are you the new man, whippersnapper? They better hire two of you to replace one of me."

"Men will be men."

"And boys will be boys."

The hard dance held us in its grip.

I spotted Lily Huong the second day in a corner of the wiring department. The women there moved their hands in practiced synchrony, looping and winding color-coded wires with such graceful dexterity and professionalism. Some chewed gum and blew bubbles, others smiled to themselves as if they were reliving the weekend. And a good number talked about the soap operas, naming off the characters as if they were family members or close friends.

Lily was in her own world. Petite, with long black hair grabbed up, stuffed beneath a net and baseball cap, her body was one fluid motion, as if it knew what it was doing and why.

"Yeah, boys will be boys," Frank said.

"What you mean?"

"You're looking at trouble, my friend."

"Maybe trouble is looking for me. And if it is, I'm not running."

"She is nothing but bona fide trouble."

I wonder if she was thinking of Vietnam while she sat bent over the table, or when she glided across the concrete floor as if she were moving through lush grass. Lily? It made me think of waterlily, lotus—how shoots and blooms were eaten in that faraway land. The lotus grows out of decay, in lagoons dark with sediment and rot.

Mornings arrived with the taste of sweet nighttime still in our mouths, when the factory smelled like the deepest ore, and the syncopation of the great heaving presses fascinated me.

The nylon and leather safety straps fit our hands like fingerless gloves and sometimes seemed as if they'd pull us into the thunderous pneumatic vacuum faster than an eye blink. These beasts pulsed hypnotically; they reminded everyone within earshot of terrifying and sobering accidents. The machinery's dance of smooth heft seemed extraordinary, a masterpiece of give-and-take precision. If a foolhardy novice wrestled with one of these metal contraptions, it would suck up the hapless soul. The trick was to give and pull back with a timing that meant the difference between life and death.

"Always use a safety block, one of these chunks of wood. Don't get careless," Frank said. "Forget the idea you can second-guess this monster. Two months ago we had a guy in here named Leo on that hunk of junk over there, the one that Chico is now riding."

"Yeah, and?"

"I don't believe it. It's crazy. I didn't know Leo was a fool. The machine got stuck, he bent down, looked underneath, and never knew his last breath. That monster flattened his head like a pancake."

One morning, I stood at the checkout counter signing out my tools for the day's work and caught a glimpse of Lily out of the corner of my eye. She stopped. Our eyes locked for a moment, and then she glided on toward her department. Did she know I had been in 'Nam? Had there been a look in my eyes that had given me away?

"You can't be interested in her," Paula said. She pushed her hair away from her face in what seemed like an assured gesture.

"Why not?" I said.

"She's nothing, nothing but trouble."

"Oh?"

"Anyway, you ain't nobody's foreman."

I took my toolbox and walked over to the punch press. The buzzer sounded. The gears kicked in. The day started.

After three weeks, I discovered certain social mechanisms ran the place. The grapevine, long, tangled, and thorny, was merciless. After a month on the job I had been wondering why Frank disappeared at lunchtime but always made it back just minutes before the buzzer.

"I bet Frank tells you why he comes back here with a smile on his mug?" Maria coaxed. She worked as a spot-welder, with most of her day spent behind heavy black goggles as the sparks danced around her.

"No."

"Why don't you ask Paula one of these mornings when you're signing out tools?"

"I don't think so," I said.

"She's the one who puts that grin on his face. They've been tearing up that rooming house over on Sycamore for years."

"Good for them," I said.

"Not if that cop husband of hers come to his senses."

It would have been cruel irony for Frank to work more than twenty years on the monster and lose his life at the hands of a mere mortal.

The grapevine also revealed that Lily had gotten on the payroll because of Rico, who was a foreman on the swing shift. They had been lovers and he had put in a good word for her. Rico was built like a lightweight boxer, his eyes bright and alert, always able to look over the whole room in a single glance. The next news said Lily was sleeping with Steve, the shipping foreman, who wore western shirts, a silver and turquoise belt buckle, and cowboy boots. His red Chevy pickup had a steer's horn on the hood. He was tall and lanky and had been in the Marines, stationed at Khe Sanh.

I wondered about Lily. What village or city had she come from—Chu Chi or Danang, Saigon or Hue? What was her story? Did she still hear the war during sleepless nights? Maybe she had had an American boyfriend, maybe she was in love with a Vietnamese once, a student, and they had intimate moments besides the Perfume River as boats with green and red lanterns passed at dusk. Or maybe she met him on the edge of a rice paddy, or in some half-lit place in Danang a few doors down from the Blue Dahlia.

She looked like so many who tried to outrun past lovers, history. "*She's nothing but trouble...* " Had she become a scapegoat? Had she tried to play a game that wasn't hers to play? Didn't anyone notice her black eye one week, the corner of her lip split the next?

I told myself I would speak to her. I didn't know when, but I would.

The women were bowed over their piecework.

As a boy I'd make bets with myself, and as a man I was still making bets, and sometimes they left me in some strange situations.

"In New Guinea those Fuzzy Wuzzies saved our asses," Frank said. "They're the smartest people I've ever seen. One moment almost in the Stone Age, and the next they're zooming around in our jeeps and firing automatic weapons like nobody's business. They gave the Japanese hell. They were so outrageously brave it still hurts to think about it."

I wanted to tell him about Vietnam, a few of the things I'd witnessed, but I couldn't. I could've told him about the South Vietnamese soldiers who were opposites of Frank's heroes.

I gazed over toward Lily.

Holding up one of the doodads—we were stamping out hundreds hourly—I said to Frank, "Do you know what this is used for?"

"No. Never crossed my mind."

"You don't know? How many do you think you've made?"

"God only knows."

"And you don't know what they're used for?"

"No."

"How much does each sell for?"

"Your guess is as good as mine. I make 'em. I don't sell 'em."

He's right, I thought. Knowing wouldn't change these workers' lives. This great symphony of sweat, oil, steel, rhythm, it all made a strange kind of sense.

"These are used in the firing mechanisms of grenade launchers," I said as I scooped up a handful. "And each costs the government almost eighty-five dollars."

The buzzer sounded.

In the cafeteria, most everybody sat in their usual clusters. A few of the women read magazines—*True Romance, Tan,* TV *Guide, Reader's Digest*—as they nibbled at sandwiches and sipped Cokes. One woman was reading her Bible. I felt like the odd man out as I took my paperback from my lunch pail: a Great Books Foundation volume, with blue-white-black cover and a circle around GB. My coworkers probably thought I was reading the same book all summer long, or that it was a religious text. I read Voltaire, Hegel, and Darwin.

Voltaire spoke to me about Equality:

All the poor are not unhappy. The greater number are born in that state, and constant labor prevents them from too sensibly feeling their situation; but when they do strongly feel it, then follow wars such as these of the popular party against the Senate at Rome, and those of the peasantry in Germany, England and France. All these wars ended sooner or later in the subjection of the people, because the great have money, and money in a state commands every thing: I say in a state, for the case is different between nation and nation. The nation that makes the best use of iron will always subjugate another that has more gold but less courage.

Maybe I didn't want to deal with those images of 'Nam still in my psyche, ones that Lily had rekindled.

"You catch on real fast, friend," Frank said. "It is hard to teach a man how to make love to a machine. It's almost got to be in your blood. If you don't watch out, you'll be doing twenty in this sweatbox too. Now mark my word."

I wanted to tell him about school. About some of the ideas filling my head. Lily would smile, but she looked as if she were gazing through me.

One morning in early August, a foreman said they needed me to work on a special unit. I was led through the security doors. The room was huge, and the man working on the big, circular-dome object seemed small and insignificant in the voluminous space. Then I was shaking hands with the guy they called Dave the Lathe. Almost everyone had a nickname here, as in the Deep South, where, it turned out, many of the workers were from. The nicknames came from the almost instinctual impulse to make language a game of insinuation.

Dave was from Paradise, California. He showed me how to polish each part, every fixture and pin. The work led to painstaking tedium. Had I posed too many questions? Was that why I was working this job?

Here everything was done by hand, with patience and silence. The room was air-conditioned. Now the clang of machines and whine of metal being cut retreated into memory. Behind this door Dave the Lathe was a master at shaping metals, alloyed with secrets, a metal that could be smoothed but wouldn't shine, take friction and heat out of this world. In fact, it looked like a fine piece of sculpture designed aeronautically, that approached perfection. Dave the Lathe had been working on this nose cone for a spacecraft for more than five months.

Dave and I seldom talked. Lily's face receded from my thoughts. Now I stood across from Dave the Lathe, thinking about two women in my class back at the University of California with the same first name. One was from New York. She had two reproductions of French nudes over her bed and was in love with Colette, the writer. The other woman was part Okinawan from Honolulu. If we found ourselves in a room alone, she always managed to disengage herself. We had never had a discussion, but here she was, undressing in my mind. At that moment, standing a few feet from Dave the Lathe, I felt that she and I were made for each other but she didn't know it yet.

I told Dave that within two weeks I'd return to graduate school. He wished me luck in a tone that suggested he knew what I'd planned to say before I said it.

"Hey, college boy!" Maria shouted across the cafeteria. "Are you in college or did you do time like Frank says?" I wanted the impossible, to disappear.

Lily's eyes caught mine. I still hadn't told her I felt I'd left part of myself in her country. Maria sat down beside me. I fished out the ham sandwich, but left Darwin in the lunch box. She said, "You gonna just soft-shoe in here and then disappear, right?"

"No. Not really."

"Not *really*, he says," she mocked.

"Well."

"Like a lousy lover who doesn't tell you every thing. Doesn't tell the fine print."

"Well."

"Cat got your tongue, college boy?"

"Are you talking to me or somebody else?"

"Yeah, you! Walk into somebody's life and then turn into a ghost. A one-night stand."

"I didn't think anyone needed to know."

"I suppose you're too damn good to tell us the truth."

She stood up, took her lunch over to another table, sat down, and continued to eat. I didn't know what to say. I was still learning.

There's good silence. There's bad silence. Growing up in rural Louisiana, along with four brothers and one sister, I began to cultivate a life of the imagination. I traveled to Mexico, Africa, and the Far East. When I was in elementary school and junior high, sometimes I knew the answers to questions, but I didn't dare raise my hand. Boys and girls danced up and down, waving their arms, with right and wrong answers. It was hard for me to chance being wrong. Also, I found it difficult to share my feelings; but I always broke the silence and stepped in if someone was being mistreated.

Now, as I sat alone, looking out the window of a Greyhound bus at 1 A.M., I felt like an initiate who had gotten cold feet and was hightailing it back to some privileged safety zone. I began to count the figures sprawled on the concrete still warm from the sun's weight on the city. There seemed to be an uneasy equality among destitutes: indigenous Americans, Mexicans, a few blacks and whites. Eleven. Twelve. I thought, a massacre of the spirit.

The sounds of the machines were still inside my head. The clanging punctuated by Frank's voice: "Are you ready to will your body to this damn beast, my friend?"

"No, Frank. I never told you I am going to college," I heard myself saying. Did education mean moving from one class to the next? My grandmothers told me again and again that one could scale a mountain with a good education. But could I still talk to them, to my parents, my siblings? I would try to live in two worlds—at the very least. That was now my task. I never wanted again to feel that my dreams had betrayed me.

Maybe the reason I hadn't spoken to Lily was I didn't want to talk about the war. I hadn't even acknowledged to my friends that I'd been there.

The bus pulled out, headed for L.A. with its headlights sweeping like slow yellow flares across drunken faces, as if images of the dead had followed Lily and me from a distant land only the heart could bridge.

Reflections and Responses

1. What images does Komunyakaa use early in his essay to link the assembly-line work, the machinery, and sexuality? Why do you think he wants to establish these links?

2. Why do you think Komunyakaa informs us about his reading? What kind of books does he seem to prefer? Why do you think he includes a long quotation from Voltaire in an essay that is almost entirely personal?

3. How does Komunyakaa present himself in this essay? How does he portray the way his fellow workers relate to him? How does he relate to his fellow workers? What role does Lily Huong play in the essay? What sense do you make of his final conversation with Maria toward the end of the essay? What is she saying about him? How do her comments link up with the sexual themes introduced early in the essay?

REBECCA MCCLANAHAN

Book Marks

Anyone who's ever bought a used book (perhaps eventually this one) has found traces of a previous reader who marked up the volume in various ways—through marginal comments, underlining, doodles, and even an occasional personal note. Sometimes the presence of the other reader still lingers in food or beverage stains, handy bookmarks such as a fast-food receipt, or even forgotten letters or photographs that once marked a pause in the reading. In "Book Marks," Rebecca McClanahan contemplates the presence of someone whose life is suggested by marginal notes scribbled in a library book. As she plays detective and tries to imagine the person who previously borrowed the book, she recollects various stages of her own life as it moved in and out of books that became closely associated with relatives, schoolmates, husbands, and lovers. McClanahan weaves these episodes together, revealing how arbitrary the lines can be that we conventionally draw between life and literature.

Rebecca McClanahan lives in New York City and has published five books of poetry, most recently Deep Light: New and Selected Poems *(2007). Her nonfiction books consist of a memoir,* The Riddle Song and Other Mysteries *(2002) and three books about writing,* One Word Deep: Lectures and Readings *(1993),* Word Painting: A Guide to Writing *More Descriptively (1999), and* Write Your Heart Out *(2001). She has received the Carter Prize for the essay from* Shenandoah, *a Pushcart award in fiction, and the Wood Prize from* Poetry *magazine. Her work was included in* The Best American Poetry *1998. First published in* Southern Review, *"Book Marks" was selected by Kathleen Norris for* The Best American Essays 2001.

I am worried about the woman. I am afraid she might hurt herself, perhaps has already hurt herself—there's no way to know which of the return dates stamped on the book of poetry was hers. The book, Denise Levertov's *Evening Train*, belongs to the New York City Public Library. I checked it out yesterday and can keep it for three weeks. Ever since my husband and I moved to the city several months ago, I've been homesick for my books, the hundreds of volumes stored in my brother's basement. I miss having them near me, running my hands over their spines, recalling when and where I acquired each one, and out of what need.

There's no way to know for certain that the phantom library patron is a woman, but all signs point in that direction. On one page is a red smear that looks like lipstick, and between two other pages, lying like a bookmark, is a long, graying hair. The underlinings, which may or may not have been made by the woman, are in pencil—pale, tentative marks I study carefully, reverently, the way an archaeologist traces a fossil's delicate imprint. The rest is dream, conjecture, the making of *my* story. It's a weird obsession, I know, studying other readers' leavings and guessing the lives lived beneath. Even as my reasonable mind is having its say (*This makes no sense. How can you assume? The marks could have been made by anyone, for any reason, over any period of time . . .*), my other self is leaving on its own journey. I've always been a hungry reader, what one friend calls a "selfish reader." But is there any other kind? Don't we all read to answer our own needs, to complete the lives we've begun, to point us toward some light?

Some of the underlinings in *Evening Train* have been partially erased (eraser crumbles have gathered in the center seams), as if the woman reconsidered her first responses or tried to cover her tracks. The markings do not strike me as those of a defiant woman but rather of one who has not only taken her blows but feels she might deserve them. She has underlined "serviceable heart" in one poem; in another, "Grey-haired, I have not grown wiser." If she exists, I would like to sit down with this woman. We seem to have a lot in common. We chose the same book, we both wear red lipstick, and though I am not so honest (the gray in my hair is hidden beneath an auburn rinse), I am probably her age or thereabouts.

And from what she has left behind on the pages of Levertov's poems, it appears that our hearts have worn down in the same places. This is the part that worries me. Though my heart has mended, for the time being at least, hers seems to be in the very act of breaking. A present-tense pain pulses through each marked-up poem, and the further I read, the clearer it becomes what she is considering. I want to reach through the pages and lead her out.

My interest in marginalia, reading between the lines, began when I was an evening student at a college in California, still living with my parents but working days to help pay my expenses. It was a lonely time. Untethered from the rock-hard rituals of high school, I'd been set adrift, floating between adolescence and Real Life, a place I'd heard about that both terrified and seduced me. As a toddler, I'd been one of those milkily content clingers who must be pulled away from the nipple; eighteen years later I was still reluctant to leave my mother's side.

My siblings had no such trouble. An older sister had married and left home, a brother was away at college, and my younger siblings, in various stages of adolescent rebellion, had struck out on their own. As for my friends, most had left to study at faraway colleges; the few who stayed, taking jobs at the local bank or training to be dental assistants, seemed even more remote than those who had left. Whatever had held us together in high school—intramural sports, glee club, the senior-class play—was light-years away. As was the boy who'd promised to marry me someday. He'd found someone else, and though part of me had always known that's how that book would end (we'd never progressed beyond kissing), nevertheless his leaving was the first hairline crack in my serviceable heart.

My only strike at independence was the paycheck I earned typing invoices at a printing shop. Though I reluctantly accepted my father's offer to pay tuition costs, I insisted on buying my own textbooks. I could afford only used ones, and the more used the book, the cheaper it was. Some had passed through several hands; the multiple marked-through names and phone numbers on the flyleaves bore witness to this fact. At first I was put off by the previous owners' underlinings, marginal comments, bright yellow highlighted sections, sophomoric doodlings and obscenities. Worse still were the unintentional markings—coffee stains, dried pizza sauce, cigarette burns.

After a while, however, I became accustomed to the markings. I even began to welcome them. Since I didn't live on campus or have college buddies—I worked all day, then went straight home after class—I appreciated the company the used books offered. I imagined the boy who had splattered pizza sauce across the map of South America. Was he lonely too? Had he eaten the pizza alone, in his tiny dorm room, while memorizing Bolivia's chief exports? What about the girl who had misspelled *orgasm* (using two s's) in the margins of John Donne's "The Canonization"? Had she ever said the word aloud? Was she a virgin like me?

The used texts served practical purposes as well. In the case of difficult subject matter (which, for me, meant political science, chemistry, and botany), it was as though I had engaged a private tutor, someone to sit at my elbow and guide me through each lesson, pointing out important concepts, underlining the principles that would show up on next week's exam. The marked-up textbook was my portable roommate, someone to sit up nights with me, to quiz me with questions I didn't know enough to ask.

Not since I was a child sharing a room with Great-Aunt Bessie, an inveterate reader, had I had a reading partner. Bessie and I would sit up late in our double bed and read mysteries and westerns aloud. We'd take turns, each reading a chapter a night, and at the end, right before Bessie removed her dentures and switched off the light (she was a disciplined reader, always stopping at the end of a chapter), right before she slipped her embroidered handkerchief into the book to mark our place, we would discuss our reactions to what we had read and make predictions about how the story would turn. Because of Aunt Bessie, I never saw books as dead, finished texts. They were living, breathing entities, unexplored territories into which we would venture the next night, and the next. Anything could happen, and we would be present when it did.

Years later, carrying this lesson into my first college class, I was amazed at what I encountered: rows of bleary-eyed students slumped around me, their limp hands spread across Norton anthologies. Most never ventured into the territory Bessie and I had explored. This stymied me, that people could read a poem by Shelley or Keats or Sylvia Plath and not want to live inside it, not want to add their words to the ones on the page. Looking back on my college literature texts, I can trace the journey of those years. In the margins of Wordsworth's sonnets, beside the lines "The world is too much with us; late and soon, / Getting and spending, we lay waste our powers," I can chart my decision to quit my day job and pursue my studies full-time, even if it meant borrowing from the savings account I'd been feeding each payday. "I am done with this," I wrote in blue ink, meaning the commerce of getting and spending, the laying waste of powers I'd yet to discover.

And in the underlined sections of Gerard Manley Hopkins's poems, I can trace the ecstasy of my first spiritual awakening ("I caught this morning morning's minion"), made all the more ecstatic since, because I was unable to understand his elliptical syntax with my *mind,* I was forced to take it in through the rhythms of my body. This was a new music for me. My heart was no longer metaphorical. It beat rapidly in my chest, my temples, in my pale, veined wrists. Suddenly, within Hopkins's lines, I was breaking in new places: "here / Buckle! And the fire that breaks from thee then, a billion / Times told lovelier, more dangerous."

At the time I encountered those lines, I had no knowledge of the fire that awaited me in the eyes of a young man I'd yet to meet. I saw myself vaguely, like a character in one of the books I fell asleep with each night. In dreams I drank black coffee at street cafés, lay beneath the branches of the campus oaks, or wandered late at night, as Whitman's narrator had wandered, looking up "in perfect silence at the stars." In daylight, I pulled another used book from the shelf and fell into its pages. Could it be that Rilke's injunction, "You must change your life," was aimed at me? I highlighted it in yellow, then wrote in the margin, in bright blue indelible ink, "THIS MEANS *YOU!*"

Had I chosen to resell these books to the campus bookstore (I didn't; they had become part of me), their new owners might one day have read my underlinings, my marginal scribblings, and wondered at the person who left such a trail. "She needs to get more sun," they might have thought, if they could deduce I was a she. Maybe they would have worried about me the way I now worry about the gray-haired woman. They might even have responded, as I sometimes do, with an answering note. It might have gone on and on like that, a serial installment of marginalia, each new reader adding his own twist to Hopkins or Wordsworth—or to me, the phantom whose pages they were turning.

When life interrupts, you close the book. Or perhaps you leave it open, facedown on the bed or table, to mark your place. Aunt

Bessie taught me never to do this. "You'll break its spine," she said, running her age-spotted hands across the book's cover, and the tenderness in her gesture made me ashamed that I'd ever considered such violence. After that I took to dog-earing pages, but after a while even that seemed too violent. Now, whenever I encounter a dog-eared page, I smooth its wounded edge.

Aunt Bessie used embroidered handkerchiefs to mark her place, though to me they seemed unnecessary since she always stopped at the end of a chapter. Some readers are like that. They regulate their reading, fitting books neatly into their lives the way some people schedule exercise or sex: five poems, twenty laps. One of my friends always stops after twenty-five pages so she can easily remember where she left off. Though I admire such discipline, I've never been able to accomplish it. I fall into books the way I fall into lust—wholly, hungrily. Often the book disappoints, or I disappoint. The first flush cools and the words grow tired and dull, or I grow tired and dull and slam the book shut. Occasionally, though, I keep reading, and lust ripens slowly into love, and I want to stay right there, at the lamplit table or in the soft, worn chair, until the last page is turned.

Then suddenly, always unexpectedly, life interferes; it is what life does best. It usually happens in mid-paragraph, sometimes even mid-sentence—a kind of biblio-interruptus—and I grab something to mark my place. Though I own many beautiful bookmarks, they are never there when I need them. So I reach for whatever is close at hand. A newspaper clipping, the phone bill, my bourbon-fossiled cocktail napkin, a note from a friend, the grocery list. Once I plucked a protruding feather from the sofa cushion where I rested my head, once I used a maple leaf that had blown in through the patio door, once I even pulled a hair from my head.

Looking back on my nineteenth year, I am amazed at how easily I closed the books I'd been living inside. What replaced them were the poems the young man handed me across a restaurant table. "Pretty Brown-Haired Girl" was the title of one; "Monday Rain" another. Some were written in German, and I used my secondhand Cassell's dictionary to translate them. The poems were not good—I remember thinking this even then—but they were the first love poems anyone had ever written for me. I ran my fingers across the words. I folded the papers, put them into my pocket, and later that night unfolded them on my bedside table. Already the poems were in my head, every ragged line break and rhyme.

At twenty-one he had one of those faces that might have looked old all along. His hair was retreating prematurely, exposing a forehead with furrows already deeply plowed. But his eyes were bright blue, center-of-a-flame blue, simultaneously cool and hot. He wore faded jeans and a rugged woolen jacket and drove a motorcycle; his mouth tasted of cigarettes. Plus he could quote Wordsworth, which weakened me even more. He was independently brilliant, a part-time student with no declared major, taking classes in subjects like German and astronomy and horticulture—nothing that fit together to form anything like a formal degree. "Come into the light of things," he teased. "Let nature be your teacher."

Nature taught me so much over the next year that it was all I could do to attend classes, let alone sit up nights with pencil in hand, scribbling notes in the margins of textbooks. He'd moved into his own apartment, and his marks were all over me—his mouth on my forehead, his tongue on my neck, my belly, the smell of his cigarettes in my hair. All else fell away. When an occasional misgiving surfaced I pushed it down. I had reason to doubt that I was his only brown-haired girl, the only one to whom he wrote poems. But I hushed the voice of reason, even when it spoke directly into my ear.

My parents disapproved of him, and though Aunt Bessie had moved back to her Midwest childhood home, I was certain she would have disapproved too. I *knew* Carolyn did. She'd told me so, in the same loving yet blatantly forthright tone she'd used on me since I was small. Carolyn was my mother's best friend, and had served as a kind of alternate mother for me as long as I could remember. Perhaps *mother* is the wrong word; *mentor* may come closer. She was a librarian who not only loved books but believed in them, even more so than Aunt Bessie. Carolyn believed that books could change our lives, could save us from ourselves.

My mother also loved books, but while she was raising her six children—sometimes single-handedly, when my pilot father was overseas—she put reading aside. I cannot recall, during those years, ever seeing my mother sit down, except to play a game of Monopoly or Old Maid, or to sew our Halloween costumes or Easter dresses. Certainly not to read. Late at night, when my father was away and she couldn't sleep, perhaps she switched on the light beside their double bed and opened a book, probably her Bible, a beautiful burgundy-leather King James my father had given her early in their marriage and that she kept close at hand. I loved to feel the cover and the onionskin pages that were tipped in gold and totally free of marginalia. The only mark I could find was a handwritten notation on the flyleaf. "Deuteronomy 29:29. The secret things belong unto the Lord our God: but those things which are revealed belong unto us and to our children for ever."

Over the years Carolyn gave me many books that she felt I needed to read at particular stages of my life. Some she'd bought on her travels; some had belonged to her mother; some had been gifts. She shared my passion for hand-me-downs, and never apologized for giving me used books. "Words don't go bad," she'd say, "like cheese. Read every thing you can get your hands on. Live inside them." On the subject of my newfound love, she was adamant: "You're too young to give it all up for a man." Carolyn had married an older, stable, kind man who adored her yet allowed the space her inquiring mind demanded. "I'm afraid you're going to lose yourself," she told me. "Besides," she added, almost as an afterthought, "I don't trust him."

"You won't be able to put it down," booksellers claim as they ring up your purchase. But of course you do, you must. The oven timer goes off, the children come in from school, your plane lands, the nurse calls your name, your lover kisses the back of your neck, your heavy eyes close in sleep. By the time you return to the book—if you return—you will be changed, will not be the same person you were ten days, or ten years, before. Life is a river, and you can't step into the same book twice.

One night after we'd made love, he lit a cigarette and leaned back onto the pillows. "I'm in trouble," he said. "There's this girl." Smoke floated around his eyes; he blinked, fanned the air. "Was this girl. It's over, but she's been calling. She says she's pregnant." Something hot flashed through my head, then was gone. All I could think was *He will marry her, and I will lose him.*

"There's this place in Mexico City," he continued. "It's nine hundred dollars for every thing, to fly her there and back. I have two hundred."

I had seen the word *abortion* in biology textbooks, but I had never uttered it. In 1969, even at the crest of the free-love movement, it was not a legal option. I had fourteen hundred dollars in my savings account, all that was left of nearly two years of typing invoices at the print shop. Each Friday I had taken the little vinyl passbook to the bank window, where the cashier recorded the deposit, half of my paycheck.

"I'll get the rest," I said, surprising even myself.

"I can't ask you to do that."

My next line was from a movie. Something out of the forties. I should have been wearing a hat with a feather. We should have been in a French café: "You're not asking. I'm offering."

"I'll make it up to you," he said.

To this day I can't recall if he repaid me. The passbook shows no record of the money being replaced. Within a year we were married, and what was left of my savings was pooled into a joint account. There was little money and much to buy—a dinette table, a TV stand, a couch. One night he suddenly sat straight up on that couch. "I'll bet she was lying all along," he said, as though continuing a conversation started just seconds before. "Maybe she just wanted a trip to Mexico. She probably spent the whole time on the beach." I wanted to believe him. I hoped the girl had spent the weekend on the sand. I hoped she'd gotten a tan. But I knew she hadn't lied. I knew because of what had been set into motion since I'd handed over the money. The shadow over our marriage had first approached in the bank's parking lot, had lengthened and darkened with each month, and has never completely lifted.

The girl's name is Barbara. She had blue eyes and long brown hair, and she lived in Garden Grove with her parents. She had a lisp. That's all he ever told me. The rest has been written in daylight imaginings and in dreams: Barbara and I are sitting beneath a beach umbrella reading books and sipping tall, cool drinks. The ocean is crashing in the distance, and the child crawling the space between our knees is a girl. She is a harlequin, seamed down the center. Not one eyelash, one fingernail, one cell of the child is his. She is the two best halves of Barbara and me, sewn with perfectly spaced stitches: this is the story I write.

*   *   *

Studying the markings in *Evening Train*, I surmise that the gray-haired woman is an honest reader, unashamed to admit her ignorance. She has drawn boxes around difficult words—*epiphanies, antiphonal, tessellations, serrations*—and placed a question mark above each box. Maybe she's merely an eager learner, the kind who sets small tasks for herself; she will go directly to the dictionary and find these words. Or maybe someone—her husband, her lover, whoever broke her serviceable heart—also criticized her vocabulary. It was too small or too large. She asked too many questions.

In the poem about the breaking heart, she has underlined "in surface fissures" and "a web / of hairline fractures." She probably didn't even notice the fissures at first. Maybe, she guessed, this webbing is the necessary landscape of every marriage, each act of love. But reading on, I sense that more has been broken than a metaphorical heart. She has circled the entire poem "The Batterers," about a man who, after beating a woman, dresses her wounds and, in so doing, begins to love her again. "Why had he never / seen, before, what she was? / What if she stops breathing?" I tell myself I wouldn't have stayed in that kind of situation. As it is, I'll never know. He never hit me, though one night, desperate for attention, I begged him to. (How do we live with the knowledge of our past selves?) He'd come home late, at two or three o'clock, with no explanation. Earlier in the evening, returning from a night class and looking for clues to his absence, I'd found a woman's jacket behind a chair. It smelled foreign yet familiar—her musky perfume mingled with the memory of his cigarettes. They had been here together, in our apartment. He had not touched me in weeks.

When his fist finally flew, it landed on the door of the filing cabinet where I kept my class notes, term papers, and poetry drafts. This should not have surprised me. For months he'd been angry that I'd returned to school. "What are you trying to prove?" he'd ask. "Where do you think this is going to get you? Just listen to yourself, can't you just hear yourself?" Though I still worked part-time at the print shop, he spent whole days on the assembly line, drilling holes into bowling balls. Anything to make ends meet. He was hoping, beyond logic, that as a married man with a full-time job, he would be saved from Vietnam. He was terrified; his draft number was low.

The force of the blow was audible: a thud, a crack. Loose sheets flew from the top of the cabinet. He cried out, then brought the fist to his mouth. Surely it was broken, I thought. I rushed toward him, but he held up his other hand to block me. Time slowed. White paper fluttered around me like birds. I stared at his hand, and something went out of me, I could feel it, a sucking force, tidal, pulling me out of myself. Then the moment was over. He turned and walked away, his wounded fist still pressed to his mouth, his blue eyes filling. I knelt on the floor and began to gather the papers. My eyes were dry, my vision clear. This is what hurt the most: the clarity of the moment, its sharp focus. Each black word, on each scattered page, distinct and singular.

Two years ago, when Carolyn was dying, when she could count the remaining months on her fingers, she wrote from her home in Virginia, asking me to come as soon as possible to help her sort through her books. "You can have whatever you want," she said. "The only thing I ask is that you don't cry. Just pretend it's a book sale. Come early, stay late. And go home with your arms full."

It took two full afternoons. Too weak to stand, Carolyn sat on a little stool, pointing and nodding, directing me shelf by shelf. Each row called forth a memory. Her life's story unfolded book by book. She told me she was glad she'd lived long enough to see a grandchild safely into the world. She was glad I had found a husband who was good to me, this time, and she wished me all the happiness she had known. When my car could hold no more books, she handed me a large envelope and explained that one of her jobs as assistant librarian had been to check the returned books before reshelving them. The envelope was labeled in Carolyn's scrawl: *Woodrow Wilson Public Library, Things Found in Books.* "You'd be surprised at what people use as bookmarks," she said.

When I got home, I emptied the envelope onto the floor, amazed at what spilled out. Bits and pieces of strangers' lives, hundreds of markers of personal histories. Love letters, folded placemats, envelopes, sympathy cards, valentines, handwritten recipes, train tickets, report cards, newspaper clippings, certificates of achievement, bills, receipts, religious tracts, swimming-pool passes, scratch-and-sniff perfume ads, canceled tickets for the bullfight, bar coasters, rice paper, happy money. Studying the bookmarks, I slid into each stranger's life, wondering which book he had checked out and whether he had finished it. What calls us away from books, then back to them?

When I am in pain, I *devour* books, often stripping the words of conceptual and metaphorical context and digging straight for the meat. The gray-haired woman seems to be doing the same thing, taking each word personally, *too* personally, as if Levertov had written them just for her, to guide her toward some terrible action. Certainly this wasn't the poet's intention, yet the more I study the markings, the more I fear what the woman is considering. In "Dream Instruction" she has underlined, twice, "gradual stillness," but appears to have missed entirely the "blessing" in the line that follows. The marks in "Contraband" are even more alarming. I want to take the woman by the hand and remind her of the poem's symbolic level, a level that's nearly impossible to see when you are in pain. Contraband, I would tell her, represents the Tree of Knowledge, the tree of reason, and the fruit is the words we stuff into our mouths, and yes, that fruit might indeed be "toxic in large quantities; fumes / swirled in our heads and around us," but those lines are not a prescription for suicide. There are other ways to live with knowledge.

For instance, you can leave, gather up what remains of yourself and set off on a journey much like the journey of faith Levertov writes of. Or, if that proves too difficult, you can send your self off on its own, wave goodbye, step back into childhood's shoes and refuse to go one step further. You can cut off your hair, take the pills the doctors prescribe and beg for more, then lose yourself daily in a gauzy sleep, surrounded by the books that have become your only food. His deferment dream did not materialize, so you have followed him to a military base where you know no one. Vietnam is still a possibility. Your heart is divided: you dread the orders yet pray for them. If they come, you will be able to retreat honorably to your parents' home. In the meantime, you have the pills and the books and the bed grown huge by his nightly absence—he is sleeping elsewhere now, with someone else, and he no longer even tries to hide it.

If you're lucky, one night your hand will find the phone, and if you are doubly lucky and have a mother like mine, she will arrive early the next day, having driven hundreds of miles alone in a car large enough to hold several children. Though she is a quiet woman who rarely interferes, in this case she will make an exception. She will locate your husband, demand that he come home, now, and when he does (this is where the details get fuzzy, you have sent yourself off somewhere), together they will lift you into the backseat of her big car and rush you to the emergency room, where the attending physician will immediately direct you to the psychiatric wing.

I would remember none of this part, which is a blessing. Had I recalled the details of the breakdown, I might have felt compelled to tell the story too soon, to anyone who would listen: strangers on buses, prospective employers, longtime family friends, men I met in bars or churches (for months I would search both places, equally, for comfort). "There's no need to tell," my mother said after my release, and she would repeat this many times, long after I was out of danger. Though I've finally decided, after nearly thirty years, to tell, I still hear her words in my head: "You don't need any more hurt. It's no one's business but yours."

This is my mother's way. Though she freely gives to anyone in need—food, comfort, time, love—there is a part of herself, the heart's most enclosed, tender core, that she guards like a secret. In this way, and others, I would like to be more like her. Less needy, more protective of private fears and desires. Less prone to look back, more single-minded in forward resolve. Though I had rehearsed his leaving for months, when he finally went, for good this time (isn't it strange how we use *good* to mean *final?*), I was devastated, terrified to imagine my future. "What should I do," I begged my mother. "What would you do?" I don't know what I expected her to say. My mother has never been one to give advice. Experience, in her view, is not transferable. It is not an inheritance you pass on to your children, no matter how much you wish you could.

If her words held no answer, I decided, then I would read her life. Certainly there were worlds it could teach me. She had left her parents and the family farm to follow her husband from one military base to the next; waited out his long absences; buried one child and raised six others; watched as loved ones suffered divorces, financial ruin, alcoholism, depression, life-threatening illnesses and accidents; nursed them through their last years. "Take me with you," I begged, meaning back home, to *her* home, to the nest she and my father had made.

My mother remembers this as one of the painful moments of her life. "I wanted more than anything to say yes," she recalls. "But I knew if I did, you'd never find your way. It was time you found your own way." So she took my face in her hands and said *no*. No, I could not follow her, I could not come back home. Then she helped me pack my suitcase, and, so I would not be alone, so I would be safe if worse once again came to worst, she made me a plane reservation to my brother's town in South Carolina. Half a world away, or so it seemed to me.

The narrator of Levertov's *Evening Train* sets off on a journey too, and though I suspect that the luggage and racks of the book's title poem are intended to be metaphorical, I cannot help but feel the heft of the bags, the steel slickness of the racks. And as I study the phantom woman's markings, it seems clear that, like mine, her journey required a real ticket on a real train or plane, and that by the time she arrived at the poem called "Arrived," she had already sat alone in a room with "Chairs, / sofa, table, a cup—" and begun the inventory of her life. Was she, like the poem's narrator, unable to call forth the face of the one she had left, who had left her? Why else mark these lines: "the shape / of his head, or / color of his eyes appear / at moments, but I can't / assemble feature with feature"?

In my pain, I prayed for such moments of forgetfulness. How pleasant it would be not to recall his hands, his tanned, furrowed forehead, the flame-cool blue of his eyes. My only release was to stuff my brain with cotton. That's how it felt when I took the pills. Though they no longer had the power to put me to sleep, they lifted me to a place of soundlessness and ether. I thought of T. S. Eliot's hollow men, their heads filled with straw. The image of scarecrows was comforting, as were thoughts of helium balloons, slow-floating dirigibles, and anything submergeed in water. I was anaquarium, enclosed. Amniotic silence surrounded me hour afterhour, and then suddenly—*What's that noise?*, I'd think, startled, amazed to discover it was my own breath in my lungs, my heart-thumping, the blood thrumming in my ears.

When this happened, when I was brought back to myself, I'd think, No, *please not that.* I had forgotten for a while that I was alive, that there were hands at the ends of my arms, fingers that could burn themselves on the gas stove, the iron, the teakettle's steam. The world was too much with me. Why bother? (*This is the way the world ends . . .*) I fell back into bed, finding comfort in Eliot, and later in Job. The New Testament was stuffed too full of promise and light, but Old Testament sufferings were redemptive, though not in the traditional sense of the word. I was long past questioning why a loving God would destroy Job's house and cattle, afflict him with boils all over his body, and kill his children. The worst is yet to come, I thought—and almost said, aloud, to Job. Happiness is what you should be fearing. Why waste your breath talking back to God, calling out for salvation? The cure might be worse than the disease. If God answers, out of the whirlwind and the chaos of destruction, beware of what will be given: healing, forgiveness, six thousand camels, a thousand she-asses, seven sons and three daughters, each fairer than the next, your life overflowing, another high place from which to fall.

I didn't want to live, but I couldn't imagine dying. How to gather the energy? I didn't own a gun and could see no way to get one. I had no courage for knives. Pills seemed an easy way out; I tried, but my stomach refused to accept them. Over the next weeks I started taking long drives on country roads, staring at the yellow lines and thinking how easy it would be to pull the wheel to the left, into the oncoming truck, which was heavy enough, I was sure, to bear the impact without killing its driver. (I didn't want to kill anyone, not even myself. I just wanted not to live. There's a difference.) Or better yet, pull the wheel to the right, into that stand of pine trees.

What terrified me was not the thought of the mangled metal, the row of wounded trunks, or even of the sheet pulled over me—a gesture that seemed almost a kindness, something a loved one would do. What terrified me that late summer day was the sudden greenness of the trees, the way their beauty insinuated itself into my vision—peripherally at first, vaguely, and without my consent. I blinked to stop what felt like tears, which I hadn't tasted for so long I'd forgotten that they were made of salt, that they were something my body was producing on its own, long after I thought I had shut down. O.K., I said to the steering wheel, the padded dashboard, the pines. If I can think of five reasons not to die, I won't.

When I got back to my room, I pulled from the pages of Eliot a blank prescription refill form I'd been using as a bookmark. I found a pencil in the nightstand, one without an eraser, I recall. I remember thinking that I couldn't go back on what I'd written, couldn't retrace my steps if I made a mistake. I turned the form over and numbered the blank side—1, 2, 3, 4, 5—with a black period after each, as if preparing to take a spelling test. It was the first time I'd put pencil to paper since I'd left California. I thought for a while, then wrote beside number one, "My parents," immediately wishing I'd split them into "Mother" and "Dad" so that I could have filled two lines. Then to my surprise the next four blanks filled quickly, and my hand was adding numbers and more numbers to accommodate the names of my siblings, my nieces and nephews, the handful of friends I still claimed and even the ones who were gone. I filled the back of the form and probably could have filled another, but I didn't want to try, I couldn't bear any more just yet—the stab of joy, the possibility.

As months passed, the world slowly continued to make itself known, appearing in small, merciful gestures, as if not wishing to startle: voices, a pair of hands, golden leaf-shadow, a suggestion of sky. Then one morning, for no reason I can recall, the world lifted her veil and showed her whole self. She looked strangely familiar— yes, I thought, it's all coming back. Put on shoes, brush teeth, smile into the mirror, pour orange juice into a glass. *This is the way the world begins. This is the way the world begins. This is the way.*

I smooth the center seam of Evening Train and run my hands over the marked-up lines. Poems can be dangerous places in which to venture, alone, and I'm not sure the woman is ready for "After Mindwalk." She has underlined "panic's black cloth falling / over our faces, over our breath." Please don't, I want to say. Don't do it, don't drink it, don't eat that apple. I want to tell her about the pine trees, the list, Mother and Bessie and Carolyn and Wordsworth and Hopkins and Job. Look, I'd say, pointing to the footnote. See, *Mindwalk* was a film by Bernt Capra, it's not a real place; don't worry. It's about Pascal and the Void. It doesn't have to be about you. But it is, of course. That's why she is not only reading the book but writing one of her own as well, with each scratch of the pencil. The printed words are Levertov's, but the other poem is the woman's—written in the margins, in the small boxes that cage the words she cannot pronounce, in the crumbled erasures, in the question marks floating above the lines. Wait up, I want to say—a crazy thought, but I can't help myself. Wait up; I want to tell you something.

Reflections and Responses

1. How do the marginal notes of others that McClanahan finds in various books affect her? What general responses do they provoke in her? What connection do they have with loneliness and the need for companionship? How are markings connected with love and sexuality?

2. "I never saw books as dead, finished texts," McClanahan writes. "They were living breathing, entities . . ." How does she throughout the essay blur the boundaries between books and people, herself included? How are books like people, and people like books? How do lines from poems intersect with her own life? What does she find so intriguing about *Evening Train*, the volume of Denise Levertov's poetry she borrowed from the library?

3. Consider the way McClanahan shapes her essay. Although it tells the story of her life, it does not proceed in an orderly chronological fashion. Go back through the essay and try putting events into a narrative timeline, starting with the earliest episodes and ending with her present time. How different does the essay seem when reassembled? Why do you think McClanahan chose to structure the essay in just the way she did?

SCOTT RUSSELL SANDERS

The Inheritance of Tools

A heritage is not only ethnic or cultural; it can also be a code of behavior, a system of manners, or even the practical skills that grandparents and parents often pass along to their children. In this widely reprinted personal essay, a writer, upon hearing of his father's sudden death, is reminded of the tools and techniques he inherited from his grandfather and father, which he in turn is now passing along to his own children. Though these tools and techniques have literally to do with carpentry, they take on extra duty in this finely crafted essay in which the hand tools themselves become equivalent to works of art: "I look at my claw hammer, the distillation of a hundred generations of carpenters, and consider that it holds up well beside those other classics—Greek vases, Gregorian chants, Don Quixote, barbed fish hooks, candles, spoons."

Scott Russell Sanders is the author of more than a dozen books of fiction, science fiction, essays, and nonfiction; these include Stone Country *(1985),* The Paradise of Bombs *(1987),* Secrets of the Universe *(1991),* Staying Put *(1993),* Hunting for Hope: A Father's Journeys *(1998),* The Force of Spirit *(2001), and* A Private History of Awe *(2006).* Writing from the Center *(1994) is a volume of essays about living and working in the Midwest. The recipient of many prestigious writing awards and fellowships, Sanders is a professor of English at Indiana University. "The Inheritance of Tools" originally appeared in* The North American Review *(1986) and was selected by Gay Talese for* The Best American Essays *1987.*

At just about the hour when my father died, soon after dawn one February morning when ice coated the windows like cataracts, I banged my thumb with a hammer. Naturally I swore at the hammer, the reckless thing, and in the moment of swearing I thought of what my father would say: "If you'd try hitting the nail it would go in a whole lot faster. Don't you know your thumb's not as hard as that hammer?" We both were doing carpentry that day, but far apart. He was building cupboards at my brother's place in Oklahoma; I was at home in Indiana, putting up a wall in the basement to make a bedroom for my daughter. By the time my mother called with news of his death—the long distance wires whittling her voice until it seemed too thin to bear the weight of what she had to say—my thumb was swollen. A week or so later a white scar in the shape of a crescent moon began to show above the cuticle, and month by month it rose across the pink sky of my thumbnail. It took the better part of a year for the scar to disappear, and every time I noticed it I thought of my father.

The hammer had belonged to him, and to his father before him. The three of us have used it to build houses and barns and chicken coops, to upholster chairs and crack walnuts, to make doll furniture and bookshelves and jewelry boxes. The head is scratched and pockmarked, like an old plowshare that has been working rocky fields, and it gives off the sort of dull sheen you see on fast creek water in the shade. It is a finishing hammer, about the weight of a bread loaf, too light, really, for framing walls, too heavy for cabinet work, with a curved claw for pulling nails, a rounded head for pounding, a fluted neck for looks, and a hickory handle for strength.

The present handle is my third one, bought from a lumberyard in Tennessee, down the road from where my brother and I were helping my father build his retirement house. I broke the previous one by trying to pull sixteen-penny nails out of floor joists—a foolish thing to do with a finishing hammer, as my father pointed out. "You ever hear of a crowbar?" he said. No telling how many handles he and my grandfather had gone through before me. My grandfather used to cut down hickory trees on his farm, saw them into slabs, cure the planks in his hayloft, and carve handles with a drawknife. The grain in hickory is crooked and knotty, and therefore tough, hard to split, like the grain in the two men who owned this hammer before me.

After proposing marriage to a neighbor girl, my grandfather used this hammer to build a house for his bride on a stretch of river bottom in northern Mississippi. The lumber for the place, like the hickory for the handle, was cut on his own land. By the day of the wedding he had not quite finished the house, and so right after the ceremony he took his wife home and put her to work. My grandmother had worn her Sunday dress for the wedding, with a fringe of lace tacked on around the hem in honor of the occasion. She removed this lace and folded it away before going out to help my grandfather nail siding on the house. "There she was in her good dress," he told me some fifty-odd years after that wedding day, "holding up them long pieces of clapboard while I hammered, and together we got the place covered up before dark." As the family grew to four, six, eight, and eventually thirteen, my grandfather used this hammer to enlarge his house room by room, like a chambered nautilus expanding its shell.

By and by the hammer was passed along to my father. One day he was up on the roof of our pony barn nailing shingles with it, when I stepped out the kitchen door to call him for supper. Before I could yell, something about the sight of him straddling the spine of that roof and swinging the hammer caught my eye and made me hold my tongue. I was five or six years old, and the world's commonplaces were still news to me. He would pull a nail from the pouch at his waist, bring the hammer down, and a moment later the *thunk* of the blow would reach my ears. And that is what had stopped me in my tracks and stilled my tongue, that momentary gap between seeing and hearing the blow. Instead of yelling from the kitchen door, I ran to the barn and climbed two rungs up the ladder—as far as I was allowed to go—and spoke quietly to my father. On our walk to the house he explained that sound takes time to make its way through air. Suddenly the world seemed larger, the air more dense, if sound could be held back like any ordinary traveler.

By the time I started using this hammer, at about the age when I discovered the speed of sound, it already contained houses and mysteries for me. The smooth handle was one my grandfather had made. In those days I needed both hands to swing it. My father would start a nail in a scrap of wood, and I would pound away until I bent it over.

"Looks like you got ahold of some of those rubber nails," he would tell me. "Here, let me see if I can find you some stiff ones."

And he would rummage in a drawer until he came up with a fistful of more cooperative nails. "Look at the head," he would tell me. "Don't look at your hands, don't look at the hammer. Just look at the head of that nail and pretty soon you'll learn to hit it square."

Pretty soon I did learn. While he worked in the garage cutting dovetail joints for a drawer or skinning a deer or tuning an engine, I would hammer nails. I made innocent blocks of wood look like porcupines. He did not talk much in the midst of his tools, but he kept up a nearly ceaseless humming, slipping in and out of a dozen tunes in an afternoon, often running back over the same stretch of melody again and again, as if searching for a way out. When the humming did cease, I knew he was faced with a task requiring great delicacy or concentration, and I took care not to distract him.

He kept scraps of wood in a cardboard box—the ends of two-by-fours, slabs of shelving and plywood, odd pieces of molding—and everything in it was fair game. I nailed scraps together to fashion what I called boats or houses, but the results usually bore only faint resemblance to the visions I carried in my head. I would hold up these constructions to show my father, and he would turn them over in his hands admiringly, speculating about what they might be. My cobbled-together guitars might have been alien spaceships, my barns might have been models of Aztec temples, each wooden contraption might have been anything but what I had set out to make.

Now and again I would feel the need to have a chunk of wood shaped or shortened before I riddled it with nails, and I would clamp it in a vise and scrape at it with a handsaw. My father would let me lacerate the board until my arm gave out, and then he would wrap his hand around mine and help me finish the cut, showing me how to use my thumb to guide the blade, how to pull back on the saw to keep it from binding, how to let my shoulder do the work.

"Don't force it," he would say, "just drag it easy and give the teeth a chance to bite."

As the saw teeth bit down, the wood released its smell, each kind with its own fragrance, oak or walnut or cherry or pine—usually pine because it was the softest, easiest for a child to work. No matter how weathered or gray the board, no matter how warped and

cracked, inside there was this smell waiting, as of something freshly
baked. I gathered every smidgen of sawdust and stored it away in
coffee cans, which I kept in a drawer of the workbench. When I
did not feel like hammering nails, I would dump my sawdust on
the concrete floor of the garage and landscape it into highways
and farms and towns, running miniature cars and trucks along
miniature roads. Looming as huge as a colossus, my father worked
over and around me, now and again bending down to inspect my
work, careful not to trample my creations. It was a landscape that
smelled dizzyingly of wood. Even after a bath my skin would carry
the smell, and so would my father's hair, when he lifted me for a
bedtime hug.

I tell these things not only from memory but also from recent observation, because my own son now turns blocks of wood into
nailed porcupines, dumps cans full of sawdust at my feet and
sculpts highways on the floor. He learns how to swing a hammer
from the elbow instead of the wrist, how to lay his thumb beside
the blade to guide a saw, how to tap a chisel with a wooden mallet,
how to mark a hole with an awl before starting a drill bit. My
daughter did the same before him, and even now, on the brink of
teenage aloofness, she will occasionally drag out my box of wood
scraps and carpenter something. So I have seen my apprenticeship
to wood and tools reenacted in each of my children, as my father
saw his own apprenticeship renewed in me.

   The saw I use belonged to him, as did my level and both of my
squares, and all four tools had belonged to his father. The blade of
the saw is the bluish color of gun barrels, and the maple handle,
dark from the sweat of hands, is inscribed with curving leaf designs. The level is a shaft of walnut two feet long, edged with brass
and pierced by three round windows in which air bubbles float in
oil-filled tubes of glass. The middle window serves for testing if a
surface is horizontal, the others for testing if a surface is plumb or
vertical. My grandfather used to carry this level on the gun rack
behind the seat in his pickup, and when I rode with him I would
turn around to watch the bubbles dance. The larger of the two
squares is called a framing square, a flat steel elbow, so beat up and
tarnished you can barely make out the rows of numbers that show
how to figure the cuts on rafters. The smaller one is called a try

square, for marking right angles, with a blued steel blade for the shank and a brass-faced block of cherry for the head.

I was taught early on that a saw is not to be used apart from a square: "If you're going to cut a piece of wood," my father insisted, "you owe it to the tree to cut it straight."

Long before studying geometry, I learned there is a mystical virtue in right angles. There is an unspoken morality in seeking the level and the plumb. A house will stand, a table will bear weight, the sides of a box will hold together, only if the joints are square and the members upright. When the bubble is lined up between two marks etched in the glass tube of a level, you have aligned yourself with the forces that hold the universe together. When you miter the corners of a picture frame, each angle must be exactly forty-five degrees, as they are in the perfect triangles of Pythagoras, not a degree more or less. Otherwise the frame will hang crookedly, as if ashamed of itself and of its maker. No matter if the joints you are cutting do not show. Even if you are butting two pieces of wood together inside a cabinet, where no one except a wrecking crew will ever see them, you must take pains to ensure that the ends are square and the studs are plumb.

I took pains over the wall I was building on the day my father died. Not long after that wall was finished—paneled with tongue-and-groove boards of yellow pine, the nail holes filled with putty and the wood all stained and sealed—I came close to wrecking it one afternoon when my daughter ran howling up the stairs to announce that her gerbils had escaped from their cage and were hiding in my brand new wall. She could hear them scratching and squeaking behind her bed. Impossible! I said. How on earth could they get inside my drum-tight wall? Through the heating vent, she answered. I went downstairs, pressed my ear to the honey-colored wood, and heard the *scritch scritch* of tiny feet.

"What can we do?" my daughter wailed. "They'll starve to death, they'll die of thirst, they'll suffocate."

"Hold on," I soothed. "I'll think of something."

While I thought and she fretted, the radio on her bedside table delivered us the headlines: Several thousand people had died in a city in India from a poisonous cloud that had leaked overnight from a chemical plant. A nuclear-powered submarine had been launched. Rioting continued in South Africa. An airplane had been hijacked in the Mediterranean. Authorities calculated that several thousand homeless people slept on the streets within sight of the Washington Monument. I felt my usual helplessness in the face of all these calamities. But here was my daughter, weeping because her gerbils were holed up in a wall. This calamity I could handle.

"Don't worry," I told her. "We'll set food and water by the heating vent and lure them out. And if that doesn't do the trick, I'll tear the wall apart until we find them."

She stopped crying and gazed at me. "You'd really tear it apart? Just for my gerbils? The wall?" Astonishment slowed her down only for a second, however, before she ran to the workbench and began tugging at drawers, saying, "Let's see, what'll we need? Crowbar. Hammer. Chisels. I hope we don't have to use them—but just in case."

We didn't need the wrecking tools. I never had to assault my handsome wall, because the gerbils eventually came out to nibble at a dish of popcorn. But for several hours I studied the tongue-and-groove skin I had nailed up on the day of my father's death, considering where to begin prying. There were no gaps in that wall, no crooked joints.

I had botched a great many pieces of wood before I mastered the right angle with a saw, botched even more before I learned to miter a joint. The knowledge of these things resides in my hands and eyes and the webwork of muscles, not in the tools. There are machines for sale—powered miter boxes and radial arm saws, for instance—that will enable any casual soul to cut proper angles in boards. The skill is invested in the gadget instead of the person who uses it, and this is what distinguishes a machine from a tool. If I had to earn my keep by making furniture or building houses, I suppose I would buy powered saws and pneumatic nailers; the need for speed would drive me to it. But since I carpenter only for my own pleasure or to help neighbors or to remake the house around the ears of my family, I stick with hand tools. Most of the ones I own were given to me by my father, who also taught me how to wield them. The tools in my workbench are a double inheritance, for each hammer and level and saw is wrapped in a cloud of knowing.

All of these tools are a pleasure to look at and to hold. Merchants would never paste new new new! signs of them in stores. Their designs are old because they work, because they serve their purpose well. Like folk songs and aphorisms and the grainy bits of language, these tools have been pared down to essentials. I look at my claw hammer, the distillation of a hundred generations of carpenters, and consider that it holds up well beside those other classics—Greek vases, Gregorian chants, *Don Quixote*, barbed fish hooks, candles, spoons. Knowledge of hammering stretches back to the earliest humans who squatted beside fires, chipping flints. Anthropologists have a lovely name for those unworked rocks that served as the earliest hammers. "Dawn stones," they are called. Their only qualification for the work, aside from hardness, is that they fit the hand. Our ancestors used them for grinding corn, tapping awls, smashing bones. From dawn stones to this claw hammer is a great leap in time, but no great distance in design or imagination.

On that iced-over February morning when I smashed my thumb with the hammer, I was down in the basement framing the wall that my daughter's gerbils would later hide in. I was thinking of my father, as I always did whenever I built anything, thinking how he would have gone about the work, hearing in memory what he would have said about the wisdom of hitting the nail instead of my thumb. I had the studs and plates nailed together all square and trim, and was lifting the wall into place when the phone rang upstairs. My wife answered, and in a moment she came to the basement door and called down softly to me. The stillness in her voice made me drop the framed wall and hurry upstairs. She told me my father was dead. Then I heard the details over the phone from my mother. Building a set of cupboards for my brother in Oklahoma, he had knocked off work early the previous afternoon because of cramps in his stomach. Early this morning, on his way into the kitchen of my brother's trailer, maybe going for a glass of water, so early that no one else was awake, he slumped down on the linoleum and his heart quit.

For several hours I paced around inside my house, upstairs and down, in and out of every room, looking for the right door to open and knowing there was no such door. My wife and children followed me and wrapped me in arms and backed away again, circling and staring as if I were on fire. Where was the door, the door, the door? I kept wondering. My smashed thumb turned purple and throbbed, making me furious. I wanted to cut it off and rush outside and scrape away the snow and hack a hole in the frozen earth and bury the shameful thing.

I went down into the basement, opened a drawer in my workbench, and stared at the ranks of chisels and knives. Oiled and sharp, as my father would have kept them, they gleamed at me like teeth. I took up a clasp knife, pried out the longest blade, and tested the edge on the hair of my forearm. A tuft came away cleanly, and I saw my father testing the sharpness of tools on his own skin, the blades of axes and knives and gouges and hoes, saw the red hair shaved off in patches from his arms and the backs of his hands. "That will cut bear," he would say. He never cut a bear with his blades, now my blades, but he cut deer, dirt, wood. I closed the knife and put it away. Then I took up the hammer and went back to work on my daughter's wall, snugging the bottom plate against a chalk line on the floor, shimming the top plate against the joists overhead, plumbing the studs with my level, making sure before I drove the first nail that every line was square and true.

Reflections and Responses

1. Consider the way Sanders opens the essay. Given the significance of his father's death, why does he mention his injured thumb in the same sentence? Why is this a relevant detail? How does it figure later in the essay?

2. Note the many concrete references to carpentry in the essay. In what ways is the language of tools and carpentry related to other aspects of life? Why is there "a mystical virtue in right angles"?

3. In rereading the essay, try to reconstruct the chronology of the February day that Sanders's father died. First, consider how Sanders constructs his narrative. Why does he deviate from a straightforward, hour-by-hour account? Why, for example, does he introduce the story about his daughter's gerbils? In what ways does that anecdote deepen the essay's theme?

LAUREN SLATER

Tripp Lake

*In this lovely, painstakingly detailed personal essay, Lauren Slater takes an
ordinary, childhood experience—her first summer away at camp—and uses it
to craft a history of an extraordinary sense of fear and maladjustment. In the
mundane details of camp life, from the mess hall to basketball bombardment,
coping for the first time alone and without her mother, Slater unfolds the beginning of a dissociation approaching mental illness. "It was as if a curtain had
been pulled back to reveal the true nature of the world," she writes, "which was
terror, through and through." But in one apparently daunting camp activity
Slater finds a peace of mind that will prove profoundly important later on.*

*Lauren Slater has written extensively and widely about psychology, memory,
and her experience. Her essays have appeared in the* New York Times, Harper's, National Geographic, Elle, *and* Nerve. *Her books include* Prozac
Diary *(1998),* Lying: A Metaphorical Memoir *(2000),* Love Works Like
This: Travels Through a Pregnant Year *(2003), and* Blue Beyond Blue:
Extraordinary Tales for Ordinary Dilemmas *(2005).* Opening Skinner's Box: Great Psychological Experiments of the Twentieth Century
*(2004) was nominated for a Los Angeles Times Book Prize in science writing
and won the Bild der Wissenschaft award in Germany for the groundbreaking
science book of the year. She has received many other awards and her work has
been translated into eighteen languages. She has a Master's degree in psychology
from Harvard and a doctorate from Boston University. "Tripp Lake" first appeared in* Swink *and was selected by Adam Gopnik for* The Best American
Essays 2008. *Lauren Slater served as guest editor for the series in 2006.*

AT THE AGE OF NINE, I went to my first and only camp, located
in Poland, Maine, way up off 95, by a kidney-shaped lake where

across the shore we could see the serrated lines of red roofs and, on sunny days, white sails walking along the water. The camp was called Tripp Lake and it was for girls, or so my parents said, who were especially competitive, girls like me, not yet pubescent, packed with all the power of a life that had yet to really unfold, that brought with it the hard parts, the shames, the sadnesses, none of that yet. I wore my hair in what was called a pixie cut, which was a nice way of saying it was short as a boy's—crewcut, really—and, at that age, white-blond so the stubble glittered silver in the summer sun. I spent my evenings playing capture the flag, an exhilarating game that requires fast feet and a bit of cunning.

Understandably, my parents thought it best to send me to a place where my energies could be shaped and expanded. I agreed. I thought I might be Olympic quality, like those skaters I'd seen, or the skiers hunched over their poles, ricocheting down mountains where ice hung from all the trees.

I remember the first night at the camp—but no, let me begin before then, at the bus stop, about to leave, and feeling, for the first time, a shudder of intense grief. My mother, an aloof woman whom I nonetheless adored, looked pale, her eyes foggy and distant. My father was a small man in the bakery business. Lately they'd been fighting. She wanted something grand out of life, something more than a muffin, whereas he was content to nozzle whipped cream on top of tarts. I loved my father, but I loved my mother more—more problematically is what I mean, in the crooked, hooked way only a daughter can love.

I hugged my parents goodbye, and when I hugged my mother I could feel a circle of sadness in her. By leaving I felt as if I were betraying her. I had heard their voices at night, his quiet, hers shrill—"you and you and you"—and I'd seen my mother sometimes sitting on the porch looking out at nothing. She was a severe and brittle woman, but even at that age I knew brittle was breakable. Sometimes, driving in the car, she crushed the accelerator to the floor, just for the feeling of speed, and other times she cried with her mouth closed. I had the feeling, there at the bus stop, that she wished she were me, about to board a bus heading for the horizon, a green-striped bus with Peter Pan dancing on its flank and girls unabashedly eating apples. And because I felt her longing, inchoate, certainly unspoken, my chest seemed to split with sadness, and also guilt. This was a new emotion, an emotion that sits in the throat, an emotion that is maybe more imagistic than all the others. Guilt made me imagine that while I was away, my mother would come undone: her arm would fall off; her hair would drift from her head. Guilt made me imagine that she would sit in the nights and cry, and what could I do about that? I wanted to say I'm sorry, but I didn't really know what for. I couldn't have said it then, what I've since felt my whole life, that separation is a sword, painful, to be avoided at all costs.

My first night at camp. I could hear the flagpole rope banging against its post; I could hear the cry of what were maybe coyotes in the woods and the susurration of thousands of tree frogs. I couldn't sleep, so I stepped outside, onto the damp dirt that surrounded the cabin, and in the single spotlight that shone down, I found a tiny toad, no bigger than a dime, with still tinier bumps on its taupe back. I lifted the amphibian up. I could not believe that God, or whoever, could make an animal so small, an animal that would have, if I cut it open, all the same organs as me, in miniature, the locket-size heart, bones like white wisps. How easy it is to break an animal. I could have crushed that frog with my fist—and part of me wanted to, while another part of me wanted to protect it, while still a third part of me wanted to let it go.

Before camp, I'd been a more or less happy girl, but that first night I couldn't sleep and by morning a wild sadness had settled in me. Where was I? Where was she? Someday I would die. Someone somewhere was sick. It was as if a curtain had been pulled back to reveal the true nature of the world, which was terror through and through.

That summer I became, for the first time in my life, truly afraid, and the fears took forms that were not good, that did not augur well for my later life, although I didn't know it then. That first day, sitting on the green lawn, watching a girl do a cartwheel and another girl mount the parallel bars, I developed an irrational fear that is still hard to explain: I became hyperaware of my own body, the swoosh of my blood and the paddling of my heart and the huh huh huhs of my breath, and it seemed amazing and tenuous to me that my body did all of this without any effort on my part. As soon as I became aware of this fact—almost as though I'd discovered my lower brain stem and how it was hitched to the spinal cord—as soon as I came to consciousness about this, I thought, *I can't breathe.* And truly it felt like I couldn't breathe. I thought, *I am thinking about my breathing, and if I think too hard about my breathing, which you're not supposed to think about, I will concentrate on it right away,* and I swallowed hard, and then I became aware of all the minute mechanisms that comprise a swallow, and so I felt I couldn't swallow anymore. It was like the lights were going out in my body, while girls in front of me did cartwheels on the green lawn, completely unaware that I was dying.

After that, the fears came fast and furious. I was afraid to think about walking, because then I would fall. Breathing, because then I would suffocaté.

Swallowing was the worst of all, to suddenly feel you have no way of bringing the world down into your throat, of taking it in, no way. And I became afraid of the dining hall, with its vicious swordfish mounted on one wall, and its huge bear head with eyes like my mother's, dull, distant eyes, eyes at once wild and flat. I became afraid of pancakes, of toothbrushes, of cutlery, of water, of counselors urging me into the lake, where fronds fingered through the murk and scads of fish darted by, making a current cool against my legs.

That first week at camp, I fished a dime out of my uniform pocket (we wore only blue-and-white standard-issue uniforms) and called my mother. From far, far away I heard her voice. When had her sadness started? With my father, or before that, with her mother, who insisted that she, the oldest of three girls, do endless tasks and child care, so she was never able to shoot marbles, too busy shining the silver. My mother, I knew, had been a good girl, exceedingly good, and because of that, she hated my grandmother. She called her Frances, and all holidays were barbed affairs, my mother sniping at her mother, making faces at the food because she, if only given the chance, could have done better.

My mother did not go to college despite the fact that she's bright. In my imagination, when I construct her history for her, because she's so closed about her own, she wants to be a singer on a lit stage or she wants to be a painter with her canvas at a quiet lakeside. She wants something larger than her own life, larger than her husband's life, larger than the house and kids, where what she does all day is clean. Much, much later, when I was near grown, after she and my father divorced, my mother would develop a passion for Israel, its military might; she became fiercely, ragefully Zionistic, and, totally bursting the caul of her confinement, she smuggled Bibles into the USSR. But this was later, when she found an outlet for her energies, and if only I'd known that was going to happen, that she was going to get something good out of life—if only I'd known, maybe my fears would have been a little less.

From far away my mother answered the phone, and I said, "I want to come home," and she said, "Don't be a quitter, Lauren." She wanted for me a larger life, a life where girls stand on stages, take charge of a team, swim the length of a lake and back in a Speedo suit. But because she didn't have these things, I felt much too guilty to take them for myself. None of this did I say.

At camp, we were divided into teams, and every activity, from drama to Newcomb, was cast as a competition. It was a summer of color war. I watched the older girls run with their lacrosse sticks, cradling them close to their sides, the ball in the gut-string pocket a soft blur. I watched as we, the younger girls, were taught to dribble and to shoot. Part of me wanted fiercely to win these games, while a still larger part of me could not even allow myself to participate, for somehow I would be betraying my mother if I did.

I was put on the Tigers team. Every morning after breakfast, standing at attention beneath that mounted swordfish, we would sing:

Shielded by orange and black
Tigers will attack
Catching every cue
Always coming through.

I remember in particular a game called bombardment, which we played in the gym on rainy days, Tigers versus Bears. In this game, each side is given a whole raft of basketballs, and the purpose is simply to hurl them at each other as hard as you can, and whoever gets hit is out. Before I'd left home, maybe I could have played this game, but certainly not now. Brown basketballs came whizzing through the air, smacked against the lacquered floor of the gym, ricocheted off a face or a flank, and one by one each girl got hit and so would sit out on the sidelines. I was so scared of bombardment that whenever we played it, I hung way in the back of the court, where the other team's balls could not reach me. And then one day, because of this, I lasted throughout the whole game; everyone on my team had been hit except me, and everyone on the other team had been hit except a senior girl named Nancy, a fourteen-year-old who had one leg longer than the other. She had custom-made shoes, her left heel stacked high enough to bring her up even so she didn't tilt. I'd watched Nancy walk out of the corners of my eyes; even with her shoes she was strangely clumsy, gangly, always giggling nervously just at the rim of a group of girls, her desire to be taken in palpable.

And now Nancy and I were the last two left in the game. Everyone on the sidelines was screaming *Go, go, go.* Nancy's skin was as pale as milk, the strands of veins visible in her neck. Her gimp foot, supported by the huge rubber heel of her sneaker, seemed to wobble. *Go, go, go,* but I couldn't do it, I couldn't hurl that ball at her; it seemed existentially horrible that we were called to do this sort of thing in the world, to live in a way where someone had to lose. I stood there, locked in place, mesmerized by her skin and her foot, while Nancy lifted the basketball high above her head and hurled it toward me with as much muster as she could muster, and I let the ball hit me on the hip. Nancy won. That was the only outcome I could tolerate.

It didn't take long for the counselors to realize something was wrong with me. I cried all the time. During free swim I retreated into the fringe of woods. The woods were next to a red barn, where horses hung their heads over stall doors and where there were golden squares of hay. Somehow, being near the horses calmed me. I liked their huge velvety lips, their thoughtful mastications. I liked the way they almost seemed to slurp up hay. I liked their rounded backsides, their plumed tails; I even liked their scat, flecked with grain and sweet-smelling. Today, whenever I enter a barn and smell that smell, I do a Proustian plunge* back to that first barn, and to the chestnut ponies.

Riding was a camp activity reserved for the older girls. I began to watch those girls cantering around the ring, the horses seeping dark sweat on their muscular chests. The riding coach's name was Kim. She was a wisp of a woman in tan jodhpurs with

---

*Proustian plunge**: French novelist Marcel Proust (1871–1922) famously wrote of how the taste of a childhood cookie sent him into a long and vivid spiral of recollections.

suede patches at the knees. Once, when I was alone in the barn, I found her riding clothes hung up on a hook near the tack room. I tried on her green hunt jacket. It hung huge on me, but it felt cozy, and on its lapel there was a tiny brooch in the shape of a dragonfly.

"Would you like to try?" Kim asked me one day.

"I'm only ten," I said.

"Well," she said, "I have a horse who's only ten, too. Maybe you would make a good match."

"What's his name?" I asked.

"What's yours?" she said.

"Lauren," I said.

"Smokey Raindrops," she said. "But we call him Rain."

Rain, Rain—what a beautiful name. It was more a sound than a designation, "Yes," I said.

In fact, I didn't get to ride Rain that day. First, all the counselors, along with Auntie Ruth, the camp director, had to discuss it. Should I have lessons even though that was not part of my camp curriculum? Would that make me happy? They thought it might.

Riding is a sport that, like any other, requires more than just the circumscribed activity. There is the ritualistic preparation, the waxing of skis or the oiling of strings or, in this case, the grooming before the tack. A few days later Kim showed me how to do it, using a currying comb, picking a hoof, leaning down and cupping the hairy fetlock, lifting the leg, seeing the shine of the silver shoe with six nail heads in it. Time passed. Days passed. Caring for the horses was soothing, and I found when I was at the stable by these big breathing animals, I could forget about my own breath and just breathe.

All through the summer Kim taught me how to ride, alone, no other girl there. She taught me how to post, how to do dressage, how to jump. I learned to hoist myself up, foot in one stirrup, other leg flung over the broad rank back. "When you post," she said, "watch the left leg. As it extends, you rise."

The trot of a horse is like a metronome. It synchronizes you. It hypnotizes you. Left foot rise. Left foot rise. Your whole mind funnels down into this foot, the flash of hoof in the summer sun. And I'll never forget the day Kim taught me to canter, how she said, "Trot out, give him a kick with your inside foot," and suddenly the horse's tight trot broke into the rocking run, around and around the ring we went, so fast it seemed, the world blurring by in a beautiful way.

Riding is largely a singular sport; although there are shows and red ribbons, first places and sixth places, it can still be done, nevertheless, with no attention to the competition aspect. You cannot really play lacrosse or soccer unless you are playing against someone, and this againstness requires that you see yourself as separate, with all that that implies. But horseback riding is something you can do alone in the woods, or in a dusty riding rink, or even in your mind, in which you can canter, too. Riding is not about separation. It is not about dominance. The only person you might hurt is you. You are, at long last, without guilt.

Riding. It is about becoming one with the animal that bears you along. It is about learning to give and take, give the horse his head, take the rein and bring him, up. It is about tack, the glorious leather saddles, and the foam-stained bits, which fascinated me, how Kim would roll them in sugar and slide them into a horse's mouth, its thick tongue clamped. It is, more than anything else, about relationship and balance, and as Kim taught me how to do these things— walk, trot, canter—a sort of peace settled in me, a working through my mother and me, a way of excelling at no one's cost.

And so the summer progressed. The only thing I could not do well was jump. Each time we approached the fence the horse seemed to sense my primordial fear, fear of the fence and fear of everything it contained, and it would bunch to a scuttering halt, or, more humiliating, the horse would stop, and then with me kicking, and kicking uselessly, it would simply walk over the bar. I watched Kim jump; she was amazing, fluid, holding on to her horse's hair as they entered the air, her face a mixture of terror and exhilaration, the balanced combination that means only one thing: mastery.

One month into the camp season was visiting day. My parents arrived carrying leathery fruit rolls and a new canteen. They seemed as separate as ever, not even looking at each other. My mother was appalled at the condition of my wardrobe. My clothes stank of sweat and fur. The soles of my boots were crammed with flaking manure. That was the summer, also, when I started to smell. "What's this?" she said, flicking through my steamer trunk. "Do you ever do your laundry?" She pulled out a white shirt with spatters of black mud on it, and stains at the armpits, slight stains, their rims barely visible.

"Lauren," she said.

"What?" I said.

She pursed her lips and shook her head. She held the shirt out as though to study it. And once again I saw that look of longing cross her face, but this time it was mixed with something else. I saw the briefest flicker of disgust.

A few minutes later, she went into our cabin bathroom, which we called the Greenie. She closed the door. I stalked up to it, pressed my ear against its wood. What did I do with my body? What did she do with hers? I heard the gush of water from the tap, the scrunch of something papery. The bathroom had a lock on my side only. Quiedy, and for a reason I still cannot quite explain, I turned the lever and the lock slid quietly into its socket.

A few minutes later, when she tried to get out, she could not. She rattled the knob. We were alone in the cabin. I stood back and watched. "Lauren?" she said. "Lauren?" Her voice hurt me. It was curved into a question, and when I didn't answer, the question took on a kind of keening. "Lauren, are you there? Open the door." I stood absolutely still. I was mesmerized, horrified by the vulnerability in her voice, how small she suddenly seemed, and how I was growing in girth by the minute. For some reason I suddenly pictured her trapped in a tiny glass bottle, and I held the bottle in my hands. I could let her out or leave her.

I let her out.

"What are you doing?" she said. She stared at me. I stared back at her. I could see her sweat now; it ran in a trickle down the side of her brow. I wanted to wipe it away.

They left in the evening, when colored clouds were streaming across the sky. I stood in the parking lot and watched their station wagon rattle over the dirt road, raising clouds of dust. The next few days, I backslid. My fears returned. There was the problem with my breathing, but now accompanying this obsession was the need to walk backward while counting. I saw for sure that I was growing while she shrank. I saw for sure that I was growing because she shrank. I also saw something pointed in me, some real desire to win. Hearing that lock sink into its socket, I had felt glee and power.

I stopped riding then. I stopped going to the stables. I stayed in my bunk. I wrote letters and letters to my mother, the act somehow soothing my conscience. *Love, Lauren XXX. Kisses and hugs. I love you.*

At last, after four days had passed, Kim came to my cabin to get me. "You disappeared," she said.

"I'm sick," I said.

"You know," she said, "I never much liked my mother."

I stared at her. How had she known?

"What will you do?" she said.

"I don't know," I said.

"Are you going to sit on a cot for the rest of your life?"

"Maybe," I said.

"Just sit there and cry?" she said, and there was, suddenly, a slight sneer to her voice.

I looked away.

"I once knew a girl," said Kim, "who spent her whole life going from hospital to hospital because she loved being sick. She was too scared to face the world. Is that you?"

I have thought of her words often—a premonition, an augury, a warning, a simple perception.

I followed her back to the barn. It was noon. The sun was high and hot. She brought Rain out into the middle of the ring, tightened his saddle strap, and tapped on the deep seat. "All aboard," she said.

Sitting high on the horse, I could smell the leaves. I could smell my own sweat and all that it contained, so many contradictions.

"We're going to jump today," she said.

She went to the center of the ring, and this time she set the fence at four feet. "Now," she said, "cross your stirrups and knot your reins. A rider has to depend on her inner balance only."

I cantered toward the jump, hands on my hips, legs grasping. But each time, at the crucial moment of departure, Rain would screech to a halt and I'd topple into his mane.

"He senses your fear," Kim said.

At last, on the third or fourth try, she went into the barn and came back out with a long black crop. Standing in the center of the ring, right next to the jump, she swizzled the crop into the air, a snapping sound. The horse's ears flashed forward. "You have to get over it," she said. I centered myself in the saddle. I cantered twice around the rink and then turned in tight toward the bar. Kim cracked the whip, a crack I still hear today whenever I feel my fears—and I do, I often do—but I rose up, arms akimbo, in this leap merged with the mammal, its heart my heart, its hooves my feet, and we sailed into the excellent air. I did it. I found a way to move forward.

Reflections and Responses

1. Slater's third paragraph begins "I remember the first night at the camp—but no, let me begin before then, at the bus stop, about to leave." How does this sudden reversal of direction set the tone for the essay as a whole? Why is the scene at the bus stop so important to the essay, and why does Slater suggest it is an afterthought? How will Slater use the order in which she recalls things to advance ideas about childhood and memory?

2. Note the variety of sensory expression Slater uses in the architecture of her images. Locate an example of a smell, a sound, a complex visual, and other senses employed during the essay. Besides making the writing generally more vivid, why does Slater find it particularly necessary in this essay to dwell on minute details and precise representations? How do these images relate to the more extrasensory, psychological memories Slater hopes to conjure?

3. Slater describes the trot of a horse as "like a metronome. It synchronizes you. It hypnotizes you." Contrast Slater's "bombardment" scene with that of riding Rain. How does Slater express the chaotic madness of the gymnasium sport on the one hand, and the calmness of riding on the other? Why is this juxtaposition central to the essay?

JANNA MALAMUD SMITH

Shipwrecked

*When Janna Malamud Smith's mother died, she felt at sea—wandering with-
out direction like a passenger in a shipwreck. But that was only the first of a
series of connections Smith makes between her bereavement and Daniel Defoe's
classic eighteenth-century novel,* Robinson Crusoe. *As she navigates the
complex series of emotions and physical responsibilities in the wake of her loss,
Smith begins to see more and more connections to Crusoe, a castaway who has
to salvage what he can of his old life in order to survive on a desert island.
Like Crusoe, Smith undergoes wild undulations of emotion in dealing with
the loss of her mother on the one hand and her physical inheritance on the
other. "The simultaneous liberation and found wealth spun my feelings," she
writes. "The ship is wrecked, yet I did not drown. Her cargo is mine."*

*Writer and psychotherapist Janna Malamud Smith has both lectured and
published widely. She is the author of* Private Matters: In Defense of the Personal Life *(1997) and* A Potent Spell: Mother Love and the Power of
Fear *(2003). Her latest,* My Father is a Book: A Memoir of Bernard Malamud *(2006) was selected as a* Washington Post *Best Book of the Year and a*
New York Times *Editor's Choice. Her writing has appeared in publications
ranging from the* New York Times *to the* Threepenny Review. *She is currently
working on books about the emotional perils of art-making, and fishing the Gulf
of Maine. "Shipwrecked" originally appeared in* The American Scholar *and
was selected by Mary Oliver for* The Best American Essays 2009.

This being within about a mile from the shore
where I was, and the boat seeming to stand upright still,
I wished myself on board, that, at least,
I might save some necessary things for my use.
—Robinson Crusoe

In the days immediately after my mother's death, as its reality slowly overtook my consciousness, I found myself recalling Robinson Crusoe. Not an association I would have anticipated, since the book holds little conscious meaning for me anymore. Yet, there it was in my mind's eye—repeatedly, an indistinct image of a stranded, barefoot man, pant legs ripped at midcalf—straining, poling a raft back to his wrecked ship to gather provisions.

Crusoe, desolate and terrified, mercifully wave-tossed onto an island after a storm has sunk his ship, crawls up a tree to sleep the first night. He feels completely unprotected; and some large part of him expects to die before dawn—savaged by a ravenous beast or a hostile human. But when he awakes the next day, sun returned, water calm, he finds that the tide has delivered his lost vessel back from the depths and stranded it within reach. Like the storm-harried Crusoe, I found myself after her death mucking through strange, flickering, opposite states of mind where, at more than a few moments, a seemingly parallel grand confusion of terror and calm, desolation and thin hope, bereftness and bounty all commingled. I felt as rattled as any half-drowned jack-tar; and like Crusoe, I understood that my first labor was to salvage.

Remarkable, really, the way the image from the book came to mind at a grievous time. How it drifted into sight, intact, uninvited, a dense, symbolic representation in the guise of a mental snapshot. A book first read . . . when? Late childhood, early adolescence? Returned years later, in this case to capture some of my complex feelings about myself, my mother, and my circumstance in the aftermath of her death. Praise the quirky mind. Present yourself at the front desk of its repository, request any volume from its stacks, and discover, once again, how the runners deliver up what suits them: "Bring her Defoe." But from where in the gray matter did they retrieve him? Was the figure on the raft constructed in the moment—in response to my emotional state? Was it borrowed from some film? Or did it linger from when, as a child first reading the book, I assembled my own picture?

Remarkable, too, how words read on a page are translated and transformed by all of us into our own archives. How does my Crusoe resemble or not resemble yours, both in profile and in the intimate psychic purpose each may serve? Of course, not everyone who has read Defoe has kept a Crusoe. (I was unaware of mine until lately.) To stay, he had to fit in, find useful work; brace some part of the psyche, the way a piece of cedar—cut, carved, steamed to curve—will rib a boat. The quick description of why I kept my Crusoe summarizes blandly: he takes care of himself in tough circumstances; he is ingenious and resourceful; his story ends well. As an overprotected daughter of a mother I deemed weak, I longed to be more like him. I borrowed a rib. Perhaps a book becomes a classic in proportion to how broadly its characters can be scavenged; how many readers find within it something they experience as desirable or even intimately necessary.

The Print Collector/Imagestate RM/PhotoLibrary

A shipwreck, now rare, but once a tragedy so common that whole schools of landscape painting prospered in detailing its vicissitudes, seems an apt metaphor for maternal death. However much you equivocate, your mother is the vessel you inhabit. And shipboard death by catastrophic storm—plunging all unselectively— holds within it something true about the strange "me and not me" of intimate loss. Several years ago at the Whitney Museum, I spent a good long time watching Bill Viola's video loop of a human fig- ure underwater in darkness very slowly surfacing, and then surfac- ing again, as if enacting my future quandary. Will I stay under, too? Is her death also mine? No, but perhaps, well, yes, if we speak not just of the past when we were one, nor of the future when I, too, shall die; but if we try to capture and describe something larger than influence, something genuinely uncanny. I'm not sure how to name it. The voyage, the direction set, the cargo carried, were my first and most basic world. I looked out through my mother's portholes. Her assumptions were the sheets I wrestled, hauled, lashed. I was her stevedore, her sailor, her AWOL midshipman, her ship's doctor, her mutinous crew, her captain—who ever knew for certain? I thought of her as my mother, but rarely of myself as her daughter. When I wrote about her for her memorial service, I was surprised to see how obviously my interests followed hers. Mourn- ing is not just a long goodbye; it is a hard labor of turning away and returning, of swimming free and then poling back.

She died between my second and third visit to the hospital on a Tuesday toward the end of March. After checking with her nurse, who, like me, thought she still had days, I had decided to attend half my evening Italian class. I departed at the break, and arrived back 20 minutes too late. The hand I grasped was still warm. But she was dead, and the conversation between us was over. Eighty-nine years old, she'd had multiple sclerosis for 20 years. For the past eight she'd lived near me year-round, and every Wednesday evening after I fin- ished seeing patients, I would walk the four or five blocks from my office to her apartment and we would eat dinner together. I never found an easy way to be with her. She longed intensely for a confid- ing intimacy that I wouldn't offer and that she couldn't seem to bear when I did. I have not known a more confounding relationship. Yet, we both kept trying, and a good portion of our love located itself within the effort.

We had our moments. I liked best when she passed along news about old friends. "I called Louise." "What did you learn?" A flat exchange. But not between us, for whom it heralded—like a sun-dapple on the shady dirt road, or a cluster of daisies against white birch—our return to the family home. The beloved summer prop-erty, so familiar that the pleasure is in revisiting together, surveying, setting things right; steadying ourselves with the known, and then contemplating the variation a season brings. Louise was my moth-er's good friend in Oregon half a century ago. Her son, Peter, an age-mate now prematurely dead, was my first playmate. We named our son Peter partly after him. Louise's husband, Chester, was my father's close friend. My mother was attracted to Chester, and on more than one occasion—car out of gas, dead mouse in the bath-tub—he rescued her. He had been a paratrooper fighting in Italy during the Second World War, and possessed a resourcefulness in crisis my father lacked. My mother liked being rescued.

Seeing it on the page, I realize this string of associations reveals an aspect of my Crusoe: I early grasped that the surest way to be with my mother was as her rescuer—not dramatically, but in small every-day ways. Childhood was a night watch. My assignment (assumed or ordered, who knows which?) was to stand between her and her self-hatred. Sometimes I gave my all. Other times, I slipped away fur-tively; I could be derelict, fractious. After she died, the figure returning to the shipwreck was a seaman suddenly unemployed; the part of my own psyche whose long labor has just ended. "My duty all ended," Gerard Manley Hopkins* wrote after another death.

What is gone and what remains? The first night, all is lost. But the next morning, the ship lies wrecked within reach, a brilliant stroke by Defoe. The reader shares Crusoe's relief. He is no longer alone—not because the boat is peopled, but because its appearance domesti-cates the alien space, offers comfort by placing within it a bit of home. Perhaps oddly, perhaps not, its reappearance resembles the return of an absent mother to her child. She disappears. He fears for his survival, dependent upon her. She reappears, and the hostile world is tempered. Better yet, she carries provisions to sustain him. The ship's hold, as Crusoe explores it, transforms into a general store

---

***Gerard Manley Hopkins (1884–1889)**: an English poet and Jesuit priest. The quo-tation is from his poem *Felix Randall.*

absent its proprietor, and he gathers up goods like a lad on a spree. What better way to please a reader, gratify basic fantasy, than with bounty found, not earned—once again, analogous to a dimension of the maternal: the full breast, the free lunch. Certainly, there is something female and mammalian about the ship as Defoe describes it when Crusoe first swims back, a large beast lying on its side, waiting to be suckled. In this case, of that manly sailor's beverage, rum:

> I swam around her twice, and the second time I spy'd a small piece of a rope, which I wondered I did not see at first, hang down by the fore-chains so low, as that with great difficulty I got hold of it, and by the help of that rope, got up into the forecastle of the ship. Here I found that the ship was bulged, and had a great deal of water in her hold, but that she lay so on the side of a bank of hard sand, or rather earth, that her stern lay lifted up upon the bank, and her head low against the water; by this means all her quarter was free, and all that was in that part was dry; for you may be sure my first work was to search and to see what was spoiled and what was free; and first I found that all the ship's provisions were dry and untouched by the water, and being well disposed to eat, I went to the bread room and filled my pockets with bisket, and ate it as I went about other things, for I had no time to lose; I also found some rum in the great cabin of which I took a large dram, and which I had indeed need enough of to spirit me for what was before me.

At once losing my mother and inheriting from her. I have kayaked places where the wind, current, and tide, the angle of underwater ledge, come together in such inscrutable, turbulent confusion it makes your head spin. There's no sure place to set your paddle, nothing to do but stroke hard and hope you don't tip into hammering ocean. The night after she died, I grabbed a bunch of cash from her wallet and took my family to dinner at a nearby bistro. She didn't need it anymore. I remember the high, so unlikely in the moment, almost giddy, of grasping coin from her purse, the pilferer's simian bark. Within hours, the elation crumpled into grief. The extreme opposite within her death, the unparalleled tenderness—my mother— the simultaneous liberation and found wealth spun my feelings: the ship is wrecked, yet I did not drown. Her cargo is mine.

I had not understood that after a person dies, her surround, her physical space retains life—the pale blue cotton nightgown clean in the dryer, the custard in the refrigerator, the open issue of The New Yorker, the bills laid out on the table waiting to be paid. Her used tissue dropped, out of reach, behind the chair. She had resisted visiting her doctor for months, but finally, too weak to protest, had been sent by ambulance to the hospital by one of the women who cared for her. I was briefly out of town. She was determined to die, and I don't know which of us she was sparing by waiting to depart until I turned away. My back to her, she hastened toward death, as if we had been playing some scrambled game of "Mother may I?" or "Red light green light." I think she knew I would try to save her. So she chose not to tell me what she foresaw—unlike herself, really, tight-lipped, determined: courageous in a way that caught me by surprise, that put paid to all clarity about where between us strength lay.

It fell to me to empty her apartment and distribute her goods. I shared Crusoe's urgency. The work couldn't wait. The weather could shift at any moment, and then the precariously resting wreck would again slide into the sea. But unlike Crusoe, I found it hard to judge utility, to know just what to keep. Something undesirable now might become crucial later. I didn't want to create a museum, even in storage boxes. Yet I didn't want to leave myself unprovisioned in a future season. The sorting, the boxing, the hauling took three months. I would drive to her apartment (it was when I pulled into her parking lot that Crusoe usually appeared). I'd let myself into her home, so familiar and now silent, and gird myself to look, touch, toss, sell, or give away; brace myself for the grief—the waves slamming the pebbled beach, then sucking back in a roar, the clamorous slush of stones. Except for one small, perfect plate, I did not keep the pieces she still owned of her grandmother's floral patterned china. I did keep a pair of gray knee socks.

Occasionally, the apartment offered animal comfort, as if it were breathing with her breath, as if it still held her body heat, or more than that, the remains of her enthusiasm, her *tendresse.* As when you walk on a quiet rural road in summer after a rain, and the humid heat wafts up all around you then drifts away. She had worked hard to sift and order while she still had strength. What she left was so condensed as to hold emotional weight disproportionate to its apparent mass. In four small rooms, her life, remnants of my father's, my brother's, my own; time past, piled, pressed dry, gathered into photo albums, into stacks of old pages recording earnings, debts paid, celebrations, bitter exchanges; mementos whose history became the sediment of hers;

photographs everywhere of my children, of Italian forebears unmet, of friends now dead. I had to disassemble a universe.

I had no idea how wrenching the labor would be. A space does not die right away when a person dies, and I was unprepared for that discovery. She was gone, yet her being still lingered within her rooms. At one point it brought to mind a story someone had told me years ago after we'd been swimming in a quarry near our summer home—about trapping and grilling the eels that lived in the water there, and the way their bodies squirmed on the grill for long minutes after their heads had been cut off. I was at once Crusoe, comforted by her hoard, a daughter overwhelmed, and some much more violent creature, ripping apart a life; plundering, feeling little of Crusoe's entitlement. A man saving his own life escapes self-doubt; my mission was more ambiguous. Her correspondence with my father*, sold to a library, may update a bathroom in our home. I like the Japanese porcelain figure from her father better in my living room than in hers. A nightmare I dreamt early on captured the psychic torque. I am in my mother's bedroom at night sitting on her bed while she is lying in it. It is very dark. Something I cannot see is threatening her life. Desperate, I dive over her to protect her. I become aware that I am both the one murdering her and the one wrestling with some shadowy intruder, trying to save her.

> It blew very hard all that night, and in
> the morning when I looked out, behold,
> no more ship was to be seen.

Crusoe disappeared in July—after I had emptied the apartment and called in the painters. In August my husband and I returned to our summer home on an island in Maine, and I began to settle. One afternoon we spotted a merlin hawk hidden in the aspen, waiting for warblers. On another, we kayaked home from an outing with the wind hard behind us and three ospreys above us, circling, diving for mackerel. Slowly, my feelings—my sorrow, my violence, my greed—came to seem less overblown, less grotesque, more like houses back on the shore, or a dock from which one has untied and departed.

---

*Her correspondence with my father: Smith's father was Bernard Malamud (1914–1986), one of the most renowned American fiction writers of the twentieth century.

I found myself thinking one day about the way people in the wild sometimes press a spider's web over an abrasion when no bandage is at hand. The sticky mass of threads staunches the bleeding until the body can take over. Crusoe webbed my wound, held my circumstance for me until I could gradually grasp it myself.

Reflections and Responses

1. Smith conjectures that a book like *Robinson Crusoe* "becomes a classic in proportion to how broadly its characters can be scavenged; how many readers find within it something they experience as desirable or even intimately necessary." Do you agree with her hypothesis? Is a work of literature more powerful the more people it brings in, or the deeper it involves its core audience? Based on Smith's description of Defoe's novel, would you find something to relate to in the story of surviving a shipwreck?

2. Do you find the metaphor Smith sets up compelling? Is she consistent in the way she treats her mother as a ship and her mother's death as a disorienting wreck? When does she veer from this interpretation and suggest other ways the Crusoe story applies to her maternal relationship? In your opinion, is Smith implying an actual connection between her experience and Crusoe's, or is she "reading into" the novel?

3. Smith observes "a space does not die right away when a person died, and I was unprepared for that discovery." How does this "discovery" fit into the Robinson Crusoe motif? Defoe's novel is one of discovery and also one about the importance of material things to survival; how does Smith's experience (or her mother's) confirm or complicate Crusoe's ordeal?

AMY TAN

Mother Tongue

For many American students, the language spoken at home is far different from the one spoken in school. For that reason, many students learn to switch back and forth between two languages, the one they use with their family and the one required for their education. Such switching, however, need not be confining or demoralizing. Rather, it can enhance one's sensitivity to language and can even be creatively enabling, as the Chinese American novelist Amy Tan suggests in this charming personal essay. "Language is the tool of my trade," Tan writes. "And I use them all—all the Englishes I grew up with."

Born into a Chinese family that had recently arrived in California, Amy Tan began writing as a child and after graduation from college worked for several years as a freelance business writer. In the mid-eighties, she began writing fiction, basing much of her work on family stories. She is the author of several best-selling novels: The Joy Luck Club *(1989), which was a finalist for both the National Book Award and National Book Critics Circle Award and was made into a motion picture directed by Wayne Wang;* The Kitchen God's Wife *(1991);* The Hundred Secret Senses *(1995);* The Bonesetter's Daughter *(2000); and* Saving Fish from Drowning *(2005). In 1992, she published a popular children's book,* The Moon Lady, *and in 2003, a collection of essays,* The Opposite of Faith: Memories of a Writing Life. *"Mother Tongue" originally appeared in the* Threepenny Review *(1990) and was selected by Joyce Carol Oates for* The Best American Essays 1991.

I am not a scholar of English or literature. I cannot give you much more than personal opinions on the English language and its variations in this country or others.

I am a writer. And by that definition, I am someone who has always loved language. I am fascinated by language in daily life. I spend a great deal of my time thinking about the power of language—the way it can evoke an emotion, a visual image, a complex idea, or a simple truth. Language is the tool of my trade. And I use them all—all the Englishes I grew up with.

Recently, I was made keenly aware of the different Englishes I do use. I was giving a talk to a large group of people, the same talk I had already given to half a dozen other groups. The nature of the talk was about my writing, my life, and my book, *The Joy Luck Club*. The talk was going along well enough, until I remembered one major difference that made the whole talk sound wrong. My mother was in the room. And it was perhaps the first time she had heard me give a lengthy speech, using the kind of English I have never used with her. I was saying things like, "The intersection of memory upon imagination" and "There is an aspect of my fiction that relates to thus-and-thus"—a speech filled with carefully wrought grammatical phrases, burdened, it suddenly seemed to me, with nominalized forms, past perfect tenses, conditional phrases, all the forms of standard English that I had learned in school and through books, the forms of English I did not use at home with my mother.

Just last week, I was walking down the street with my mother, and I again found myself conscious of the English I was using, the English I do use with her. We were talking about the price of new and used furniture and I heard myself saying this: "Not waste money that way." My husband was with us as well, and he didn't notice any switch in my English. And then I realized why. It's because over the twenty years we've been together I've often used that same kind of English with him, and sometimes he even uses it with me. It has become our language of intimacy, a different sort of English that relates to family talk, the language I grew up with.

So you'll have some idea of what this family talk I heard sounds like, I'll quote what my mother said during a recent conversation which I videotaped and then transcribed. During this conversation, my mother was talking about a political gangster in Shanghai who had the same last name as her family's, Du, and how the gangster in his early years wanted to be adopted by her family, which was rich by comparison. Later, the gangster became more powerful, far richer than my mother's family, and one day showed up at my mother's wedding to pay his respects. Here's what she said in part:

"Du Yusong having business like fruit stand. Like off the street kind. He is Du like Du Zong—but not Tsung-ming Island people. The local people call putong, the river east side, he belong to that side local people. That man want to ask Du Zong father take him in like become own family. Du Zong father wasn't look down on him, but didn't take seriously, until that man big like become a mafia. Now important person, very hard to inviting him. Chinese way, came only to show respect, don't stay for dinner. Respect for making big celebration, he shows up. Mean gives lots of respect. Chinese custom. Chinese social life that way. If too important won't have to stay too long. He come to my wedding. I didn't see, I heard it. I gone to boy's side, they have YMCA dinner. Chinese age I was nineteen."

You should know that my mother's expressive command of English belies how much she actually understands. She reads the *Forbes* report, listens to *Wall Street Week*, converses daily with her stockbroker, reads all of Shirley MacLaine's books with ease—all kinds of things I can't begin to understand. Yet some of my friends tell me they understand 50 percent of what my mother says. Some say they understand 80 to 90 percent. Some say they understand none of it, as if she were speaking pure Chinese. But to me, my mother's English is perfectly clear, perfectly natural. It's my mother tongue. Her language, as I hear it, is vivid, direct, full of observation and imagery. That was the language that helped shape the way I saw things, expressed things, made sense of the world.

Lately, I've been giving more thought to the kind of English my mother speaks. Like others, I have described it to people as "broken" or "fractured" English. But I wince when I say that. It has always bothered me that I can think of no way to describe it other than "broken," as if it were damaged and needed to be fixed, as if it lacked a certain wholeness and soundness. I've heard other terms used, "limited English," for example. But they seem just as bad, as if everything is limited, including people's perceptions of the limited English speaker.

I know this for a fact, because when I was growing up, my mother's "limited" English limited *my* perception of her. I was ashamed of her English. I believed that her English reflected the quality of what she had to say. That is, because she expressed them imperfectly her thoughts were imperfect. And I had plenty of empirical evidence to support me: the fact that people in department stores, at banks, and at restaurants did not take her seriously, did not give her good service, pretended not to understand her, or even acted as if they did not hear her.

My mother has long realized the limitations of her English as well. When I was fifteen, she used to have me call people on the phone to pretend I was she. In this guise, I was forced to ask for information or even to complain and yell at people who had been rude to her. One time it was a call to her stockbroker in New York. She had cashed out her small portfolio and it just so happened we were going to go to New York the next week, our very first trip outside California. I had to get on the phone and say in an adolescent voice that was not very convincing, "This is Mrs. Tan."

And my mother was standing in the back whispering loudly, "Why he don't send me check, already two weeks late. So mad he lie to me, losing me money."

And then I said in perfect English, "Yes, I'm getting rather concerned. You had agreed to send the check two weeks ago, but it hasn't arrived."

Then she began to talk more loudly. "What he want, I come to New York tell him front of his boss, you cheating me?" And I was trying to calm her down, make her be quiet, while telling the stockbroker, "I can't tolerate any more excuses. If I don't receive the check immediately, I am going to have to speak to your manager when I'm in New York next week." And sure enough, the following week there we were in front of this astonished stockbroker, and I was sitting there red-faced and quiet, and my mother, the real Mrs. Tan, was shouting at his boss in her impeccable broken English.

We used a similar routine just five days ago, for a situation that was far less humorous. My mother had gone to the hospital for an appointment, to find out about a benign brain tumor a CAT scan had revealed a month ago. She said she had spoken very good English, her best English, no mistakes. Still, she said, the hospital did not apologize when they said they had lost the CAT scan and she had come for nothing. She said they did not seem to have any sympathy when she told them she was anxious to know the exact diagnosis, since her husband and son had both died of brain tumors. She said they would not give her any more information until the next time and she would have to make another appointment for that. So she said she would not leave until the doctor called her daughter. She wouldn't budge. And when the doctor finally called her daughter, me, who spoke in perfect English—lo and behold—we had assurances the CAT scan would be found, promises that a conference call on Monday would be held, and apologies for any suffering my mother had gone through for a most regrettable mistake.

I think my mother's English almost had an effect on limiting my possibilities in life as well. Sociologists and linguists probably will tell you that a person's developing language skills are more influenced by peers. But I do think that the language spoken in the family, especially in immigrant families which are more insular, plays a large role in shaping the language of the child. And I believe that it affected my results on achievement tests, IQ tests, and the SAT. While my English skills were never judged as poor, compared to math, English could not be considered my strong suit. In grade school I did moderately well, getting perhaps B's, sometimes B-pluses, in English and scoring perhaps in the sixtieth or seventieth percentile on achievement tests. But those scores were not good enough to override the opinion that my true abilities lay in math and science, because in those areas I achieved A's and scored in the ninetieth percentile or higher.

This was understandable. Math is precise; there is only one correct answer. Whereas, for me at least, the answers on English tests were always a judgment call, a matter of opinion and personal experience. Those tests were constructed around items like fill-in-the-blank sentence completion, such as, "Even though Tom was ———, Mary thought he was ———." And the correct answer always seemed to be the most bland combinations of thoughts, for example, "Even though Tom was shy, Mary thought he was charming," with the grammatical structure "even though" limiting the correct answer to some sort of semantic opposites, so you wouldn't get answers like, "Even though Tom was foolish, Mary thought he was ridiculous." Well, according to my mother, there were very few limitations as to what Tom could have been and what Mary might have thought of him. So I never did well on tests like that.

The same was true with word analogies, pairs of words in which you were supposed to find some sort of logical, semantic relationship—for example, "*Sunset* is to *nightfall* as ——— is to ———." And here you would be presented with a list of four possible pairs, one of which showed the same kind of relationship: *red is to stoplight, bus is to arrival, chills is to fever, yawn is to boring*. Well, I could never think that way. I knew what the tests were asking, but I could not block out of my mind the images already created by the first pair, "*sunset is to nightfall*"—and I would see a burst of colors against a darkening sky, the moon rising, the lowering of a curtain of stars. And all the other pairs of words—red, bus, stoplight, boring—just threw up a mass of confusing images, making it impossible for me to sort out something as logical as saying: "A sunset precedes nightfall" is the same as "a chill precedes a fever." The only way I would have gotten that answer right would have been to imagine an associative situation, for example, my being disobedient and staying out past sunset, catching a chill at night, which turns into feverish pneumonia as punishment, which indeed did happen to me.

I have been thinking about all this lately, about my mother's English, about achievement tests. Because lately I've been asked, as a writer, why there are not more Asian Americans represented in American literature. Why are there few Asian Americans enrolled in creative writing programs? Why do so many Chinese students go into engineering? Well, these are broad sociological questions I can't begin to answer. But I have noticed in surveys—in fact, just last week—that Asian students, as a whole, always do significantly better on math achievement tests than in English. And this makes me think that there are other Asian-American students whose English spoken in the home might also be described as "broken" or "limited." And perhaps they also have teachers who are steering them away from writing and into math and science, which is what happened to me.

Fortunately, I happen to be rebellious in nature and enjoy the challenge of disproving assumptions made about me. I became an English major my first year in college, after being enrolled as premed. I started writing nonfiction as a freelancer the week after I was told by my former boss that writing was my worst skill and I should hone my talents toward account management.

But it wasn't until 1985 that I finally began to write fiction. And at first I wrote using what I thought to be wittily crafted sentences, sentences that would finally prove I had mastery over the English language. Here's an example from the first draft of a story that later made its way into *The Joy Luck Club*, but without this line: "That was my mental quandary in its nascent state." A terrible line, which I can barely pronounce.

Fortunately, for reasons I won't get into today, I later decided I should envision a reader for the stories I would write. And the reader I decided upon was my mother, because these were stories about mothers. So with this reader in mind—and in fact she did read my early drafts—I began to write stories using all the Englishes I grew up with: the English I spoke to my mother, which for lack of a better term might be described as "simple"; the English she used with me, which for lack of a better term might be described as "broken"; my translation of her Chinese, which could certainly be described as "watered down"; and what I imagined to be her translation of her Chinese if she could speak in perfect English, her internal language, and for that I sought to preserve the essence, but neither an English nor a Chinese structure. I wanted to capture what language ability tests can never reveal: her intent, her passion, her imagery, the rhythms of her speech and the nature of her thoughts.

Apart from what any critic had to say about my writing, I knew I had succeeded where it counted when my mother finished reading my book and gave me her verdict: "So easy to read."

Reflections and Responses

1. What "Englishes" did Amy Tan grow up with? Why does she feel uncomfortable with the term "broken English"? Why do you think she still uses that term toward the end of her essay?

2. What point is Tan making about language tests? Why did she perform less well on them than she did on math and science tests? In her opinion, what aspects of language do the tests fail to take into account?

3. Tan cites a sentence—"That was my mental quandary in its nascent state"—that she deleted from *The Joy Luck Club*. What do you think she dislikes about that sentence? What kind of English does it represent? Does it or does it not demonstrate a "mastery" of the English language?

RYAN VAN METER

First

Many essays reflect on an experience from early childhood and how the often-confused way that children relate to their immediate world carries repercussions into the essayist's grownup life. In this brief but poignant essay, Ryan Van Meter remembers the first time he felt love—as a five-year-old for his neighbor Ben—and the reaction his expression of that love garnered from his mother. Van Meter dwells on the "one last second" in which he and his mother could "look at each other without anything wrong between us," before she reprimands his feelings in a way that fundamentally confuses the sense of love she herself has instilled in him. By taking a clear, objective tone, the author implies that he still feels the same confusion about the way society judges his affection.

Ryan Van Meter studied nonfiction writing at the University of Iowa, and has published essays in Gulf Coast, Colorado Review, Indiana Review, Gettsyburg Review, *and* The Iowa Review, *among others. His work has also appeared in anthologies including* Touchstone Anthology of Contemporary Creative Nonfiction: Work from 1970 to Present *(2007), edited by Lex Williford and Michael Martone, and* You Must Be This Tall to Ride: Contemporary *Writers Take You Inside the Story (2009), edited by B. J. Hollars. His collection called* If You Knew Then What I Know Now, *which contains this essay, will be published in April 2011. "First" originally appeared in* The Gettysburg Review *and was selected by Mary Oliver for* The Best American Essays 2009.

Ben and I are sitting side by side in the very back of his mother's station wagon. We face glowing white headlights of cars following us, our sneakers pressed against the back hatch door. This is our joy—his and mine—to sit turned away from our moms and dads in this place that feels like a secret, as though they are not even in the car with us. They have just taken us out to dinner, and now we are driving home. Years from this evening, I won't actually be sure that this boy sitting beside me is named Ben. But that doesn't matter tonight. What I know for certain right now is that I love him, and I need to tell him this fact before were turn to our separate houses, next door to each other. We are both five.

Ben is the first brown-eyed boy I will fall for but will not be the last. His hair is also brown and always needs scraping off his forehead, which he does about every five minutes. All his jeans have dark squares stuck over the knees where he has worn through the denim. His shoelaces are perpetually undone, and he has a magic way of tying them with a quick, weird loop that I study and try myself, but can never match. His finger nails are ragged because he rips them off with his teeth and spits out the pieces when our moms aren't watching. Somebody always has to fix his shirt collars.

Our parents face the other direction, talking about something, and it is raining. My eyes trace the lines of water as they draw down the glass. Coiled beside my legs are the thick black and red cords of a pair of jumper cables. Ben's T-ball bat is also back here, rolling around and clunking as the long car wends its way through town. Ben's dad is driving, and my dad sits next to him, with our mothers in the back seat; I have recently observed that when mothers and fathers are in the car together, the dad always drives. My dad has also insisted on checking the score of the Cardinals game, so the radio is tuned to a staticky AM station, and the announcer's rich voice buzzes out of the speakers up front.

The week before this particular night, I asked my mother, "Why do people get married?" I don't recall the impulse behind my curiosity, but I will forever remember every word of her answer—she stated it simply after only a moment or two of thinking—because it seemed that important: "Two people get married when they love each other."

I had that hunch. I am a kindergartener, but the summer just before this rainy night, I learned most of what I know about love from watching soap operas with my mother. She is a gym teacher and during her months off, she catches up on the shows she has watched since college. Every summer weekday, I couldn't wait until they came on at two o'clock. My father didn't think I should be watching them—boys should be outside, playing—but he was rarely home early enough to know the difference, and according to my mother, I was too young to really understand what was going on anyway.

What I enjoyed most about soap opera was how exciting and beautiful life was. Every lady was pretty and had wonderful hair, and all the men had dark eyes and big teeth and faces as strong as bricks, and every week, there was a wedding or a man hunt or a birth. The people had grand fights where they threw vases at wall sand slammed doors and chased each other in cars. There were villains locking up the wonderfully haired heroines and suspending them in gold cages above enormous acid vats. And, of course, it was love that inspired every one of these stories and made life on the screen as thrilling as it was. That was what my mother would say from the sofa when I turned from my spot on the carpet in front of her and faced her, asking, "Why is he spying on that lady?"

"Because he loves her."

In the car, Ben and I hold hands. There is something sticky on his fingers, probably the strawberry syrup from the ice cream sundaes we ate for dessert. We have never held hands before; I have simply reached for his in the dark and held him while he holds me. I want to see our hands on the rough floor, but they are only visible every block or so when the car passes beneath a streetlight, and then, for only a flash. Ben is my closest friend because he lives next door, we are the same age, and we both have little brothers who are babies. I wish he were in the same kindergarten class as me, but he goes to a different school—one where he has to wear a uniform all day and for which there is no school bus.

"I love you," I say. We are idling, waiting for a red light to be green; a shining car has stopped right behind us, so Ben's face is pale and brilliant.

"I love you too," he says.

The car becomes quiet as the voice of the baseball game shrinks smaller and smaller.

"Will you marry me?" I ask him. His hand is still in mine; on the soap opera, you are supposed to have a ring, but I don't have one.

He begins to nod, and suddenly my mother feels very close. I look over my shoulder, my eyes peeking over the back of the last row of seats that we are leaning against. She has turned around, facing me. Permed hair, laugh lines not laughing.

"What did you just say?" she asks.

"I asked Ben to marry me."

The car starts moving forward again, and none of the parents are talking loud enough for us to hear them back here. I brace myself against the raised carpeted hump of the wheel well as Ben's father turns left onto the street before the turn onto our street. Sitting beside my mom is Ben's mother, who keeps staring forward, but I notice that one of her ears keeps swiveling back here, a little more each time. I am still facing my mother, who is still facing me, and for one last second, we look at each other without anything wrong between us.

"You shouldn't have said that," she says. "Boys don't marry other boys. Only boys and girls get married to each other."

She can't see our hands, but Ben pulls his away. I close my fingers into a loose fist and rub my palm to feel, and keep feeling, how strange his skin has made mine.

"Okay?" she asks.

"Yes," I say, but by accident my throat whispers the words.

She asks again. "Okay? Did you hear me?"

"Yes!" this time nearly shouting, and I wish we were already home so I could jump out and run to my bedroom. To be back here in the dark, private tail of the car suddenly feels wrong, so Ben and I each scoot off to our separate sides. "Yes," I say again, almost normally, turning away to face the rainy window. I feel her turn too as the radio baseball voice comes back up out of the quiet. The car starts to dip as we head down the hill of our street; our house is at the bottom. No one speaks for the rest of the ride. We all just sit and wait and watch our own views of the road—the parents see what is ahead of us while the only thing I can look at is what we have just left behind.

Reflections and Responses

---

1. What is the importance of the observation the narrator makes early on that "when mothers and fathers are in the car together, the dad always drives." Is this just an idle observation, or is Van Meter saying something more profound about gender? Where else in the essay is this theme enforced? How does this relate to the larger themes of sexuality and gender roles in the essay?

2. What does the last sentence of the essay ("We all just sit and wait and watch our own views of the road—the parents see what is ahead of us while the only thing I can look at is what we have just left behind.") mean in the context of the epiphany the narrator has had that he loves Ben, and the "lesson" he's learned that boys can only marry girls?

3. Does this essay have a political or social agenda, or is it meant as a story whose moral, even to the author, may be vague and multi-faceted? Do you think this intensely personal essay is more effective than, say, an argument in favor of legalizing gay marriage? Explain why or why not.

2

*The Attentive Mind:
Observation,
Reflection, Insight*

ANNIE DILLARD

The Stunt Pilot

*Creative expression can take many forms; it need not refer only to literature,
painting, or music. We can find creativity in craft and design, in the movements of dancers and athletes, and even — as the following essay reveals — in
the aerobatics of a stunt pilot. Observing the breathtaking dives and spins,
the "loops and arabesques" of a celebrated pilot, Annie Dillard is struck by
their resemblance to artistic expression. She finds in the pilot's use of space a
new kind of beauty, one that seems to encompass all the arts — poetry, painting, music, sculpture: "The black plane dropped spinning, and flattened
out spinning the other way; it began to carve the air into forms that built
wildly and musically on each other and never ended."*

> *Annie Dillard is one of America's preeminent essayists, someone for
> whom, as she puts it, the essay is not an occasional piece but her "real
> work." Her many award-winning books of essays and nonfiction include*
> Pilgrim at Tinker Creek, *which won the Pulitzer Prize for General
> Nonfiction in 1975;* Holy the Firm *(1977);* Living by Fiction *(1982);*
> Teaching a Stone to Talk *(1982);* An American Childhood *(1987);*
> The Writing Life *(1989); and* For the Time Being *(1999). Dillard
> has taught creative writing at Wesleyan University in Middletown, Con-
> necticut, and currently lives in Key West, Florida. Dillard has also pub-
> lished two novels,* The Living *(1992) and* The Maytrees *(2007). "The
> Stunt Pilot" originally appeared in* Esquire *(1989) and was selected by
> Justin Kaplan for* The Best American Essays 1990.

Dave Rahm lived in Bellingham, Washington, north of Seattle.
Bellingham, a harbor town, lies between the alpine North Cascade
Mountains and the San Juan Islands in Haro Strait above Puget

Sound. The latitude is that of Newfoundland. Dave Rahm was a
stunt pilot, the air's own genius.

In 1975, with a newcomer's willingness to try anything once, I
attended the Bellingham Air Show. The Bellingham airport was a
wide clearing in a forest of tall Douglas firs; its runways suited small
planes. It was June. People wearing blue or tan zipped jackets
stood loosely on the concrete walkways and runways outside the
coffee shop. At that latitude in June, you stayed outside because
you could, even most of the night, if you could think up something
to do. The sky did not darken until ten o'clock or so, and it never
got very dark. Your life parted and opened in the sunlight. You
tossed your dark winter routines, thought up mad projects, and
improvised everything from hour to hour. Being a stunt pilot
seemed the most reasonable thing in the world; you could wave
your arms in the air all day and night, and sleep next winter.

I saw from the ground a dozen stunt pilots; the air show scheduled
them one after the other, for an hour of aerobatics. Each pilot
took up his or her plane and performed a batch of tricks. They
were precise and impressive. They flew upside down, and straightened out; they did barrel rolls, and straightened out; they drilled
through dives and spins, and landed gently on a far runway.

For the end of the day, separated from all other performances of
every sort, the air show director had scheduled a program titled
"Dave Rahm." The leaflet said that Rahm was a geologist who taught
at Western Washington University. He had flown for King Hussein
in Jordan. A tall man in the crowd told me Hussein had seen Rahm
fly on a visit the king made to the United States; he had invited him
to Jordan to perform at ceremonies. Hussein was a pilot, too. "Hussein thought he was the greatest thing in the world."

Idly, paying scant attention, I saw a medium-sized, rugged man
dressed in brown leather, all begoggled, climb in a black biplane's open cockpit. The plane was a Bücker Jungman, built in
the thirties. I saw a tall, dark-haired woman seize a propeller tip
at the plane's nose and yank it down till the engine caught. He
was off; he climbed high over the airport in his biplane, very
high until he was barely visible as a mote, and then seemed to
fall down the air, diving headlong, and streaming beauty in spi-
rals behind him.

The black plane dropped spinning, and flattened out spinning the other way; it began to carve the air into forms that built wildly and musically on each other and never ended. Reluctantly, I started paying attention. Rahm drew high above the world an inexhaustibly glorious line; it piled over our heads in loops and arabesques. It was like a Saul Steinberg[*] fantasy; the plane was the pen. Like Steinberg's contracting and billowing pen line, the line Rahm spun moved to form new, punning shapes from the edges of the old. Like a Klee[†] line, it smattered the sky with landscapes and systems.

The air show announcer hushed. He had been squawking all day, and now he quit. The crowd stilled. Even the children watched dumbstruck as the slow, black biplane buzzed its way around the air. Rahm made beauty with his whole body; it was pure pattern, and you could watch it happen. The plane moved every way a line can move, and it controlled three dimensions, so the line carved massive and subtle slits in the air like sculptures. The plane looped the loop, seeming to arch its back like a gymnast; it stalled, dropped, and spun out of it climbing; it spiraled and knifed west on one side's wings and back east on another; it turned cartwheels, which must be physically impossible; it played with its own line like a cat with yarn. How did the pilot know where in the air he was? If he got lost, the ground would swat him.

Rahm did everything his plane could do: tailspins, four-point rolls, flat spins, figure eights, snap rolls, and hammerheads. He did pirouettes on the plane's tail. The other pilots could do these stunts too, skillfully, one at a time. But Rahm used the plane inexhaustibly, like a brush marking thin air.

His was pure energy and naked spirit. I have thought about it for years. Rahm's line unrolled in time. Like music, it split the bulging rim of the future along its seam. It pried out the present. We watchers waited for the split-second curve of beauty in the present to reveal itself. The human pilot, Dave Rahm, worked in the cockpit right at the plane's nose; his very body tore into the future for us and reeled it down upon us like a curling peel.

[*]**Saul Steinberg:** Contemporary artist (1914–1999) who also created numerous covers for *The New Yorker magazine*.

[†]**Klee:** Paul Klee (1879–1940), a Swiss artist known for his highly distinctive abstract paintings.

Like any fine artist, he controlled the tension of the audience's longing. You desired, unwittingly, a certain kind of roll or climb, or a return to a certain portion of the air, and he fulfilled your hope slantingly, like a poet, or evaded it until you thought you would burst, and then fulfilled it surprisingly, so you gasped and cried out.

The oddest, most exhilarating and exhausting thing was this: he never quit. The music had no periods, no rests or endings; the poetry's beautiful sentence never ended; the line had no finish; the sculptured forms piled overhead, one into another without surcease. Who could breathe, in a world where rhythm itself had no periods?

It had taken me several minutes to understand what an extraordinary thing I was seeing. Rahm kept all that embellished space in mind at once. For another twenty minutes I watched the beauty unroll and grow more fantastic and unlikely before my eyes. Now Rahm brought the plane down slidingly, and just in time, for I thought I would snap from the effort to compass and remember the line's long intelligence; I could not add another curve. He brought the plane down on a far runway. After a pause, I saw him step out, an ordinary man, and make his way back to the terminal.

The show was over. It was late. Just as I turned from the runway, something caught my eye and made me laugh. It was a swallow, a blue-green swallow, having its own air show, apparently inspired by Rahm. The swallow climbed high over the runway, held its wings oddly, tipped them, and rolled down the air in loops. The inspired swallow. I always want to paint, too, after I see the Rembrandts. The blue-green swallow tumbled precisely, and caught itself and flew up again as if excited, and looped down again, the way swallows do, but tensely, holding its body carefully still. It was a stunt swallow.

I went home and thought about Rahm's performance that night, and the next day, and the next.

I had thought I knew my way around beauty a little bit. I knew I had devoted a good part of my life to it, memorizing poetry and focusing my attention on complexity of rhythm in particular, on force, movement, repetition, and surprise, in both poetry and prose. Now I had stood among dandelions between two asphalt runways in Bellingham, Washington, and begun learning about beauty. Even the Boston Museum of Fine Arts was never more inspiriting than this small northwestern airport on this time-killing Sunday afternoon in June. Nothing on earth is more gladdening than knowing we must roll up our sleeves and move back the boundaries of the humanly possible once more.

Later I flew with Dave Rahm; he took me up. A generous geographer, Dick Smith, at Western Washington University, arranged it, and came along. Rahm and Dick Smith were colleagues at the university. In geology, Rahm had published two books and many articles. Rahm was handsome in a dull sort of way, blunt-featured, wide-jawed, wind-burned, keen-eyed, and taciturn. As anyone would expect. He was forty. He wanted to show me the Cascade Mountains; these enormous peaks, only fifty miles from the coast, rise over nine thousand feet; they are heavily glaciated. Whatcom County has more glaciers than the lower forty-eight states combined; the Cascades make the Rocky Mountains look like hills. Mount Baker is volcanic, like most Cascade peaks. That year, Mount Baker was acting up. Even from my house at the shore I could see, early in the morning on clear days, volcanic vapor rise near its peak. Often the vapor made a cloud that swelled all morning and hid the snows. Every day the newspapers reported on Baker's activity: Would it blow? (A few years later, Mount St. Helens did blow.)

Rahm was not flying his trick biplane that day, but a faster enclosed plane, a single-engine Cessna. We flew from a bumpy grass airstrip near my house, out over the coast and inland. There was coastal plain down there, but we could not see it for clouds. We were over the clouds at five hundred feet and inside them too, heading for an abrupt line of peaks we could not see. I gave up on everything, the way you do in airplanes; it was out of my hands. Every once in a while Rahm saw a peephole in the clouds and buzzed over for a look. "That's Larsen's pea farm," he said, or "That's Nooksack Road," and he changed our course with a heave.

When we got to the mountains, he slid us along Mount Baker's flanks sideways.

Our plane swiped at the mountain with a roar. I glimpsed a windshield view of dirty snow traveling fast. Our shaking, swooping belly seemed to graze the snow. The wings shuddered; we peeled away and the mountain fell back and the engines whined. We felt flung, because we were in fact flung; parts of our faces and internal organs trailed pressingly behind on the curves. We came back for another pass at the mountain, and another. We dove at the snow headlong like suicides; we jerked up, down, or away at the last second, so late we left our hearts, stomachs, and lungs behind. If I forced myself to hold my heavy head up against the G's,* and to raise my eyelids, heavy as barbells, and to notice what I saw, I could see the wrinkled green crevasses cracking the glaciers' snow.

Pitching snow filled all the windows, and shapes of dark rock. I had no notion which way was up. Everything was black or gray or white except the fatal crevasses; everything made noise and shook. I felt my face smashed sideways and saw rushing abstractions of snow in the windshield. Patches of cloud obscured the snow fleetingly. We straightened out, turned, and dashed at the mountainside for another pass, which we made, apparently, on our ear, an inch or two away from the slope. Icefalls and cornices jumbled and fell away. If a commercial plane's black box, such as the FAA painstakingly recovers from crash sites, could store videotapes as well as pilots' last words, some videotapes would look like this: a mountainside coming up at the windows from all directions, ice and snow and rock filling the screen up close and screaming by.

Rahm was just being polite. His geographer colleague wanted to see the fissure on Mount Baker from which steam escaped. Everybody in Bellingham wanted to see that sooty fissure, as did every geologist in the country; no one on earth could fly so close to it as Rahm. He knew the mountain by familiar love and feel, like a face; he knew what the plane could do and what he dared to do.

When Mount Baker inexplicably let us go, he jammed us into cloud again and soon tilted. "The Sisters!" someone shouted, and I saw the windshield fill with red rock. This mountain looked infernal, a drear and sheer plane of lifeless rock. It was red and sharp; its gritty blades cut through the clouds at random. The mountain was quiet. It was in shade. Careening, we made sideways passes at these brittle peaks too steep for snow. Their rock was full of iron, somebody shouted at me then or later; the iron had rusted, so they

---

*G's: A measure of gravitational force.

were red. Later, when I was back on the ground, I recalled that, from a distance, the two jagged peaks called the Twin Sisters looked translucent against the sky; they were sharp, tapered, and fragile as arrowheads.

I talked to Rahm. He was flying us out to the islands now. The islands were fifty or sixty miles away. Like many other people, I had picked Bellingham, Washington, by looking at an atlas. It was clear from the atlas that you could row in the salt water and see snow-covered mountains; you could scale a glaciated mountainside with an ice ax in August, skirting green crevasses two hundred feet deep, and look out on the islands in the sea. Now, in the air, the clouds had risen over us; dark forms lay on the glinting water. There was almost no color to the day, just blackened green and some yellow. I knew the islands were forested in dark Douglas firs the size of skyscrapers. Bald eagles scavenged on the beaches; robins the size of herring gulls sang in the clearings. We made our way out to the islands through the layer of air between the curving planet and its held, thick clouds.

"When I started trying to figure out what I was going to do with my life, I decided to become an expert on mountains. It wasn't much to be, it wasn't everything, but it was something. I was going to know everything about mountains from every point of view. So I started out in geography." Geography proved too pedestrian for Rahm, too concerned with "how many bushels of wheat an acre." So he ended up in geology. Smith had told me that geology departments throughout the country used Rahm's photographic slides—close-ups of geologic features from the air.

"I used to climb mountains. But you know, you can get a better feel for a mountain's power flying around it, flying all around it, than you can from climbing it tied to its side like a flea."

He talked about his flying performances. He thought of the air as a line, he said. "This end of the line, that end of the line—like a rope." He improvised. "I get a rhythm going and stick with it." While he was performing in a show, he paid attention, he said, to the lighting. He didn't play against the sun. That was all he said about what he did.

In aerobatic maneuvers, pilots pull about seven positive G's on some stunts and six negative G's on others. Some gyrations push; others pull. Pilots alternate the pressures carefully, so they do not gray out or black out.

Later I learned that some stunt pilots tune up by wearing gravity boots. These are boots made to hook over a doorway; wearing them, you hang in the doorway upside down. It must startle a pilot's children to run into their father or mother in the course of their home wanderings—the parents hanging wide-eyed, upside down in the doorway like a bat.

We were landing; here was the airstrip on Stuart Island—that island to which Ferrar Burn was dragged by the tide. We put down, climbed out of the plane, and walked. We wandered a dirt track through fields to a lee shore where yellow sandstone ledges slid into the sea. The salt chuck, people there called salt water. The sun came out. I caught a snake in the salt chuck; the snake, eighteen inches long, was swimming in the green shallows.

I had a survivor's elation. Rahm had found Mount Baker in the clouds before Mount Baker found the plane. He had wiped it with the fast plane like a cloth and we had lived. When we took off from Stuart Island and gained altitude, I asked if we could turn over—could we do a barrel roll? The plane was making a lot of noise, and Dick Smith did not hear any of this, I learned later. "Why not?" Rahm said, and added surprisingly, "It won't hurt the plane." Without ado he leaned on the wheel and the wing went down and we went somersaulting over it. We upended with a roar. We stuck to the plane's sides like flung paint. All the blood in my body bulged on my face; it piled between my skull and skin. Vaguely I could see the chrome sea twirling over Rahm's head like a baton, and the dark islands sliding down the skies like rain.

The G's slammed me into my seat like thugs and pinned me while my heart pounded and the plane turned over slowly and compacted each organ in turn. My eyeballs were newly spherical and full of heartbeats. I seemed to hear a crescendo; the wing rolled shuddering down the last 90 degrees and settled on the flat. There were the islands, admirably below us, and the clouds, admirably above. When I could breathe, I asked if we could do it again, and we did. He rolled the other way. The brilliant line of the sea slid up the side window bearing its heavy islands. Through the shriek of my blood and the plane's shakes I glimpsed the line of the sea over the windshield, thin as a spear. How in performance did Rahm keep track while his brain blurred and blood roared in his ears without ceasing? Every performance was a tour de force and a show of will, a *Machtspruch.** I had seen the other stunt pilots straighten out after a trick or two; their blood could drop back and the planet simmer down. An Olympic gymnast, at peak form, strings out a line of spins ten stunts long across a mat, and is hard put to keep his footing at the end. Rahm endured much greater pressure on his faster spins using the plane's power, and he could spin in three dimensions and keep twirling till he ran out of sky room or luck.

When we straightened out, and had flown straightforwardly for ten minutes toward home, Dick Smith, clearing his throat, brought himself to speak. "What was that we did out there?"

"The barrel rolls?" Rahm said. "They were barrel rolls." He said nothing else. I looked at the back of his head; I could see the serious line of his cheek and jaw. He was in shirtsleeves, tanned, strong-wristed. I could not imagine loving him under any circumstance; he was alien to me, unfazed. He looked like GI Joe. He flew with that matter-of-fact, bored gesture pilots use. They click overhead switches and turn dials as if only their magnificent strength makes such dullness endurable. The half circle of wheel in their big hands looks like a toy they plan to crush in a minute; the wiggly stick the wheel mounts seems barely attached.

A crop-duster pilot in Wyoming told me the life expectancy of a crop-duster pilot is five years. They fly too low. They hit buildings and power lines. They have no space to fly out of trouble, and no space to recover from a stall. We were in Cody, Wyoming, out on the north fork of the Shoshone River. The crop duster had wakened me that morning flying over the ranch house and clearing my bedroom roof by half an inch. I saw the bolts on the wheel assembly a few feet from my face. He was spraying with pesticide the plain old grass. Over breakfast I asked him how long he had been dusting crops. "Four years," he said, and the figure stalled in the air between us for a moment. "You know you're going to die at it someday," he added. "We all know it. We accept that; it's part of it." I think now that, since the crop duster was in his twenties, he accepted only that he had to say such stuff; privately he counted on skewing the curve.

***Machtspruch:** German, meaning "power speech."

I suppose Rahm knew the fact too. I do not know how he felt about it. "It's worth it," said the early French aviator Mermoz. He was Antoine de Saint-Exupéry's friend. "It's worth the final smashup."

Rahm smashed up in front of King Hussein, in Jordan, during a performance. The plane spun down and never came out of it; it nosedived into the ground and exploded. He bought the farm. I was living then with my husband out on that remote island in the San Juans, cut off from everything. Battery radios picked up the Canadian Broadcasting Company out of Toronto, half a continent away; island people would, in theory, learn if the United States blew up, but not much else. There were no newspapers. One friend got the Sunday *New York Times* by mail boat on the following Friday. He saved it until Sunday and had a party, every week; we all read the Sunday *Times* and no one mentioned that it was last week's.

One day, Paul Glenn's brother flew out from Bellingham to visit; he had a seaplane. He landed in the water in front of the cabin and tied up to our mooring. He came in for coffee, and he gave out news of this and that, and—Say, did we know that stunt pilot Dave Rahm had cracked up? In Jordan, during a performance: he never came out of a dive. He just dove right down into the ground, and his wife was there watching. "I saw it on CBS News last night." And then—with a sudden sharp look at my filling eyes—"What, did you know him?" But no, I did not know him. He took me up once. Several years ago. I admired his flying. I had thought that danger was the safest thing in the world, if you went about it right.

Later, I found a newspaper. Rahm was living in Jordan that year; King Hussein invited him to train the aerobatics team, the Royal Jordanian Falcons. He was also visiting professor of geology at the University of Jordan. In Amman that day he had been flying a Pitt Special, a plane he knew well. Katy Rahm, his wife of six months, was sitting beside Hussein in the viewing stands, with her daughter. Rahm died performing a Lomcevak combined with a tail slide and hammerhead. In a Lomcevak, the pilot brings the plane up on a slant and pirouettes. I had seen Rahm do this: the falling plane twirled slowly like a leaf. Like a ballerina, the plane seemed to hold its head back stiff in concentration at the music's slow, painful beauty. It was one of Rahm's favorite routines. Next the pilot flies straight up, stalls the plane, and slides down the air on his tail. He brings the nose down—the hammerhead—kicks the engine, and finishes with a low loop.

It is a dangerous maneuver at any altitude, and Rahm was doing it low. He hit the ground on the loop; the tail slide had left him no height. When Rahm went down, King Hussein dashed to the burning plane to pull him out, but he was already dead.

A few months after the air show, and a month after I had flown with Rahm, I was working at my desk near Bellingham, where I lived, when I heard a sound so odd it finally penetrated my concentration. It was the buzz of an airplane, but it rose and fell musically, and it never quit; the plane never flew out of earshot. I walked out on the porch and looked up: it was Rahm in the black and gold biplane, looping all over the air. I had been wondering about his performance flight: could it really have been so beautiful? It was, for here it was again. The little plane twisted all over the air like a vine. It trailed a line like a very long mathematical proof you could follow only so far, and then it lost you in its complexity. I saw Rahm flying high over the Douglas firs, and out over the water, and back over farms. The air was a fluid, and Rahm was an eel.

It was as if Mozart could move his body through his notes, and you could walk out on the porch, look up, and see him in periwig and breeches, flying around in the sky. You could hear the music as he dove through it; it streamed after him like a contrail.

I lost myself; standing on the firm porch, I lost my direction and reeled. My neck and spine rose and turned, so I followed the plane's line kinesthetically. In his open-cockpit black plane, Rahm demonstrated curved space. He slid down ramps of air, he vaulted and wheeled. He piled loops in heaps and praised height. He unrolled the scroll of air, extended it, and bent it into Möbius strips; he furled line in a thousand new ways, as if he were inventing a script and writing it in one infinitely recurring utterance until I thought the bounds of beauty must break.

From inside, the looping plane had sounded tinny, like a kazoo. Outside, the buzz rose and fell to the Doppler effect as the plane looped near or away. Rahm cleaved the sky like a prow and tossed out time left and right in his wake. He performed for forty minutes; then he headed the plane, as small as a wasp, back to the airport inland. Later I learned Rahm often practiced acrobatic flights over this shore. His idea was that if he lost control and was going to go down, he could ditch in the salt chuck, where no one else would get hurt.

If I had not turned two barrel rolls in an airplane, I might have fancied Rahm felt good up there, and playful. Maybe Jackson Pollock felt a sort of playfulness, in addition to the artist's usual deliberate and intelligent care. In my limited experience, painting, unlike writing, pleases the senses while you do it, and more while you do it than after it is done. Drawing lines with an airplane, unfortunately, tortures the senses. Jet bomber pilots black out. I knew Rahm felt as if his brain were bursting his eardrums, felt that if he let his jaws close as tight as centrifugal force pressed them, he would bite through his lungs.

"All virtue is a form of acting," Yeats said. Rahm deliberately turned himself into a figure. Sitting invisible at the controls of a distant airplane, he became the agent and the instrument of art and invention. He did not tell me how he felt when we spoke of his performance flying; he told me instead that he paid attention to how his plane and its line looked to the audience against the lighted sky. If he had noticed how he felt, he could not have done the work. Robed in his airplane, he was as featureless as a priest. He was lost in his figural aspect like an actor or a king. Of his flying, he had said only, "I get a rhythm and stick with it." In its reticence, this statement reminded me of Veronese's[*] "Given a large canvas, I enhanced it as I saw fit." But Veronese was ironic, and Rahm was not; he was as literal as an astronaut; the machine gave him tongue.

When Rahm flew, he sat down in the middle of art and strapped himself in. He spun it all around him. He could not see it himself. If he never saw it on film, he never saw it at all—as if Beethoven could not hear his final symphonies not because he was deaf but because he was inside the paper on which he wrote. Rahm must have felt it happen, that fusion of vision and metal, motion and idea. I think of this man as a figure, a college professor with a PhD upside down in the loud band of beauty. What are we here for? *Propter chorum*, the monks say: for the sake of the choir.

---

[*]**Veronese:** Paolo Veronese (1528–1588), famous Venetian painter.

"Purity does not lie in separation from but in deeper penetration into the universe," Teilhard de Chardin* wrote. It is hard to imagine a deeper penetration into the universe than Rahm's last dive in his plane, or than his inexpressible wordless selfless line's inscribing the air and dissolving. Any other art may be permanent. I cannot recall one Rahm sequence. He improvised. If Christo† wraps a building or dyes a harbor, we join his poignant and fierce awareness that the work will be gone in days. Rahm's plane shed a ribbon in space, a ribbon whose end unraveled in memory while its beginning unfurled as surprise. He may have acknowledged that what he did could be called art, but it would have been, I think, only in the common misusage, which holds art to be the last extreme of skill. Rahm rode the point of the line to the possible; he discovered it and wound it down to show. He made his dazzling probe on the run. "The world is filled, and filled with the Absolute," Teilhard de Chardin wrote. "To see this is to be made free."

Reflections and Responses

1. How does Dillard establish a connection between stunt piloting and artistic performance? Identify the various moments in her essay when she makes such a connection. What do these moments have in common? What images do they share?

2. Note that Dillard doesn't wait until the very end of her essay to introduce Rahm's death. Why do you think she avoids this kind of climax? What advantage does this give her?

3. "The Stunt Pilot" also appears as an untitled chapter in Dillard's book *The Writing Life*. Why is this an appropriate context for the essay? What does the essay tell us about expression and composition?

*Teilhard de Chardin: Pierre Teilhard de Chardin (1881–1953), a noted paleontologist and Catholic priest whose most famous book, *The Phenomenon of Man*, attempts to bridge the gap between science and religion.

†Christo: A contemporary Bulgarian artist known for staging spectacular environmental effects.

BRIAN DOYLE

Joyas Voladoras

Certain essays are composed like poetry, with a lyric intensity in which every word, every phrase, and every image seems critical. Such essays are usually quite short (often only a few paragraphs) since, for one thing, it is extremely difficult to sustain such verbal intensity over many pages, and for another, if extended too long, the style could become tiresome. Critics sometimes call such works "prose poems," suggesting that their prose style is enriched by such poetic characteristics as cadence and imagery. Attention to the sound of the prose and its phrasal rhythms is crucial, as is metaphorical originality. Suggestiveness of the theme is often favored over explicit statement. All of these literary characteristics can be seen in Brian Doyle's "Joyas Voladoras" as he looks lyrically into matters of the heart ranging from hummingbirds to humans.

Brian Doyle is the editor of Portland Magazine *at the University of Portland, in Oregon. He is the author of five collections of essays, among them* Spirited Men *(about writers and musicians, 2004) and* Leaping *(about everything else, 2003). His most recent books are* The Wet Engine *(2005), about the "muddle & music of hearts"; and* The Grail *(2006), about a year in an Oregon vineyard. A collection of poems called* Epiphanies & Elegies *was published in the fall of 2006 by Rowman and Littlefield. "Joyas Voladoras"—which means "flying jewels," the name the first Spanish explorers gave to hummingbirds—originally appeared in* The American Scholar *and was selected by Susan Orlean for* The Best American Essays 2005.

Consider the hummingbird for a long moment. A hummingbird's heart beats ten times a second. A hummingbird's heart is the size of a pencil eraser. A hummingbird's heart is a lot of the hummingbird. *Joyas voladoras,* flying jewels, the first white explorers in the

Americas called them, and the white men had never seen such creatures, for hummingbirds came into the world only in the Americas, nowhere else in the universe, more than three hundred species of them whirring and zooming and nectaring in hummer time zones nine times removed from ours, their hearts hammering faster than we could clearly hear if we pressed our elephantine ears to their infinitesimal chests.

Each one visits a thousand flowers a day. They can dive at sixty miles an hour. They can fly backward. They can fly more than five hundred miles without pausing to rest. But when they rest they come close to death: on frigid nights, or when they are starving, they retreat into torpor, their metabolic rate slowing to a fifteenth of their normal sleep rate, their hearts sludging nearly to a halt, barely beating, and if they are not soon warmed, if they do not soon find that which is sweet, their hearts grow cold, and they cease to be. Consider for a moment those hummingbirds who did not open their eyes again today, this very day, in the Americas: bearded helmetcrests and booted racket-tails, violet-tailed sylphs and violet-capped woodnymphs, crimson topazes and purplecrowned fairies, red-tailed comets and amethyst woodstars, rainbow-bearded thornbills and glittering-bellied

Tom Brakefield/Stockbyte/Jupiter Images

emeralds, velvet-purple coronets and golden-bellied star-frontlets, fiery-tailed awlbills and Andean hillstars, spatuletails and pufflegs,* each the most amazing thing you have never seen, each thunderous wild heart the size of an infant's fingernail, each mad heart silent, a brilliant music stilled.

Hummingbirds, like all flying birds but more so, have incredible enormous immense ferocious metabolisms. To drive those metabolisms they have racecar hearts that eat oxygen at an eyepopping rate. Their hearts are built of thinner, leaner fibers than ours. Their arteries are stiffer and more taut. They have more mitochondria in their heart muscles—anything to gulp more oxygen. Their hearts are stripped to the skin for the war against gravity and inertia, the mad search for food, the insane idea of flight. The price of their ambition is a life closer to death; they suffer more heart attacks and aneurysms and ruptures than any other living creature. It's expensive to fly. You burn out. You fry the machine. You melt the engine. Every creature on earth has approximately two billion heartbeats to spend in a lifetime. You can spend them slowly, like a tortoise, and live to be two hundred years old, or you can spend them fast, like a hummingbird, and live to be two years old.

The biggest heart in the world is inside the blue whale. It weighs more than seven tons. It's as big as a room. It *is* a room, with four chambers. A child could walk around in it, head high, bending only to step through the valves. The valves are as big as the swinging doors in a saloon. This house of a heart drives a creature a hundred feet long. When this creature is born it is twenty feet long and weighs four tons. It is waaaaay bigger than your car. It drinks a hundred gallons of milk from its mama every day and gains two hundred pounds a day, and when it is seven or eight years old it endures an unimaginable puberty and then it essentially disappears from human ken, for next to nothing is known of the mating habits, travel patterns, diet, social life, language, social structure, diseases, spirituality, wars, stories, despairs, and arts of the blue whale. There are perhaps ten thousand blue whales in the world, living in every ocean on earth, and of the largest mammal who ever lived we know nearly nothing. But we know this: the animals

*A list of some species of hummingbirds; the majority of hummingbirds are found in the tropics. Only one species is commonly seen in the eastern region of the United States: the ruby-throated hummingbird.

Denis Scott/Corbis

with the largest hearts in the world generally travel in pairs, and their penetrating moaning cries, their piercing yearning tongue, can be heard underwater for miles and miles.

Mammals and birds have hearts with four chambers. Reptiles and turtles have hearts with three chambers. Fish have hearts with two chambers. Insects and mollusks have hearts with one chamber. Worms have hearts with one chamber, although they may have as many as eleven single-chambered hearts. Unicellular bacteria have no hearts at all; but even they have fluid eternally in motion, washing from one side of the cell to the other, swirling and whirling. No living being is without interior liquid motion. We all churn inside. So much held in a heart in a lifetime. So much held in a heart in a day, an hour, a moment. We are utterly open with no one, in the end—not mother and father, not wife or husband, not lover, not child, not friend. We open windows to each but we live alone in the house of the heart. Perhaps we must. Perhaps we could not bear to be so naked, for fear of a constantly harrowed heart. When young we think there will come one person who will savor and sustain us always; when we are older we know this is the dream of a child, that all hearts finally are bruised and scarred, scored and torn, repaired by time and will, patched by force of character, yet fragile and rickety forevermore, no matter how ferocious the defense and how many bricks you bring to the wall. You can brick up your heart as stout and tight and hard and cold and impregnable as you possibly can and down it comes in an instant, felled by a woman's second glance, a child's apple breath, the shatter of glass in the road, the words "I have something to tell you," a cat with a broken spine dragging itself into the forest to die, the brush of your mother's papery ancient hand in the thicket of your hair, the memory of your father's voice early in the morning echoing from the kitchen where he is making pancakes for his children.

Reflections and Responses

1. A common poetic device used often in prose is known as *anaphora*. In prose it is often seen as the repetition of the same words (sometimes with slight variations) at the start of a sentence or clause. Try underlining the use of anaphora in Doyle's short essay. How many examples do you find? Select one sequence of examples and try to explain the effect this device has on your response to the essay.

2. Why do you think Doyle contrasts the hearts of hummingbirds and blue whales? What physical details does he introduce to make you aware of their relative sizes? To what extent do his descriptive details of both creatures' hearts surprise you? What expressions do you find especially original or imaginative?

3. What happens when you reach the final paragraph? In what ways does an essay that at first appeared to be about creatures great and small suddenly turn into an essay about human nature? What has happened to the word *heart*? Do you think "Joyas Voladoras" could be considered a personal essay, even a private one? How would you account for all the specific details that the author introduces in the concluding paragraph apparently to support a generalization about the human heart?

KITTY BURNS FLOREY

Sister Bernadette's Barking Dog

It's said that we live in an increasingly visual culture, surrounded by imagery everywhere we turn. Our phones now have cameras; our computer screen is a collage of icons and flashing screen savers; our information often comes in colorful layouts and graphical formats. Yet one form of visualization has disappeared: We no longer picture sentences. The days are long gone, as Kitty Burns Florey reminds us in "Sister Bernadette's Barking Dog," when elementary school students learned the rules of grammar and parts of speech through the use of visual diagrams. "The diagram," Florey vividly remembers, "was a bit like art, a bit like mathematics. It was much more than words uttered or words written: it was a picture of language."

Kitty Burns Florey is the author of ten novels, most recently The Sleep Specialist *(2007) and* Solos *(2004). In 2009, she published* Script and Scribble: The Rise and Fall of Handwriting. *Her short stories and essays have been published in the* New York Times, Harper's Magazine, The North American Review, The Greensboro Review, *and* House Beautiful. *"Sister Bernadette's Barking Dog" was reprinted from Harper's Magazine (a version also appeared in* The Vocabula Review*) and was selected by Susan Orlean for* The Best American Essays 2005. *Readers who enjoy this essay will surely enjoy the expanded book-length treatment of this subject in* Sister Bernadette's Barking Dog: The Quirky History and Lost Art of Diagramming Sentences *(2006).*

Diagramming sentences is one of those lost skills, like darning socks or playing the sackbut, that no one seems to miss. Invented, or at least codified, in an 1877 text called *Higher Lessons in English*, by Alonzo Reed and Brainerd Kellogg, it swept through American public schools like the measles, and was embraced by teachers as the way to reform students who were engaged in "the cold-blooded murder of the English tongue" (to take Henry Higgins* slightly out of context). By promoting the beautifully logical rules of syntax, diagramming would root out evils like "it's me" and "I ain't got none," until everyone wrote like Ralph Waldo Emerson, or at least James Fenimore Cooper.

In my own youth, many years after 1877, diagramming was still serious business. I learned it in the sixth grade from Sister Bernadette. I can still see her: a tiny nun with a sharp pink nose, confidently drawing a dead-straight horizontal line like a highway across the blackboard, flourishing her chalk in the air at the end of it, her veil flipping out behind her as she turned back to the class. "We begin," she said, "with a straight line." And then, in her firm and saintly script, she put words on the line, a noun and a verb—probably something like *dog barked*. Between the words she drew a short vertical slash, bisecting the line. Then she made a road that forked off at an angle—a short country lane under the word *dog*—and on it she wrote *The*.

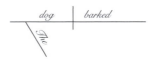

That was it: subject, predicate, and the little modifying article that civilized the sentence—all of it made into a picture that was every bit as clear and informative as an actual portrait of a beagle in mid-woof. The thrilling part was that this was a picture not of the animal but of the words that stood for the animal and its noises. It was a representation of something both concrete and abstract. The diagram was a bit like art, a bit like mathematics. It was much more than words uttered or words written: it was a picture of language.

I was hooked. So, it seems, were many of my contemporaries. Among the myths that have attached themselves to memories of being educated in the fifties is the notion that activities like

---

*Henry Higgins** is the leading character in George Bernard Shaw's famous play *Pygmalion* (1912), which was made into the popular musical comedy *My Fair Lady*. A phonetics professor, Higgins wins a bet that he can transform Liza Doolittle's accent into such perfect-sounding English that she could be mistaken for a duchess.

diagramming sentences (along with memorizing poems and adding long columns of figures without a calculator) were pointless
and monotonous. I thought diagramming was fun, and most of my
friends who were subjected to it look back with varying degrees of
delight. Some of us were better at it than others, but it was considered a kind of treat, a game that broke up the school day. You took
a sentence, threw it against the wall, picked up the pieces, and put
them together again, slotting each word into its pigeonhole. When
you got it right, you made order and sense out of what we used all
the time and took for granted: sentences.

Gertrude Stein,* of all people, was a great fan of diagramming.
"I really do not know that anything has ever been more exciting
than diagramming sentences," she wrote in the early 1930s. "I like
the feeling the everlasting feeling of sentences as they diagram
themselves."

In my experience they didn't exactly diagram themselves; they
had to be coaxed, if not wrestled. But—the feeling the everlasting
feeling: if Gertrude Stein wasn't just riffing on the words, the love-
song sound of them, she must have meant the glorious definite-
ness of the process. I remember loving the look of the sentences,
short or long, once they were tidied into diagrams—the curious
maplike shapes they made, the way the words settled primly along
their horizontals like houses on a road, the way some roads were
culs-de-sac and some were long meandering interstates with many
exit ramps and scenic lookouts. And the clarity of it all, the ease
with which—once they were laid open, their secrets exposed—
those sentences could be comprehended.

On a more trivial level, part of the fun was being summoned to
the blackboard to show off. There you stood, chalk in hand, while,
with a glint in her eye, Sister Bernadette read off an especially tricky
sentence. Compact, fastidious handwriting was an asset. A good
spatial sense helped you arrange things so that the diagram didn't
end up with the words jammed together against the edge of the
blackboard like commuters in a subway car. The trick was to think
fast, write fast, and not get rattled if you failed in the attempt.

*__Gertrude Stein__ (1874–1946) was a prolific novelist and essayist known for her
experimental and innovative prose. She wrote extensively on the subject of composition and today is perhaps best known for her best-selling book *The Autobiography of
Alice B. Toklas* (1933).

As we became more proficient, the tasks got harder. There was great appeal in the Shaker-like simplicity of sentences like *The dog chased a rabbit* (subject, predicate, direct object), with their plain, no-nonsense diagrams:

But there were also lovable subtleties, like the way the line that set off a predicate adjective slanted back like a signpost toward the subject it modified:

Or the thorny rosebush created by diagramming a prepositional phrase modifying another prepositional phrase:

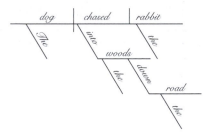

Or the elegant absence of the preposition when using an indirect object, indicated by a short road with no house on it:

The missing preposition—in this case *to*—could also be placed on that road in parentheses, but this always seemed to me a clumsy solution, right up there with explaining a pun. In a related situation, however, the void where the subject of an imperative sentence would go was better filled, to my mind, with the graphic and slightly menacing parenthesized pronoun, as in:

Questions were a special case. For diagramming, they had to be turned inside out, the way a sock has to be eased onto a foot: *What is the dog doing?* transformed into the more dramatic *The dog is doing what?*

Mostly we diagrammed sentences out of a grammar book, but sometimes we were assigned the task of making up our own, taking pleasure in coming up with wild Proustian* wanderings that— kicking and screaming—had to be corralled, harnessed, and made to trot into the barn in neat rows.

Part of the fun of diagramming sentences was that it didn't matter what they said. The dog could bark, chew gum, play chess—in the world of diagramming, sentences weren't about meaning so much as they were about subject, predicate, object, and their various dependents or modifiers. If they were diagrammed properly, they always illustrated correct syntax, no matter how silly their content. We hung those sentences out like a wash until we understood every piece of them. We could see for ourselves the difference between *who* and *whom.* We knew what an adverb was, and we knew where in a sentence it went, and why it went there. We were aware of dangling modifiers because we could see them, quite literally, dangle.

Today, diagramming is not exactly dead, but for many years it has been in sharp decline. This is partly because diagramming sentences seems

---

Proustian: A reference to the prose style of the influential French novelist Marcel Proust (1871–1922), who was known for his fluid and meandering sentences.

to double the task of the student, who has to learn a whole new set of rules—where does that pesky line go, and which way does it slant?—in order to illustrate a set of rules that, in fact, has been learned pretty thoroughly simply by immersion in the language from birth. It's only the subtleties that are difficult—*who* versus *whom*, adjective versus adverb, *it's I* versus *it's me*—and most of those come from the mostly doomed attempt, in the early days of English grammar, to stuff English into the well-made boxes of Latin and Greek, which is something like forcing a struggling cat into the carrier for a trip to the vet.

Another problem is that teachers—and certainly students—have become more willing to accept the idea that the sentences that can be popped into a diagram aren't always sentences anyone wants to write. One writer friend of mine says that she disliked diagramming because it meant "forcing sentences into conformity." And indeed language can be more supple and interesting than the patterns that perfect syntax forces on it. An attempt to diagram a sentence by James Joyce, or one by Henry James (whose style H. G. Wells compared so memorably to "a magnificent but painful hippopotamus resolved at any cost . . . upon picking up a pea"), will quickly demonstrate the limitations of Sister Bernadette's methods. Diagramming may have taught us to write more correctly— and maybe even to think more logically—but I don't think anyone would claim that it taught us to write well. And besides, any writer knows that the best way to learn to write good sentences is not to diagram them but to read them.

Still, like pocket watches and Gilbert and Sullivan operas, diagramming persists, alternately reviled and championed by linguists and grammarians. It can be found in university linguistics courses and on the Web sites of a few diehard enthusiasts. There are teachers' guides, should any teacher want one; it's taught in ESL courses and in progressive private schools. There's a video, *English Grammar: The Art of Diagramming Sentences,* that features a very 1950s-looking teacher named Miss Lamb working at a blackboard. There's even a computer program, apparently, that diagrams.

Sometimes, on a slow subway or a boring car trip, I mentally diagram a sentence, just as I occasionally try to remember the declension of *hic, haec, hoc* or the words to the second verse of "The Star-Spangled Banner." I have no illusions that diagramming sentences in my youth did anything for me, practically speaking.

But in an occasional fit of nostalgia, I like to bring back those golden afternoons when

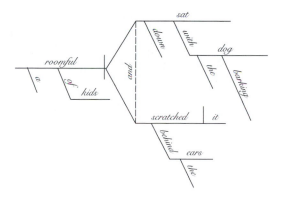

Reflections and Responses

1. Note the author's use of figurative language throughout the essay. For example, she recalls Sister Bernadete "confidently drawing a dead-straight horizontal line like a highway across the blackboard. . . ." Why is the horizontal line likened to a "highway"? Why is it an appropriate metaphor? How does the author continue this metaphor throughout the essay?

2. Besides the extensive use of figurative language, what other elements does Florey employ to emphasize the role of visualization? How does the idea of art and perception enter into her love of diagramming? How does it help her appreciate the architecture of a sentence?

3. After reading Kitty Burns Florey's nostalgic tribute to diagramming, do you think diagramming is an effective method for learning English grammar that ought to be restored? Why or why not? What advantages do you see in learning to diagram? What are the limitations of this method? In what ways does Florey cover both the advantages and the limitations in her essay? Can you restore her final sentence to the way it would have originally read had she not diagrammed it?

IAN FRAZIER

A Lovely Sort of Lower Purpose

In the middle of the eighteenth century, the great English essayist Samuel Johnson regularly published a series of essays known as The Idler. *The title was carefully chosen; from Montaigne on, essayists have traditionally culti-vated a leisurely pace and written many pieces in praise of idleness or what in today's terms would be called "hanging out" and "fooling around." In "A Lovely Sort of Lower Purpose," Ian Frazier revisits this time-tested topic and, in his inimitable fashion, celebrates the virtues of doing nothing. Fra-zier warns us, however, that this virtue is rapidly declining as our restless society continually finds ways to make everything busy, useful, and purpose-ful. As Frazier suggests, the terrible question grown-ups often ask children, "What are you doing?" now haunts us all.*

Besides several collections of humorous essays and two award-winning books of nonfiction, Family *(1994) and* Great Plains *(1989), Ian Frazier has published* On the Rez *(1999), a look at life on a reservation;* The Fish's Eye *(2002), a collection of his fishing essays; and* Gone to New York: Adventures in the City *(2005), a collection of his essays on New York City and environs. His latest collection of essays is* Lamentations of the Father *(2008). His writing has appeared in* The New Yorker, Out-side, The Atlantic Monthly, *and many other magazines. Frazier was the guest editor of* The Best American Essays *1997. "A Lovely Sort of Lower Purpose" originally appeared in* Outside *magazine and was selected by Edward Hoagland for* The Best American Essays *1999.*

As kids, my friends and I spent a lot of time out in the woods. "The woods" was our part-time address, destination, purpose, and ex-cuse. If I went to a friend's house and found him not at home, his mother might say, "Oh, he's out in the woods," with a tone of airy acceptance. It's similar to the tone people sometimes use nowa-days to tell me that someone I'm looking for is on the golf course or at the hairdresser's or at the gym, or even "away from his desk." The combination of vagueness and specificity in the answer gives a sense of somewhere romantically incommunicado. I once attended an awards dinner at which Frank Sinatra was supposed to appear, and when he didn't, the master of ceremonies explained that Frank had called to say he was "filming on location." Ten-year-olds suffer from a scarcity of fancy-sounding excuses to do whatever they feel like for a while. For us, saying we were "out in the woods" worked just fine.

We sometimes told ourselves that what we were doing in the woods was exploring. Exploring was a more prominent idea back then than it is today. History, for example, seemed to be mostly about explorers, and the semirural part of Ohio where we lived still had a faint recollection of being part of the frontier. At the town's two high schools, the sports teams were the Explorers and the Pioneers. Our explorations, though, seemed to have less sys-tem than the historic kind: something usually came up along the way. Say we began to cross one of the little creeks plentiful in the second-growth forests we frequented and found that all the creek's moisture had somehow become a shell of milk-white ice about eight inches above the now-dry bed. No other kind of ice is as satis-fying to break. The search for the true meridian would be post-poned while we spent the afternoon breaking the ice, stomping it underfoot by the furlong, and throwing its bigger pieces like Fris-bees to shatter in excellent, war-movie-type fragmentation among the higher branches of the trees.

Stuff like that—throwing rocks at a fresh mudflat to make cra-ters, shooting frogs with slingshots, making forts, picking blackber-ries, digging in what we were briefly persuaded was an Indian burial mound—occupied much of our time in the woods. Our purpose there was a higher sort of un-purpose, a free-form aimlessness that would be beyond me now. Once as we tramped for miles along Tinker's Creek my friend Kent told me the entire plot of two Bob Hope movies, *The Paleface* and *Son of Paleface*, which he had just seen on a double bill. The joke-filled monotony of his synopsis went well with the soggy afternoon, the muddy water, the endless tangled brush. (Afterward, when I saw the movies themselves, I found a lot to prefer in Kent's version.) The woods were ideal for those trains of thought that involved tedium and brooding. Often when I went by myself I would climb a tree and just sit.

I could list a hundred pointless things we did in the woods. Climbing trees, though, was a common one. Often we got "lost" and had to climb a tree to get our bearings. If you read a story in which someone does that successfully, be skeptical; the topmost branches are usually too skinny to hold weight, and we could never climb high enough to see anything except other trees. There were four or five trees that we visited regularly—tall beeches, easy to climb and comfortable to sit in. We spent hours at a time in trees, afflicting the best perches with so many carved-in names, hearts, arrows, and funny sayings from the comic strips that we ran out of room for more.

It was in a tree, too, that our days of fooling around in the woods came to an end. By then some of us had reached seventh grade and had begun the bumpy ride of adolescence. In March, the month when we usually took to the woods again after winter, two friends and I set out to go exploring. Right away, we climbed a tree, and soon were indulging in the spurious nostalgia of kids who have only short pasts to look back upon. The "remember whens" faltered, finally, and I think it occurred to all three of us at the same time that we really were rather big to be up in a tree. Some of us had started wearing unwoodsy outfits like short-sleeved madras shirts and penny loafers, even after school. Soon there would be the spring dances on Friday evenings in the high school cafeteria. We looked at the bare branches around us receding into obscurity, and suddenly there was nothing up there for us. Like Adam and Eve, we saw our own nakedness, and that terrible grown-up question "What are you *doing*?" made us ashamed.

We went back to the woods eventually—and when I say "we," I'm speaking demographically, not just of my friends and me. Millions of us went back, once the sexual and social business of early adulthood had been more or less sorted out. But significantly, we brought that same question with us. Now we had to be seriously doing—racing, strengthening, slimming, traversing, collecting, achieving, catching-and-releasing. A few parts per million of our concentrated purpose changed the chemistry of the whole outdoors. Even those rare interludes of actually doing nothing in the woods took on a certain fierceness as we reinforced them with personal dramas, usually of a social or sexual kind: the only way we could justify sitting motionless in an A-frame cabin in the north woods of Michigan, for example, was if we had just survived a really messy divorce.

"What are you *doing?*" The question pursues me still. When I go fishing and catch no fish, the idea that it's fun simply to be out on the river consoles me for not one second. I must catch fish; and if I do, I must then catch more and bigger fish. On a Sunday afternoon last summer I took my two young children fishing with me on a famous trout stream near my house. My son was four and my daughter was eight, and I kidded myself that in their company I would be able to fish with my usual single-minded mania. I suited up in my waders and tackle-shopful of gear and led my kids from the parking area down toward the water. On the way, however, we had to cross a narrow, shallow irrigation ditch dating from when this part of the valley had farms. Well, the kids saw that little ditch and immediately took off their shoes and waded in and splashed and floated pine cones. My son got an inexplicable joy from casting his little spinning rod far over the ditch into the woods and reeling the rubber casting weight back through the trees. My daughter observed many tent caterpillars—a curse of yard-owners that year—falling from bushes into the ditch and floating helplessly along, and she decided to rescue them. She kept watching the water carefully, and whenever she spotted a caterpillar she swooped down and plucked it out and put it carefully on the bank. I didn't have the heart to drag the kids away, and as I was sitting in all my fishing gear beside the unlikely trickle, a fly fisherman about my age and just as geared-up came along. He took me in at a glance, noticed my equipment and my idleness, and gave a small but unmistakable snort of derision. I was offended, but I understood how he felt as he and his purpose hurried on by.

Here, I'd like to consider a word whose meaning has begun to drift like a caterpillar on a stream. That word is *margin*. Originally its meaning—the blank space around a body of type or the border of a piece of ground—had neutral connotations. But its adjective form, *marginal*, now has a negative tinge. Marginal people or places or activities are ones that don't quite work out, don't sufficiently account of themselves in the economic world. From the adjective sprouted a far-fetched verb, *marginalize*, whose meaning is only bad. To be marginalized is to be a victim, and to marginalize someone else is an act of exclusion that can cost you tenure. Today's so-called marginal people are the exact equivalents, etymologically, of the old-time heathens. A heathen was a savage, wild, un-Christian person who lived out on a heath. The heath was the margin of Christendom. No one today would ever use the word *heathen* except ironically, but we call certain people and activities marginal without a hint of irony all the time.

I've never been on a heath, but to judge from accounts of coal-smogged London in the days when *heathen* was in vogue, a wind-swept place full of heather and salmon streams sounds like the better place to be. And if the modern version of the margin is somewhere in western Nebraska, and the un-margin, the coveted red-hot center, is a site like Rodeo Drive, I wouldn't know which to choose. We need both, but especially as the world gets more jammed up, we need margins. A book without margins is impossible to read. And marginal behavior can be the most important kind. Every purpose-filled activity we pursue in the woods began as just fooling around. The first person to ride his bicycle down a mountain trail was doing a decidedly marginal thing. The margin is where you can try out odd ideas that you might be afraid to admit to with people looking on. Scientists have a term for research carried on with no immediate prospects of economic gain: "blue-sky research." Marginal places are the blue-sky research zones of the outdoors.

Unfortunately, there are fewer and fewer of them every day. Now a common fate of a place on the margin is to have a convenience store or a windowless brick building belonging to a telephone company built on it. Across the country, endless miles of exurbia now overlap and spill into one another with hardly a margin at all. There's still a lot of open space out there, of course, but usually it's far enough from home that just getting to it requires purpose and premeditation. As the easy-to-wander-into hometown margins disappear, a certain kind of wandering becomes endangered too.

On the far west side of the small western city where I live, past the town-killer discount stores, is an open expanse of undeveloped ground. Its many acres border the Bitterroot River, and its far end abuts a fence surrounding a commercial gravel pit. It is a classic marginal, anything-goes sort of place, and at the moment I prefer it to just about anywhere I know.

Army reservists sometimes drive tanks there on weekends. The camouflaged behemoths slithering across the ground would make my skin crawl if I didn't suspect that the kids driving them were having such a good time. The dirt-bike guys certainly are, as they zip all over, often dawn to dusk, exuberantly making a racket. Dads bring their kids to this place to fly kites and model airplanes, people in a converted school bus camp there for weeks on end, coin-shooters cruise around with metal detectors, hunters just in off the river clean game, college kids party and leave heaps of cigarette butts and beer cans and occasionally pieces of underwear. I fish there, of course, but remarkably I don't always feel I have to. Sometimes I also pick up the trash, and I pull my kids around on a sled in the winter, and I bring friends just off the plane to sit on the riverbank and drink wine and watch the sunset.

Soon, I'm sure, Development will set its surveyor's tripod on this ground and make it get with one program or another. Rumblings of this have already begun to sound in the local newspaper. I foresee rows of condominiums, or an expansion of the gravel pit, or a public park featuring hiking trails and grim pieces of exercise equipment every twenty yards. That last choice, in all its worthy banality, somehow is the most disheartening of all. A plan will claim the empty acres and erase the spotted knapweed and the tank tracks and the beer-can heaps. The place's possibilities, which at the moment are approximately infinite, will be reduced to merely a few. And those of uncertain purpose will have to go elsewhere when they feel like doing nothing in particular, just fooling around.

Reflections and Responses

1. What do you think Frazier means by a "lower purpose"? What would a higher purpose be? Give a few examples of lower-purpose activities that appear in the essay.

2. What is Frazier opposed to in this essay? Do you think he opposes all kinds of purposeful activity? Explain in your own words what he objects to.

3. Why is the idea of margins important to the development of his essay? How has the term taken on negative meanings? Why does Frazier want to retain the word's other meanings? How do Frazier's final three paragraphs illustrate his use of the word *marginal*?

PATRICIA HAMPL

The Dark Art of Description

Patricia Hampl is a writer who also teaches writing, and "The Dark Art of Description" is in many ways an essay about what she's learned from her students. At two critical points in this well-crafted essay, which careens smoothly between exposition and narrative, her students address the problem of writing about oneself when one's life is boring—when there doesn't seem to be much to write. Hampl has concluded that the basis of modern memoir is that "fundamentally it isn't about having a more interesting life than someone else." An important illustration of her point is the power of description, especially visual description, in memoir. But her rumination on this link leads to a meditation on the power of description itself—not merely an ornamental picturing of things, description can be the key to storytelling. "Description, written from the personal voice of my own perception," Hampl writes, "proved even to be the link with the world's story, with history itself."

Patricia Hampl is Regents Professor and McKnight Distinguished Professor at the University of Minnesota in Minneapolis and has written critically acclaimed fiction, poetry, essays, and autobiography. Her books include A Romantic Education *(1981),* Virgin Time: In Search of the Contemplative Life *(1992),* I Could Tell You Stories: Sojourns in the Land of Memory *(1999),* Blue Arabesque: A Search for the Sublime *(2006). Her most recent book is* The Florist's Daughter, *which was selected by the* New York Times *as one of the one hundred notable books of 2007.*

I was coming down the last lap of my most recent book, a memoir about my mother and father, and I was painfully aware of just how specific every bit of writing is, full of choices and chances, not theoretical at all, not the business of sweeping statements or smart ideas about "form" or "genre" or anything remotely theoretical. Just subject-verb-object and the hope of meaning.

Two nights away from the finish of my book, I was working late. I looked away from the computer screen for a moment and there was my dog staring at me intently. She was on the verge of speech. I could see it. *Come to bed.* Her eyes said this clearly. It was almost 2 A.M. and for the past four hours I've been obsessively changing commas to dashes and then back again to commas with the obsessive focus only a fanatic can sustain.

You've become a crazy person again, I said right out loud. The dog padded away.

The great short story writer J.F. Powers was once asked how things were going by a colleague in the corridor at their university. Powers allowed that it had been a tough day—"I spent the morning trying to decide whether to have my character call his friend *pal* or *chum*," he said.

That's where I often find myself—thinking how important the choice of *pal* or *chum* is, how whatever truth writing lays claim to resides in a passion for just such quite mad distinctions. This monomania* is what a friend of mine calls the 600-pound gorilla of a book. Once the 600-pound gorilla gets hold of you, you're his (or hers). "Those last weeks of finishing a book are a world in themselves," he said. "I think that gorilla is the reason most of us write—it's a real high, but it's also a subconscious agreement not to be available or even normal for as long as it takes."

But as soon as you—or I, anyway—break away from the gorilla's embrace of a particular book, those big, rangy theoretical questions begin to make their approach again. Maybe this is especially true of memoir, the odd enterprise of "writing a life" that has captivated our literary life for the last two decades or so. We tend to think of the novel as the classic narrative form—ever evolving, but familiar, its stately provenance long the preserve of academic interest and the center of trade publishing. Whereas the memoir seems new or somehow "modern," a rather suspect literary upstart. And therefore a form that invites interrogation.

But strictly speaking, autobiography is a genre far older than the novel, and is hard-wired into Western literary history. Perhaps

---

*monomania:** An obsession with, or fixation on, one idea or object.

from that first injunction of the oracle at Delphi—*Know thyself*—Western culture has been devoted to the exploration of the individual consciousness and the unspooling of the individual life.

That commandment to *know thyself* was central to antiquity. Plato uttered a version of it; Cicero used it in a tract on the development of social concord. It was such a pillar of cultural, even spiritual value that in the early Christian period Clement of Alexandria felt compelled to claim that the saying had been borrowed by the Greeks from scripture, thus binding the two developing spiritualities—pagan and monotheistic—together in a seamless endeavor.

Closer to modernity, Goethe is supposed to have said with a shudder, "Know thyself? If I knew myself, I'd run away." And Andre Gide probably expressed this revulsion best: "Know thyself! A maxim as pernicious as it is ugly. Whoever observes himself arrests his own development. A caterpillar who wanted to know itself well would never become a butterfly."

But the strongest indictment of the form I have ever encountered came from a student in Indiana who had been conscripted by his Freshman Comp teacher to attend a reading I gave some years ago. He sprawled in his chair with its baseball cap on backwards, his eloquent body language making it clear he was far, far away. Can't win them all, I decided, and carried on, my eye straying back to him like a tongue drawn to the absence of a just-pulled tooth. During the Q&A I fielded the decorous questions the students posed. And then, suddenly, apparently in response to something I'd said, my anti-hero sat bold-upright, and was waving his hand urgently, his face alight with interest. Ah—a convert. I called on him, smiling.

"I get it," he said. "Nothin's ever happened to you—and you write books about it."

He was right, of course. And in pronouncing this acute literary critical remark, he touched on the most peculiar aspect of the rise of the memoir in our times—namely, that fundamentally it isn't about having a more interesting life than someone else. True, there is a strand of autobiographical writing that relies on the documentation of extraordinary circumstances, lives lived in extremity, often at great peril. But such memoirs have always been part of literary history. What characterizes the rise of memoir in recent times is precisely the opposite condition—not a gripping "narrative arc," but the quality of voice, the story of perception rather than action.

The self is not the subject of memoir, in this kind of book, but its instrument. And the work of the self is not to "narrate" but to describe. There is something fundamentally photographic about memoir, photographic rather than cinematic. Not a story, but a series of tableaus we are given to consider. No memoirist is surprised by the absences and blanks in action, for another unavoidable quality of autographical as I am thinking of it—as lyrical quest literature—is that it is as much about reticence as it is about revelation.

It is often remarked that the advent of the movies and the ever faster pace of modern life have conspired to make description a less essential part of prose narrative in our own times. We don't need to be told what things look like—we are inundated with images, pictures, moving or static. In this view, we need the opposite of the photographic quality so beloved of nineteenth century descriptive writing in which the landscape is rolled out, sentence after sentence, the interior of a room and the interior of the character's mind are meticulously presented.

We require writing, instead, that subsumes description, leaps right over it to frame episode and to create the much sough-after "narrative arc." The motto—even the mantra—of this narrative model is of course the commandment of introductory fiction writing workshops: *Show, don't tell.*

But as recent memoir writing shows, descriptive writing abounds. And it proves, finally, not to be about the object described. Or not only. Description in memoir is where the consciousness of the writer and the material of the story are established in harmony, where the self is lost in the material, in a sense. In fiction of the show-don't-tell variety narrative scenes that "show" and dutifully do not "tell," are advanced by volleys of dialogue in which the author's presence is successfully obscured by the dramatic action of the dialogue of his characters. But in description we hear and feel the absorption of the author in the material. We sense the presence of the creator of the scene.

This personal absorption is what we mean by "style." It is strange that we would choose so oddly surfacey a word—style—for this most soulful aspect of writing. We could, perhaps more exactly, call this relation between consciousness and its subject "integrity." What else is the articulation of perception?

Style is a word usually claimed by fashion and the most passing aesthetic values. But maybe that's as it should be because style in writing is terribly perishable. It can rot—that is what we mean when we recognize writing to be "precious," for example. But at its best and most essential, style is the register between a writer's consciousness and the material he is committed to wrestling to the page. It is the real authority of a writer, more substantial than plot, less ego-dependent than voice.

In 1951, Alfred Kazin published his memoir of his boyhood in Brooklyn, *A Walker in the City*, the book that establishes modern American memoir. The critic Leslie Fiedler admired the book was also frustrated by it. It "perversely refuses to be a novel," he said with some annoyance, as if Kazin's book, deeply dependent on descriptive writing, were refusing to behave. And it was. It was refusing to obey the commandment to Show, don't tell.

When you read "The Block and Beyond," a much-anthologized chapter from Kazin's memoir, it is impossible to discuss the main characters and certainly not its plot or even its narrative structure. It is a rhapsodic evocation of a place and time. And once read, it is impossible to forget, as indelible and inevitable as a poem.

What Kazin was able to do—what every memoirist can attempt—in liberating himself from the rigid demands of show-don't-tell narrative was to enter into reflection, into speculation, into interpretation, and to use the fragment, the image, the vignette, rather than narratively linked scenes to form his world and his book. He was able to show *and* tell. To write a story and write an essay—all in the same tale, braided and twined together. The root of this double power lies in description.

* * *

I was one of those enthralled teenage readers of long nineteenth-century English novels. I toiled my way through dense descriptions of gloomy heaths and bogs to get to the airy volleys of dialogue that lofted back and forth down the page to give me what I wanted—would Jane* and Mr. Rochester . . . or would they not? Would

---

*Jane . . . Lydgate: Jane and Mr. Rochester are characters from Charlotte Brontë's *Jane Eyre*; Dorothea and Lydgate from George Eliot's *Middlemarch*, both influential nineteenth-century novels by British women.

Dorothea Brooke awaken—would Mr. Lydgate? I didn't relish the descriptive passages. I endured them. Just as Jane and Dorothea endured their parched lives, as if these endless descriptive passages were the desert to be crossed before the paradise of dialogue and the love story could be entered.

Yet all this description was, after all, the *world* of the book—not simply because it gave the book "a sense of place" as the old literary cliché puts it. It wasn't a "sense of place" I cared about in these passages, but the meeting place of perception with story—the place where someone *claimed* the story, where I could glimpse the individual consciousness, the creator of the scene. The person pulling the wires and making Jane and Dorothea move. I was looking, I suppose, for a sign of intimacy with the invisible author. That "dear reader" moment so familiar in nineteenth century novels—think of Thackeray pausing to have a chat with the reader—with you!—about how to live on nothing a year. Think of George Eliot breaking off to describe the furnishings of Dorothea's ardent mind.

Henry James* is probably the crown prince of nineteenth century describers, a *flâneur* of the sentence, a lounge lizard of the paragraph, taking his own sweet time to unfurl an observation, smoking the cheroot of his thought in the contemplative after-dinner puffery of a man who knows how to draw out the pleasure of his rare tobacco. Or—because James himself never hesitates to pile up opposing figures of speech until he has sliced his thought to the refracted transparency he adores—maybe I'll just switch metaphors and say that James sits mildly at his torture apparatus, turning the crank in meticulously calibrated movements as the reader lies helplessly strained upon the rack of his ever-expanding sentences, the exquisite pain of the lengthening description almost breaking the bones of attention. In short (as James often says after gassing on for a nice fat paragraph or two on the quality of a Venetian sunset or the knowing lift of a European eyebrow glimpsed across a table by an artless American ingénue), in short, he loves to carry on.

Carrying on, I was discovering, is what it is to describe. A lot. At length. To trust description above plot, past character development, and even theme. To understand that to describe is both

---

*__Henry James__: A nineteenth- and early-twentieth-century American-born British novelist famous for his expansive prose style.

humbler and more essential than to think of compositional impon-
derables such as "voice" or to strain toward superstructures like
"narrative arc." To trust that the act of description will *find* voice
and out of its streaming attention will take hold of narration.

By the time I was considering all of this, I had passed from being
a reader and had become that more desperate literary type—a
writer trying to figure out how to do it myself. I had no idea how
to "sustain a narrative," and didn't even understand at the time
(the late 1970s) that I was writing something called "a memoir."
Yet when I read *Speak, Memory* by Vladimir Nabokov* and later
read his command—*Caress the detail, the divine detail*—I knew I had
found the motto I could live by, the one that prevailed over "Show,
Don't Tell."

Perhaps only someone as thoroughly divested of his paradise as
Nabokov had been of his boyhood Russia and his family, his native
language and all his beloved associations and privileged expecta-
tions, could enshrine the detail, the fragment, as the divinity of his
literary religion, could trust the truths to be found in the DNA of
detail, attentively rendered in ardent description. The dutiful observation that is the yeoman's work of description finally ascended,
Nabokov demonstrated, to the transcendent reality of literature,
to metaphor itself.

Nabokov was asked in an interview if his characters ever "took
over." He replied icily that *his* characters were his galley slaves.

Yet when it was a matter of locating the godhead of literary endeavor, even a writer as unabashedly imperious as Nabokov did not
point to himself and his intentions but to the lowly detail. *Caress the
detail, the divine detail.* Next to grand conceptions like plot, which is
the legitimate government of most stories, or character, which is
the crowned sovereign, the detail looks like a ragged peasant with
a half-baked idea of revolution and a crazy, sure glint in its eye. But
here, according to Nabokov, resides divinity.

Henry James put his faith in something at least as insubstantial.
"If one was to undertake to . . . report with truth on the human
scene," he wrote, "it could but be because notes had been from
the cradle the ineluctable consequence of one's greatest inward

---

*Vladimir Nabokov**: A twentieth-century Russian-born American novelist. *Speak,
Memory* was his memoir.

energy . . . to take them was as natural as to look, to think, to feel, to recognize, to remember. " He considered his habit the basis of literature and called it "the rich principle of the Note."

Such "notes" are of course details, observations. Description. In attending to these details, in the act of description, the more dynamic aspects of narrative have a chance to reveal themselves— not as "action" or "conflict" or any of the theoretical and technical terms we persist in thinking of as the sources of form. Rather, description gives the authorial mind a place to be in relation with the reality of the world.

It was surely this desire for the world—that is for the world's memoir, which is history—that drew me to memoir, that seemingly personal form. And it was to description I tended, not to narrative, not to story. Maybe the root of the desire to write is always lost—properly lost—in the non-literary earth of our real lives. And craft, as we think of it, is just the jargon we give to that darker, earthier medium.

I know it was my mother who was the storyteller in our house. I was her audience. Her dear reader, in a way. I dimly—and sometimes bitterly—understood that nothing much was happening in our modest Midwestern lives, yet I clung to the drama with which she infused every vignette, every encounter at the grocery store.

And when I sought to make sense of the world that kept slipping away to the past, to loss and forgetfulness, when I protested inwardly at that disappearance, it was to description I instinctively turned. Coming from a background in poetry and therefore being a literalist, it didn't occur to me to copy other prose writers. It I wanted to learn to write descriptively, I needed—what else?— pictures.

I took myself off to the Minneapolis Institute of Arts and plunked myself down in front of a Bonnard.* I wrote the painting. Described it. I went home and looked at a teacup on my table—I wrote that too. Still life descriptions that ran on for several pages. I wrote and wrote, describing my way through art galleries and the inadvertent still lives of my house and my memory, my grandmother's garden, her Sunday dinners.

To my growing astonishment, these long descriptive passages, sometimes running two, three pages or longer, had a way of sheering

---

***Bonnard**: Pierre Bonnard was a twentieth-century French painter and printmaker.

off into narrative after all. The teacup I was describing had been given to me by my mother. And once I thought of the fact that she had bought these cups, made in Czechoslovakia, as a bride just before the Second World War, I was writing about that war, about my mother and her later disappointments which somehow were—and were not—part of this fragile cup. Description—which had seemed like background in novels, static and inert as a butterfly pinned to the page of my notebook, proved to be a dynamic engine that stoked voice and even more propelled the occasional narrative arc. Description, written from the personal voice of my own perception, proved even to be the link with the world's story, with history itself. Here was my mother's teacup, made in Czechoslovakia before the War, and here, therefore, was not only my mother's heartbreak but Europe's. The detail was surely divine, offering up miracle after miracle of connections out of the faithful consideration of the fragments before me.

We sense this historical power at the heart of autobiographical writing in the testaments from the Holocaust, from the Gulag, from every marginal and abused life that has found the courage to speak its truth which is often its horror, to preserve its demonic details—and in so doing has seen them become divine. Nadezhda Mandelstam, Anne Frank, Primo Levi—to name only a very few. In time we will, surely, see such documents from Guantanamo[*] and the unknown places of extreme rendition.

The history of whole countries, of an entire era and even lost populations depends sometimes on a little girl faithfully keeping her diary. The great contract of literature consists in this: you tell me your story and somehow I get my story. If we are looking for another reason to explain the strangely powerful grip of the first-person voice on contemporary writing perhaps we need look no farther than the power of Anne Frank's equation—that to write one's life enables the world to preserve its history.

But what of lives lived in the flyover? Lives that don't have that powerful, if terrible, historical resonance of radical suffering. Ordinary lives, in a word. Alfred Kazin's life—or yours. And certainly mine in middling Minnesota in the middle of the twentieth century. Why bother to describe it? Because of course, all details are divine,

---

[*]**Guantanamo**: Guantanamo Bay, Cuba, was the site of a controversial American detention center for accused terrorists opened after 9/11.

not just Nabokov's. In fact, perhaps the poorer the supposed value, the more the detail requires description to assure its divinity.

Which brings me to—if not a story, at least a fragment, a vignette. Early in my teaching life, I went (foolishly) through a killer snowstorm in Minneapolis to get to my University office because I had student conferences scheduled. By the time I arrived, the University had closed and the campus was empty, whipped by white shrouds of blizzard snow, the wind whistling down the Mall. I sat in my office in the empty building, cursing my ruinous work ethic, and wondering if the buses would keep running so I could get home.

Then a rap on my office door. I opened it and there, like an extra out of *Doctor Zhivago**, stood my 11 A.M. appointment, a quiet sophomore named Tommy.

He looked anxious. He was really glad I was there, he said, because he had a big problem with the assignment. I had asked the students to write short autobiographies. "I just can't write anything about my life," he said miserably, his head down, his overshoes puddling on the floor.

I waited for the disclosure. What would it be—child abuse, incest, what murder or mayhem could this boy not divulge? What had brought him trooping through the blizzard to get help with his life story? How would I get him to Student Counseling?

"See, I come from Fridley," he said, naming one of the nowhere-suburbs sprawling drearily beyond the freeway north of Minneapolis.

I stared at him. I didn't, for a moment, comprehend that this was the dark disclosure, this the occasion of his misery: being from Fridley meant, surely, that he had nothing worth writing about.

There it was again—nothin' had ever happened to him and I was asking him to write about it.

"I have good news for you, Tommy," I said. "The field's wide open—nobody has told what it's like to grow up in Fridley yet. It's all yours."

All he needed to do was sit down and describe. And because the detail is divine, if you caress it into life, you find the world you have lost or ignored, the world ruined or devalued. The world you alone can bring into being, bit by broken bit. Your voice, your style—which is to say your integrity.

Doctor Zhivago: A 1965 American movie based on Boris Pasternak's novel.

Reflections and Responses

1. How would you categorize "The Dark Art of Description"? Is it a memoir? (It does, after all, contain a rich personal story.) Or is it an expository essay aimed at making a point about writing? Is it some sort of hybrid? Do you think it is a particularly descriptive essay itself? How does the way the essay straddles description, narrative, and argument help advance its agenda?

2. Hampl writes that when she "tried to make sense of the world that kept slipping away into the past, to loss and forgetfulness, when I protested inwardly at that disappearance, it was to description that I instinctively turned." Do you think her assessment of her life—or of her student from Fridley's life—as relatively uneventful is earnest? Or is she suggesting in this paragraph that there can be more narrative to a story than meets the eye?

3. Parse the essay's title: Why does Hampl call description a "Dark Art"? Is there something almost sinister about the way an image can conceal or bolster a story?

ARIEL LEVY

The Lesbian Bride's Handbook

In 2009, the New York state legislature took steps toward legalizing same-sex marriage. Two years earlier, Ariel Levy and her partner got married anyway. But how did the fact that their wedding was not sanctioned by civil society affect the wedding itself? Instead of a ponderous argument on the merits of gay marriage, Levy writes a light, comic essay on planning the nuptials, considering questions from what a gay bride should wear to what the couple should even call the ceremony. In the process, Levy begins to wonder if her wedding (which she calls a "party about love") is real, or just a parody of heterosexual marriage—and what that means about her relationship and her identity. In trying to please her future mother-not-quite-in-law, Levy realizes that "it was my secret wish that if my party about love was as flawless as the gowns in that store, it would subsume the humiliation of its own existence . . . subsume the horror of my homosexuality."

Ariel Levy's work has appeared in the Washington Post, Vogue, *and* Slate *among other publications. She's also the author of* Female Chauvinist Pigs: Women and the Rise of Raunch Culture *(2005), which criticizes the modern feminist establishment. She was a contributing editor at* New York *magazine, where* The Lesbian Bride's Handbook *first appeared, for twelve years; since 2008 she's been a staff writer at* The New Yorker.

What is the right thing to wear to a wedding? Women have been asking themselves this question for generations and, I suppose, coming up with many of the same answers as I have. Black and gray, the colors I usually wear, are obviously too somber. Red is a bad idea: too garish, too iconic—the whore instead of the virgin—and, as a saleswoman at Saks explained to me, one doesn't want to draw attention away from the bride. But then I am the bride. Sort of.

For several months, admitting that detail filled me with a flickering dread. I knew what would inevitably follow: "Why aren't you wearing white?" Eventually, I realized that, obviously, I could just tell Katie at Barneys or Jen at Chloé, "Because I prefer color." But at first, I felt compelled to tell the whole mortifying truth: "Because it's a gay wedding." Or, if I couldn't quite get those words out of my mouth: "Because it's not a real wedding."

A real wedding was not something I was raised to want. My parents were bohemians of a sort, and real weddings were like real jobs: square. As my mother has managed to mention on numerous occasions, she would have liked to elope, but to please her parents, there was a modest reception; she told them to do whatever they wanted and that she and my father would show up. When Amy and I announced that we intended to have a wedding—not a real wedding, of course, but something festive, something that expressed the scale of our glee—my mother's response was less than gushing. "How can you feel okay about spending all that money on one day?" she wanted to know.

Joanne West/Queerstock, Inc/Alamy

Naturally, I yelled at her for saying that, but the truth is I didn't. By the time things starting getting specific and estimated costs of various things started combining to form enormous estimated sums, money was only one of many things I did not feel okay about. I did not feel okay about the word marriage, for instance, partly because it didn't describe a legal option for me, and partly because the closer that something quite like it loomed the less it seemed like an attractive condition with which to be afflicted. (This was relatively easy to sidestep, at least in a technical sense: Our invitations promised "a party about love," and you can't really argue with that.) I also didn't feel okay about spending all my free time on the phone with the flower guy and the tent man, or about making little checklists of who was coming, and who was not coming, and who was staying at the Goodstone Inn. And I definitely did not feel okay about telling the sales staff of half the better clothing retailers in New York City that I needed something fetching to wear to my big fat gay wedding.

Now that I know what is involved in throwing such an event, it is difficult to remember exactly how we decided to do so . . . hard to retrace the steps that led to my standing in front of a three-way mirror in a $3,700 canary-yellow Donna Karan trapeze dress, completely panicked, knowing that soon, very soon, everyone I knew and loved would be joining me for this hell of my own making, this festival of gayness and commitment.

All I can say for sure is that it started on the blackout*. When I met Amy on a friend's balcony that night, I never wanted the lights to come back on. With all the stoplights dead, traffic moved on the streets below to its own ghostly, unpredictable rhythm—everything was different. The idea that we wouldn't be together from then on seemed unnatural, almost immediately. And so it was unsurprising that despite the considerable obstacles of other relationships and opposite coasts, eventually we had one life. We were pretty pleased with ourselves. "Look!" we wanted to say to everyone. "Look how fun! Look what's possible! Let's have a cocktail!" We would celebrate with our friends—our families, even. There should be music

---

*the blackout: New York City, along with much of the northeast, suffered a major, day-long blackout in August 2003.

and dancing. We'd need hyacinths and shrimps! Let the wild rumpus begin.

I am not a total idiot. I always had the sense to say no wedding cake, no officiant, no first dance, no here comes the bride, no Times announcement, and absolutely no white dress. Who are we kidding? And why? We just wanted a big, awesome party where everyone could meet and go bananas. It's a special opportunity, you know: The only other time everyone you love will assemble in one place is at your funeral. (At most weddings, some people you don't actually love will also be in attendance. But the silver lining of my parents' being irreverent and Amy's parents' being in denial is that we didn't have to invite anyone we didn't want to.) The thing is, though, you have to serve something, and you can't very well go naked. You can call it a party about love all you want, but you still have to make all the same decisions that every other bride has to make, and you have to make them very carefully unless you want everyone you know to schlep to some crummy party in the middle of nowhere.

And I do not believe in crummy parties. I believe in glamour. I believe that when you are on your deathbed clinging to the murk of your memories, some will stay with you purely on the power of atmosphere: the way a punch bowl looked surrounded by daisies at your 5th-birthday party, the feel of a certain set of blue sheets the first time you traveled alone. There was no way I was going to let this thing be shoddy—some pathetic hers-and-hers imitation of the real thing or some vaguely patchouli-scented ceremony. If I was going to have a party about love, it was going to be the classiest party about love ever. I did not experience this imperative as relaxing.

This was not the first large, square, optional ceremony I'd insisted on having despite my mother's warnings. As a 10-year-old, I decided that I wanted to have a bat mitzvah. I was the only kid in the history of Westchester County who demanded Hebrew school. And as I stood in front of the racks of red at Bergdorf Goodman, I recalled the feeling I'd had at some point in my preteen Jewish odyssey when I looked down at the sacred ancient letters on the scroll: What have I done?

But in both cases, by the time the magnitude of my folly revealed itself to me, it was way, way too late to undo. As my stepmother put it with terrifying accuracy when we went to see how many cocktail tables would fit on the porch of the house where she and my dad live in the Blue Ridge Mountains, "This horse is out of the gate." It was too late to cancel those lovely and meticulously worded invitations. Too late to tell Amy's 80-year-old father, a man who served in MacArthur's honor guard after World War II, that the vibratingly tense dinner at which we'd declared our intention to faux wed was a waste of a good steak and two hours of his remaining time on planet Earth. It was too late to do anything but find a dress.

Normally, I love clothes. Really love them. I feel about clothes the way I feel about flowers: They sing to me. But I understand tulips and boots; I understand little jackets. I am a stranger to formalwear. The first dress I brought home was a kind of Grecian muumuu in a cheery shade of coral. It looked like something Mrs. Robinson would have worn to a pool party in The Graduate. "Chic, right?" I said to Amy. "Perky and festive."

She appeared confused. "You want to wear a nightgown to our wedding?"

"It's not a wedding!" I shrieked. "It's a party about love!"

Amy rolled her eyes. "I didn't realize it was a pajama party about love."

Back it went. A few days later, I modeled a low-cut pale-gold dress with spaghetti straps and a gauzy skirt from Missoni. "Nice!" said Amy. "You look like a fancy hooker. In Capri." This was not the look I wanted.

Then one day, I went to a doctor's appointment uptown. It was a sunny spring morning and I wore sneakers and track pants so I could walk home to the East Village when it was over. Amy was at Jussara Lee, the custom shop on Little West 12th Street where she was having her suit made for the big event, the P.A.L. As I made my way down Madison Avenue, I envied her. (And by envied I mean, obviously, resented.) Of course Amy would wear a suit; Amy always wears a suit. Everything about this situation seemed simpler for her—she was neither ambivalent nor insane, while I was rapidly flipping my lid. She didn't care about how uncool it was that we were doing this; Amy has always been cool. While I obsessed about how lame it was to seek public acceptance, to crave ritual, and grew queasy at the mention of marriage, Amy was excited.

Then something in a shop window caught my eye. A dress the color of grass, the shape of a mermaid. A dress that would flash before your eyes on your deathbed and in your dreams. I could no longer think about being cool or being mortified or being heteronormative. I could no longer think. The doorman looked at my sneakers skeptically as I shuffled past him into the Carolina Herrera boutique.

"Hello," I said to the salesgirl, a water lily of a woman. "I need a dress to wear to my wedding. I do not want to wear white. I want to wear that one."

"A gown," she told me. "That one is a gown

I stood still in my sneakers. "Great."

If you are unfamiliar with the price points at Carolina Herrera, here's a good way to get a sense of them: Think of the absolute most you can imagine an article of clothing costing. Now triple that. I must have tried on a hundred-thousand dollars' worth of fabric that day. But every dress was exquisite, astounding. Each one made me look thinner and more expensive. And then the saleswoman brought me something I would never have even looked twice at: It was made of pale-blue oxford cloth with ribbons for straps and a corseted bodice. The skirt was tight at the top and then exploded with volume and hand-painted floral appliqués. When I put it on, I appeared to be in full bloom. "There's your bouquet," she said.

"I'll take it."

If my mother knew how much money I paid for that dress, I do believe she would disown me. But I wasn't thinking about my mother when the seamstress started pinning me in. I was thinking about Amy's.

Like me, Mrs. Norquist was a journalist before she got married. Like me, she is a chatterbox and a gardener. And like me, she is a clotheshorse. But that's it. Mrs. Norquist is a staunch conservative and a churchgoer, as are two of the three sons she raised. (Her oldest, Bruce, is an Evangelical minister, and her youngest, Todd, works for the creationist movement.) When Amy came out in college (two decades ago), Mrs. Norquist didn't speak to her for a year. In fact, as much as she likes to gab, Mrs. Norquist does not talk about anything that really bothers her, except to say the words "Oh, honestly." She likes to talk about who's had a baby and who's been on a trip, and she likes to talk about weddings, a lot. She talks about weddings as much as my mother talks about shiatsu. Where my family is freaky and loose, foulmouthed and freewheeling, Mrs. Norquist is nurturing and restrained, a woman who makes toasted cheese sandwiches and tomato soup. I fell for her immediately.

When we go to visit Amy's parents, generally Amy and her dad watch sports, and Mrs. Norquist and I drink tea and look at fashion magazines together. This is not something I find boring. It is a shared passion and a neutral territory—we avoid discussing politics, sexuality, ethnicity, and religion (except once, when I let loose an "oy vey" and she said, "What?" And I said, "That's what my people say when we mean 'Oh, honestly.'"). Fashion is what we agree upon, the thing we share besides Amy (who does not look at fashion magazines, unless maybe there were a special issue on mantailored suits). "That's a darling heel!" Mrs. Norquist will say. "It would be good in a dark suede," I reply. It's honest communication. We are both ourselves when we talk about clothes, telling each other, for once, the whole truth.

When I saw myself in the mirror in that blue gown with its graceful silhouette and giddy flowers, I could hear Mrs. Norquist gasping and saying, "Isn't that gorgeous!" It was my secret wish that she would look at it and see in our lives sparkle instead of shame. It was my secret wish that if my party about love was as flawless as the gowns in that store, it would subsume the humiliation of its own existence . . . subsume the horror of my homosexuality.

"What do you care what other people think?" is what my own mother would say, of course—has said, many times over the course of my life. And that is the difference between us. My mother is a woman who moved to Cape Cod on a whim. Who has giant green marbles stuck in the plaster of her walls for decoration and an extensive collection of Buddha-like objects she has amassed in her travels through China, Tibet, and the gift shops of the lower cape. She wears pajamas to work and is nicknamed Rocky and was, in her day, a pretty serious practitioner of non-monogamy. My mother is (still) a bad-ass, because she just doesn't give a shit what anybody else thinks. I care what everybody thinks. So does Mrs. Norquist. I am not sure which one of them I find more mysterious.

I'm not going to lie to you: My gay wedding rocked. My oldest friend, Jesse, played "Crimson and Clover" on his electric guitar when we walked down the mountain, and I can still feel the sound of that song reverberating in my chest. My mother wore high heels and makeup for the first time I can remember and danced until one in the morning. There were these amazing pink margaritas everyone kept drinking. Mrs. Norquist gave Amy the handkerchief her mother gave her on her wedding day: "Something blue," she said, and that's all she said on the subject. That and "Isn't that gorgeous!" when she saw my gown. She still can't quite bring herself to call what happened in September a wedding. But then, for a long time, neither could I.

The dress is still hanging in my closet, which has less to do with my being sentimental than it does with eBay's being really complicated. I can't imagine that I'll ever wear it again, partly because mine is not a black-tie life, and also because I doubt very much that I could get back into it. (When conservatives discuss the perils of gay marriage, they fail to mention its most pernicious consequence: Gay marriage, like all marriage, is extremely fattening.) One of these days I'll sell it, though: That thing cost a fortune, and who could feel okay about keeping something so expensive hanging in a garment bag? Amy I'm keeping.

Reflections and Responses

1. "I believe," Levy writes, "that when you are on your deathbed clinging to the murk of your memories, some will stay with you purely on the power of atmosphere." What does she mean by this, and how does the story of her wedding confirm her point? Notice that in an essay about a wedding, there's only a little more than a paragraph about the wedding itself; how does that brief description, contrasted with a long meditation about planning for the event, illustrate (or subvert) Levy's ideas about the meaning of ceremonies?

2. Levy stays away from the politics of gay marriage for the most part, but does forward something of an emotional argument for it in the scenes with Mrs. Norquist. How is the form of Levy's essay more (or less) effective than a politically oriented argument for gay marriage?

3. Levy uses humor, especially about the cost of the ceremony, the stresses of planning it, how "fattening" it is, etc., throughout her essay. Identify some of Levy's jokes and consider their function. Do they serve some purpose in the essay? Think especially about the tradition of similar wedding-themed humor in the context of traditional, straight weddings. Is Levy suggesting that her wedding is—or that she wants it to be—despite what she tells store clerks, a "real wedding"?

BARRY LOPEZ

The Stone Horse

Great works of art do not always hang in museums, accessible to anyone who cares to see them. When Barry Lopez wanted to see a mysterious stone horse carved perhaps some four hundred years ago by the Quechan people, his journey took him far off the beaten track. What he finds in the deserts of southern California near the Mexican border is the kind of large ground carving (an intaglio) that some think was intended as a sign to extraterrestrials. But, upon seeing the horse, Lopez does not believe it was "meant to be seen by gods in the sky above," nor does he think it can even be properly appreciated in an aerial photograph. How we see this work of art, Lopez suggests, is as important as what we see. And how we see it requires the journey to it.

One of America's most distinguished nonfiction writers, Lopez is the author of Arctic Dreams, *which won the National Book Award in 1986, and* Of Wolves and Men, *which won the John Burroughs Medal in 1979. His other publications include* Desert Notes *(1979),* River Notes *(1979),* Winter Count *(1981),* Crossing Open Ground *(1988),* Coyote Love *(1989),* The Rediscovery of North America *(1990),* Field Notes *(1994), and* Lessons from the Wolverine *(1997). He has also recently published* About This Life: Journeys on the Threshold of Memory *(1998) and a collection of stories,* Resistance *(2004). He received an award for fiction from the Friends of American Writers in 1982 and the Award in Literature from the American Academy and Institute of Arts and Letters in 1986. "The Stone Horse" originally appeared in* Antaeus *(1986) and was selected by Gay Talese for* The Best American Essays 1987.

I

The deserts of southern California, the high, relatively cooler and wetter Mojave and the hotter, dryer Sonoran to the south of it, carry the signatures of many cultures. Prehistoric rock drawings in the Mojave's Coso Range, probably the greatest concentration of petroglyphs in North America, are at least three thousand years old. Big-game-hunting cultures that flourished six or seven thousand years before that are known from broken spear tips, choppers, and burins left scattered along the shores of great Pleistocene lakes, long since evaporated. Weapons and tools discovered at China Lake may be thirty thousand years old; and worked stone from a quarry in the Calico Mountains is, some argue, evidence that human beings were here more than 200,000 years ago.

Flight Images LLP/Britain on View/PhotoLibrary

An example of a horse cut into a hillside in England over 200 years ago. Although not the same figure the author finds in the southern California desert, this white horse was formed by removing the hillside vegetation to expose the chalk beneath.

Because of the long-term stability of such arid environments, much of this prehistoric stone evidence still lies exposed on the ground, accessible to anyone who passes by—the studious, the acquisitive, the indifferent, the merely curious. Archaeologists do not agree on the sequence of cultural history beyond about twelve thousand years ago, but it is clear that these broken bits of chalcedony, chert, and obsidian, like the animal drawings and geometric designs etched on walls of basalt throughout the desert, anchor the earliest threads of human history, the first record of human endeavor here.

Western man did not enter the California desert until the end of the eighteenth century, 250 years after Coronado brought his soldiers into the Zuni pueblos in a bewildered search for the cities of Cibola. The earliest appraisals of the land were cursory, hurried. People traveled *through* it, en route to Santa Fe or the California coastal settlements. Only miners tarried. In 1823 what had been Spain's became Mexico's, and in 1848 what had been Mexico's became America's; but the bare, jagged mountains and dry lake beds, the vast and uniform plains of creosote bush and yucca plants, remained as obscure as the northern Sudan until the end of the nineteenth century.

Before 1940 the tangible evidence of twentieth-century man's passage here consisted of very little—the hard tracery of travel corridors; the widely scattered, relatively insignificant evidence of mining operations; and the fair expanse of irrigated fields at the desert's periphery. In the space of a hundred years or so the wagon roads were paved, railroads were laid down, and canals and high-tension lines were built to bring water and electricity across the desert to Los Angeles from the Colorado River. The dark mouths of gold, talc, and tin mines yawned from the bony flanks of desert ranges. Dust-encrusted chemical plants stood at work on the lonely edges of dry lake beds. And crops of grapes, lettuce, dates, alfalfa, and cotton covered the Coachella and Imperial valleys, north and south of the Salton Sea, and the Palo Verde Valley along the Colorado.

These developments proceeded with little or no awareness of earlier human occupations by cultures that preceded those of the historic Indians—the Mojave, the Chemehuevi, the Quechan. (Extensive irrigation began actually to change the climate of the

Sonoran Desert, and human settlements, the railroads, and farming introduced many new, successful plants into the region.)

During World War II, the American military moved into the desert in great force, to train troops and to test equipment. They found the clear weather conducive to year-round flying, the dry air and isolation very attractive. After the war, a complex of training grounds, storage facilities, and gunnery and test ranges was permanently settled on more than three million acres of military reservations. Few perceived the extent or significance of the destruction of the aboriginal sites that took place during tank maneuvers and bombing runs or in the laying out of highways, railroads, mining districts, and irrigated fields. The few who intuited that something like an American Dordogne Valley lay exposed here were (only) amateur archaeologists; even they reasoned that the desert was too vast for any of this to matter.

After World War II, people began moving out of the crowded Los Angeles basin into homes in Lucerne, Apple, and Antelope valleys in the western Mojave. They emigrated as well to a stretch of resort land at the foot of the San Jacinto Mountains that included Palm Springs, and farther out to old railroad and military towns like Twentynine Palms and Barstow. People also began exploring the desert, at first in military-surplus jeeps and then with a variety of all-terrain and off-road vehicles that became available in the 1960s. By the mid-1970s, the number of people using such vehicles for desert recreation had increased exponentially. Most came and went in innocent curiosity; the few who didn't wreaked a havoc all out of proportion to their numbers. The disturbance of previously isolated archaeological sites increased by an order of magnitude. Many sites were vandalized before archaeologists, themselves late to the desert, had any firm grasp of the bounds of human history in the desert. It was as though in the same moment an Aztec library had been discovered intact various lacunae had begun to appear.

The vandalism was of three sorts: the general disturbance usually caused by souvenir hunters and by the curious and the oblivious; the wholesale stripping of a place by professional thieves for black-market sale and trade; and outright destruction, in which vehicles were actually used to ram and trench an area. By 1980, the Bureau of Land Management estimated that probably 35 percent of the archaeological sites in the desert had been vandalized. The destruction at some places by rifles and shotguns, or by power winches mounted on vehicles, was, if one cared for history, demoralizing to behold.

In spite of public education, land closures, and stricter law enforcement in recent years, the BLM estimates that, annually, about 1 percent of the archaeological record in the desert continues to be destroyed or stolen.

II

A BLM archaeologist told me, with understandable reluctance, where to find the intaglio. I spread my Automobile Club of Southern California map of Imperial County out on his desk, and he traced the route with a pink felt-tip pen. The line crossed Interstate 8 and then turned west along the Mexican border.

"You can't drive any farther than about here," he said, marking a small X. "There's boulders in the wash. You walk up past them."

On a separate piece of paper he drew a route in a smaller scale that would take me up the arroyo to a certain point where I was to cross back east, to another arroyo. At its head, on higher ground just to the north, I would find the horse.

"It's tough to spot unless you know it's there. Once you pick it up . . ." He shook his head slowly, in a gesture of wonder at its existence.

I waited until I held his eye. I assured him I would not tell anyone else how to get there. He looked at me with stoical despair, like a man who had been robbed twice, whose belief in human beings was offered without conviction.

I did not go until the following day because I wanted to see it at dawn. I ate breakfast at four A.M. in El Centro and then drove south. The route was easy to follow, though the last section of road proved difficult, broken and drifted over with sand in some spots. I came to the barricade of boulders and parked. It was light enough by then to find my way over the ground with little trouble. The contours of the landscape were stark, without any masking vegetation. I worried only about rattlesnakes.

I traversed the stone plain as directed, but, in spite of the frankness of the land, I came on the horse unawares. In the first moment of recognition I was without feeling. I recalled later being startled, and that I held my breath. It was laid out on the ground

with its head to the east, three times life size. As I took in its outline I felt a growing concentration of all my senses, as though my
attentiveness to the pale rose color of the morning sky and other
peripheral images had now ceased to be important. I was aware
that I was straining for sound in the windless air, and I felt the uneven pressure of the earth hard against my feet. The horse, out-
lined in a standing profile on the dark ground, was as vivid before
me as a bed of tulips.

I've come upon animals suddenly before, and felt a similar tension, a precipitate heightening of the senses. And I have felt the
inexplicable but sharply boosted intensity of a wild moment in the
bush, where it is not until some minutes later that you discover the
source of electricity—the warm remains of a grizzly bear kill, or
the still moist tracks of a wolverine.

But this was slightly different. I felt I had stepped into an unoccupied corridor. I had no familiar sense of history, the temporal structure in which to think: this horse was made by Quechan people three
hundred years ago. I felt instead a headlong rush of images: people
hunting wild horses with spears on the Pleistocene veld of southern
California; Cortés riding across the causeway into Montezuma's Ten-
ochtitlán; a short-legged Comanche, astride his horse like some sort
of ferret, slashing through cavalry lines of young men who rode like
farmers; a hoof exploding past my face one morning in a corral in
Wyoming. These images had the weight and silence of stone.

When I released my breath, the images softened. My initial feeling, of facing a wild animal in a remote region, was replaced with a
calm sense of antiquity. It was then that I became conscious, like
an ordinary tourist, of what was before me, and thought: this horse
was probably laid out by Quechan people. But when? I wondered.
The first horses they saw, I knew, might have been those that came
north from Mexico in 1692 with Father Eusebio Kino. But Cocopa
people, I recalled, also came this far north on occasion, to fight
with their neighbors, the Quechan. And *they* could have seen
horses with Melchior Diaz, at the mouth of the Colorado River in
the fall of 1540. So, it could be four hundred years old. (No one in
fact knows.)

I still had not moved. I took my eyes off the horse for a moment
to look south over the desert plain into Mexico, to look east past
its head at the brightening sunrise, to situate myself. Then, finally,

I brought my trailing foot slowly forward and stood erect. Sunlight was running like a thin sheet of water over the stony ground and it threw the horse into relief. It looked as though no hand had ever disturbed the stones that gave it its form.

The horse had been brought to life on ground called desert pavement, a tight, flat matrix of small cobbles blasted smooth by sand-laden winds. The uniform, monochromatic blackness of the stones, a patina of iron and magnesium oxides called desert varnish, is caused by long-term exposure to the sun. To make this type of low-relief ground glyph, or intaglio, the artist either selectively turns individual stones over to their lighter side or removes areas of stone to expose the lighter soil underneath, creating a negative image. This horse, about eighteen feet from brow to rump and eight feet from withers to hoof, had been made in the latter way, and its outline was bermed at certain points with low ridges of stone a few inches high to enhance its three-dimensional qualities. (The left side of the horse was in full profile; each leg was extended at 90 degrees to the body and fully visible, as though seen in three-quarter profile.)

I was not eager to move. The moment I did I would be back in the flow of time, the horse no longer quivering in the same way before me. I did not want to feel again the sequence of quotidian events—to be drawn off into deliberation and analysis. A human being, a four-footed animal, the open land. That was all that was present—and a "thoughtless" understanding of the very old desires bearing on this particular animal: to hunt it, to render it, to fathom it, to subjugate it, to honor it, to take it as a companion.

What finally made me move was the light. The sun now filled the shallow basin of the horse's body. The weighted line of the stone berm created the illusion of a mane and the distinctive roundness of an equine belly. The change in definition impelled me. I moved to the left, circling past its rump, to see how the light might flesh the horse out from various points of view. I circled it completely before squatting on my haunches. Ten or fifteen minutes later I chose another view. The third time I moved, to a point near the rear hooves, I spotted a stone tool at my feet. I stared at it a long while, more in awe than disbelief, before reaching out to pick it up. I turned it over in my left palm and took it between my fingers to feel its cutting edge. It is always difficult, especially with something so portable, to rechannel the desire to steal.

I spent several hours with the horse. As I changed positions and as the angle of the light continued to change I noticed a number of things. The angle at which the pastern carried the hoof away from the ankle was perfect. Also, stones had been placed within the image to suggest at precisely the right spot the left shoulder above the foreleg. The line that joined thigh and hock was similarly accurate. The muzzle alone seemed distorted—but perhaps these stones had been moved by a later hand. It was an admirably accurate representation, but not what a breeder would call perfect conformation. There was the suggestion of a bowed neck and an undershot jaw, and the tail, as full as a winter coyote's, did not appear to be precisely to scale.

The more I thought about it, the more I felt I was looking at an individual horse, a unique combination of generic and specific detail. It was easy to imagine one of Kino's horses as a model, or a horse that ran off from one of Coronado's columns. What kind of horses would these have been? I wondered. In the sixteenth century the most sought-after horses in Europe were Spanish, the offspring of Arabian stock and Barbary horses that the Moors brought to Iberia and bred to the older, eastern European strains brought in by the Romans. The model for this horse, I speculated, could easily have been a palomino, or a descendant of horses trained for lion hunting in North Africa.

A few generations ago, cowboys, cavalry quartermasters, and draymen would have taken this horse before me under consideration and not let up their scrutiny until they had its heritage fixed to their satisfaction. Today, the distinction between draft and harness horses is arcane knowledge, and no image may come to mind for a blue roan or a claybank horse. The loss of such refinement in everyday conversation leaves me unsettled. People praise the Eskimo's ability to distinguish among forty types of snow but forget the skill of others who routinely differentiate between overo and tobiano pintos. Such distinctions are made for the same reason. You have to do it to be able to talk clearly about the world.

For parts of two years I worked as a horse wrangler and packer in Wyoming. It is dim knowledge now; I would have to think to remember if a buckskin was a kind of dun horse. And I couldn't throw a double-diamond hitch over a set of panniers—the packer's basic tie-down—without guidance. As I squatted there in the desert, however,

these more personal memories seemed tenuous in comparison with
the sweep of this animal in human time. My memories had no depth.
I thought of the Hittite cavalry riding against the Syrians 3,500 years
ago. And the first of the Chinese emperors, Ch'in Shih Huang, buried in Shensi Province in 210 B.C. with thousands of life-size horses
and soldiers, a terra-cotta guardian army. What could I know of what
was in the mind of whoever made this horse? Was there some racial
memory of it as an animal that had once fed the artist's ancestors
and then disappeared from North America? And then returned in
this strange alliance with another race of men?

Certainly, whoever it was, the artist had observed the animal
very closely. Certainly the animal's speed had impressed him.
Among the first things the Quechan would have learned from an
encounter with Kino's horses was that their own long-distance
runners—men who could run down mule deer—were no match
for this animal.

From where I squatted I could look far out over the Mexican
plain. Juan Bautista de Anza passed this way in *1774*, extending El
Camino Real into Alta California from Sinaloa. He was followed by
others, all of them astride the magical horse; *gente de razón*, the
people of reason, coming into the country of *los primitivos*. The
horse, like the stone animals of Egypt, urged these memories upon
me. And as I drew them up from some forgotten corner of my
mind—huge horses carved in the white chalk downs of southern
England by an Iron Age people; Spanish horses rearing and wheel-
ing in fear before alligators in Florida—the images seemed teth-
ered before me. With this sense of proportion, a memory of my
own—the morning I almost lost my face to a horse's hoof—now
had somewhere to fit.

I rose up and began to walk slowly around the horse again. I had
taken the first long measure of it and was now looking for a way to
depart, a new angle of light, a fading of the image itself before the
rising sun, that would break its hold on me. As I circled, feeling both
heady and serene at the encounter, I realized again how strangely
vivid it was. It had been created on a barren bajada between two ar-
royos, as nondescript a place as one could imagine. The only plant
life here was a few wands of ocotillo cactus. The ground beneath my
shoes was so hard it wouldn't take the print of a heavy animal even
after a rain. The only sounds I heard here were the voices of quail.

The archaeologist had been correct. For all its forcefulness, the horse is inconspicuous. If you don't care to see it you can walk right past it. That pleases him, I think. Unmarked on this bleak shoulder of the plain, the site signals to no one; so he wants no protective fences here, no informative plaque, to act as beacons. He would rather take a chance that no motorcyclist, no aimless wanderer with a flair for violence and a depth of ignorance, will ever find his way here.

The archaeologist had given me something before I left his office that now seemed peculiar—an aerial photograph of the horse. It is widely believed that an aerial view of an intaglio provides a fair and accurate depiction. It does not. In the photograph the horse looks somewhat crudely constructed; from the ground it appears far more deftly rendered. The photograph is of a single moment, and in that split second the horse seems vaguely impotent. I watched light pool in the intaglio at dawn; I imagine you could watch it withdraw at dusk and sense the same animation I did. In those prolonged moments its shape and so, too, its general character changed—noticeably. The living quality of the image, its immediacy to the eye, was brought out by the light-in-time, not, at least here, in the camera's frozen instant.

Intaglios, I thought, were never meant to be seen by gods in the sky above. They were meant to be seen by people on the ground, over a long period of shifting light. This could even be true of the huge figures on the Plain of Nazca in Peru, where people could walk for the length of a day beside them. It is our own impatience that leads us to think otherwise.

This process of abstraction, almost unintentional, drew me gradually away from the horse. I came to a position of attention at the edge of the sphere of its influence. With a slight bow I paid my respects to the horse, its maker, and the history of us all, and departed.

III

A short distance away I stopped the car in the middle of the road to make a few notes. I could not write down what I was thinking when I was with the horse. It would have seemed disrespectful, and it would have required another kind of attention. So now I patiently drained my memory of the details it had fastened itself upon. The road I'd stopped on was adjacent to the All American Canal, the major source of water for the Imperial and Coachella valleys. The water flowed west placidly. A disjointed flock of coots, small, dark birds with white bills, was paddling against the current, foraging in the rushes.

I was peripherally aware of the birds as I wrote, the only movement in the desert, and of a series of sounds from a village a half-mile away. The first sounds from this collection of ramshackle houses in a grove of cottonwoods were the distracted dawn voices of dogs. I heard them intermingled with the cries of a rooster. Later, the high-pitched voices of children calling out to each other came disembodied through the dry desert air. Now, a little after seven, I could hear someone practicing on the trumpet, the same rough phrases played over and over. I suddenly remembered how as children we had tried to get the rhythm of a galloping horse with hands against our thighs, or by fluttering our tongues against the roofs of our mouths.

After the trumpet, the impatient calls of adults summoning children. Sunday morning. Wood smoke hung like a lens in the trees. The first car starts—a cold eight-cylinder engine, of Chrysler extraction perhaps, goosed to life, then throttled back to murmur through dual mufflers, the obbligato music of a shade-tree mechanic. The rote bark of mongrel dogs at dawn, the jagged outcries of men and women, an engine coming to life. Like a thousand villages from West Virginia to Guadalajara.

I finished my notes—where was I going to find a description of the horses that came north with the conquistadors? Did their manes come forward prominently over the brow, like this one's, like the forelocks of Blackfeet and Assiniboin men in nineteenth-century paintings? I set the notes on the seat beside me.

The road followed the canal for a while and then arced north, toward Interstate 8. It was slow driving and I fell to thinking how the desert had changed since Anza had come through. New plants and animals—the MacDougall cottonwood, the English house sparrow, the chukar from India—have about them now the air of the native-born. Of the native species, some—no one knows how many—are extinct. The populations of many others, especially the animals, have been sharply reduced. The idea of a desert impoverished by agricultural poisons and varmint hunters, by off-road vehicles and military operations, did not seem as disturbing to me, however, as this other horror, now that I had been those hours with the horse. The vandals, the few who crowbar rock art off the desert's walls, who dig up graves, who punish the ground that holds intaglios, are people who devour history. Their self-centered scorn, their disrespect for ideas and images beyond their ken, create the awful atmosphere of loose ends in which totalitarianism thrives, in which the past is merely curious or wrong.

I thought about the horse sitting out there on the unprotected plain. I enumerated its qualities in my mind until a sense of its vulnerability receded and it became an anchor for something else. I remembered that history, a history like this one, which ran deeper than Mexico, deeper than the Spanish, was a kind of medicine. It permitted the great breadth of human expression to reverberate, and it did not urge you to locate its apotheosis in the present.

Each of us, individuals and civilizations, has been held upside down like Achilles in the River Styx. The artist mixing his colors in the dim light of Altamira; an Egyptian ruler lying still now, wrapped in his byssus,* stored against time in a pyramid; the faded Dorset culture of the Arctic; the Hmong and Samburu and Walbiri of historic time; the modern nations. This great, imperfect stretch of human expression is the clarification and encouragement, the urging and the reminder, we call history. And it is inscribed everywhere in the face of the land, from the mountain passes of the Himalayas to a nameless bajada in the California desert.

Small birds rose up in the road ahead, startled, and flew off. I prayed no infidel would ever find that horse.

Reflections and Responses

1. Lopez divides his essay into three parts. How does each of these parts differ? What purpose does each serve?

2. Examine Lopez's choice of words. When does he introduce technical terms into the essay? Go through the essay and identify

---

*byssus: Ancient cloth.

the various technical terms. From what diverse disciplines are they drawn? How do these terms affect your response to both the author and his subject?

3. When this essay originally appeared, it included no photographs of the carving. Why do you think that decision was made? What distortions would photography introduce? What would a photograph not be able to show us? What is Lopez's attitude toward photography in this instance?

KYOKO MORI

Yarn

Many fine essays deal with ordinary, routine matters. In fact, as a genre, the essay is usually more comfortable in our habitual worlds than it is in worlds we may imagine. Our hobbies, daily schedules, everyday interests and amusements, preoccupations (whether kayaking, knitting, or karate)—these will supply the building blocks that the essayist will assemble, disassemble, and reassemble. The trick of making our ordinary lives and concerns of interest to others, however, is what aspiring essayists must learn. In "Yarn," Kyoko Mori provides a solid demonstration of the way an experienced essayist can toggle between the micro and the macro, the personal and the historical. As she writes about her lifelong passion for knitting, Mori at the same time makes us aware of the way life and art are shaped by the pursuit, the improvisation, and the dissolution of patterns.

*Kyoko Mori is the author of two nonfiction books—*The Dream of Water: A Memoir *(1995) and* Polite Lies: On Being a Woman Caught Between Cultures *(1998)—as well as three novels, the most recent of which is* Stone Field, True Arrow *(2000). Born in Kobe, Japan, Mori has lived in the American Midwest for most of her adult life. She has taught creative nonfiction at Harvard University and fiction in Lesley University's low-residency MFA program. Mori is currently on the MFA faculty at George Mason University. "Yarn" originally appeared in the* Harvard Review *and was selected by Louis Menand for* The Best American Essays 2004.

1

The yellow mittens I made in seventh-grade home economics proved that I dreamed in color. For the unit on knitting, we were supposed to turn in a pair of mittens. The two hands had to be precisely the same size so that when we held them together, palm to palm, no extra stitches would stick out from the thumb, the tips of the fingers, or the cuff. Somewhere between making the fourth and the fifth mitten to fulfill this requirement, I dreamed that the ball of yellow yarn in my bag had turned green. Chartreuse, leaf, Granny Smith, lime, neon, acid green. The brightness was electric. I woke up knowing that I was, once again, doomed for a D in home ec.

I don't remember what possessed me to choose yellow yarn for that assignment. Yellow was a color I never liked; perhaps I was conceding defeat before I started. Mittens, as it turns out, are just about the worst project possible for a beginner. Each hand has to be knitted as a very small tube, with the stitches divided among four pointed needles that twist and slip unless you are holding them with practiced confidence. The pair won't be the same size if you drop or pick up extra stitches along the way, skip a couple of decreases in shaping the top, or knit too tightly in your nervousness and then let up in relief as you approach the end. You might inadvertently make two right mittens or two lefts because you forgot that the thumb has to be started in a different position for each hand. I ended up with two right hands of roughly the same size and three left hands that could have been illustrations for a fairy tale. *Once upon a time there lived three brothers, each with only one hand—large, medium and very small—and, even though the villagers laughed at them and called them unkind names, the brothers, could do any thing when they put their three left hands together. . . .*

I didn't knit again until graduate school when I met a woman from Germany with a closetful of beautiful sweaters. Sabina came to our seminar wearing a soft angora cardigan one week, a sturdy fisherman's pullover the next.

"I make all my sweaters," she said. "I can teach you."

I told her about my mitten fiasco.

"Knitting is easy," Sabina insisted. "A sweater's bigger than a mitten but much simpler."

"The patterns will confuse me."

"You don't need patterns. You can make things up as you go."

Sabina took me to a local yarn store, where I bought skeins of red cotton yarn. Following her instructions, I first knit the body of the sweater: two flat pieces, front and back, with a few simple decreases to shape the shoulders and the neck. The pieces were surprisingly easy to sew together. Sabina showed me how to pick up the stitches along the arm opening, connect the new yarn, and knit the sleeves, going from the shoulder to the wrist. I finished the sweater in a month, The result was slightly lopsided—one sleeve was half an inch wider than the other around the elbow—but the arms looked more or less even once I put the sweater on. The small mistakes in a knitted garment disappear when the garment is on the body, where it belongs. That might have been the most important thing I learned from my first sweater.

In the twenty years since then, I've made sweaters, vests, hats, bedspreads, lap blankets, shawls, scarves, socks, and mittens. Like most people who knit, I have bags of yarn stashed in my closet for future projects. The bags are a record of the cities where I've wandered into yarn stores: Madison, Portland, Cambridge, New Orleans. Evanston, Washington, DC. Like hair salons, yarn stores have slightly witty names: Woolgathering, Woolworks, Woolcotts, the Knitting Tree, the Quarter Stitch (New Orleans), Fiber Space. Inside each store, the walls are lined with plastic crates bursting with color. My friend Yenkuei took up knitting because she fell in love with the fuchsia sleeveless sweater in the window of Woolcotts in Harvard Square, floating, she thought, and beckoning to her. Another friend, who doesn't knit, comes along just to touch. She goes from shelf to shelf fingering the rayon chenilles, angoras, alpacas, and silk-cotton blends while I'm trying to figure out how much yarn I need. When I was five, in kindergarten, I was horrified to see other kids stick their fingers in the library paste, scoop up the pale glop, and put it in their mouths, but I tried to eat the raspberry-colored crayon on my teacher's desk because it looked so delicious. Knitting is about that same hunger for color. I never again picked up yellow yarn.

2

Knitting is a young craft. The oldest surviving examples—blue and white cotton socks and fabric fragments discovered in an Egyptian tomb—are dated around A.D. 1200. Knitting probably originated in Egypt or another Arabic country around that time and reached

Europe through Spain. Two knitted cushions, found in the tomb of a thirteenth-century Castilian prince and princess, are the oldest known European artifacts of knitting. Once it reached Europe, the craft spread quickly. By the fourteenth century, Italian and German artists were painting the Virgin Mary knitting in a domestic setting.

Most of the early knitting in Europe was for socks and stockings. Elizabeth I preferred the knitted silk stockings from France to the woven-and-sewn foot coverings made in England. Mary, Queen of Scots, wore two pairs of French stockings—one plain white and the other patterned with gold stitches—on the day of her execution; the stockings were held up with green garters. By the end of the sixteenth century, cheap metal needles became widely available, enabling the rural families throughout England to knit socks and stockings during the winter months to supplement their income.

In the cities, guilds controlled the licensing of knitting workshops. An apprentice would spend three years working under one master and three more traveling as a "journeyman," to learn new techniques from various masters, before he could submit samples of his work for the guild's approval. In Vienna at the beginning of the seventeenth century, the samples had to include a six-colored tablecloth, a beret, a pair of silk stockings, and a pair of gloves.

Sweaters are not on this list because in Vienna at that time, as in most of Europe, upper-body garments such as shirts, tunics, vests, and jackets were cut and sewn from woven fabrics only. The first knitted upper-body garments were made in the fifteenth century, in the Channel Islands of Guernsey and Jersey, where fishermen and sailors needed thick tunics made of wool to repel water and protect against the cold. Although these garments spread slowly across the rest of Europe among laborers, they did not become popular as "sweaters" until the 1890s when American athletes wore heavy, dark blue pullovers before and after contests to ward off the chills.

Knitting is an activity that can be performed anywhere, while weaving requires a loom, a complicated piece of equipment that takes up space and is difficult to move. Still, the earliest proof of woven cloth predates knitting by more than eight thousand years. Clay balls found in Iraq and dated around 7000 B.C. have clear impressions of woven textiles on them. Numerous images of weavers are preserved on papyruses and tomb paintings from ancient Egypt. In the *Odyssey*, Penelope weaves and unweaves a funeral cloth to ward off the suitors; in Greek mythology, Aracne is turned into a spider when she challenges Athena to a weaving contest and loses. The knitting Madonnas of the fourteenth century represent some of the earliest depictions of women knitting, and no Greek hero's wife or foolish mortal ever won praise or punishment for this simple activity.

3

As with people, so with garments: the strengths and the weaknesses are often one and the same. A knitted garment, whose loose construction traps air next to the body, is warmer but more fragile than a woven one, and the stretching property of yarn makes knitting a less precise but more forgiving craft than sewing. On a knitted fabric, one broken loop can release all the loops, causing the fabric to "run." This same quality allows a knitter to unravel the yarn on purpose, undo a few inches of work, and correct a mistake she has discovered. Even after the garment is finished, a knitter can snip one of the stitches, carefully unravel one round of knitting, put the loops back on a needle, and redo the bottom of the sweater or the sleeve to make it smaller, larger, or a different shape. Sewing doesn't allow the same flexibility.

My first home ec sewing project was no better than the mittens: an Oxford shirt with cuffs, buttonholes, darts along the bust line, and square collars; a pleated skirt with a zipper closure, I'm sure there are much easier things to sew. Still, in sewing, you can't get away from cutting, assembling, and fitting. If you cut the pieces wrong, you'll have to buy more cloth and lay out the pattern again. If the finished shirt is half an inch too small, it's not going to stretch the way a sweater will.

Even the words "thread" (the stringlike material we sew with) and "yarn" (the stringlike material we knit with) convey different degrees of flexibility. Thread holds together and restricts, while yarn stretches and gives. Thread is the overall theme that gives meaning to our words and thoughts—to lose the thread is to be incoherent or inattentive. A yarn is a long, pointless, but usually amusing story whose facts have been exaggerated. It is infinitely more relaxing to listen to a yarn than to a lecture whose thread we must follow.

In my first ten years of knitting, I took full advantage of the forgiving quality of yarn and made hats and scarves from patterns that had only five- to ten-sentence directions. For sweaters, I made three tubes (one big tube for the body, two smaller tubes for the sleeves) and then knitted them together at the yoke and shoulders so I didn't have to sew the pieces together at the end. If, halfway through the body or the sleeve, I noticed the piece getting wider faster than I'd expected, I simply stopped increasing stitches; if the piece looked too small, I increased more. It was just as Sabina had told me: I could make things up as I went along.

My favorite project was a hat from a pattern I found in a yarn store on a visit to Portland, Oregon. I bought the thick mohair yarn and extra needles so I could start knitting the first one in my hotel room. The hat, which I finished on the flight home the next day, looked more like a lampshade; the brim came down to my shoulders. At home, I threw this enormous hat in the washer, set it on hot wash and cold rinse, and ran the cycle twice. Just as the pattern promised, the hat came out shrunk and "felted"; the stitches had contracted till they were invisible, leaving a dense, fuzzy nap. I reshaped the hat on a mixing bowl about the size of my head, and by the time it dried, it looked like a professionally made bowler.

The washing-machine hat became a staple of my gift-giving. A few years later, I visited an antiques mall with a couple who had fallen in love with an oak dresser they though was too expensive. Every weekend for two months, they brought a different friend to look at the dresser, to ooh and aah over it, and help them work up the nerve to spend the money. The antiques mall was a huge place out in the country, and we had to walk what felt like three city blocks crammed with furniture and knickknacks. When we finally got to the right section, I failed my friends completely by not noticing the dresser because to the right of it, on a small table, was a wooden hat form. To an untrained eye, the hat form looks like a wooden head, but I knew what it was. Tired of reshaping hats over a bowl, I had been trying to order one (except all the modern hat forms were made of Styrofoam and I didn't think I could stand the squeaky noise they would make), I grabbed the wooden head and walked around with it tightly clutched under my arm while my friends showed me all the other oak dressers, every one of them inferior to the one they wanted. At the counter, I paid $12 for my find.

This fall, I brought the wooden head with me to Wisconsin because I still make those hats for gifts. But in the past five years, I've graduated to more complicated patterns. I had gotten tired of the rugged look of the make-it-as-you-go kind of sweater, but more than that, my reasons for knitting have changed. In my twenties and thirties, I wanted everything I did to express what I considered my essential nature: casual, relaxed, and intuitively creative, rather than formal, precise, and meticulous. That's why I chose knitting over sewing, running and cycling over tennis or golf. Now, in my mid-forties, I look instead for balance. If following step-by-step instructions doesn't come naturally to me, that is all the more reason for me to try it. I would rather knit from a complicated pattern and make a few mistakes than execute an easier one flawlessly.

The folklore among knitters is that everything handmade should have at least one mistake so an evil spirit will not become trapped in the maze of perfect stitches. A missed increase or decrease, a crooked seam, a place where the tension is uneven—the mistake is a crack left open to let in the light. The evil spirit I want to usher out of my knitting and my life is at once a spirit of laziness and of overachieving. It's that little voice in my head that says, I won't even try this because it doesn't come naturally to me and I won't be very good at it.

4

A friend of mine fell in love with a young man at college because he was knitting a sweater between classes the first time she saw him. She concluded that he must be an extraordinarily sensitive and creative man, though eventually she found out he was neither. This man, whom I never met, is the only contemporary male knitter I know of, besides Kaffe Fasset, the British sweater designer.

Knitting wasn't always a feminine craft. The knitting masters and apprentices of the medieval guilds were all men, since women were not admitted into guilds. Before the Industrial Revolution, both men and women, of all ages, knitted socks in the countryside. The fishermen and the sailors from the English Channel Islands made their own sweaters during their long sea voyages. In the late nineteenth century, the Japanese samurai whose clans were faltering tried to supplement their income by knitting *tabi*, split-toed Japanese socks (essentially, mittens for feet). Even so, knitting—like sewing, spinning, weaving, and embroidery—has been historically associated with women's household skills and marriageability. One of the most remarkable examples involves the mitten.

In Latvia, until the early twentieth century, every girl learned to knit by the age of six so she could get an early start on her dowry chest. A full dowry chest would decrease the number of cattle her family would have to pay the groom's family when it came time for her to marry. The main contents of the dowry chest were mittens with multicolored, geometrical designs. On the day of the wedding, these mittens were distributed to all the participants from the carriage driver to the minister, as well as to the numerous relatives, in-laws, and neighbors. At the feast after the ceremony, the bride and the groom ate with mittened hands to invite good luck. At the end of the day, the bride walked around the inside and outside of her new home, laying mittens (to be collected later by her mother-in-law) on all the important locations: the hearth, the doors, the windows, the cow barn, the sheep shed, the beehives, and the garden. To properly complete these marriage rites, a bride needed one to two hundred pairs of mittens. The mittens were treasured as heirlooms, and the complicated knitting patterns were meant to show off a young woman's patience—her ability to perform meticulous and repetitive work—as well as her skill.

When my Japanese home ec teacher decided to teach us how to knit mittens, the assignment was, in a sense, grimly appropriate, since the not-so-hidden purpose of home ec was also to give us skills that showed off our patience and meticulousness. After the semester of knitting and sewing, we were required to take several semesters of cooking) in which we made elaborate casseroles and soufflés and desserts, food to impress people, food for parties, not the kind of food I would cook for myself when I moved out to live on my own.

In most schools in the United States and Japan now, home ec is an elective, open to both girls and boys. Young women in Latvia no longer make two hundred pairs of mittens in order to get married. Of course I'm happy for these changes, though a part of me worries whether anyone will preserve these centuries-old crafts. I have not met one man who has ever knitted, sewn, or embroidered clothes for his partner or children—or a woman knitter, quilter, garment maker, or embroiderer who has not made something for the men and the children among her family and friends. I don't know what to do with the weight of history and the way it affects our daily lives.

At least on a purely personal level, I've reconciled myself to the mitten. Last year in Cambridge, I tackled the ultimate mitten. The pattern, marked for "experienced knitters." called them "flip-flop mittens" because the top half could be made to flip back like a hinged lid, exposing the fingers in a fingerless glove. I thought of them as cat mittens: at the necessary moment, the sheath pulled back and out came the claws. It was a slow and complicated project. To achieve the gauge for the pattern, I had to use number zero needles, which were thinner than satay sticks, The fuzzy mohair yarn made the stitches difficult to see, and each finger had to be knitted separately. It took me two months to make myself a pair. Then I started another pair for my friend Junko, whose hands are smaller than the smallest measurement in the directions. I was proud of having managed to follow the directions and, at the same time, make a few adjustments on my own, until I finished the second mitten and realized that—only on that hand—I had made the top flip forward instead of back. After thirty years, I was back where I'd started; I had been blown back into the mitten purgatory of mismatched hands.

The next morning, I sat down and thought of the various tricks I'd learned. I looked at knitting books, went over the notes I'd made in the margins of some patterns. Finally I figured out how to unravel just a few rows of stitches and detach the flip at the front, make a new edging for it, and graft the stitches to the back of the hand so that the flip now faced the right way. The procedure left a small scar, hardly noticeable in the fuzzy mohair. When I gave the mittens to Junko, I showed her my mistake. Across the back of her left hand stretched a faint broken line, like a rural road on a map of the desert, a path across unknown terrain.

Reflections and Responses

1. The essay begins with a reference to the author's inability to knit mittens properly when she was a young girl. How does Kyoko

Mori continue this image through the essay? In what ways do mittens emerge as an important part of the essay's theme?

2. Why do you think Kyoko Mori weaves as much history as she does into her rather short essay? Why doesn't she concentrate entirely on her own knitting and what it means to her? What do the historical details add to the essay?

3. In what ways does "Yarn" suggest matters larger than the enjoyment and satisfaction of knitting? What pun is intended in the essay's title? How does Mori connect knitting with art and life in general? Can you infer the author's attitude toward life and art from her account of knitting? For example, can you see any similarities between knitting mittens and writing an essay?

JOYCE CAROL OATES

They All Just Went Away

The essay has long been the perfect form for the reflective mind. In the hands of a great writer, the process of reflection can be stimulated by a single incident or image and then veer off in so many different directions that, by the end of the essay, the reader is amazed at how much ground has been covered. "They All Just Went Away" does everything a superb reflective essay can do because it moves from the personal eccentricities of a lonely young girl who finds herself drawn to abandoned houses and desolate families into a consideration of American art, class boundaries, sexual abuse, and strange erotic attachments. It is not a cheerful or placid piece of writing, however. "As I am not drawn to art that makes me feel good, comfortable, or at ease," Joyce Carol Oates writes, "so I am not drawn to essays that 'smile,' except in the context of larger, more complex ambitions."

One of the country's most distinguished authors, Joyce Carol Oates has published over two dozen novels and numerous collections of poems, plays, short stories, criticism, and essays. Equipped with her work alone, the scholar and essayist Henry Louis Gates Jr. claimed, a future archaeologist could "easily piece together the whole postwar America." The recipient of countless literary awards, she was at thirty-one the youngest writer ever to receive the prestigious National Book Award for fiction when her novel them *was chosen in 1969. She currently teaches writing at Princeton University. Among her most recent works of fiction are* Blonde *(2000),* I'll Take You There *(2002),* The Tattooed Girl *(2003),* The Falls *(2004),* Missing Mom *(2005),* Black Girl/White Girl *(2006),* The Gravedigger's Daughter *(2007),* My Sister, My Love *(2008),* Dear Husband: Stories *(2009). "They All Just Went Away" originally appeared in* The New Yorker *(1995) and was selected by Geoffrey C. Ward for* The Best American Essays 1996.

I must have been a lonely child. Until the age of twelve or thirteen, my most intense, happiest hours were spent tramping desolate fields, woods, and creek banks near my family's farmhouse in Millersport, New York. No one knew where I went. My father, working most of the day at Harrison's, a division of General Motors in Lockport, and at other times preoccupied, would not have asked; if my mother asked, I might have answered in a way that would deflect curiosity. I was an articulate, verbal child. Yet I could not have explained what drew me to the abandoned houses, barns, silos, corncribs. A hike of miles through fields of spiky grass, across outcroppings of shale as steeply angled as stairs, was a lark if the reward was an empty house.

Some of these houses had been inhabited as "homes" fairly recently—they had not yet reverted to the wild. Others, abandoned during the Depression, had long since begun to rot and collapse, engulfed by vegetation (trumpet vine, wisteria, rose of Sharon, willow) that elsewhere, on our property for instance, was kept neatly trimmed. I was drawn to both kinds of houses, though the more recently inhabited were more forbidding and therefore more inviting.

Cindy Creighton/iStockphoto.com

To push open a door into such silence: the absolute emptiness of a house whose occupants have departed. Often, the crack of broken glass underfoot. A startled buzzing of flies, hornets. The slithering, ticklish sensation of a garter snake crawling across floorboards.

Left behind, as if in haste, were remnants of a lost household. A broken toy on the floor, a baby's bottle. A rain-soaked sofa, looking as if it has been gutted with a hunter's skilled knife. Strips of wallpaper like shredded skin. Smashed crockery, piles of tin cans; soda, beer, whiskey bottles. An icebox, its door yawning open. Once, on a counter, a dirt-stiffened rag that, unfolded like precious cloth, revealed itself to be a woman's cheaply glamorous "see-through" blouse, threaded with glitter-strips of gold.

This was a long time ago, yet it is more vivid to me than anything now.

This was when I was too young to think the house is the mother's body, you have been expelled and are forbidden now to reenter.

Always, I was prepared to see a face at a high, empty window. A woman's hand uplifted in greeting, or in warning. *Hello! Come in! Stay away! Run! Who are you?* A movement in the corner of my eye: the blurred motion of a person passing through a doorway, or glimpsed through a window. There might be a single shriek of laughter from a barn—piercing as a bird's cry. Murmurous, teasing voices confused with wind rippling through tall, coarse, gone-to-seed grass. Voices that, when you pause to listen, fade immediately and are gone.

The sky in such places of abandonment was always of the hue and brightness of tin, as if the melancholy rural poverty of tin roofs reflected upward.

A house: a structural arrangement of space, geometrically laid out to provide what are called rooms, these divided from one another by verticals and horizontals called walls, ceilings, floors. The house contains the home but is not identical with it. The house anticipates the home and will very likely survive it, reverting again simply to house when home (that is, life) departs. For only where there is life can there be home.

I have never found the visual equivalent of these abandoned farmhouses of upstate New York, of northern Erie County, in the area of the long, meandering Tonawanda Creek and the Barge

Canal. You think most immediately of the canvases of Edward Hopper: those dreamily stylized visions of a lost America, houses never depicted as homes, and human beings, if you look closer, never depicted as other than mannequins. For Hopper is not a realist but a surrealist. His dreams are of the ordinary, as if, even in imagination, the artist were trapped in an unyielding daylight consciousness. There seems almost a kind of rage, a revenge against such restraints, in Hopper's studied, endlessly repeated *simplicity*. By contrast, Charles Burchfield, with his numerous oils and watercolors—frequently of upstate New York landscapes, houses, and farms—rendered the real as visionary and luminous, suffused with a Blakean rapture and a kind of radical simplicity, too. Then there are the shimmering New England barns, fields, and skies of our contemporary Wolf Kahn—images evoked by memory, almost on the verge of dissolution. But the "real"—what assaults the eye before the eye begins its work of selection—is never on the verge of dissolution, still less of appropriation. The real is raw, jarring, unexpected, sometimes trashy, sometimes luminous. Above all, the real is arbitrary. For to be a realist (in art or in life) is to acknowledge that all things might be other than they are. That there is no design, no intention, no aesthetic or moral or teleological imprimatur but, rather, the equivalent of Darwin's great vision of a blind, purposeless, ceaseless evolutionary process that yields no "products"—only temporary strategies against extinction.

Yet, being human, we think, To what purpose these broken-off things, if not to be gathered up, at last, in a single ecstatic vision?

There is a strange and profound and unknowable reality to these abandoned houses where jealously guarded, even prized possessions have become mere trash: windowpanes long ago smashed, and the spaces where they had been festooned with cobwebs, and cobwebs brushing against your face, catching in your hair like caresses. The peculiar, dank smell of wood rot and mildew, in one of the houses I most recall that had partly burned down, the smell of smoke and scorch, in early summer pervading even the lyric smell of honeysuckle—these haunting smells, never, at the time of experiencing, given specific sources, names.

Where a house has been abandoned—unworthy of being sold to new tenants, very likely seized by the county for default on taxes

and the property held in escrow—you can be sure there has been
a sad story. There have been devastated lives. Lives to be spoken of
pityingly. How they went wrong. Why did she marry him, why did
she stay with him? Just desperate people. Ignorant. Poor white
trash. Runs in the family. A wrong turn.

Shall I say for the record that ours was a happy, close-knit, and un-
extraordinary family for our time, place, and economic status? Yet
what was vividly real in the solid-built old farmhouse that contained my home (my family consisted of my father, mother,
younger brother, grandfather, and grandmother, who owned the
property—a slow-failing farm whose principal crop had become
Bartlett pears by the time I was a girl) was of far less significance to
me than what was real elsewhere. A gone-to-seed landscape had an
authority that seemed to me incontestable: the powerful authority
of silence in houses from which the human voice had vanished.
For the abandoned house contained the future of any house—the
lilac tree pushing through the rotted veranda, hornets' nests beneath eaves, windows smashed by vandals, human excrement left
to dry on a parlor floor once scrubbed on hands and knees.

The abandoned, the devastated, was the profound experience,
whereas involvement in family life—the fever, the bliss, the abrasions,
the infinite distractions of human love—was so clearly temporary. Like
a television screen upon which antic images (at this time, in the fifties,
minimally varying gradations of gray) appear fleetingly and are gone.

I have seemed to suggest that the abandoned houses were all
distant from our house, but in fact the one that had been partly
gutted by fire—which I will call the Weidel house—was perhaps a
half mile away. If you drove, turning right off Transit Road, which
was our road, onto the old Creek Road, it would have been a distance of a mile or more, but if you crossed through our back po-
tato field and through the marshy woods which no one seemed to
own, it was a quick walk.

The Weidels' dog, Slossie, a mixed breed with a stumpy, energetic tail and a sweet disposition, sand-colored, rheumy-eyed, as
hungry for affection as for the scraps we sometimes fed her, trot-
ted over frequently to play with my brother and me. Though,
strictly speaking, Slossie was not wanted at our house. None of the
Weidels were wanted.

The "Weidel house," it would be called for years. The "Weidel property." As if the very land—which the family had not owned in any case, but only rented, partly with county-welfare support—were somehow imprinted with that name, a man's identity. Or infamy.

For tales were told of the father who drank, beat and terrorized his family, "did things to" his daughters, and finally set the house on fire and fled and was arrested, disappearing forever from the proper, decent life of our community. There was no romance in Mr. Weidel, whom my father knew only slightly and despised as a drinker, and as a wife- and child-beater. Mr. Weidel was a railway worker in Lockport, or perhaps an ex-railway worker, for he seemed to work only sporadically, though he always wore a railway-man's cap. He and his elder sons were hunters, owning a shotgun among them and one or two deer rifles. His face was broad, fair, vein-swollen, with a look of flushed, alcoholic reproach. He was tall and heavyset, with graying black whiskers that sprouted like quills. His eyes had a way of swerving in their sockets, seeking you out when you could not slip away quickly enough. *H'lo there, little Joyce! Joycie! Joycie Oates, h'lo!* He wore rubber boots that flapped, unbuckled, about his feet.

Mrs. Weidel was a faded-pretty, apologetic woman with a body that seemed to have become bloated, as with a perpetual pregnancy. Her bosom had sunk to her waist. Her legs were encased, sausagelike, in flesh-colored support hose. *How can that woman live with him? That pig.* There was disdain, disgust, in this frequent refrain. *Why doesn't she leave him? Did you see that black eye? Did you hear them the other night? Take the girls away, at least.* It was thought that she could, for Mrs. Weidel was the only one in the family who seemed to work at all regularly. She was hired for seasonal canning in a tomato factory in lower Lockport and may have done house-cleaning in the city.

A shifting household of relatives and rumored "boarders" lived in the Weidel house. There were six Weidel children, four sons and two daughters. Ruth was a year older than I, and Dorothy two years younger. There was an older brother of Mr. Weidel's, who walked with a cane and was said to be an ex-convict, from Attica. The eldest Weidel son, Roy, owned a motorcycle, and friends of his often visited, fellow bikers. There were loud parties, frequent disputes, and tales of Mr. Weidel's chasing his wife with a butcher knife, a claw hammer, the shotgun, threatening to "blow her head off." Mrs. Weidel and the younger children fled outdoors in terror and hid in the hayloft. Sheriff's deputies drove out to the house, but no charges were ever pressed against Mr. Weidel. Until the fire, which was so public that it couldn't be denied.

There was the summer day—I was eleven years old—that Mr. Weidel shot Slossie. We heard the poor creature yelping and whimpering for what seemed like hours. When my father came home from work, he went to speak to Mr. Weidel, though my mother begged him not to. By this time, the dog had dragged herself beneath the Weidels' house to die. Mr. Weidel was furious at the intrusion, drunk, defensive—Slossie was his goddam dog, he said, she'd been getting in the way, she was "old." But my father convinced him to put the poor dog out of her misery. So Mr. Weidel made one of his sons drag Slossie out from beneath the house, and he straddled her and shot her a second time, and a third, at close range. My father, who'd never hunted, who'd never owned a gun, backed off, a hand over his eyes.

Afterward, my father would say of that day that walking away from that drunken son of a bitch with a rifle in his hands was about the hardest thing he'd ever done. He'd expected a shot between his shoulders.

The fire was the following year, around Thanksgiving.

After the Weidels were gone from Millersport and the house stood empty, I discovered Slossie's grave. I'm sure it was Slossie's grave. It was beyond the dog hutch, in the weedy back yard, a sunken patch of earth measuring about three feet by four with one of Mrs. Weidel's big whitewashed rocks at the head.

Morning glories grew in clusters on the posts of the front porch. Mrs. Weidel had planted hollyhocks, sunflowers, and trumpet vine in the yard. Tough, weedlike flowers that would survive for years.

It had been said of Ruth and her sister Dorothy that they were "slow." Yet Ruth was never slow to fly into a rage when she was teased by neighborhood boys or by her older brothers. She waved her fists and stammered obscenities, words that stung like hail. Her face darkened with blood, and her full, thick lips quivered with a strange sort of pleasure. How you loved to see Ruth Weidel fly into one of her rages; it was like holding a lighted match to flammable material.

The Weidel house was like any other rundown woodframe house, said by my grandfather to have been "thrown up" in the 1920s. It had no cellar, only a concrete-block foundation—an emptiness that gradually filled with debris. It had an upstairs with several small bedrooms. There was no attic. No insulation. Steep, almost vertical stairs. The previous tenant had started to construct a front porch of raw planks, never completed or painted. (Though Mrs. Weidel added "touches" to the porch—chairs, a woven-rush rug, geraniums in flowerpots.) The roof of the house was made of sheets of tin, scarred and scabbed like skin, and the front was covered in simulated-brick asphalt siding pieced together from lumberyard scraps. All year round, a number of the windows were covered in transparent duct tape and never opened. From a distance, the house was the fading dun color of a deer's winter coat.

Our house had an attic and a cellar and a deep well and a solid cement foundation. My father did all the carpentry on our house, most of the shingling, the painting, the masonry. I would not know until I was an adult that he'd come from what's called a "broken home" himself—what an image, luridly visual, of a house literally broken, split in two, its secrets spilled out onto the ground for all to see, like entrails.

My mother, unlike Mrs. Weidel, had time to houseclean. It was a continuous task, a mother's responsibility. My mother planted vegetables, strawberries, beds of flowers. Petunias and pansies and zinnias. Crimson peonies that flowered for my birthday, in mid-June.

I remember the night of the fire vividly, as if it had been a festive affair to which I'd been invited.

There was the sound of a siren on the Creek Road. There were shouts, and an astonishing burst of flame in the night, in the direction of the Weidel house. The air was moist, and reflected and magnified the fire, surrounding it like a nimbus. My grandparents would claim there had never been such excitement in Millersport, and perhaps that was true. My father dressed hurriedly and went to help the firefighters, and my mother and the rest of us watched from upstairs windows. The fire began at about 1 A.M., and it would be past 4 A.M. before my seven-year-old brother and I got back to bed.

Yet what was so exciting an event was, in fact, an ending, with nothing to follow. Immediately afterward, the Weidels disappeared from Millersport and from our lives. It was said that Mr. Weidel fled "as a fugitive" but was captured and arrested the next day, in Buffalo. The family was broken up, scattered, the younger children placed in foster homes. That quickly, the Weidels were gone.

For a long time, the smell of wood smoke, scorch, pervaded the air of Millersport, the fresh, damp smell of earth sullied by its presence. Neighbors complained that the Weidel house should be razed at the county's expense, bulldozed over, and the property sold. But nothing was done for years. Who knows why? When I went away to college, the old falling-down house was still there.

How swiftly, in a single season, a human habitation can turn wild. The bumpy cinder driveway over which the eldest Weidel son had ridden his motorcycle was soon stippled with tall weeds.

What had happened to Roy Weidel? It was said he'd joined the navy. No, he had a police record and could not have joined the navy. He'd disappeared. Asked by the police to give a sworn statement about the night of his father's "arson," he'd panicked and fled.

Signs were posted—NO TRESPASSING, THIS PROPERTY CONDEMNED BY ERIE CO.—and they, too, over a period of months, became shabby and faded. My parents warned me never to wander onto the Weidel property. There was a well with a loose-fitting cover, among other dangers. As if I would fall into a well! I smiled to think how little my parents knew me. How little anyone knew me.

Have I said that my father never struck his children, as Mr. Weidel struck his? And did worse things to them, to the girls sometimes, it was whispered. Yes, and Mrs. Weidel, who seemed so soft and apologetic and sad, she too had beaten the younger children when she'd been drinking. County social workers came around to question neighbors, and spread the story of what they learned along the way.

In fact, I may have been disciplined, spanked, a few times. Like most children, I don't remember. I remember Mr. Weidel spanking his children until they screamed (though I wasn't a witness, was I?), but I don't remember being spanked by my parents, and in any case, if I was, it was no more than I deserved.

I'd seen Mr. Weidel urinating once at the roadside. The loose-flying skein of the kerosene he'd flung around the house before setting the fire must have resembled the stream of his urine, transparent and glittering. But they laughed, saying Mr. Weidel had been too drunk, or too careless, to have done an adequate job of sprinkling kerosene through the downstairs of the house. Wasn't it like him, such a slovenly job. Only part of the house had burned, a wall of the kitchen and an adjoining woodshed.

Had Mr. Weidel wanted to burn his family alive in their beds? Mrs. Weidel testified no, they'd all been awake, they'd run out into the yard before the fire began. They'd never been in any danger, she swore. But Mr. Weidel was indicted on several counts of attempted murder, along with other charges.

For so many years the Weidel house remained standing. There was something defiant about it, like someone who has been mortally wounded but will not die. In the weedy front yard, Mrs. Weidel's display of whitewashed rocks and plaster-of-Paris gnomes and the clay pedestal with the shiny blue glass ball disappeared from view within a year or so. Brambles grew everywhere. I forced myself to taste a small bitter red berry but spat it out, it made my mouth pucker so.

What did it mean that Erie County had "condemned" the Weidel property? The downstairs windows were carelessly boarded over, and both the front and rear doors were unlocked, collapsing on their hinges. Broken glass underfoot and a sickish stench of burn, mildew, decay. Yet there were "touches"—on what remained of a kitchen wall, a Holstein calendar from a local feed store, a child's crayon drawing. Upstairs, children's clothes, socks and old shoes heaped on the floor. I recognized with a thrill of repugnance an old red sweater of Ruth's, angora-fuzzy. There were broken Christmas tree ornaments, a naked pink plastic doll. Toppled bedsprings, filthy mattresses streaked with yellow and rust-colored stains. The mattresses looked as if they'd been gutted, their stuffing strewn about. The most terrible punishment, I thought, would be to be forced to lie down on such a mattress.

I thought of Mrs. Weidel, her swollen, blackened eyes, her bruised face. Shouts and sirens in the night, the sheriff's patrol car. But no charges filed. The social worker told my mother how Mrs. Weidel had screamed at the county people, insisting her husband hadn't done anything wrong and shouldn't go to jail. The names she'd called them! Unrepeatable.

She was the wife of that man, they'd had babies together. The law had no right to interfere. The law had nothing to do with them.

As a woman and as a writer, I have long wondered at the wellsprings of female masochism. Or what, in despair of a more subtle, less reductive phrase, we can call the congeries of predilections toward self-hurt, self-erasure, self-repudiation in women. These predilections are presumably "learned"—"acquired"—but perhaps also imprinted in our genes, of biological necessity, neuro-physiological fate, predilections that predate culture. Indeed, may shape culture. Do not say, "Yes, but these are isolated, peripheral examples. These are marginal Americans, uneducated. They tell us nothing about ourselves." They tell us everything about ourselves, and even the telling, the exposure, is a kind of cutting, an inscription in the flesh.

Yet what could possibly be the evolutionary advantage of self-hurt in the female? Abnegation in the face of another's cruelty? Acquiescence to another's will? This loathsome secret that women do not care to speak of, or even acknowledge.

Two or three years later, in high school, twelve miles away in a consolidated district school to which, as a sophomore, I went by school bus, Ruth Weidel appeared. She was living now with relatives in Lockport. She looked, at sixteen, like a woman in her twenties; big-breasted, with full, strong thighs and burnished-brown hair inexpertly bleached. Ruth's homeroom was "special education," but she took some classes with the rest of us. If she recognized me, in our home economics class, she was careful to give no sign.

There was a tacit understanding that "something had happened" to Ruth Weidel, and her teachers treated her guardedly. Ruth was special, the way a handicapped person is special. She was withdrawn, quiet; if still prone to violent outbursts of rage, she might have been on medication to control it. Her eyes, like her father's, seemed always about to swerve in their sockets. Her face was round, fleshy, like a pudding, her nose oily-pored. Yet she wore lipstick, she was "glamorous"—almost. In gym class, Ruth's large breasts straining against her T-shirt and the shining rippled muscles and fatty flesh of her thighs were amazing to us; we were so much thinner and less female, so much younger.

I believed that I should protect Ruth Weidel, so I told none of the other students about her family. Even to Ruth, for a long time I pretended not to know who she was. I can't explain how Ruth could have possibly believed me, yet this seems to have been so.

Quite purposefully, I befriended Ruth. I thought her face would lose its sallow hardness if she could be made to smile, and so it became a kind of challenge to me to induce Ruth Weidel to smile. She was lonely and miserable at school, and flattered by my attention. For so few "normal" girls sought out "specialed" girls. At first she may have been suspicious, but by degrees she became trusting. I thought of Slossie: trust shows in the eyes.

I sat with Ruth at lunch in the school cafeteria and eventually I asked her about the house on the old Creek Road, and she lied bluntly, to my face, insisting that an uncle of hers had owned that house. She'd only visited a few times. She and her family. I asked, "How did the fire start?" and Ruth said, slowly, each word sucked like a pebble in the mouth, "Lightning. Lightning hit it. One night in a storm." I asked, "Are you living with your mother now, Ruth?" and Ruth shrugged, and made a face, and said, "She's OK. I see her sometimes." I asked about Dorothy. I asked where Mrs. Weidel was. I said that my mother had always liked her mother, and missed her when she went away. But Ruth seemed not to hear. Her gaze had drifted. I said, "Why did you all move away?" Ruth did not reply, though I could hear her breathing hard. "Why did you abandon your house? It could have been fixed. It's still there. Your mom's hollyhocks are still there. You should come out and see it sometime. You could visit me." Ruth shrugged, and laughed. She gave me a sidelong glance, almost flirtatiously. It was startling to see how good-looking she could be, how sullen-sexy; to know how men would stare at her who would never so much as glance at a girl like me. Ruth said slowly, as if she'd come to a final, adamant conclusion to a problem that had long vexed her, "They all just went away."

Another time, after lunch with Ruth. I left a plastic change purse with a few coins in it on the ledge in one of the girls' lavatories, where Ruth was washing her hands. I don't recall whether I left it on purpose or not. But when I returned, after waiting for Ruth to leave the lavatory, the change purse was gone.

Once or twice, I invited Ruth Weidel to come home with me on the school bus some afternoon, to Millersport, to have supper with my family and stay the night. I must not have truly believed she might accept, for my mother would have been horrified and would have forced me to rescind the invitation. Ruth had hesitated, as if she wanted to say yes, wanted very badly to say yes, but finally she said, "No. I guess I better not."

Reflections and Responses

1. How does Joyce Carol Oates introduce the issue of class into the essay? How does her background differ from Ruth Weidel's? How would you describe her attitude toward the Weidel family? Why is she drawn to them? What does she find attractive about them?

2. How can you account for the abrupt introduction in the ninth paragraph of houses as the subject for famous American painters? Why do you think the author suddenly interjected this information? What does it contribute to the essay as a whole?

3. Where does the essay's title come from? Why do you think Joyce Carol Oates used this expression as the title? What does it suggest about the overall experience of the essay?

SUSAN ORLEAN

Lifelike

Although essays have been published in newspapers since the eighteenth century and in magazines since the middle of the nineteenth, it wasn't until the early twentieth century that the essay began to form a full partnership with periodical journalism. American writers such as Stephen Crane and Jack London were instrumental in taking the conventional essay out of the library and study, where it had been at ease for decades, and putting the form to reportorial work as they covered shipwrecks, earthquakes, big-time sporting events, and life in America's squalid cities. By the 1920s, the reportorial essay had become a staple of the American magazine and was in the process of being brought to perfection in one new periodical, The New Yorker, *which had been founded in 1925. Since then, the magazine has become a literary institution, featuring the essay and nonfiction of some of the nation's finest writers. One of these writers is Susan Orlean (pronounced with two syllables: "Or-leen"), whose work regularly appears in current issues. In "Lifelike" she demonstrates her mastery of the reportorial essay as she attends a taxidermy championship and closely observes the meticulous skill and weird dedication to craft that go into the "questionable enterprise of making dead things look like live things."*

Susan Orlean has been a staff writer for The New Yorker *since 1992. In addition, she has contributed to* Vogue, Outside, Rolling Stone, *and the* New York Times Magazine. *Her books include* Saturday Night *(1990),* The Orchid Thief *(1998),* The Bullfighter Checks Her Makeup *(2001), and* My Kind of Place *(2004). In 2004, she was a fellow at the Nieman Foundation for Journalism at Harvard University. Currently at work on a biography of Rin Tin Tin, she served as guest editor of* The Best American Essays 2005. *"Lifelike" originally appeared in* The New Yorker *and was selected by Louis Menand for* The Best American Essays 2004.

As soon as the 2003 World Taxidermy Championships opened, the heads came rolling in the door. There were foxes and moose and freeze-dried wild turkeys; mallards and buffalo and chipmunks and wolves; weasels and buffleheads and bobcats and jackdaws; big fish and little fish and razor-backed boar. The deer came in herds, in carloads, and on pallets: dozens and dozens of whitetail and roe; half deer and whole deer and deer with deformities, sneezing and glowering and nuzzling and yawning; does chewing apples and bucks nibbling leaves. There were millions of eyes, boxes and bowls of them; some as small as a lentil and some as big as a poached egg. There were animal mannequins, blank-faced and brooding, earless and eyeless and utterly bald: ghostly gray duikers and spectral pine martens and black-bellied tree ducks from some other world. An entire exhibit hall was filled with equipment, all the gear required to bring something dead back to life: replacement noses for grizzlies, false teeth for beavers, fish-fin cream, casting clay, upholstery nails.

The championships were held in April at the Springfield, Illinois, Crowne Plaza hotel, the sort of nicely appointed place that seems more suited to regional sales conferences and rehearsal dinners than to having wolves in the corridors and people crossing the lobby shouting, "Heads up! Buffalo coming through!" A thousand taxidermists converged on Springfield to have their best pieces judged and to attend such seminars as "Mounting Flying Waterfowl," "Whitetail Deer—From a Master!," and "Using a Fleshing Machine." In the Crowne Plaza lobby, across from the concierge desk, a grooming area had been set up. The taxidermists were bent over their animals, holding flashlights to check problem areas like tear ducts and nostrils, and wielding toothbrushes to tidy flyaway fur. People milled around, greeting fellow taxidermists they hadn't seen since the last world championships, held in Springfield two years ago, and talking shop:

"Acetone rubbed on a squirrel tail will fluff it right back up."

"My feeling is that it's quite tough to do a good tongue."

"The toes on a real competitive piece are very important. I think Bondo works nicely, and so does Super Glue."

"I knew a fellow with cattle, and I told him, 'If you ever have one stillborn, I'd really like to have it.' I thought it would make a really nice mount."

Walter Bibikow//Danita Delimont, Agent//Alamy

That there is a taxidermy championship at all is something of an astonishment, not only to the people in the world who have no use for a Dan-D-Noser and Soft Touch Duck Degreaser but also to taxidermists themselves. For a long time, taxidermists kept their own counsel. Taxidermy, the three-dimensional representation of animals for permanent display, has been around since the eighteenth century, but it was first brought into popular regard by the Victorians, who thrilled to all tokens of exotic travel and especially to any domesticated representations of wilderness—the glassed-in miniature rain forest on the tea table, the mounted antelope by the front door. The original taxidermists were upholsterers who tanned the hides of hunting trophies and then plumped them up with rags and cotton, so that they reassumed their original shape and size; those early poses were stiff and simple, and the expressions fairly expressionless. The practice grew popular in this country, too: by 1882, there was a Society of American Taxidermists, which held annual meetings and published scholarly reports, especially on the matter of preparing animals for museum display. As long as taxidermy served to preserve wild animals and make them available for study, it was

viewed as an honorable trade, but most people were still discomfited by it. How could you not be? It was the business of dealing
with dead things, coupled with the questionable enterprise of
making dead things look like live things. In spite of its scientific
value, it was usually regarded as almost a black art, a wholly owned
subsidiary of witchcraft and voodoo. By the early part of the twentieth century, taxidermists such as Carl E. Akeley, William T.
Horneday, and Leon Pray had refined techniques and begun
emphasizing artistry. But the more the techniques of taxidermy
improved, the more it discomfited: instead of the lumpy moose
head that was so artless that it looked fake, there were mounts of
pouncing bobcats so immaculately and exactly preserved they
made you flinch.

For the next several decades, taxidermy existed in the margins—a few practitioners here and there, often self-taught, and
usually known only by word of mouth. Then, in the late 1960s, a
sort of transformation began: the business started to seem cleaner
and less creepy—or maybe, in that messy, morbid time, popular
culture started to again appreciate the messy, morbid business
of mounting animals for display. An ironic reinterpretation of
cluttered, bourgeois Victoriana and its strained juxtapositions of
the natural and the man-made was in full revival—what hippie
outpost didn't have a stuffed owl or a moose head draped with a
silk shawl?—so, once again, taxidermy found a place in the public eye. Supply houses concocted new solvents and better tanning
compounds, came out with lightweight mannequins, produced
modern formulations of resins and clays. Taxidermy schools
opened; previously, any aspiring taxidermist could only hope to
learn the trade by apprenticing or by taking one of a few correspondence courses available. In *1971*, the National Taxidermy
Association was formed (the old society had moldered long before). In 1974, a trade magazine called Taxidermy Review began
sponsoring national competitions. For the first time, most taxidermists had a chance to meet one another and share advice on
how to glue tongues into jaw sets or accurately measure the carcass of a squirrel.

The competitions were also the first time that taxidermists could
compare their skills and see who in the business could sculpt the
best moose septum or could most perfectly capture the look on a

prowling coyote's face. Taxidermic skill is a function of how deft you are at skinning an animal and then stretching its hide over a mannequin and sewing it into place. Top-of-the-line taxidermists sculpt their own mannequins; otherwise they will buy a ready-made polyurethane-foam form and tailor the skin to fit. Body parts that can't be preserved (ears, eyes, noses, lips, tongues) can be either store-bought or handmade. How good the mount looks—that is, how alive it looks—is a function of how assiduously the taxidermist has studied reference material (photographs, drawings, and actual live animals) so that he or she knows the particular creature literally and figuratively inside out.

To be good at taxidermy, you have to be good at sewing, sculpting, painting, and hairdressing, and mostly you have to be a little bit of a zoology nerd. You have to love animals—love looking at them, taking photographs of them, hunting them, measuring them, casting them in plaster of Paris when they're dead so that you have a reference when you're, say, attaching ears or lips and want to get the angle and shape exactly right. Some taxidermists raise the animals they most often mount, so they can just step out in the back yard when they're trying to remember exactly how a deer looks when it's licking its nose, especially because modern taxidermy emphasizes mounts with interesting expressions, rather than the stunned-looking creations of the past. Taxidermists seem to make little distinction between loving animals that are alive and loving ones that are not. "I love deer," one of the champions in the Whitetail division said to me. "They're my babies."

Taxidermy is now estimated to be a $570-million annual business, made up of small operators around the country who mount animals for museums, for decorators, and mostly for the thirteen million or so Americans who are recreational hunters and on occasion want to preserve and display something they killed and who are willing to shell out anywhere from $200 to mount a pheasant to several thousand for a kudu or a grizzly bear. There are state and regional taxidermy competitions throughout the year and the world championships, which are held every other year; two trade magazines; a score of taxidermy schools; and three thousand visits to Taxidermy.net every day, where taxidermists can trade information and goods with as little self-consciousness as you would find on a knitting Web site:

"I am in need of several pair of frozen goat feet!"

"Hi! I have up to 300 sets of goat feet and up to 1000 set of sheep feet per month. Drop me an email at frozencritters.com . . . or give me a call and we can discuss your needs."

"I have a very nice small raccoon that is frozen whole. I forgot he was in the freezer. Without taking exact measurements I would guess he is about twelve inches or so—very cute little one. Will make a very nice mount."

"Can I rinse a boar hide good and freeze it?"

"Bob, if it's salted, don't worry about it!"

"Can someone please tell me the proper way to preserve turkey legs and spurs? Thanks!"

"Brian, I inject the feet with Preservz-It . . . Enjoy!"

The word in the grooming area was that the piece to beat was Chris Krueger's happy-looking otters swimming in a perpetual circle around a leopard frog. A posting on Taxidermy.net earlier in the week declared, "EVERYTHING about this mount KICKS BUTT!!" Kicking butt, in this era of taxidermy, requires having a mount that is not just lifelike but also artistic. It used to be enough to do what taxidermists call "fish on a stick" displays; now a serious competitor worries about things like flow and negative space and originality. One of this year's contenders, for instance, Ken Walker's giant panda, had artistry and accuracy going for it, along with the element of surprise. The thing looked 100 percent pure panda, but you can't go out and shoot a panda, and you aren't likely to get hold of a panda that has met a natural end, so everyone was dying to know how he had done it. The day the show opened, Walker was in the grooming area, gluing bamboo into place behind the animal's back paws, and a crowd had gathered around him. Walker works as a staff taxidermist for the Smithsonian. He is a breezy, shaggy-haired guy whose hands are always busy. One day, I saw him holding a piece of clay while waiting for a seminar to begin, and within thirty seconds or so, without actually paying much attention to it, he had molded the clay into a little minklike creature.

"The panda was actually pretty easy," he was saying. "I just took two black bears and bleached one of them—I think I used Clairol Basic. Then I sewed the two skins together into a panda pattern." He took out a toothbrush and fluffed the fur on the panda's face. "At the world championship two years ago, a guy came in with an extinct Labrador duck. I was in awe. I thought, What could beat that—an extinct duck? And I came up with this idea." He said he thought that the panda would get points for creativity alone. "You can score a ninety-eight with a squirrel, but it's still a squirrel," he said. "So that means I'm going with a panda."

"What did you do for toenails, Ken?" someone asked.

"I left the black bear's toenails in," he said. "They looked pretty good."

Another passerby stopped to admire the panda. He was carrying a grooming kit, which appeared to contain Elmer's glue, brown and black paint, a small tool set, and a bottle of Suave mousse. "I killed a blond bear once," he said to Ken. "A two-hundred-pound sow. Whew, she made a beautiful mount."

"I'll bet," Ken said. He stepped back to admire the panda. "I like doing re-creations of these endangered animals and extinct animals, since that's the only way anyone's going to have one. Two years ago, I did a saber-toothed cat. I got an old lioness from a zoo and bleached her."

The panda was entered in the Re-Creation (Mammal) division, one of the dozens of divisions and subdivisions and sub-subcategories, ranging from the super-specific (Whitetail Deer Long Hair, Open Mouth division) to the sweepingly colossal (Best in World), that would share in $25,000 worth of prizes. (There is even a sub-sub-subspecialty known as "fish carving," which uses no natural fish parts at all; it is resin and wood sculpted into a fish form and then painted.) Nearly all the competitors are professionals, and they publicize their awards wherever possible. For instance, instead of ordering just any Boar Eye-Setting Reference Head out of a taxidermy catalogue, you can order the Noonkester's #NRB-ERH head sculpted by Bones Johnson, which was, as the catalogue notes, the 2000 National Taxidermy Association Champion Gamehead.

The taxidermists take the competition very seriously. During the time I was in Springfield, I heard conversations analyzing such arcane subjects as exactly how much a javelina's snout wrinkles when it snarls and which molars deer use to chew acorns as opposed to which ones they use to chew leaves. This is important because the ultimate goal of a taxidermist is to make the animal look as if it had never died, as if it were still in the middle of doing ordinary animal things like plucking berries off a bush or taking a nap. When I walked around with the judges one morning, I heard discussions that were practically Talmudic,* about whether the eyelids on a bison mount were overdetailed, and whether the nostrils on a springbok were too wide, and whether the placement of whiskers on an otter appeared too deliberate. "You do get compulsive," a taxidermist in the exhibit hall explained to me one afternoon. At the time, he was running a feather duster over his entry—a bobcat hanging off an icicle-covered rock—in the last moments before the judging would begin. "When you're working on a piece, you forget to eat, you forget to drink, you even forget to sleep. You get up in the middle of the night and go into the shop so you can keep working. You get completely caught up in it. You want it to be perfect. You're trying to make something come back to life."

I said that his bobcat was beautiful, and that even the icicles on the piece looked completely real. "I made them myself," he said. "I used clear acrylic toilet-plunger handles. The good Lord sent the idea to me while I was in a hardware store. I just took the handles and put them in the oven at four hundred degrees." He tapped the icicles and then added, "My wife was pretty worried, but I did it on a nonstick cookie sheet."

So who wants to be a taxidermist? "I was a meat cutter for fifteen years," a taxidermist from Kentucky said to me. "That whole time, no one ever said to me, 'Boy, that was a wonderful steak you cut me.' Now I get told all the time what a great job I've done." Steve Faechner, who is the president and chairman of the Academy of Realistic Taxidermy, in Havre, Montana, started mounting animals in 1989, after years spent working on the railroad. "I had gotten hurt, and was looking for something to do," he said. "I was with a friend who did taxidermy and I thought to myself, I have got to get a life. And this was it." Larry Blomquist, who is the owner of the World Taxidermy Championships and of Breakthrough, the trade magazine that sponsors the competition, was a schoolteacher for three years before setting up his business. There are a number of

---

*Talmudic: Refers to the collection of ancient Jewish writings that form the basis of Judaic law; the adjective suggests a highly specified and hair-splitting system of rules and regulations.

women taxidermists (one was teaching this year's seminar on Problem Areas in Mammal Taxidermy), and there are budding junior taxidermists, who had their own competition division, for kids fourteen and younger, at the show.

The night the show opened, I went to dinner with three taxidermists who had driven in from Kentucky, Michigan, and Maryland. They were all married, and all had wives who complained when they found one too many antelope carcasses in the family freezer, and all worked full time mounting animals—mostly deer, for local hunters, but occasional safari work, for people who had shot something in Africa. When I mentioned that I had no idea that a person could make a living as a taxidermist, they burst out laughing, and the guy from Kentucky pointed out that he lived in a little town and there were two other full-time taxidermists in business right down the road.

"What's the big buzz this year?" the man from Michigan asked.

"I don't know. Probably something new with eyes," the guy from Maryland answered. "That's where you see the big advances. Remember at the last championship, those Russian eyes?" These were glass animal eyes that had a reflective paint embedded in them, so that if you shone a light they would shine back at you, sort of like the way real animals' eyes do. The men discussed those for a while, then talked about the new fish eyes being introduced this year, which have photographic transfers of actual fish eyes printed on plastic lenses. We happened to be in a restaurant with a sports theme, and there were about a hundred televisions on around the room, broadcasting dozens of different athletic events, but the men never glanced at them, and never stopped talking about their trade. We had all ordered barbecued ribs. When dinner was over, all three of them were fiddling around with the bones before the waitress came to clear our plates.

"Look at these," the man from Kentucky said, holding up a rib. "You could take these home and use them to make a skeleton."

In the seminars, the atmosphere was as sober and exacting as a tax-law colloquium. "Whiskers," one of the instructors said to the group, giving them a stern look. "I pull them out. I label them. There are left whiskers and there are right whiskers. If you want to get those top awards, you're going to have to think about whiskers."

Everyone took notes. In the next room: "Folks, remember, your carcass is your key. The best thing you can do is to keep your carcass in the freezer. Freeze the head, cast it in plaster. It's going to really help if your head is perfect." During the breaks, the group made jokes about a T-shirt that had been seen at one of the regional competitions. The shirt said "PETA" in big letters, but when you got up close you saw that PETA didn't spell out People for the Ethical Treatment of Animals, the bane of all hunters and, by extension, all taxidermists; it spelled out People Eating Tasty Animals. Chuckles all around, then back to the solemn business of Mounting Flying Waterfowl: "People, follow what the bird is telling you. Study it, do your homework. When you've got it ready, fluff the head, shake it, and then get your eyes. There are a lot of good eyes out there on the market today. Do your legwork, and you can have a beautiful mount."

It was brisk and misty outside—the antler venders in the parking lot looked chilled and miserable—and the modest charms of Springfield, with its mall and the Oliver P. Parks Telephone Museum and Abraham Lincoln's tomb, couldn't compete with the strange and wondrous sights inside the hotel. The mere experience of waiting for the elevator—knowing that the doors would peel back to reveal maybe a man and a moose, or a bush pig, or a cougar—was much more exciting than the usual elevator wait in the usual Crowne Plaza hotel. The trade show was a sort of mad tea party of body parts and taxidermy supplies, things for pulling flesh off a carcass, for rinsing blood out of fur—a surreal carnality, but all conveyed with the usual trade-show earnestness and hucksterism, with no irony and no acknowledgment that having buckets of bear noses for sale was anything out of the ordinary. "Come take a look at our beautiful synthetic fur! We're the hair club for lions! If you happen to shoot a lion who is out of season or bald, we can provide you with a gorgeous replacement mane!" "Too many squirrels? Are they driving you nuts? Let us mount them for you!" "Divide and Conquer animal forms—an amazing advance in small-mammal mannequins, patent pending!"

The big winner at the show turned out to be a tiny thing—a mount of two tree sparrows, submitted by a strapping German named Uwe Bauch, who had grown up in the former East Germany dreaming of competing in an American taxidermy show. The piece was precise and lovely, almost haunting, since the more you looked at it the more certain you were that the birds would just stop building their nest, spread their wings, and fly away. Early one morning, before I left Springfield, I took a last walk around the competition hall. It was quiet and uncanny, with hundreds of mounts arranged on long tables throughout the room; the deer heads clustered together, each in a slightly different pose and angle, looked like a kind of animal Roman forum caught in mid-debate. A few of the mounts were a little gory—a deer with a mailbox impaled on an antler, another festooned with barbed wire, and one with an arrow stuck in its brisket—and one display, a coyote whose torso was split open to reveal a miniature scene of the destruction of the World Trade Center, complete with little firemen and rubble piles, was surpassingly weird. Otherwise, the room was biblically tranquil, the lion at last lying down with the Corsican lamb, the family of jackdaws in everlasting, unrequited pursuit of a big green beetle, and the stillborn Bengal tiger cub magically revived, its face in an eternal snarl, alive-looking although it had never lived.

Reflections and Responses

1. Every month in the United States there are perhaps a thousand professional conventions and trade shows that a reporter could cover. Why do you think Susan Orlean chose to attend a taxidermists' championship and convention? She doesn't acknowledge a prior interest or expertise in taxidermy, so what in particular do you think attracted her to this event? Why do you think *The New Yorker* would be interested in publishing this essay?

2. *The New Yorker* is an urban, liberal-oriented, sophisticated magazine that appeals to a like-minded readership. What attitude would you expect it to take toward nonurban Americans who enjoy hunting and displaying their stuffed trophies? Do you think Orlean brings any "attitude" or predisposition into her coverage? How would you summarize her general approach to the trade show? For example, do you find anything condescending in her report?

After reading the essay, what image do you carry away of taxidermy? What do the details she introduces in her final paragraph suggest about Orlean's general attitude towards the taxidermists' exhibit?

3. Reporters can play a range of roles in their essays: They can be invisible, be constantly present, or move quietly in and out of the reader's attention. How would you describe Orlean's presence in her coverage? Does she provide any background identity for herself? What would we know about her from the essay alone? What appear to be the sources of her information? Examine her opening paragraphs: There is no "I" reporting, yet how do you feel her presence?

DAVID SEDARIS

This Old House

Describing one's childhood house is such a common subject for a personal essay it has become a cliché. After all, what can be a more tangible manifestation of one's relationship to the past than one's memories of the house he or she grew up in? In this essay humorist David Sedaris subverts the trope, almost glossing completely over his practical parents' suburban house, where furniture was chosen "for its durability rather than for its beauty." In its place he ruminates on a house where he rented a room as a young adult—an older, dingier place filled with antiques and characters so eccentric and colorful they seem to come from television. In particular, Sedaris forms a bond with his landlady Rosemary, a maternal figure who stokes his romanticization of the past. But as Sedaris explores his old house, he considers its bizarre and profound alienation. "The idea was that we were different, not like the rest of America, with its Fuzzbusters and shopping malls and rotating showerheads," he writes. And he quotes Rosemary: "'If it's not new and shiny, they don't want anything to do with it. . . . Give them the Liberty Bell and they'd bitch about the crack. That's how folks are nowadays.'"

David Sedaris is perhaps the most popular humor writer in America. He is best known for his sardonic reflections on his childhood, reflections that often involve biting social commentary. He contributes frequently to The New Yorker, *where* This Old House *first appeared, and to* This American Life *on National Public Radio. His collections of essays include* Barrel Fever *(1994),* Naked *(1997),* Holidays on Ice *(1997),* Me Talk Pretty One Day *(2000),* Dress Your Family in Corduroy and Denim *(2004), and* When You Are Engulfed in Flames *(2008). "This Old House" was selected by Adam Gopnik for* The Best American Essays *2008.*

When it came to decorating her home, my mother was nothing if not practical. She learned early on that children will destroy whatever you put in front of them, so for most of my youth our furniture was chosen for its durability rather than for its beauty. The one exception was the dining-room set, which my parents bought shortly after they were married. Should a guest eye the buffet for longer than a second, my mother would notice and jump in to prompt a compliment. "You like it?" she'd ask. "It's Scandinavian!" This, we learned, was the name of a region—a cold and forsaken place where people stayed indoors and plotted the death of knobs.

The buffet, like the table, was an exercise in elegant simplicity. The set was made of teak, and had been finished with tung oil. This brought out the character of the wood, allowing it, at certain times of day, to practically glow. Nothing was more beautiful than our dining room, especially after my father covered the walls with cork. It wasn't the kind you use on bulletin boards but something coarse and dark, the color of damp pine mulch. Light the candles beneath the chafing dish, lay the table with the charcoal-textured dinnerware we hardly ever used, and you had yourself a real picture.

This dining room, I liked to think, was what my family was all about. Throughout my childhood, it brought me great pleasure, but then I turned sixteen and decided that I didn't like it anymore. What happened was a television show,* a weekly drama about a close-knit family in Depression-era Virginia. The family didn't have a blender or a country-club membership, but they did have one another—that and a really great house, an old one, built in the twenties or something. All their bedrooms had slanted clapboard walls and oil lamps that bathed everything in fragile golden light. I wouldn't have used the word "romantic," but that's how I thought of it.

"You think those prewar years were cozy?" my father once asked. "Try getting up at 5 A.M. to sell newspapers on the snow-covered streets. That's what I did and it stunk to high heaven."

"Well," I told him, "I'm just sorry that you weren't able to appreciate it."

---

*a television show: The allusion is to *The Waltons,* a popular 1960s TV series.

Like anyone nostalgic for a time he didn't live through, I chose to weed out the little inconveniences: polio, say, or the thought of eating stewed squirrel. The world was simply grander back then, somehow more civilized, and nicer to look at. Wasn't it crushing to live in a house no older than our cat?

"No," my father said. "Not at all."

My mother felt the same: "Boxed in by neighbors, having to walk through my parents' bedroom in order to reach the kitchen. If you think that was fun, you never saw your grandfather with his teeth out."

They were more than willing to leave their pasts behind them, and reacted strongly when my sister Gretchen and I began dragging it home. " The *Andrews* Sisters*?" my father groaned. "What the hell do you want to listen to them for?"

When I started buying clothes from Goodwill, he really went off, and for good reason, probably. The suspenders and knickers were bad enough, but when I added a top hat he planted himself in the doorway and physically prevented me from leaving the house. "It doesn't make sense," I remember him saying. "That hat with those pants, worn with the damn platform shoes . . ." His speech temporarily left him, and he found himself waving his hands, no doubt wishing that they held magic wands. "You're just . . . a mess is what you are."

The way I saw it, the problem wasn't my outfit but my context. Sure I looked out of place beside a Scandinavian buffet, but put me in the proper environment and I'd undoubtedly fit right in.

"The environment you're looking for is called a psychiatric hospital," my father said. "Now give me the damn hat before I burn it off."

I longed for a home where history was respected—and, four years later, I finally found one. This was in Chapel Hill, North Carolina. I'd gone there to visit an old friend from high school—and because I was between jobs, and had no real obligations, I decided to stay for a while and maybe look for some dishwashing work. The restaurant that hired me was a local institution, all dark wood and windowpanes the size of playing cards. The food was O.K., but

---

*The Andrews Sisters: An enormously popular trio whose career straddled World War II.

what the place was really known for was the classical music that the man in charge, someone named Byron, pumped into the dining room. Anyone else might have thrown in a compilation tape, but he took his responsibilities very seriously, and planned each meal as if it were an evening at Tanglewood. I hoped that dishwashing might lead to a job in the dining room, busing tables, and, eventually, waiting on them, but I kept these aspirations to myself. Dressed as I was, in jodhpurs and a smoking jacket, I should have been grateful that I was hired at all.

After getting my first paycheck, I scouted out a place to live. My two requirements were that it be cheap and close to where I worked, and on both counts I succeeded. I couldn't have dreamed that it would also be old and untouched, an actual boarding house. The owner was adjusting her "Room for Rent" sign as I passed, and our eyes locked in an expression that said, "Hark, stranger, you are one of me!" Both of us looked like figures from a scratchy newsreel: me the unemployed factory worker in tortoiseshell safety glasses and a tweed overcoat two sizes too large, and her, the feisty widow lady, taking in boarders in order to make ends meet. "Excuse me," I called, "but is that hat from the forties?"

The woman put her hands to her head and adjusted what looked like a fistful of cherries spilling from a velveteen saucer. "Why, yes it is," she said. "How canny of you to notice." I'll say that her name was Rosemary Dowd, and, as she introduced herself, I tried to guess her age. What foxed me was her makeup, which was on the heavy side, and involved a great deal of peach-colored powder. From a distance, her hair looked white, but now I could see that it was streaked with yellow, almost randomly, like snow that had been peed on. If she seemed somewhat mannish, it was the fault of her clothing rather than her features. Both her jacket and her blouse were kitted out with shoulder pads, and when they were worn together she could barely fit through the door. This might be a problem for others, but Rosemary didn't get out much. And why would she want to?

I hadn't even crossed the threshold when I agreed to take the room. What sold me was the look of the place. Some might have found it shabby—"a dump," my father would eventually call it— but, unless you ate them, a few thousand paint chips never hurt anyone. The same could be said for the groaning front porch and the occasional missing shingle. It was easy to imagine that the house, set as it was, on the lip of a student parking lot, had dropped from the sky, like Dorothy's in "The Wizard of Oz," but with a second story. Then there was the inside, which was even better. The front door opened into a living room, or, as Rosemary called it, "the parlor." The word was old-fashioned, but fitting. Velvet curtains framed the windows. The walls were papered in a faint, floral pattern, and doilies were everywhere, laid flat on tabletops and sagging like cobwebs from the backs of overstuffed chairs. My eyes moved from one thing to another, and, like my mother with her dining-room set, Rosemary took note of where they landed. "I see you like my davenport," she said, and, "You don't find lamps like that anymore. It's a genuine Stephanie."

It came as no surprise that she bought and sold antiques, or "dabbled" in them, as she said. Every available surface was crowded with objects: green-glass candy dishes, framed photographs of movie stars, cigarette boxes with monogrammed lids. An umbrella leaned against an open steamer trunk, and, when I observed that its handle was Bakelite, my new landlady unpinned her saucer of cherries and predicted that the two of us were going to get along famously.

And for many months we did. Rosemary lived on the ground floor, in a set of closed-off rooms she referred to as her chambers. The door that led to them opened onto the parlor, and when I stood outside I could sometimes hear her television. This seemed to me a kind of betrayal, like putting a pool table inside the Great Pyramid, but she assured me that the set was an old one—"My 'Model Tee Vee,'" she called it.

My room was upstairs, and in letters home I described it as "hunky-dory." How else to capture my peeling, buckled wallpaper, and the way that it brought everything together. The bed, the desk, the brass-plated floor lamp: it was all there waiting for me, and though certain pieces had seen better days—the guest chair, for instance, was missing its seat—at least everything was uniformly old. From my window I could see the parking lot and, beyond that, the busy road leading to the restaurant. It pleased Rosemary that I worked in such a venerable place. "It suits you," she said. "And don't feel bad about washing dishes. I think even Gable* did it for a while."

---

*Gable: Clark Gable was one of the most famous actors in the early period of American cinema.

"Did he?"

I felt so clever, catching all her references. The other boarder didn't even know who Charlie Chan* was, and the guy was half Korean! I'd see him in the hall from time to time—a chemistry major, I think he was. There was a third room as well, but owing to some water damage Rosemary was having a hard time renting it. "Not that I care so much," she told me. "In my business, it's more about quality than quantity."

I moved in at the beginning of January, and throughout that winter my life felt like a beautiful dream. I'd come home at the end of the day and Rosemary would be sitting in the parlor, both of us fully costumed. "Aha!" she'd say. "Just the young man I was looking for." Then she'd pull out some new treasure she'd bought at an estate sale and explain what made it so valuable: "On most of the later Fire King loaf pans, the trademark helmet is etched rather than embossed."

The idea was that we were different, not like the rest of America, with its Fuzzbusters† and shopping malls and rotating showerheads. "If it's not new and shiny, they don't want anything to do with it," Rosemary would complain. "Give them the Liberty Bell and they'd bitch about the crack. That's how folks are nowadays. I've seen it."

There was a radio station in Raleigh that broadcast old programs, and sometimes at night, when the reception was good, we'd sit on the davenport and listen to Jack Benny or "Fibber McGee and Molly." Rosemary might mend a worn Wac uniform with her old-timey sewing kit, while I'd stare into the fireplace and wish that it still worked. Maybe we'd leaf through some old *Look* magazines. Maybe the wind would rattle the windows and we'd draw a quilt over our laps and savor the heady scent of mothballs.

I hoped that our lives would continue this way forever, but inevitably the past came knocking. Not the good kind that was collectible but the bad kind that had arthritis. One afternoon in early April, I returned home from work to find a lost-looking white-haired woman sitting in the parlor. Her fingers were stiff and

*__Charlie Chan__: A fictional Chinese-American detective created during the 1920s and perennially popular in novels, radio, and movies.

†__Fuzzbusters__: Radar detectors used to evade highway patrol.

gnarled, so rather than shake hands I offered a little salute. "Sister Sykes" was how she introduced herself. I thought that was maybe what they called her in church, but then Rosemary walked out of her chambers and told me through gritted teeth that this was a professional name.

"Mother here was a psychic," she explained. "Had herself a tarot deck and a crystal ball and told people whatever stupid malarkey they wanted to hear."

"That I did," Sister Sykes said, chuckling.

You'd think that someone who occasionally wore a turban herself would like having a psychic as a mom, but Rosemary was over it. "If she'd forecast thirty years ago that I'd wind up having to take care of her, I would have put my head in the oven and killed myself," she told me.

When June rolled around, the chemistry student graduated, and his room was rented to a young man I'll call Chaz, who worked on a road-construction crew. "You know those guys that hold the flags?" he said. "Well, that's me. That's what I do."

His face, like his name, was chiselled and memorable, and, after deciding that he was too handsome, I began to examine him for flaws. The split lower lip only added to his appeal, so I moved on to his hair, which had clearly been blow-dried, and to the strand of turquoise pebbles visible through his unbuttoned shirt.

"What are you looking at?" he asked, and before I had a chance to blush he started telling me about his ex-girlfriend. They'd lived together for six months, in a little apartment behind Fowler's grocery store, but then she cheated on him with someone named Robby, an asshole who went to U.N.C. and majored in fucking up other people's lives. "You're not one of those college snobs, are you?" he asked.

I probably should have said "No," rather than "Not presently."

"What did you study?" he asked. "Bank robbing?"

"Excuse me?"

"Your clothes," he said. "You and that lady downstairs look like those people from 'Bonnie and Clyde,'* not the stars but the other ones. The ones who fuck everything up."

---

*Bonnie and Clyde: An acclaimed 1967 film by director Arthur Penn about the Great Depression–era bank-robbing duo.

"Yes, well, we're individuals."

"Individual freaks," he said, and then he laughed, suggesting that there were no hard feelings. "Anyway, I don't have time to stand around and jaw. A friend and me are hitting the bars."

He'd do this every time: start a conversation and end it abruptly, as if it had been me who was running his mouth. Before Chaz moved in, the upstairs was fairly quiet. Now I heard the sound of his radio through the wall, a rock station that made it all the harder to pretend I was living in gentler times. When he was bored, he'd knock on my door and demand that I give him a cigarette. Then he'd stand there and smoke it, complaining that my room was too clean, my sketches were too sketchy, my old-fashioned bathrobe was too old-fashioned. "Well, enough of this," he'd say. "I have my own life to lead." Three or four times a night this would happen.

As Chaz changed life on the second floor, Sister Sykes changed it on the first. I went to check my mail one morning and found Rosemary dressed just like anyone else her age: no hat or costume jewelry, just a pair of slacks and a ho-hum blouse with unpadded shoulders. She wasn't wearing makeup, either, and had neglected to curl her hair. "What can I tell you?" she said. "That kind of dazzle takes time, and I just don't seem to have any lately." The parlor, which had always been just so, had gone downhill as well. Now there were cans of iced-tea mix sitting on the Victrola, and boxed pots and pans parked in the corner where the credenza used to be. There was no more listening to Jack Benny, because that was Sister Sykes's bath time. "The queen bee," Rosemary called her.

Later that summer, just after the Fourth of July, I came downstairs and found a pair of scuffed white suitcases beside the front door. I hoped that someone was on his way out—Chaz, specifically—but it appeared that the luggage was coming rather than going. "Meet my daughter," Rosemary said, this with the same grudging tone she'd used to introduce her mother. The young woman—I'll call her Ava—took a rope of hair from the side of her head and stuck it in her mouth. She was a skinny thing, and very pale, dressed in jeans and a Western-style shirt. "In her own little world," Sister Sykes said.

Rosemary told me later that her daughter had just been released from a mental institution, and though I tried to act surprised,

I don't think I was very convincing. It was like she was on acid almost, the way she'd sit and examine something long after it had lost its mystery: an ashtray, a dried-up moth, Chaz's blow-dryer in the upstairs bathroom—everything got equal attention, including my room. There were no lockable doors on the second floor. The keys had been lost years earlier, so Ava just wandered in whenever she felt like it. I'd come home after a full day of work—my clothes smelling of wet garbage, my shoes squishy with dishwater—and find her sitting on my bed, or standing like a zombie behind my door.

"You scared me," I'd say, and she'd stare into my face until I turned away.

The situation at Rosemary's sank to a new low when Chaz lost his job. "I was overqualified," he told me, but, as the days passed, his story became more elaborate, and he felt an ever-increasing urge to share it with me. He started knocking more often, not caring that it was 6 A.M. or well after midnight. "And another thing . . ." he'd say, stringing ten separate conversations into one. He got into a fight that left him with a black eye. He threw his radio out the window and then scattered the broken pieces throughout the parking lot.

Late one evening, he came to my door, and when I opened it he grabbed me around the waist and lifted me off the floor. This might sound innocent, but his was not a celebratory gesture. We hadn't won a game or been granted a stay of execution, and carefree people don't call you a "hand puppet of the Dark Lord" when they pick you up without your consent. I knew then that there was something seriously wrong with the guy, but I couldn't put a name to it. I guess I thought that Chaz was too good-looking to be crazy.

When he started slipping notes under my door, I decided it was time to update my thinking. "Now I'm going to *die* and come back on the same day," one of them read. It wasn't just the messages but the writing itself that spooked me, the letters all jittery and butting up against one another. Some of his notes included diagrams, and flames rendered in red ink. When he started leaving them for Rosemary, she called him down to the parlor and told him he had to leave. For a minute or two, he seemed to take it well, but then he thought better of it and threatened to return as a vapor.

"Did he say 'viper'?" Sister Sykes asked.

Chaz's parents came a week later, and asked if any of us had seen him. "He's a schizophrenic, you see, but sometimes he goes off his medication."

I'd thought that Rosemary would be sympathetic, but she was sick to death of mental illness, just as she was sick of old people, and of having to take in boarders to make ends meet. "If he was screwy you should have told me before he moved in," she said to Chaz's father. "I can't have people like that running through my house. What with these antiques, it's just not safe." The man's eyes wandered around the parlor, and through them I saw what he did: a dirty room full of junk. It had never been anything more than that, but for some reason—the heat, maybe, or the couple's heavy, almost contagious sense of despair—every gouge and smudge jumped violently into focus. More depressing still was the thought that I belonged here, that I fit in.

For years, the university had been trying to buy Rosemary's property. Representatives would come to the door, and her accounts of these meetings seemed torn from a late-night movie: "So I said to him, 'But don't you see? This isn't just a house. It's my home, sir. My home.'"

They didn't want the building, of course, just the land. With every passing semester, it became more valuable, and she was smart to hold out for as long as she did. I don't know what their final offer was, but Rosemary accepted it. She signed the papers with a vintage fountain pen, and was still holding it when she came to give me the news. This was in August, and I was lying on my floor, making a sweat angel. A part of me was sad that the house was being sold, but another, bigger part—the part that loved air-conditioning—was more than ready to move on. It was pretty clear that as far as the restaurant was concerned I was never going to advance beyond dishwashing. Then, too, it was hard to live in a college town and not go to college. The students I saw out my window were a constant reminder that I was just spinning my wheels, and I was beginning to imagine how I would feel in another ten years, when they started looking like kids to me.

A few days before I left, Ava and I sat together on the front porch. It had just begun to rain when she turned and asked, "Did I ever tell you about my daddy?"

This was more than I'd ever heard her say, and before continuing she took off her shoes and socks and set them on the floor beside her. Then she drew a hank of hair into her mouth, and told me that her father had died of a heart attack. "Said he didn't feel well and an hour later he just plunked over."

I asked a few follow-up questions, and learned that he had died on November 19, 1963.[*] Three days after that, the funeral was held, and while riding from the church to the cemetery Ava looked out the window and noticed that everyone she passed was crying. "Old people, college students, even the colored men at the gas station— the soul brothers, or whatever we're supposed to call them now."

It was such an outmoded term, I just had to use it myself. "How did the soul brothers know your father?"

"That's just it," she said. "No one told us until after the burial that Kennedy had been shot. It happened when we were in the church, so that's what everyone was so upset about. The President, not my father."

She then put her socks back on and walked into the parlor, leaving both me and her shoes behind.

When I'd tell people about this later, they'd say, "Oh, come on," because it was all too much, really. An arthritic psychic, a ramshackle house, and either two or four crazy people, depending on your tolerance for hats. Harder to swallow is that each of us was such a cliché. It was as if you'd taken a Carson McCullers[†] novel, mixed it with a Tennessee Williams play, and dumped all the sets and characters into a single box. I didn't even add that Sister Sykes used to own a squirrel monkey, as it only amounted to overkill. Even the outside world seems suspect here: the leafy college town, the restaurant with its classical music.

I never presumed that Kennedy's death was responsible for Ava's breakdown. Plenty of people endure startling coincidences with no lasting aftereffects, so I imagine that her troubles started years earlier. As for Chaz, I later learned that it was fairly common for schizophrenics to go off their medication. I'd think it strange that the boarding

---

[*]**November 19, 1963**: Three days before the assassination of President John F. Kennedy in Dallas.

[†]**Carson McCullers . . . Tennessee Williams**: Both southern American writers known for their portrayal of the psychology of everyday life.

house attracted both him and me, but that's what cheap places do—draw in people with no money. An apartment of my own was unthinkable at that time of my life, and, even if I'd found an affordable one, it wouldn't have satisfied my fundamental need: to live in a communal past, or what I imagined the past to be like—a world full of antiques. What I could never fathom, and still can't, really, is that at one point all those things were new—the wheezing Victrola, the hulking davenport. How were they any different from the eight-track tape player, or my parents' Scandinavian dining-room set? Given enough time, I guess, anything can look good. All it has to do is survive.

Responses and Reflections

1. Sedaris is best known as a humor writer, and the content of *This Old House* is ostensibly humorous. But the tone of the essay is more ambiguous, floating between zinging one-liners and poignant nostalgia. How would you characterize the overall tone of the essay? How is this hybrid, or at least difficult, tone a particularly effective vehicle for the essay's content?

2. Sedaris concludes by writing "When I'd tell people about this later, they'd say, 'Oh, come on,' because it was all too much, really. . . . Even the outside world seems suspect here: the leafy college town, the restaurant with its classical music." What exactly does Sedaris mean is "suspect"? Why does he compare his story to works of fiction? Do you think elements of it might be exaggerated or fictitious? Review the essay for clues that Sedaris may be mixing memoir with fictive, or at least cinematic, elements.

3. Sedaris writes that he considered the TV Waltons' house "romantic." What aspects of the past does Sedaris romanticize, and how do his parents react to this romanticization? How does Sedaris' relationship with his parents play on the typical dynamic between generations? How does this tension add to the humor, and the broader themes, of the essay as a whole?

GAY TALESE

Ali in Havana

When one of America's leading journalists was assigned to profile one of the world's biggest celebrities on a humanitarian-aid visit to one of the world's most controversial political figures, the result was bound to be a fascinating piece of writing and disclosure. In "Ali in Havana," Gay Talese accompanies the great fighter Muhammad Ali as he travels with his wife and entourage, along with many other visitors, to a reception at Havana's Palace of the Revolution to meet aging communist leader Fidel Castro. What ensues is both comic and poignant, as the magical Ali, stricken with Parkinson's disease, leaves Castro—who has been struggling to keep the small talk flowing—with a very odd parting token. A connoisseur of the unnoticed detail, Talese captures all of the humor, tension, and awkwardness of this nearly surrealistic scene.

Gay Talese is one of the founders of the New Journalism, a literary movement that irrevocably altered both the art of reporting and the art of the essay. He is the best-selling author of books about the New York Times, The Kingdom and the Power *(1969); the inside story of a Mafia family,* Honor Thy Father *(1971); the changing moral values of America,* Thy Neighbor's Wife *(1981); and a historical memoir,* Unto the Sons *(1992). Other nonfiction books include* The Bridge, New York: A Serendipiter's Journey *(1964) and* Fame and Obscurity *(1970). In 2006, he published a memoir,* A Writer's Life. *Talese served as guest editor of* The Best American Essays 1987. *"Ali in Havana" originally appeared in* Esquire *and was selected by Ian Frazier for the 1997 volume.*

It is a warm, breezy, palm-flapping winter evening in Havana, and the leading restaurants are crowded with tourists from Europe, Asia, and South America being serenaded by guitarists relentlessly

singing "*Guan-tan-a-mera . . . guajira . . . Guan-tan-a-mera*"; and at
the Café Cantante there are clamorous salsa dancers, mambo
kings, grunting, bare-chested male performers lifting tables with
their teeth, and turbaned women swathed in hip-hugging skirts,
blowing whistles while gyrating their glistening bodies into an
erotic frenzy. In the café's audience as well as in the restaurants,
hotels, and other public places throughout the island, cigarettes
and cigars are smoked without restraint or restriction. Two prostitutes are smoking and talking privately on the corner of a dimly lit
street bordering the manicured lawns of Havana's five-star Hotel
Nacional. They are copper-colored women in their early twenties
wearing faded miniskirts and halters, and as they chat, they are
watching attentively while two men—one white, the other black—
huddle over the raised trunk of a parked red Toyota, arguing
about the prices of the boxes of black-market Havana cigars that
are stacked within.

The white man is a square-jawed Hungarian in his mid-thirties,
wearing a beige tropical suit and a wide yellow tie, and he is one of
Havana's leading entrepreneurs in the thriving illegal business of
selling top-quality hand-rolled Cuban cigars below the local and
international market price. The black man behind the car is a well-
built, baldish, gray-bearded individual in his mid-fifties from Los
Angeles named Howard Bingham; and no matter what price the
Hungarian quotes, Bingham shakes his head and says, "No, no—
that's too much!"

"You're crazy!" cries the Hungarian in slightly accented English,
taking one of the boxes from the trunk and waving it in Howard Bingham's face. "These are Cohiba Esplendidos! The best in the world!
You will pay one thousand dollars for a box like this in the States."

"Not me," says Bingham, who wears a Hawaiian shirt with a camera strapped around his neck. He is a professional photographer,
and he is staying at the Hotel Nacional with his friend Muhammad
Ali. "I wouldn't give you more than fifty dollars."

"You really are crazy," says the Hungarian, slicing through the
box's paper seal with his fingernail, opening the lid to reveal a
gleaming row of labeled Esplendidos.

"Fifty dollars," says Bingham.

"A hundred dollars," insists the Hungarian. "And hurry! The
police could be driving around." The Hungarian straightens up

and stares over the car toward the palm-lined lawn and stanchioned
lights that glow in the distance along the road leading to the hotel's ornate portico, which is now jammed with people and vehicles; then he turns and flings a glance back toward the nearby
public street, where he notices that the prostitutes are now blowing smoke in his direction. He frowns.

"Quick, quick," he says to Bingham, handing him the box. "One
hundred dollars."

Howard Bingham does not smoke. He and Muhammad Ali and
their traveling companions are leaving Havana tomorrow, after
participating in a five-day American humanitarian-aid mission that
brought a planeload of medical supplies to hospitals and clinics
depleted by the United States' embargo, and Bingham would like
to return home with some fine contraband cigars for his friends.
But, on the other hand, one hundred is still too much.

"Fifty dollars," says Bingham determinedly, looking at his watch.
He begins to walk away.

"O.K., O.K.," the Hungarian says petulantly. "Fifty."

Bingham reaches into his pocket for the money, and the Hungarian grabs it and gives him the Esplendidos before driving off in
the Toyota. One of the prostitutes takes a few steps toward Bingham, but the photographer hurries on to the hotel. Fidel Castro is
having a reception tonight for Muhammad Ali, and Bingham has
only a half hour to change and be at the portico to catch the char-
tered bus that will take them to the government's headquarters.
He will be bringing one of his photographs to the Cuban leader:
an enlarged, framed portrait showing Muhammad Ali and Malcolm
X walking together along a Harlem sidewalk in 1963. Malcolm X
was thirty-seven at the time, two years away from an assassin's
bullet; the twenty-one-year-old Ali was about to win the heavyweight
title in a remarkable upset over Sonny Liston in Miami. Bingham's
photograph is inscribed, TO PRESIDENT FIDEL CASTRO, FROM MUHAMMAD
ALI. Under his signature, the former champion has sketched a little
heart.

Although Muhammad Ali is now fifty-four and has been retired
from boxing for more than fifteen years, he is still one of the most
famous men in the world, being identifiable throughout five conti-
nents; and as he walks through the lobby of the Hotel Nacional

toward the bus, wearing a gray sharkskin suit and a white cotton
shirt buttoned at the neck without a tie, several guests approach
him and request his autograph. It takes him about thirty seconds
to write "Muhammad Ali," so shaky are his hands from the effects
of Parkinson's syndrome; and though he walks without support,
his movements are quite slow, and Howard Bingham and Ali's
fourth wife, Yolanda, are following nearby.

Bingham met Ali thirty-five years ago in Los Angeles, shortly
after the fighter had turned professional and before he discarded
his "slave name" (Cassius Marcellus Clay) and joined the Black
Muslims. Bingham subsequently became his closest male friend
and has photographed every aspect of Ali's life: his rise and fall
three times as the heavyweight champion; his three-year expulsion
from boxing, beginning in 1967, for refusing to serve in the American military during the Vietnam War ("I ain't got no quarrel with
them Vietcong"); his four marriages; his fatherhood of nine children (one adopted, two out of wedlock); his endless public appearances in all parts of the world—Germany, England, Egypt (sailing
on the Nile with a son of Elijah Muhammad's), Sweden, Libya,
Pakistan (hugging refugees from Afghanistan), Japan, Indonesia,
Ghana (wearing a dashiki and posing with President Kwame Nkru-
mah), Zaire (beating George Foreman), Manila (beating Joe Frazier) . . . and now, on the final night of his 1996 visit to Cuba, he is
en route to a social encounter with an aging contender he has long
admired—one who has survived at the top for nearly forty years
despite the ill will of nine American presidents, the CIA, the Mafia,
and various militant Cuban Americans.

Bingham waits for Ali near the open door of the charter bus that
is blocking the hotel's entrance; but Ali lingers within the crowd in
the lobby, and Yolanda steps aside to let some people get closer to
her husband.

She is a large and pretty woman of thirty-eight, with a radiant
smile and a freckled, fair complexion that reflects her interracial
ancestry. A scarf is loosely draped over her head and shoulders,
her arms are covered by long sleeves, and her well-designed dress
in vivid hues hangs below her knees. She converted to Islam from
Catholicism when she married Ali, a man sixteen years her senior
but one with whom she shared a familial bond dating back to her
girlhood in their native Louisville, where her mother and Ali's

mother were sisterly soul mates who traveled together to attend his fights. Yolanda had occasionally joined Ali's entourage, becoming acquainted with not only the boxing element but with Ali's female contemporaries who were his lovers, his wives, the mothers of his children; and she remained in touch with Ali throughout the 1970s, while she majored in psychology at Vanderbilt and later earned her master's degree in business at UCLA. Then—with the end of Ali's boxing career, his third marriage, and his vibrant health—Yolanda intimately entered his life as casually and naturally as she now stands waiting to reclaim her place at his side.

She knows that he is enjoying himself. There is a slight twinkle in his eyes, not much expression on his face, and no words forthcoming from this once most talkative of champions. But the mind behind his Parkinson's mask is functioning normally, and he is characteristically committed to what he is doing: he is spelling out his full name on whatever cards or scraps of paper his admirers are handing him. "Muhammad Ali." He does not settle for a time-saving "Ali" or his mere initials. He has never shortchanged his audience.

And in this audience tonight are people from Latin America, Canada, Africa, Russia, China, Germany, France. There are two hundred French travel agents staying at the hotel in conjunction with the Cuban government's campaign to increase its growing tourist trade (which last year saw about 745,000 visitors spending an estimated one billion dollars on the island). There is also on hand an Italian movie producer and his lady friend from Rome and a onetime Japanese wrestler, Antonio Inoki, who injured Ali's legs during a 1976 exhibition in Tokyo (but who warmly embraced him two nights ago in the hotel's lounge as they sat listening to Cuban pianist Chucho Valdes playing jazz on a Russian-made Moskva baby grand); and there is also in the crowd, standing taller than the rest, the forty-three-year-old, six-foot five-inch Cuban heavyweight hero Teófilo Stevenson, who was a three-time Olympic gold medalist, in 1972, 1976 and 1980, and who, on this island at least, is every bit as renowned as Ali or Castro.

Though part of Stevenson's reputation derives from his erstwhile power and skill in the ring (although he never fought Ali), it is also attributable to his not having succumbed to the offers of professional boxing promoters, stubbornly resisting the Yankee dollar—although Stevenson hardly seems deprived. He dwells among his countrymen like a towering Cuban peacock, occupying high positions within the government's athletic programs and gaining sufficient attention from the island's women to have garnered four wives so far, who are testimony to his eclectic taste.

His first wife was a dance instructor. His second was an industrial engineer. His third was a medical doctor. His fourth and present wife is a criminal attorney. Her name is Fraymari, and she is a girlishly petite olive-skinned woman of twenty-three who, standing next to her husband in the lobby, rises barely higher than the midsection of his embroidered guayabera—a tightly tailored, short-sleeved shirt that accentuates his tapered torso, his broad shoulders, and the length of his dark, muscular arms, which once prevented his opponents from doing any injustice to his winning Latin looks.

Stevenson always fought from an upright position, and he maintains that posture today. When people talk to him, his eyes look downward, but his head remains high. The firm jaw of his oval-shaped head seems to be locked at a right angle to his straight-spined back. He is a proud man who exhibits all of his height. But he does listen, especially when the words being directed up at him are coming from the perky little attorney who is his wife. Fraymari is now reminding him that it is getting late—everyone should be on the bus; Fidel may be waiting.

Stevenson lowers his eyes toward her and winks. He has gotten the message. He has been Ali's principal escort throughout this visit. He was also Ali's guest in the United States during the fall of 1995; and though he knows only a few words of English, and Ali no Spanish, they are brotherly in their body language.

Stevenson edges himself into the crowd and gently places his right arm around the shoulders of his fellow champion. And then, slowly but firmly, he guides Ali toward the bus.

The road to Fidel Castro's Palace of the Revolution leads through a memory lane of old American automobiles chugging along at about twenty-five miles an hour—springless, pre-embargo Ford coupes and Plymouth sedans, DeSotos and LaSalles, Nashes and Studebakers, and various vehicular collages created out of Cadillac grilles and Oldsmobile axles and Buick fenders patched with pieces of oil-drum metal and powered by engines interlinked with kitchen utensils and pre-Batista lawn mowers and other gadgets that have elevated the craft of tinkering in Cuba to the status of high art.

The relatively newer forms of transportation seen on the road are, of course, non-American products—Polish Fiats, Russian Ladas, German motor scooters, Chinese bicycles, and the glistening, newly imported, air-conditioned Japanese bus from which Muhammad Ali is now gazing through a closed window out toward the street. At times, he raises a hand in response to one of the waving pedestrians or cyclists or motorists who recognize the bus, which has been shown repeatedly on the local TV news conveying Ali and his companions to the medical centers and tourist sites that have been part of the busy itinerary.

On the bus, as always, Ali is sitting alone, spread out across the two front seats in the left aisle directly behind the Cuban driver. Yolanda sits a few feet ahead of him to the right; she is adjacent to the driver and within inches of the windshield. The seats behind her are occupied by Teófilo Stevenson, Fraymari, and the photographer Bingham. Seated behind Ali, and also occupying two seats, is an American screenwriter named Greg Howard, who weighs more than three hundred pounds. Although he has traveled with Ali for only a few months while researching a film on the fighter's life, Greg Howard has firmly established himself as an intimate sidekick, and as such is among the very few on this trip who have heard Ali's voice. Ali speaks so softly that it is impossible to hear him in a crowd, and as a result whatever public comments or sentiments he is expected to, or chooses to, express are verbalized by Yolanda, or Bingham, or Teófilo Stevenson, or even at times by this stout young screenwriter.

"Ali is in his Zen period," Greg Howard has said more than once, in reference to Ali's quiescence. Like Ali, he admires what he has seen so far in Cuba—"There's no racism here"—and as a black man he has long identified with many of Ali's frustrations and confrontations. His student thesis at Princeton analyzed the Newark race riots of 1967, and the Hollywood script he most recently completed focuses on the Negro baseball leagues of the pre–World War II years. He envisions his new work on Ali in the genre of Gandhi.

* * *

The two-dozen bus seats behind those tacitly reserved for Ali's inner circle are occupied by the secretary-general of the Cuban Red Cross and the American humanitarian personnel who have entrusted him with $500,000 worth of donated medical supplies; and there are also the two Cuban interpreters and a dozen members of the American media, including the CBS-TV commentator Ed Bradley and his producers and camera crew from 60 Minutes.

Ed Bradley is a gracious but reserved individualist who has appeared on television for a decade with his left earlobe pierced by a small circular ring—which, after some unfavorable comment initially expressed by his colleagues Mike Wallace and Andy Rooney, prompted Bradley's explanation: "It's *my* ear." Bradley also indulges in his identity as a cigar smoker; and as he sits in the midsection of the bus next to his Haitian lady friend, he is taking full advantage of the Communist regime's laissez-faire attitude toward tobacco, puffing away on a Cohiba Robusto, for which he paid full price at the Nacional's tobacco shop—and which now exudes a costly cloud of fragrance that appeals to his friend (who occasionally also smokes cigars) but is not appreciated by the two California women who are seated two rows back and are affiliated with a humanitarian-aid agency.

Indeed, the women have been commenting about the smoking habits of countless people they have encountered in Havana, being especially disappointed to discover earlier this very day that the pediatric hospital they visited (and to which they committed donations) is under the supervision of three tobacco-loving family physicians. When one of the American women, a blonde from Santa Barbara, reproached one of the cigarette-smoking doctors indirectly for setting such a poor example, she was told in effect that the island's health statistics regarding longevity, infant mortality, and general fitness compared favorably with those in the United States and were probably better than those of Americans residing in the capital city of Washington. On the other hand, the doctor made it clear that he did not believe that smoking was good for one's health—after all, Fidel himself had given it up; but unfortunately, the doctor added, in a classic understatement, "Some people have not followed him."

Nothing the doctor said appeased the woman from Santa Barbara. She did not, however, wish to appear confrontational at the hospital's news conference, which was covered by the press; nor during her many bus rides with Ed Bradley did she ever request that he discard his cigar. "Mr. Bradley intimidates me," she confided to her California coworker. But he was of course living within the law on this island that the doctor had called "the cradle of the best tobacco in the world." In Cuba, the most available American periodical on the newsstands is *Cigar Aficionado.*

The bus passes through the Plaza de la Revolución and comes to a halt at a security checkpoint near the large glass doors that open onto the marble-floored foyer of a 1950s modern building that is the center of communism's only stronghold in the Western Hemisphere.

As the bus door swings open, Greg Howard moves forward in his seat and grabs the 235-pound Muhammad Ali by the arms and shoulders and helps him to his feet; and after Ali has made his way down to the metal step, he turns and stretches back into the bus to take hold of the extended hands and forearms of the 300-pound screenwriter and pulls him to a standing position. This routine, repeated at each and every bus stop throughout the week, is never accompanied by either man's acknowledging that he had received any assistance, although Ali is aware that some passengers find the pas de deux quite amusing, and he is not reluctant to use his friend to further comic effect. After the bus had made an earlier stop in front of the sixteenth-century Morro Castle—where Ali had followed Teófilo Stevenson up a 117-step spiral staircase for a rooftop view of Havana Harbor—he spotted the solitary figure of Greg Howard standing below in the courtyard. Knowing that there was no way the narrow staircase could accommodate Howard's wide body, Ali suddenly began to wave his arms, summoning Howard to come up and join him.

Castro's security guards, who know in advance the names of all the bus passengers, guide Ali and the others through the glass doors and then into a pair of waiting elevators for a brief ride that is followed by a short walk through a corridor and finally into a large white-walled reception room, where it is announced that Fidel Castro will soon join them. The room has high ceilings and potted palms in every corner and is sparsely furnished with modern tan leather furniture. Next to a sofa is a table with two telephones, one gray and the other red. Overlooking the sofa is an oil painting of the Viñales valley, which lies west of Havana; and among the primitive art displayed on a circular table in front of the sofa is a grotesque tribal figure similar to the one Ali had examined earlier in the week at a trinket stand while touring with the group in Havana's Old Square. Ali had then whispered into the ear of Howard Bingham, and Bingham had repeated aloud what Ali had said: "Joe Frazier."

Ali now stands in the middle of the room, next to Bingham, who carries under his arm the framed photograph he plans to give Castro. Teófilo Stevenson and Fraymari stand facing them. The diminutive and delicate-boned Fraymari has painted her lips scarlet and has pulled back her hair in a matronly manner, hoping no doubt to appear more mature than her twenty-three years suggest, but standing next to the three much older and heavier and taller men transforms her image closer to that of an anorexic teenager. Ali's wife and Greg Howard are wandering about within the group that is exchanging comments in muted tones, either in English or Spanish, sometimes assisted by the interpreters. Ali's hands are shaking uncontrollably at his sides; but since his companions have witnessed this all week, the only people who are now paying attention are the security guards posted near the door.

Also waiting near the door for Castro is the four-man CBS camera team, and chatting with them and his two producers is Ed Bradley, without his cigar. There are no ashtrays in this room! This is a most uncommon sight in Cuba. Its implications might be political. Perhaps the sensibilities of the blond woman from Santa Barbara were taken into account by the doctors at the hospital and communicated to Castro's underlings, who are now making a conciliatory gesture toward their American benefactress.

Since the security guards have not invited the guests to be seated, everybody remains standing—for ten minutes, for twenty minutes, and then for a full half hour. Teófilo Stevenson shifts his weight from foot to foot and gazes over the heads of the crowd toward the upper level of the portal through which Castro is expected to enter—if he shows up. Stevenson knows from experience that Castro's schedule is unpredictable. There is always a crisis of some sort in Cuba, and it has long been rumored on the island that Castro constantly changes the location of where he sleeps. The identity of his bed partners is, of course, a state secret. Two nights ago, Stevenson and Ali and the rest were kept waiting until midnight for an expected meeting with Castro at the Hotel Biocaribe (to which Bingham had brought his gift photograph). But Castro never appeared. And no explanation was offered.

Now in this reception room, it is already 9 P.M. Ali continues to shake. No one has had dinner. The small talk is getting smaller: A few people would like to smoke. The regime is not assuaging anyone in this crowd with a bartender. It is a cocktail party without cocktails. There are not even canapés or soft drinks. Everyone is becoming increasingly restless—and then suddenly there is a collective sigh. The very familiar man with the beard strides into the room, dressed for guerrilla combat; and in a cheerful, high-pitched voice that soars beyond his whiskers, he announces, "*Buenas noches!*"

In an even higher tone, he repeats, "*Buenas noches,*" this time with a few waves to the group while hastening toward the guest of honor; and then, with his arms extended, the seventy-year-old Fidel Castro immediately obscures the lower half of Ali's expressionless face with a gentle embrace and his flowing gray beard.

"I am glad to see you," Castro says to Ali, via the interpreter who followed him into the room, a comely, fair-skinned woman with a refined English accent. "I am very, very glad to see you," Castro continues, backing up to look into Ali's eyes while holding on to his trembling arms, "and I am thankful for your visit." Castro then releases his grip and awaits a possible reply. Ali says nothing. His expression remains characteristically fixed and benign, and his eyes do not blink despite the flashbulbs of several surrounding photographers. As the silence persists, Castro turns toward his old friend Teófilo Stevenson, feigning a jab. The Cuban boxing champion lowers his eyes and, with widened lips and cheeks, registers a smile. Castro then notices the tiny brunette standing beside Stevenson.

"Stevenson, who is this young woman?" Castro asks aloud in a tone of obvious approval. But before Stevenson can reply, Fraymari steps forward with a hint of lawyerly indignation: "You mean you don't remember me?"

Castro seems stunned. He smiles feebly, trying to conceal his confusion. He turns inquiringly toward his boxing hero, but Stevenson's eyes only roll upward. Stevenson knows that Castro has met Fraymari socially on earlier occasions, but unfortunately the Cuban leader has forgotten, and it is equally unfortunate that Fraymari is now behaving like a prosecutor.

"You held my son in your arms before he was one year old!" she reminds him while Castro continues to ponder. The crowd is attentive; the television cameras are rolling.

"At a volleyball game?" Castro asks tentatively.

"No, no," Stevenson interrupts, before Fraymari can say anything more, "that was my former wife. The doctor."

Castro slowly shakes his head in mock disapproval. Then he abruptly turns away from the couple, but not before reminding Stevenson, "You should get name tags."

Castro redirects his attention to Muhammad Ali. He studies Ali's face.

"Where is your wife?" he asks softly. Ali says nothing. There is more silence and turning of heads in the group until Howard Bingham spots Yolanda standing near the back and waves her to Castro's side.

Before she arrives, Bingham steps forward and presents Castro with the photograph of Ali and Malcolm X in Harlem in 1963. Castro holds it up level with his eyes and studies it silently for several seconds. When this picture was taken, Castro had been in control of Cuba for nearly four years. He was then thirty-seven. In 1959, he defeated the U.S.-backed dictator Fulgencio Batista, overcoming odds greater than Ali's subsequent victory over the supposedly unbeatable Sonny Liston. Batista had actually announced Castro's death back in 1956. Castro, then hiding in a secret outpost, thirty years old and beardless, was a disgruntled Jesuit-trained lawyer who was born into a landowning family and who craved Batista's job. At thirty-two, he had it. Batista was forced to flee to the Dominican Republic.

During this period, Muhammad Ali was only an amateur. His greatest achievement would come in 1960, when he received a gold medal in Rome as a member of the United States Olympic boxing team. But later in the sixties, he and Castro would share the world stage as figures moving against the American establishment—and now, in the twilight of their lives, on this winter's night in Havana, they meet for the first time: Ali silent and Castro isolated on his island.

"*Que bien!*" Castro says to Howard Bingham before showing the photograph to his interpreter. Then Castro is introduced by

Bingham to Ali's wife. After they exchange greetings through the interpreter, he asks her, as if surprised, "You don't speak Spanish?"

"No," she says softly. She begins to caress her husband's left wrist, on which he wears a $250 silver Swiss Army watch she bought him. It is the only jewelry Ali wears.

"But I thought I saw you speaking Spanish on the TV news this week," Castro continues wonderingly before acknowledging that her voice had obviously been dubbed.

"Do you live in New York?"

"No, we live in Michigan."

"Cold," says Castro.

"Very cold," she repeats.

"In Michigan, don't you find many people that speak Spanish?"

"No, not many," she says. "Mostly in California, New York . . ." and, after a pause, "Florida."

Castro nods. It takes him a few seconds to think up another question. Small talk has never been the forte of this man who specializes in nonstop haranguing monologues that can last for hours; and yet here he is, in a room crowded with camera crews and news photographers—a talk-show host with a guest of honor who is speechless. But Fidel Castro plods on, asking Ali's wife if she has a favorite sport.

"I play a little tennis," Yolanda says, and then asks him, "Do you play tennis?"

"Ping-Pong," he replies, quickly adding that during his youth he had been active in the ring. "I spent hours boxing . . . " he begins to reminisce, but before he finishes his sentence, he sees the slowly rising right fist of Muhammad Ali moving toward his chin! Exuberant cheering and handclapping resound through the room, and Castro jumps sideways toward Stevenson, shouting, "*Asesorame!*"— "Help me!"

Stevenson's long arms land upon Ali's shoulders from behind, squeezing him gently; and then, after he releases him, the two ex-champions face each other and begin to act out in slow motion the postures of competing prizefighters—bobbing, weaving, swinging, ducking—all of it done without touching and all of it accompanied by three minutes of ongoing applause and the clicking of cameras, and also some feelings of relief from Ali's friends because, in his own way, he has decided to join them. Ali still says nothing, his face still inscrutable, but he is less remote, less alone, and he does not pull away from Stevenson's embrace as the latter eagerly tells Castro about a boxing exhibition that he and Ali had staged earlier in the week at the Balado gym, in front of hundreds of fans and some of the island's up-and-coming contenders.

Stevenson did not actually explain that it had been merely another photo opportunity, one in which they sparred openhanded in the ring, wearing their street clothes and barely touching each other's bodies and faces; but then Stevenson had climbed out of the ring, leaving Ali to the more taxing test of withstanding two abbreviated rounds against one and then another young bully of grade school age who clearly had not come to participate in a kiddie show. They had come to floor the champ. Their bellicose little bodies and hot-gloved hands and helmeted hell-bent heads were consumed with fury and ambition; and as they charged ahead, swinging wildly and swaggering to the roars of their teenage friends and relatives at ringside, one could imagine their future boastings to their grandchildren: On one fine day back in the winter of '96, I whacked Muhammad Ali! Except, in truth, on this particular day,

Ali was still too fast for them. He backpedaled and shifted and swayed, stood on the toes of his black woven-leather pointed shoes, and showed that his body was made for motion—his Parkinson's problems were lost in his shuffle, in the thrusts of his butterfly sting that whistled two feet above the heads of his aspiring assailants, in the dazzling dips of his rope-a-dope that had confounded George Foreman in Zaire, in his ever-memorable style, which in this Cuban gym moistened the eyes of his ever-observant photographer friend and provoked the overweight screen writer to cry out in a voice that few in this noisy Spanish crowd could understand, "Ali's on a high! Ali's on a high!"

Teófilo Stevenson raises Ali's right arm above the head of Castro, and the news photographers spend several minutes posing the three of them together in flashing light. Castro then sees Fraymari watching alone at some distance. She is not smiling. Castro nods toward her. He summons a photographer to take a picture of Fraymari and himself. But she relaxes only after her husband comes over to join her in the conversation, which Castro immediately directs to the health and growth of their son, who is not yet two years old.

"Will he be as tall as his father?" Castro asks.

"I assume so," Fraymari says, glancing up toward her husband. She also has to look up when talking to Fidel Castro, for the Cuban leader is taller than six feet and his posture is nearly as erect as her husband's. Only the six-foot three-inch Muhammad Ali, who is standing with Bingham on the far side of her husband—and whose skin coloring, oval-shaped head, and burr-style haircut are very similar to her husband's—betrays his height with the slope-shouldered forward slouch he has developed since his illness.

"How much does your son weigh?" Castro continues.

"When he was one year old, he was already twenty-six pounds," Fraymari says. "This is three above normal. He was walking at nine months."

"She still breast-feeds him," Teófilo Stevenson says, seeming pleased.

"Oh, that's very nourishing," agrees Castro.

"Sometimes the kid becomes confused and thinks my chest is his mother's breast," Stevenson says, and he could have added that his son is also confused by Ali's sunglasses. The little boy engraved teeth marks all over the plastic frames while chewing on them during the days he accompanied his parents on Ali's bus tour.

As a CBS boom pole swoops down closer to catch the conversation, Castro reaches out to touch Stevenson's belly and asks, "How much do you weigh?"

"Two hundred thirty-eight pounds, more or less."

"That's thirty-eight more than me," Castro says, but he complains, "I eat very little. Very little. The diet advice I get is never accurate. I eat around fifteen hundred calories—less than thirty grams of protein, less than that."

Castro slaps a hand against his own midsection, which is relatively flat. If he does have a potbelly, it is concealed within his well-tailored uniform. Indeed, for a man of seventy, he seems in fine health. His facial skin is florid and unsagging, his dark eyes dart around the room with ever-alert intensity, and he has a full head of lustrous gray hair not thinning at the crown. The attention he pays to himself might be measured from his manicured fingernails down to his square-toed boots, which are unscuffed and smoothly buffed without the burnish of a lackey's spit shine. But his beard seems to belong to another man and another time. It is excessively long and scraggly. Wispy white hairs mix with the faded black and dangle down the front of his uniform like an old shroud, weatherworn and drying out. It is the beard from the hills. Castro strokes it constantly, as if trying to revive the vitality of its fiber.

Castro now looks at Ali.

"How's your appetite?" he asks, forgetting that Ali is not speaking.

"Where's your wife?" he then asks aloud, and Howard Bingham calls out to her. Yolanda has once more drifted back into the group.

When she arrives, Castro hesitates before speaking to her. It is as if he is not absolutely sure who she is. He has met so many people since arriving, and with the group rotating constantly due to the jostling of the photographers, Castro cannot be certain whether the woman at his side is Muhammad Ali's wife or Ed Bradley's friend or some other woman he has met moments ago who has left him with an unlasting impression. Having already committed a faux pas regarding one of the wives of the two multimarried ex-champions standing nearby, Castro waits for some hint from his interpreter. None is offered. Fortunately, he does not have to worry in this country about the women's vote—or any vote, for that matter—but he does sigh in mild relief when Yolanda reintroduces herself as Ali's wife and does so by name.

"Ah, Yolanda," Castro repeats, "what a beautiful name. That's the name of a queen somewhere."

"In our household," she says.

"And how is your husband's appetite?"

"Good, but he likes sweets."

"We can send you some of our ice cream to Michigan," Castro says. Without waiting for her to comment, he asks, "Michigan is very cold?"

"Oh, yes," she replies, not indicating that they had already discussed Michigan's winter weather.

"How much snow?"

"We didn't get hit with the blizzard," Yolanda says, referring to a storm in January, "but it can get three, four feet—"

Teófilo Stevenson interrupts to say that he had been in Michigan during the previous October.

"Oh," Castro says, raising an eyebrow. He mentions that during the same month he had also been in the United States (attending the United Nations' fiftieth-anniversary tribute). He asks Stevenson the length of his American visit.

"I was there for nineteen days," says Stevenson.

"Nineteen days!" Castro repeats. "Longer than I was."

Castro complains that he was limited to five days and prohibited from traveling beyond New York.

"Well, *comandante*," Stevenson responds offhandedly, in a slightly superior tone, "if you like, I will sometime show you my video."

Stevenson appears to be very comfortable in the presence of the Cuban leader, and perhaps the latter has habitually encouraged this; but at this moment, Castro may well be finding his boxing hero a bit condescending and worthy of a retaliatory jab. He knows how to deliver it.

"When you visited the United States," Castro asks pointedly, "did you bring your wife, the lawyer?"

Stevenson stiffens. He directs his eyes toward his wife. She turns away.

"No," Stevenson answers quietly. "I went alone."

Castro abruptly shifts his attention to the other side of the room, where the CBS camera crew is positioned, and he asks Ed Bradley, "What do you do?"

"We're making a documentary on Ali," Bradley explains, "and we followed him to Cuba to see what he was doing in Cuba and . . ."

Bradley's voice is suddenly overwhelmed by the sounds of laughter and handclapping. Bradley and Castro turn to discover that Muhammad Ali is now reclaiming everyone's attention. He is holding his shaky left fist in the air; but instead of assuming a boxer's pose, as he had done earlier, he is beginning to pull out from the top of his upraised fist, slowly and with dramatic delicacy, the tip of a red silk handkerchief that is pinched between his right index finger and thumb.

After he has pulled out the entire handkerchief, he dangles it in the air for a few seconds, waving it closer and closer to the forehead of the wide-eyed Fidel Castro. Ali seems bewitched. He continues to stare stagnantly at Castro and the others, surrounded by applause that he gives no indication he hears. Then he proceeds to place the handkerchief back into the top of his cupped left hand—pecking with the pinched fingers of his right—and then quickly opens his palms toward his audience and reveals that the handkerchief has disappeared.

"Where is it?" cries Castro, who seems to be genuinely surprised and delighted. He approaches Ali and examines his hands, repeating, "Where is it? Where have you put it?"

Everyone who has traveled on Ali's bus during the week knows where he has hidden it. They have seen him perform the trick repeatedly in front of some of the patients and doctors at the hospitals and clinics as well as before countless tourists who have recognized him in his hotel lobby or during his strolls through the town square. They have also seen him follow up each performance with a demonstration that exposes his method. He keeps hidden in his fist a flesh-colored rubber thumb that contains the handkerchief that he will eventually pull out with the fingers of his other hand; and when he is reinserting the handkerchief, he is actually shoving the material back into the concealed rubber thumb, into which he then inserts his own right thumb. When he opens his hands, the uninformed among his onlookers are seeing his empty palms and missing the fact that the handkerchief is tucked within the rubber thumb that is covering his outstretched right thumb. Sharing with his audience the mystery of his magic always earns him additional applause.

After Ali has performed and explained the trick to Castro, he gives Castro the rubber thumb to examine—and, with more zest than he has shown all evening, Castro says, "Oh, let me try it, I want to try—it's the first time I have seen such a wonderful thing!" And after a few minutes of coaching from Howard Bingham, who long ago learned how to do it from Ali, the Cuban leader performs with sufficient dexterity and panache to satisfy his magical ambitions and to arouse another round of applause from the guests.

Meanwhile, more than ten minutes have passed since Ali began his comic routine. It is already after 9:30 P.M., and the commentator Ed Bradley, whose conversation with Castro had been interrupted, is concerned that the Cuban leader might leave the room without responding to the questions Bradley has prepared for his show. Bradley edges close to Castro's interpreter, saying in a voice that is sure to be heard, "Would you ask him if he followed . . . was able to follow Ali when he was boxing professionally?"

The question is relayed and repeated until Castro, facing the CBS cameras, replies, "Yes, I recall the days when they were discussing the possibilities of a match between the two of them"—he nods toward Stevenson and Ali—"and I remember when he went to Africa."

"In Zaire," Bradley clarifies, referring to Ali's victory in 1974 over George Foreman. And he follows up: "What kind of impact did he have in this country, because he was a revolutionary as well as . . . ?"

"It was great," Castro says. "He was very much admired as a sportsman, as a boxer, as a person. There was always a high opinion of him. But I never guessed one day we would meet here, with this kind gesture of bringing medicine, seeing our children, visiting our polyclinics. I am very glad, I am thrilled, to have the opportunity to meet him personally, to appreciate his kindness. I see he is strong. I see he has a very kind face."

Castro is speaking as if Ali were not in the room, standing a few feet away. Ali maintains his fixed façade even as Stevenson whispers into his ear, asking in English, "Muhammad, Muhammad, why you no speak?" Stevenson then turns to tell the journalist who stands behind him, "Muhammad does speak. He speaks to me." Stevenson says nothing more because Castro is now looking at him while continuing to tell Bradley, "I am very glad that he and Stevenson have met." After a pause, Castro adds, "And I am glad that they never fought."

"He's not so sure," Bradley interjects, smiling in the direction of Stevenson.

"I find in that friendship something beautiful," Castro insists softly.

"There is a tie between the two of them," Bradley says.

"Yes," says Castro. "It is true." He again looks at Ali, then at Stevenson, as if searching for something more profound to say.

"And how's the documentary?" he finally asks Bradley.

"It'll be on *60 Minutes.*"

"When?"

"Maybe one month," Bradley says, reminding Castro's interpreter, "This is the program on which the *comandante* has been interviewed by Dan Rather a number of times in the past, when Dan Rather was on *60 Minutes.*"

"And who's there now?" Castro wants to know.

"I am," Bradley answers.

"You," Castro repeats, with a quick glance at Bradley's earring. "So you are there—the boss now?"

Bradley responds as a media star without illusions: "I'm a worker."

Trays containing coffee, tea, and orange juice finally arrive, but only in amounts sufficient for Ali and Yolanda, Howard Bingham, Greg Howard, the Stevensons, and Castro—although Castro tells the waiters he wants nothing.

Castro motions for Ali and the others to join him across the room, around the circular table. The camera crews and the rest of the guests follow, standing as near to the principals as they can. But throughout the group there is a discernible restlessness. They have been standing for more than an hour and a half. It is now approaching 10 P.M. There has been no food. And for the vast majority, it is clear that there will also be nothing to drink. Even among the special guests, seated and sipping from chilled glasses or hot cups, there is a waning level of fascination with the evening. Indeed, Muhammad Ali's eyes are closed. He is sleeping.

Yolanda sits next to him on the sofa, pretending not to notice. Castro also ignores it, although he sits directly across the table, with the interpreter and the Stevensons.

"How large is Michigan?" Castro begins a new round of questioning with Yolanda, returning for the third time to a subject they had explored beyond the interest of anyone in the room except Castro himself.

"I don't know how big the state is as far as demographics," Yolanda says. "We live in a very small village [Barrien Springs] with about two thousand people."

"Are you going back to Michigan tomorrow?"

"Yes."

"What time?"

"Two-thirty."

"Via Miami?" Castro asks.

"Yes."

"From Miami, where do you fly?"

"We're flying to Michigan."

"How many hours' flight?"

"We have to change at Cincinnati—about two and a half hours."

"Flying time?" asks Castro.

Muhammad Ali opens his eyes, then closes them.

"Flying time," Yolanda repeats.

"From Miami to Michigan?" Castro continues.

"No," she again explains, but still with patience, "we have to go to Cincinnati. There are no direct flights."

"So you have to take two planes?" Castro asks.

"Yes," she says, adding for clarification, "Miami to Cincinnati— and then Cincinnati to South Bend, Indiana."

"From Cincinnati . . . ?"

"To South Bend," she says. "That's the closest airport."

"So," Fidel goes on, "it is on the outskirts of the city?"

"Yes."

"You have a farm?"

"No," Yolanda says, "just land. We let someone else do the growing."

She mentions that Teófilo Stevenson has traveled through this part of the Midwest. The mention of his name gains Stevenson's attention.

"I was in Chicago," Stevenson tells Castro.

"You were at their home?" Castro asks.

"No," Yolanda corrects Stevenson, "you were in Michigan."

"I was in the countryside," Stevenson says. Unable to resist, he adds, "I have a video of that visit. I'll show it to you sometime."

Castro seems not to hear him. He directs his attention back to Yolanda, asking her where she was born, where she was educated, when she became married, and how many years separate her age from that of her husband, Muhammad Ali.

After Yolanda acknowledges being sixteen years younger than Ali, Castro turns toward Fraymari and with affected sympathy says that she married a man who is twenty years her senior.

"*Comandante!*" Stevenson intercedes, "I am in shape. Sports keep you healthy. Sports add years to your life and life to your years!"

"Oh, what conflict she has," Castro goes on, ignoring Stevenson and catering to Fraymari—and to the CBS cameraman who steps forward for a closer view of Castro's face. "She is a lawyer, and she does not put this husband in jail." Castro is enjoying much more than Fraymari the attention this topic is now getting from the group. Castro had lost his audience and now has it back and seemingly wants to retain it, no matter at what cost to Stevenson's harmony with Fraymari. Yes, Castro continues, Fraymari had the misfortune to select a husband "who can never settle down. . . . Jail would be an appropriate place for him."

"*Comandante,*" Stevenson interrupts in a jocular manner that seems intended to placate both the lawyer who is his spouse and the lawyer who rules the country, "I might as well be locked up!" He implies that should he deviate from marital fidelity, his lawyer wife "will surely put me in a place where she is the only woman who can visit me!"

Everyone around the table and within the circling group laughs. Ali is now awake. The banter between Castro and Stevenson resumes until Yolanda, all but rising in her chair, tells Castro, "We have to pack."

"You're going to have dinner now?" he asks.

"Yes, sir," she says. Ali stands, along with Howard Bingham.

Yolanda thanks Castro's interpreter directly, saying, "Be sure to tell him, 'You're always welcome in our home.'" The interpreter quotes Castro as again complaining that when he visits America, he is usually restricted to New York, but he adds, "Things change."

The group watches as Yolanda and Ali pass through, and Castro follows them into the hallway. The elevator arrives, and its door is held open by a security guard. Castro extends his final farewell with handshakes—and only then does he discover that he holds Ali's rubber thumb in his hand. Apologizing, he tries to hand it back to Ali, but Bingham politely protests. "No, no," Bingham says, "Ali wants you to have it."

Castro's interpreter at first fails to understand what Bingham is saying.

"He wants you to keep it," Bingham repeats.

Bingham enters the elevator with Ali and Yolanda. Before the door closes, Castro smiles, waves goodbye, and stares with curiosity at the rubber thumb. Then he puts it in his pocket.

Reflections and Responses

1. Read Gay Talese's comments "On Certain Magazine Interviews" and "Listening to People Think" (page 36). How do you think his journalistic procedures in this essay compare to his comments about the art of interviewing?

2. How would you describe Talese's role in the essay? Where does he seem visible? Where does he seem almost invisible? How does he fit himself as a participant or as an observer into different situations?

3. Consider how Talese sets up the drama at the palace reception. How does he build tension? How does he mix both the leading and minor roles? Why do you think he focuses so closely on the different conversations? What do you think he wants the conversations to convey in general about the overall event? Consider, too, the strange gift Ali leaves with Castro. Do you think the gift can have any larger significance? Do you think Talese finds it significant? What exactly is it, and what might it represent?

3

The Public Sphere: Advocacy, Argument, Controversy

ALAN M. DERSHOWITZ

Shouting "Fire!"

Artists and performers are not the only ones who explore the boundaries of free expression. Lawyers and judges, too, frequently find themselves struggling to ascertain the limits of free speech. In the following essay, one of America's best-known trial lawyers, Alan M. Dershowitz, takes a close look at one of the most commonly used arguments against free speech, the idea that some speech should be suppressed because it is "just like" falsely shouting fire in a crowded theater. In his investigation into the source of this famous analogy, Dershowitz demonstrates how it has been widely misused and abused by proponents of censorship. Indeed, it was an "inapt analogy even in the context in which it was originally offered." As an expression to suppress expression, the "shouting fire" analogy, Dershowitz maintains, has been "invoked so often, by so many people, in such diverse contexts, that it has become part of our national folk language."

Alan M. Dershowitz is Felix Frankfurter Professor of Law at Harvard Law School. He is the author of many books, including The Best Defense *(1982),* Taking Liberties *(1988),* Chutzpah *(1991),* Contrary to Public Opinion *(1992),* The Abuse Excuse *(1994),* Reasonable Doubts *(1996), and* Sexual McCarthyism *(1998). His most recent books include* Supreme Injustice *(2001),* Letters to a Young Lawyer *(2001),* Why Terrorism Works *(2002),* America on Trial *(2004),* Rights from Wrongs *(2004), and* Preemption: A Knife That Cuts Both Ways *(2006). In 2007 Dershowitz published* Finding Jefferson: A Lost Letter, a Remarkable Discovery, and the First Amendment in an Age of Terrorism *and* Blasphemy: How the Religious Right Is Hijacking the Declaration of Independence. *In addition to his teaching and writing, Professor Dershowitz is an active criminal defense and civil liberties lawyer. "Shouting 'Fire!'" originally appeared in* The Atlantic *(1989) and was selected by Justin Kaplan for* The Best American Essays 1990.

When the Reverend Jerry Falwell learned that the Supreme Court had reversed his $200,000 judgment against *Hustler* magazine for the emotional distress that he had suffered from an outrageous parody, his response was typical of those who seek to censor speech: "Just as no person may scream 'Fire!' in a crowded theater when there is no fire, and find cover under the First Amendment, likewise, no sleazy merchant like Larry Flynt should be able to use the First Amendment as an excuse for maliciously and dishonestly attacking public figures, as he has so often done."

Justice Oliver Wendell Holmes's classic example of unprotected speech—falsely shouting "Fire!" in a crowded theater—has been invoked so often, by so many people, in such diverse contexts, that it has become part of our national folk language. It has even appeared—most appropriately—in the theater: in Tom Stoppard's play *Rosencrantz and Guildenstern Are Dead* a character shouts at the audience, "Fire!" He then quickly explains: "It's all right—I'm demonstrating the misuse of free speech." Shouting "Fire!" in the theater may well be the only jurisprudential analogy that has assumed the status of a folk argument. A prominent historian recently characterized it as "the most brilliantly persuasive expression that ever came from Holmes' pen." But in spite of its hallowed position in both the jurisprudence of the First Amendment and the arsenal of political discourse, it is and was an inapt analogy, even in the context in which it was originally offered. It has lately become—despite, perhaps even because of, the frequency and promiscuousness of its invocation—little more than a caricature of logical argumentation.

The case that gave rise to the "Fire!"-in-a-crowded-theater analogy, *Schenck* v. *United States*, involved the prosecution of Charles Schenck, who was the general secretary of the Socialist party in Philadelphia, and Elizabeth Baer, who was its recording secretary. In 1917 a jury found Schenck and Baer guilty of attempting to cause insubordination among soldiers who had been drafted to fight in the First World War. They and other party members had circulated leaflets urging draftees not to "submit to intimidation" by fighting in a war being conducted on behalf of "Wall Street's chosen few."

Schenck admitted, and the Court found, that the intent of the pamphlets' "impassioned language" was to "influence" draftees to resist the draft. Interestingly, however, Justice Holmes noted that unlawful or violent means to oppose conscription: "In form at least [the pamphlet] confined itself to peaceful measures, such as a petition for the repeal of the act" and an exhortation to exercise "your right to assert your opposition to the draft." Many of its most impassioned words were quoted directly from the Constitution.

Justice Holmes acknowledged that "in many places and in ordinary times the defendants, in saying all that was said in the circular, would have been within their constitutional rights." "But," he added, "the character of every act depends upon the circumstances in which it is done." And to illustrate that truism he went on to say:

> The most stringent protection of free speech would not protect a man in falsely shouting fire in a theater, and causing a panic. It does not even protect a man from an injunction against uttering words that may have all the effect of force.

Justice Holmes then upheld the convictions in the context of a wartime draft, holding that the pamphlet created "a clear and present danger" of hindering the war effort while our soldiers were fighting for their lives and our liberty.

The example of shouting "Fire!" obviously bore little relationship to the facts of the Schenck case. The Schenck pamphlet contained a substantive political message. It urged its draftee readers to *think* about the message and then—if they so chose—to act on it in a lawful and nonviolent way. The man who shouts "Fire!" in a crowded theater is neither sending a political message nor inviting his listener to think about what he has said and decide what to do in a rational, calculated manner. On the contrary, the message is designed to force action *without* contemplation. The message "Fire!" is directed not to the mind and the conscience of the listener but, rather, to his adrenaline and his feet. It is a stimulus to immediate *action*, not thoughtful reflection. It is—as Justice Holmes recognized in his follow-up sentence—the functional equivalent of "uttering words that may have all the effect of force."

Indeed, in that respect the shout of "Fire!" is not even speech, in any meaningful sense of that term. It is a *clang* sound, the equivalent of setting off a nonverbal alarm. Had Justice Holmes been more honest about his example, he would have said that freedom of speech does not protect a kid who pulls a fire alarm in the absence of a fire. But that obviously would have been irrelevant to the case at hand. The proposition that pulling an alarm is not protected speech certainly leads to the conclusion that shouting the word "fire" is also not protected. But the core analogy is the nonverbal alarm, and the derivative example is the verbal shout. By cleverly substituting the derivative shout for the core alarm, Holmes made it possible to analogize one set of words to another—as he could not have done if he had begun with the self-evident proposition that setting off an alarm bell is not free speech.

The analogy is thus not only inapt but also insulting. Most Americans do not respond to political rhetoric with the same kind of automatic acceptance expected of schoolchildren responding to a fire drill. Not a single recipient of the Schenck pamphlet is known to have changed his mind after reading it. Indeed, one draftee, who appeared as a prosecution witness, was asked whether reading the pamphlet asserting that the draft law was unjust would make him "immediately decide that you must erase that law." Not surprisingly, he replied, "I do my own thinking." A theatergoer would probably not respond similarly if asked how he would react to a shout of "Fire!"

Another important reason why the analogy is inapt is that Holmes emphasizes the factual falsity of the shout "Fire!" The Schenck pamphlet, however, was not factually false. It contained political opinions and ideas about the causes of the war and about appropriate and lawful responses to the draft. As the Supreme Court recently reaffirmed (*in Falwell* v. *Hustler*), "The First Amendment recognizes no such thing as a 'false' idea." Nor does it recognize false opinions about the causes of or cures for war.

A closer analogy to the facts of the Schenck case might have been provided by a person's standing outside a theater, offering the patrons a leaflet advising them that in his opinion the theater was structurally unsafe, and urging them not to enter but to complain to the building inspectors. That analogy, however, would not have served Holmes's argument for punishing Schenck. Holmes needed an analogy that would appear relevant to Schenck's political speech but that would invite the conclusion that censorship was appropriate.

Unsurprisingly, a war-weary nation—in the throes of a know-nothing hysteria over immigrant anarchists and socialists—welcomed the comparison between what was regarded as a seditious political pamphlet and a malicious shout of "Fire!" Ironically, the "Fire!" analogy is nearly all that survives from the Schenck case; the ruling itself is almost certainly not good law. Pamphlets of the kind that resulted in Schenck's imprisonment have been circulated with impunity during subsequent wars.

Over the past several years I have assembled a collection of instance[s]—cases, speeches, arguments—in which proponents of censorship have maintained that the expression at issue is "just like" or "equivalent to" falsely shouting "Fire!" in a crowded theater and ought to be banned, "just as" shouting "Fire!" ought to be banned. The analogy is generally invoked, often with self-satisfaction, as an absolute argument-stopper. It does, after all, claim the high authority of the great Justice Oliver Wendell Holmes. I have rarely heard it invoked in a convincing, or even particularly relevant, way. But that, too, can claim lineage from the great Holmes.

Not unlike Falwell, with his silly comparison between shouting "Fire!" and publishing an offensive parody, courts and commentators have frequently invoked "Fire!" as an analogy to expression that is not an automatic stimulus to panic. A state supreme court held that "Holmes' aphorism . . . applies with equal force to pornography"—in particular to the exhibition of the movie *Carmen Baby* in a drive-in theater in close proximity to highways and homes. Another court analogized "picketing . . . in support of a secondary boycott" to shouting "Fire!" because in both instances "speech and conduct are brigaded." In the famous Skokie case one of the judges argued that allowing Nazis to march through a city where a large number of Holocaust survivors live "just might fall into the same category as one's 'right' to cry fire in a crowded theater."

Outside court the analogies become even more badly stretched. A spokesperson for the New Jersey Sports and Exposition Authority complained that newspaper reports to the effect that a large number of football players had contracted cancer after playing in the Meadowlands—a stadium atop a landfill—were the "journalistic equivalent of shouting fire in a crowded theater." An insect researcher acknowledged that his prediction that a certain amusement park might become roach-infested "may be tantamount to shouting fire in a crowded theater." The philosopher Sidney Hook, in a letter to the *New York Times* bemoaning a Supreme Court decision that required a plaintiff in a defamation action to prove that the offending statement was actually false, argued that the First Amendment does not give the press carte blanche to accuse innocent persons "anymore than the First Amendment protects the right of someone falsely to shout fire in a crowded theater."

Some close analogies to shouting "Fire!" or setting off an alarm are, of course, available: calling in a false bomb threat; dialing 911 and falsely describing an emergency; making a loud, gunlike sound in the presence of the President; setting off a voice-activated sprinkler system by falsely shouting "Fire!" In one case in which the "Fire!" analogy was directly to the point, a creative defendant tried to get around it. The case involved a man who calmly advised an airline clerk that he was "only here to hijack the plane." He was charged, in effect, with shouting "Fire!" in a crowded theater, and his rejected defense—as quoted by the court—was as follows: "If we built fireproof theaters and let people know about this, then the shouting of 'Fire!' would not cause panic."

Here are some more-distant but still related examples: the recent incident of the police slaying in which some members of an onlooking crowd urged a mentally ill vagrant who had taken an officer's gun to shoot the officer; the screaming of racial epithets during a tense confrontation; shouting down a speaker and preventing him from continuing his speech.

Analogies are, by their nature, matters of degree. Some are closer to the core example than others. But any attempt to analogize political ideas in a pamphlet, ugly parody in a magazine, offensive movies in a theater, controversial newspaper articles, or any of the other expressions and actions catalogued above to the very different act of shouting "Fire!" in a crowded theater is either self-deceptive or self-serving.

The government does, of course, have some arguably legitimate bases for suppressing speech which bear no relationship to shouting "Fire!" It may ban the publication of nuclear-weapon codes, of information about troop movements, and of the identity of undercover agents. It may criminalize extortion threats and conspiratorial agreements. These expressions may lead directly to serious harm, but the mechanisms of causation are very different from that at work when an alarm is sounded. One may also argue—less persuasively, in my view—against protecting certain forms of public obscenity and defamatory statements. Here, too, the mechanisms of causation are very different. None of these exceptions to the First Amendment's exhortation that the government "shall make no law . . . abridging the freedom of speech, or of the press" is anything like falsely shouting "Fire!" in a crowded theater; they all must be justified on other grounds.

A comedian once told his audience, during the stand-up routine, about the time he was standing around a fire with a crowd of people and got in trouble for yelling "Theater, theater!" That, I think, is about as clever and productive a use as anyone has ever made of Holmes's flawed analogy.

Reflections and Responses

1. Consider Dershowitz's analysis of Justice Holmes's decision in the Schenck case. What does Dershowitz find wrong with Holmes's reasoning? In what ways is Holmes's analogy "flawed"?

2. To what kinds of expression does Dershowitz find Holmes's analogy applicable? Go through Dershowitz's examples of protected and unprotected speech. Why is the "falsely shouting fire" analogy appropriate in some instances and not in others?

3. Consider Dershowitz's anecdote in the last paragraph about the comedian who yells "Theater, theater!" What was the comedian expressing? Why does Dershowitz find this response to Holmes's analogy "clever and productive"?

ANNE FADIMAN

Mail

Anne Fadiman's "Mail" grows out of a long literary tradition. Such essays, with their attention to everyday detail, their casual humor, intellectual curiosity, occasional idiosyncratic stance, and mixture of information, criticism, and entertainment, were once known as "familiar" essays. That literary designation disappeared more than a half-century ago; in fact, Fadiman's father, the distinguished American essayist Clifton Fadiman, noted this disappearance back in 1955 when he wrote "A Gentle Dirge for the Familiar Essay." The "familiar" essay took its name from the essayist's use of ordinary topics—such familiar subjects as taking walks or observing facial expressions or table manners—and from an agreeable style or tone that was neither too formal or too informal. Unlike today's confessional or autobiographically oriented personal essays, the familiar essay had a subject other than the self, though the writer usually approached the subject from a decidedly personal perspective. In "Mail," Anne Fadiman looks at a new phenomenon that has become familiar to millions—electronic mail—and ruminates on its relation to her father's old-fashioned habits of letter writing and even the history of the postal service. Along the way, she raises some significant questions about modern technology and the price we sometimes pay for its efficiency and convenience.

Anne Fadiman's The Spirit Catches You and You Fall Down *(1997) won the National Book Critics Circle Award for general nonfiction.* Ex Libris *(1998) is a collection of essays on reading and language. A winner of the National Magazine Award for both reporting and essays, she has contributed articles and essays to* Civilization, The New Yorker, Harper's, *and the* New York Times, *among other publications. She lives in western Massachusetts and teaches writing at Yale University. She was the editor of* The Best American Essays *2003. Her most recent collection is* At Large and At Small: Familar Essays *(2007). "Mail" originally appeared in* The American Scholar, *a magazine she edited for seven years, and was selected by Kathleen Norris for* The Best American Essays *2001.*

Some years ago, my parents lived at the top of a steep hill. My father kept a pair of binoculars on his desk with which, like a pirate captain hoisting his spyglass to scan the horizon for treasure ships, he periodically inspected the mailbox to see if the flag had been raised. When it finally went up, he trudged down the driveway and opened the extra-large black metal box, purchased by my mother in the same accommodating spirit with which some wives buy their husbands extra-large trousers. The day's load—a mountain of letters and about twenty pounds of review books packed in Jiffy bags, a few of which had been pierced by their angular contents and were leaking what my father called "mouse dirt"—was always tightly

Howard Grey/Getty Images

wedged. But he was a persistent man, and after a brief show of resistance the mail would surrender, to be carried up the hill in a tight clinch and dumped onto a gigantic desk. Until that moment, my father's day had not truly begun.

His desk was made of steel, weighed more than a refrigerator, and bristled with bookshelves and secret drawers and sliding panels and a niche for a cedar-lined humidor. (He believed that cigar-smoking and mail-reading were natural partners, like oysters and Muscadet.) I think of it as less a writing surface than a mail-sorting table. He hated Sundays and holidays because there was nothing new to spread on it. Vacations were taxing, the equivalent of forced relocations to places without food. His homecomings were always followed by day-long orgies of mail-opening—feast after famine—at the end of which all the letters were answered; all the bills were paid; the outgoing envelopes were affixed with stamps from a brass dispenser heavy enough to break your toe; the books and manuscripts were neatly stacked; and the empty Jiffy bags were stuffed into an extra-large copper wastebasket, cheering confirmation that the process of postal digestion was complete.

"One of my unfailing minor pleasures may seem dull to more energetic souls: opening the mail," he once wrote.

> Living in an advanced industrial civilization is a kind of near-conquest over the unexpected. . . . Such efficiency is of course admirable. It does not, however, by its very nature afford scope to that perverse human trait, still not quite eliminated, which is pleased by the accidental. Thus to many tame citizens like me the morning mail functions as the voice of the unpredictable and keeps alive for a few minutes a day the keen sense of the unplanned and the unplannable. The letter opener is an instrument that has persisted from some antique land of chance and adventure into our ordered world of the perfectly calculated.

What chance and adventure might the day's haul contain? My brother asked him, when he was in his nineties, what kind of mail he liked best. "In my youth," he replied, "a love letter. In middle age, a job offer. Today, a check." (That was false cynicism, I think. His favorite letters were from his friends.) Whatever the accidental pleasure, it could not please until it arrived. Why were deliveries so few and so late (he frequently grumbled), when, had he lived in

central London in the late seventeenth century, he could have received his mail between ten and twelve times a day?

We get what we need. In 1680, London had mail service nearly
every hour because there were no telephones. If you wished to invite someone to tea in the afternoon, you could send him a letter
in the morning and receive his reply before he showed up at your
doorstep. Postage was one penny.

If you wished to send a letter to another town, however, delivery
was less reliable and postage was gauged on a scale of staggering
complexity. By the mid-1830s,

> the postage on a single letter delivered within eight miles of the office
> where it was posted was . . . twopence, the lowest rate beyond that limit
> being fourpence. Beyond fifteen miles it became fivepence; after which
> it rose a penny at a time, but by irregular augmentation, to one shilling,
> the charge for three hundred miles. There was as a general rule an ad-
> ditional charge of a half penny on a letter crossing the Scotch border;
> while letters to or from Ireland had to bear, in addition, packet rates,
> and rates for crossing the bridges over the Conway and the Menai.

So wrote Rowland Hill, the greatest postal reformer in history, who
in 1837 devised a scheme to reduce and standardize postal rates and
to shift the burden of payment from the addressee to the sender.

Until a few years ago I had no idea that if you sent a letter out of
town—and if you weren't a nobleman, a member of Parliament, or
other VIP who had been granted the privilege of free postal franking—the postage was paid by the recipient. This dawned on me
when I was reading a biography of Charles Lamb, whose employer,
the East India House, allowed clerks to receive letters gratis until
1817: a substantial perk, sort of like being able to call your friends
on your office's 800 number. (Lamb, who practiced stringent
economies, also wrote much of his personal correspondence on
company stationery. His most famous letter to Wordsworth, for instance—the one in which he refers to Coleridge as "an Archangel
a little damaged"—is inscribed on a page whose heading reads
"Please to state the Weights and Amounts of the following Lots.")

Sir Walter Scott liked to tell the story of how he had once had to
pay "five pounds odd" in order to receive a package from a young
New York lady he had never met: an atrocious play called *The Cherokee*

Lovers, accompanied by a request to read it, correct it, write a prologue, and secure a producer. Two weeks later another large package arrived for which he was charged a similar amount. "Conceive my horror," he told his friend Lord Melville, "when out jumped the same identical tragedy of *The Cherokee Lovers*, with a second epistle from the authoress, stating that, as the winds had been boisterous, she feared the vessel entrusted with her former communication might have foundered, and therefore judged it prudent to forward a duplicate." Lord Melville doubtless found this tale hilarious, but Rowland Hill would have been appalled. He had grown up poor, and, as Christopher Browne notes in *Getting the Message*, his splendid history of the British postal system, "Hill had never forgotten his mother's anxiety when a letter with a high postal duty was delivered, nor the time when she sent him out to sell a bag of clothes to raise 3*s* for a batch of letters."

Hill was a born Utilitarian who, at the age of twelve, had been so frustrated by the irregularity of the bell at the school where his father was principal that he had instituted a precisely timed bell-ringing schedule. In 1837 he published a report called "Post Office Reform: Its Importance and Practicability." Why, he argued, should legions of accountants be employed to figure out the Byzantine postal charges? Why should Britain's extortionate postal rates persist when France's revenues had risen, thanks to higher mail volume, after its rates were lowered? Why should postmen waste precious time waiting for absent addressees to come home and pay up? A national Penny Post was the answer, with postage paid by the senders, "using a bit of paper . . . covered at the back with a glutinous wash, which the bringer might, by the application of a little moisture, attach to the back of the letter."

After much debate, Parliament passed a postal reform act in 1839. On January 10, 1840, Hill wrote in his diary, "Penny Postage extended to the whole kingdom this day! . . . I guess that the number despatched to-night will not be less than 100,000, or more than three times what it was this day twelve-months. If less I shall be disappointed." On January 11, he wrote, "The number of letters despatched exceeded all expectation. It was 112,000, of which all but 13,000 or 14,000 were prepaid." In May, after experimentation to produce a canceling ink that could not be surreptitiously removed, the Post Office introduced the Penny Black, bearing a profile of

Queen Victoria: the first postage stamp. The press, pondering the process of cancellation, fretted about the "untoward disfiguration of the royal person," but Victoria became an enthusiastic philatelist, and renounced the royal franking privilege for the pleasure of walking to the local post office from Balmoral Castle to stock up on stamps and gossip with the postmaster. When Rowland Hill—by that time, *Sir* Rowland Hill—retired as Post Office Secretary in 1864, *Punch* asked, "SHOULD ROWLAND HILL have a Statue? Certainly, if OLIVER CROMWELL should. For one is celebrated for cutting off the head of a bad King, and the other for sticking on the head of a good Queen."

The Penny Post, wrote Harriet Martineau, "will do more for the circulation of ideas, for the fostering of domestic affections, for the humanizing of the mass generally, than any other single measure that our national wit can devise." It was incontrovertible proof, in an age that embraced progress on all fronts ("the means of locomotion and correspondence, every mechanical art, every manufacture, every thing that promotes the convenience of life," as Macaulay put it in a typical gush of national pride), that the British were the most civilized people on earth. Ancient Syrian runners, Chinese carrier pigeons, Persian post riders, Egyptian papyrus bearers, Greek *hemerodromes*, Hebrew dromedary riders, Roman equestrian relays, medieval monk-messengers, Catalan *troters*, international couriers of the House of Thurn and Taxis, American mail wagons—what could these all have been leading up to, like an ever-ascending staircase, but the Victorian postal system?

And yet (to raise a subversive question), might it be possible that, whatever the profit in efficiency, there may have been a literary cost associated with the conversion from payment by addressee to payment by sender? If you knew that your recipient would have to bear the cost of your letter, wouldn't courtesy motivate you to write an extra-good one? On the other hand, if you paid for it yourself, wouldn't you be more likely to feel you could get away with "Having a wonderful time, wish you were here"?

I used to think my father's attachment to the mail was strange. I now feel exactly the way he did. I live in an apartment building and, with or without binoculars, I cannot see my mailbox, one of thirteen dinky aluminum cells bolted to the lobby wall. The mail usually comes around four in the afternoon (proving that the postal staircase that reached its highest point with Rowland Hill has been descending ever since), which means that at around three, *just in case*, I'm likely to visit the lobby for the first of several reconnaissance missions. There's no flag, but over the years my fingers have become postally sensitive, and I can tell if the box is full by giving it the slightest of pats. If there's a hint of convexity—it's very subtle, nothing as obvious, let us say, as the bulge of a can that might harbor botulism—I whip out my key with the same excitement with which my father set forth down his driveway.

There the resemblance ends. The thrill of the treasure hunt is followed all too quickly by the glum realization that the box contains only four kinds of mail: (1) junk, (2) bills, (3) work, and (4) letters that I will read with enjoyment, place in a folder labeled "To Answer," leave there for a geologic interval, and feel guilty about. The longer they languish, the more I despair of my ability to live up to the escalating challenge of their response. It is a truism of epistolary psychology that, for example, a Christmas thank-you note written on December 26 can say any old thing, but if you wait until February, you are convinced that nothing less than *Middlemarch* will do.

In October of 1998 I finally gave in and signed up for e-mail. I had resisted for a long time. My husband and I were proud of our retrograde status. Not only did we lack a modem, but we didn't have a car, a microwave, a Cuisinart, an electric can opener, a cellular phone, a CD player, or cable television. It's hard to give up that sort of backward image; I worried that our friends wouldn't have enough to make fun of. I also worried that learning how to use e-mail would be like learning how to program our VCR, an unsuccessful project that had confirmed what excellent judgment we had shown in not purchasing a car, etc.

As millions of people had discovered before me, e-mail was fast. Sixteenth-century correspondents used to write "Haste, haste, haste, for lyfe, for lyfe, haste!" on their most urgent letters; my "server," a word that conjured up a delicious sycophancy, treated *every* message as if someone's life depended on it. Not only did it get there instantly, caromed in a series of analog cyberpackets along the nodes of the Internet and reconverted to digital form via its recipient's modem. (I do not understand a word of what I just wrote, but that is immaterial. Could the average Victorian have diagrammed the mail coach route from Swansea to Tunbridge

Wells?) More important, I *answered* e-mail fast—almost always on the day it arrived. No more guilt! I used to think I did not like to write letters. I now realize that what I didn't like was folding the paper, sealing the envelope, looking up the address, licking the stamp, getting in the elevator, crossing the street, and dropping the letter in the postbox.

At first I made plenty of mistakes. I clicked on the wrong icons, my attachments didn't stick, and, not having learned how to file addresses, I sent an X-rated message to my husband (I thought) at gcolt @aol.com instead of georgecolt@aol.com. I hope Gerald or Gertrude found it flattering. But the learning curve was as steep as my father's driveway, and pretty soon I was batting out fifteen or twenty e-mails a day in the time it had once taken me to avoid answering a single letter. My box was nearly always full—no waiting, no binoculars, no convexity checks, no tugging—and when it wasn't, the reason was not that the mail hadn't *arrived*, it was that it hadn't been *sent*. I began to look forward every morning to the festive green arrow with which AT&T WorldNet welcomed me into my father's "antique land of chance and adventure." Would I be invited to purchase Viagra, lose thirty pounds, regrow my thinning hair, obtain electronic spy software, get an EZ loan, retire in three years, or win a Pentium III 500 MHz computer (presumably in order to receive such messages even faster)? Or would I find a satisfying little clutch of friendly notes whose responses could occupy me until I awoke sufficiently to tackle something that required intelligence? As Hemingway wrote to Fitzgerald, describing the act of letter-writing: "Such a swell way to keep from working and yet feel you've done something."

My computer, without visible distension, managed to store a flood tide of mail that in nonvirtual form would have silted up my office to the ceiling. This was admirable. And when I wished to commune with my friend Charlie, who lives in Taipei, not only could I disregard the thirteen-hour time difference, but I was billed the same amount as if I had dialed his old telephone number on East 22nd Street. The German critic Bernhard Siegert has observed that the breakthrough concept behind Rowland Hill's Penny Post was "to think of all Great Britain as a single city, that is, no longer to give a moment's thought to what had been dear to Western discourse on the nature of the letter from the beginning:

the idea of distance." E-mail is a modern Penny Post: the world is a single city with a single postal rate.

Alas, our Penny Post, like Hill's, comes at a price. If the transfer of postal charges from sender to recipient was the first great demotivator in the art of letter-writing, e-mail was the second. "It now seems a good bet," Adam Gopnik has written, "that in two hundred years people will be reading someone's collected e-mail the way we read Edmund Wilson's diaries or Pepys's letters." Maybe—but will what they read be any good? E-mails are brief. (One doesn't blather; an overlong message might induce carpal tunnel syndrome in the recipient from excessive pressure on the Down arrow.) They are also—at least the ones I receive—frequently devoid of capitalization, minimally punctuated, and creatively spelled. E-mail's greatest strength—speed—is also its Achilles' heel. In effect, it's always December 26; you are not expected to write *Middlemarch*, and therefore you don't.

In a letter to his friend William Unwin, written on August 6, 1780, William Cowper noted that "a Letter may be written upon any thing or Nothing." This observation is supported by the index of *The Faber Book of Letters,* 1578–1939. Let us examine some entries from the *d* section:

damnation, 87
dances and entertainments, 33, 48, 59, 97, 111, 275
dentistry, 220
depressive illness, 81, 87
Dictionary of the English Language, Johnson's, 61
Diggers, 22
dolphins, methods of cooking, 37

I have never received an e-mail on any of these topics. Instead, I am informed that *Your browser is not Y2K-compliant. Your son left his Pokémon turtle under our sofa. Your column is 23 lines too long.* Important pieces of news, but, as Lytton Strachey (one of the all-time great letter writers) pointed out, "No good letter was ever written to convey information, or to please its recipient: it may achieve both these results incidentally; but its fundamental purpose is to express the personality of its writer." *But wait!* you pipe up. *Someone just e-mailed me a joke!* So she did, but wasn't the personality of the sender slightly muffled by the fact that she forwarded it from an e-mail *she* received, and sent it to seventeen additional addressees?

I also take a dim, or perhaps a buffaloed, view of electronic slang. Perhaps I should view it as a linguistic milestone, as historic as the evolution of Cockney rhyming slang in the 1840s. But will the future generations who reopen our hard drives be stirred by the eloquence of the e-acronyms recommended by a Web site on "netiquette"?

BTDT	been there done that
FC	fingers crossed
IITYWTMWYBMAD	if I tell you what this means will you buy me a drink?
MTE	my thoughts exactly
ROTFL	rolling on the floor laughing
RTFM	read the f—— manual
TAH	take a hint
TTFN	ta-ta for now

Or by the "emoticons," otherwise known as "smileys"—punctuational images, read sideways—that "help readers interpret the e-mail writer's attitude and tone"?

:-)	ha ha
:-(	boo hoo
(-:	I am left-handed
%-)	I have been staring at a green screen for 15 hours straight
:-&	I am tongue-tied
{:-)	I wear a toupee
:-[	I am a vampire
:-F	I am a bucktoothed vampire with one tooth missing
=l:-)=	I am Abraham Lincoln

"We are of a different race from the Greeks, to whom beauty was everything," wrote Thomas Carlyle, a Victorian progress-booster. "Our glory and our beauty arise out of our inward strength, which makes us victorious over material resistance." We have achieved a similar victory of efficiency over beauty. I wouldn't give up e-mail if you paid me, but I'd feel a pang of regret if the epistolary novels of the future were to revolve around such messages as

Subject: **R U Kidding?**
From: Clarissa Harlowe <claha@virtue.com>
To: Robert Lovelace <lovelaceandlovegirlz@vice.com

hi bob, TAH. if u think i'm gonna run off w/ u, :-F, do u really think i'm
that kind of girl?? if you're looking 4 a trollop, CLICK HERE NOW:
http://www.hotpix.html. TTFN.

I own a letter written by Robert Falcon Scott, the polar explorer, to
G. T. Temple, Esq., who helped procure the footgear for Scott's
first Antarctic expedition. The date is February 26, 1901. The
envelope and octavo stationery have black borders because Queen
Victoria had died in January. The paper is yellowed, the handwriting is messy, and the stamp bears the Queen's profile—and the
denomination ONE PENNY. I bought the letter many years ago
because, unlike a Cuisinart, which would have cost about the same,
it was something I believed I could not live without. I could never
feel that way about an e-mail.

I also own my father's old wastebasket, which now holds my own
empty Jiffy bags. Several times a day I use his stamp dispenser; it is
tarnished and dinged, but still capable of unspooling its contents
with a singular smoothness. And my file cabinets hold hundreds of
his letters, the earliest written in his sixties in small, crabbed handwriting, the last in his nineties, after he lost much of his sight,
penned with a Magic Marker in huge capital letters. I hope my
children will find them someday, as Hart Crane once found his
grandmother's love letters in the attic,

> pressed so long
> Into a corner of the roof
> That they are brown and soft,
> And liable to melt as snow.

Reflections and Responses

1. Note the perspective from which Anne Fadiman opens her essay.
Can you find other sections of the essay that you think could also

have served as a beginning? Why do you think she doesn't begin
with the earliest time and end in the present?

2. A portion of the essay is taken up by her brief history of the British postal system. How does she integrate this information into the
essay? What associations does she make between that history and
our present system of communication? How is her movement
between various time periods reflected in the way she crafts her
sentences? Find examples of how she constructs single sentences
that link various eras.

3. What specific images does Fadiman use to contrast her father's
time with her own? How does she evaluate each era? What aspects
of her father's time does she appear to prefer? How does she avoid
being completely nostalgic about the past? In what ways does
Fadiman's essay resemble Scott Russell Sanders's "The Inheritance
of Tools"?

GEORGE GESSERT

An Orgy of Power

In May 2004, the New Yorker *magazine published shocking photos showing United States military personnel treating prisoners at the Abu Ghraib prison in occupied Baghdad in ways that most people classified immediately as torture. Americans have always prided themselves in the fair treatment of even their worst enemies; consequently the photos appalled the world community and called into question many of the premises on which the invasion of Iraq had been launched the previous year. In this remarkable essay, part personal and part political, George Gessert examines his own reaction to the revelations of Abu Ghraib, and considers the horror of torture itself. Quoting Austrian essayist Jean Améry, Gessert concludes that torture is borne of our "innate drive for unchecked self-expansion," and that the torturers, like their victims, are human beings, "capable of beautiful behavior and terrible behavior, individually and collectively."*

George Gessert is an artist prominent in the bio-art movement, which uses living matter as a medium. His work has been exhibited widely in the United States, Australia, and Europe. His writing, meanwhile, has appeared in several anthologies, including Biomediale, Art et Biotechnologies, *and* The Aesthetics of Care. *He is an editor at the journal* Leonardo, *and won a Pushcart Prize in 2005.* "An Orgy of Power" *was selected by David Foster Wallace for* The Best American Essays 2007.

I am reluctant to write about torture. It holds no special fascination for me—on the contrary, I find the subject repellent. But I did not choose the times I live in, nor do I choose what I am compelled to write. As a writer I am committed to speaking from my own experience, which may seem to counsel silence. I have not been to Iraq, Afghanistan, or Guantánamo Bay. I am not a journalist or an authority on the history of torture. But the perimeters of experience do not end with what is immediate. In today's world, almost everything connects with everything else. The coffee that fuels my editing was raised in Kenya, my shirt was made in China. Reports arrive daily from around the world. The problem is sorting the relevant from the irrelevant, the true from the false, and assigning each bit of information something like its proper weight. These things make learning gradual, writing slow, and these notes very late.

In August 2002, following the battle of Konduz in Afghanistan, I read puzzling reports on the Internet. More than two hundred prisoners taken at Konduz had been found dead in a mass grave. They had died of heat, dehydration, and suffocation after being sealed in metal containers for transport to Shabarghan prison. The U.S. role in the deaths was unclear, and to date has not been properly investigated, although the number of victims is now put at a thousand. However, the U.S. Army's Special Forces seems to have been involved.[1]

The media gave extensive attention to one captive, John Walker Lindh. He was a twenty-one-year-old Californian who had converted to Islam, and trained in Afghanistan to fight the Northern Alliance. He had arrived at the front lines before September 11. We now know that he had no advance knowledge of the attacks on New York and Washington, D.C., and that reports he heard afterward were sketchy. Following his capture he was separated from other prisoners and allegedly tortured.

The accounts that I read at the time said that Lindh had been handcuffed, blindfolded, and photographed. Some of his captors were hostile to him and did not treat a wound in his leg. But how was this torture? I wondered if Lindh's family and lawyer were making exaggerated claims in an attempt to win public sympathy for the young man and save him from the death sentence he could face if charged with aiding the enemy. Only much later did I read that Lindh had had a bullet in his leg, and U.S. agents had left the bullet there while they interrogated him, which had gone on until the wound became "seeping and malodorous." Lindh received death threats, and his hands were cuffed so tightly that he was in intense pain. He was confined in a metal shipping container, and suffered extended exposure to cold.[2]

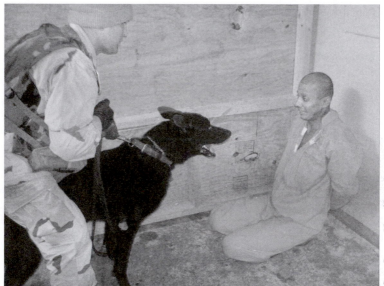

Getty Images News/Getty Images

For almost a year after the battle of Konduz I read sketchy and ambiguous reports of prisoner mistreatment. I was not sure what to make of them. Then came the pictures from Abu Ghraib and overwhelming evidence that detainees had been tortured. They had been tortured not only in Iraq, but in Afghanistan and an archipelago of prisons around the world. Documents surfaced, such as the so-called torture memo of August 1, 2002, showing that very close associates of President Bush, apparently with his full approval, had encouraged torture.[3]

Lions and hyenas kill swiftly. Housecats play with their victims, but only to practice pouncing, not to cause pain. Tapeworms and the shingles virus keep their victims alive as sources of sustenance, not to cause pain. Only humans torture.

In many societies torture was open and acceptable. The Romans made elaborate forms of animal and human torture into public entertainments. During the Inquisition torture served the Church. But

from the earliest days of the republic Americans have defined themselves as the people who are opposed to "cruel and unusual punishments." The Eighth Amendment to the Constitution provides a legal
groundwork for putting this ideal into practice. By the twentieth century, the United States had become an international leader in outlaw-
ing torture. Along the way some Americans engaged in torture, but
cruel and unusual punishments, variously defined, have been forbidden for so long as to seem somehow foreign and un-American. Consequently most Americans are unaccustomed to discussing torture,
much less torture done with encouragement from the president.

A few days ago a letter appeared in our local newspaper repeating
the familiar claim that nothing worse happened at Abu Ghraib than
happens in fraternity hazings. This simile has cropped up in local
and national media ever since Rush Limbaugh gave it his imprimatur on May 4, 2004, on his show "It's Not About Us; This Is War."

> CALLER: It was like a college fraternity prank that stacked up
>   naked men . . .
> LIMBAUGH: Exactly. Exactly my point. This is no different than what hap-
>   pens at the Skull and Bones* initiation . . . I'm talking about
>   people having a good time, these people, you ever heard of
>   emotional release? You ever heard of need to blow off some
>   steam?

No doubt stress relief was a factor in what happened, and not
only at Abu Ghraib. An army sergeant, describing events at Camp
Mercury, near Fallujah, reported that "everyone in camp knew if
you wanted to work out your frustrations you show up" at the PUC
tent. PUC, pronouced "puck," stands for person under control,
the term that has replaced POW, or prisoner of war, which evokes
the Geneva Conventions. As an example of someone working out
his frustrations, the sergeant told of a cook who on his day off
went to the PUC tent and broke a prisoner's leg with a Louisville
Slugger, a metal baseball bat.[4]

I am not shocked by war photographs. They are all too familiar. I
have seen too many images of the dead and wounded, too many

---

*Skull and Bones: an exclusive, fraternity-like society at Yale University.

mutilated children, too many body parts in black-and-white and in color, and far too many grief-stricken survivors. Long ago, without ever making a conscious decision, I became detached. But my automatic defenses did not work with the photographs from Abu Ghraib. Their extraordinary power arose from the novelty of their subject matter, their striking resemblance to pornography, and their absolute authenticity. I doubt that any professional photographer or trained artist could have created such damning images.

The tormenters are my fellow countrymen and -women. They look like people on the street, and from all reports they are ordinary citizens. But the prisoners, in their fear, anguish, and humiliation, are more immediately recognizable as human beings—even with digitally blanked-out faces.

Of the many photographs from Abu Ghraib (the Pentagon may hold thousands), so far only about two dozen have entered the public realm.[5] After seeing a dozen or so photographs, I began to follow news about torture. This led me to pay attention to how public discussion was being framed. Beginning in March 2004, when the first photographs became public, the media adopted the administration's preferred word, "abuse," to describe what had happened at Abu Ghraib. "Abuse" covers a range of activities, but is not ordinarily used to describe attempted male rape, which is what some of the photographs show. We do not ordinarily call homicide "abuse," and yet one of the photographs is of a man who had evidently been beaten to death. The media could have corrected itself when those reports were confirmed, and when evidence emergéd that detainees at Abu Ghraib, Guantánamo Bay, Bagram Air Base, and elsewhere had been forced to maintain stress positions until passing out, reports of cigarettes being put out in a detainee's ears, evidence of blows that liquefied muscles and produced strokes, and of many other clear instances of torture. But even today the media persists in using the unmodified word "abuse." Why? Perhaps reporters and media executives fear the administration. Fear is not unreasonable. The Bush administration has been unsparingly hostile and vindictive toward critics. Or perhaps mainstream reporters and those who manage the media fear the public, the greater part of which until very recently has supported the president. As I write, a *Newsweek* poll shows that about half of the American public approve of torture.[6] But whatever the reasons for the media's reluctance to use the word "torture," at what point do denial, fear, and caution shade into complicity?

To the media's credit, it has brought news of torture to the attention of U.S. citizens and to the world. Who is ultimately responsible, the major media or individuals, for determining the moral weight of tossing the body of a murdered man into his sister's cell, as reported by the *Los Angeles Times*? Is it torture when a man is nearly drowned by having his head forced into a toilet, as we learn happened at Guantánamo Bay from an article in the *Washington Post*? Is a broken jaw less painful if it is noted on page 10 than on page 1?

The United States may not have as monumental a literature of war as Russia, or as desolating a one as Germany, but in any good public library one can find vivid descriptions of Americans at war, read about the ordeals and boredom and camaraderie of soldiers, gain some sense of the appeals and horrors of combat, and learn about its aftermath. We also have literature about the home front, about the women and children, the parents waiting for the knock on the door—typically with neighbors determinedly oblivious of what is happening.

But torture plays only the most minor role in our literature. *The Pit and the Pendulum,* if It can be said to describe torture at all, reads like an overheated fantasy. In Faulkner's *Sanctuary* an impotent gangster named Popeye rapes a girl with a corncob. A mob mutilates and murders Joe Christmas in *Light in August.* In Robert Stone's *Dog Soldiers* two drug dealers use a heated clotiies iron to terrorize a man into surrendering heroin that he has smuggled into California. In *A Flag for Sunrise an* American nun is tortured in a fictitious Central American country. But such passages only underscore a near absence in our literature. Our literature does not fathom torture. Torture by Americans has spread in a vacuum of language.

Painting and filmmaking have prepared us slightly better. Leon Golub devoted much of his career to painting torturers and their victims. During the Vietnam War Peter Saul painted terrifying, cartoonlike fantasies that map a peculiarly American approach to torture. And *Reservoir Dogs* brought unaestheticized images and sounds of torture to a mass audience. In small ways, perhaps, our visual culture has helped educate us to see the photographs from Abu Ghraib.

Susan Sontag observed that the grins on the faces of U.S. soldiers
in photographs from Abu Ghraib resemble those on white faces in
photographs of lynchings.[7] Schoolyard bullies have the same smile.
The truth that the bully and the torturer share is the truth of unre-
strained power, but the bully only glimpses it, while the lyncher
and the torturer realize it.

Jean Améry, who was tortured by the Gestapo in Fort Breendonk
in Belgium in 1943, remembered the faces of his torturers as "not
'Gestapo faces' with twisted noses, hypertrophied chins, pock-
marks and knife scars, as they might appear in a book, but rather
faces like anyone else's. Plain, ordinary faces." During torture,
these plain, ordinary faces became "concentrated in murderous
self-realization. With heart and soul they went about their business,
and the name of it was power, domination over spirit and flesh, an
orgy of unchecked self-expansion."[8]

Hannah Arendt's insight into the banality of evil applies to bureau-
crats and ordinary citizens far removed from the suffering that they
cause, but according to Améry does not apply to the men and women
who do the actual work of destruction. Améry claims an authority in
this regard that exceeds Arendt's, since Arendt was never tortured.
The act of torture, he writes, destroys ordinary social bonds and relationships, and propels the torturer far beyond the realm of daily life.
The torturer engages in what Elaine Scarry calls "the unmaking of
civilization . . . [and the] uncreating of the created world."[9]

"An orgy of unchecked self-expansion": Améry's phrase, with its
Sadean* grandiosity, is consistent with the smiles on American faces at
Abu Ghraib. The reward of torture, according to Améry, is "murderous
self-realization." Self-realization in this context suggests a return,
however brief, to infantile omnipotence. The smile of the torturer is la-
tent within everyone.

The torturer and his or her superiors mimic God. They and they
alone determine who is guilty, what is right, and what is wrong. It
comes as no surprise, then, that according to the International
Committee of the Red Cross, between 70 and 90 percent of the
thousands detained at Abu Ghraib had been arrested "by

***Sadean:** like the Marquis de Sade, who wrote of sexual torture in 18th-century
France.

mistake."[10] Reportedly these were among the victims of torture. At least one hundred prisoners were children. We have less information about the prisoners at Guantánamo Bay, but we know that among them are children and demented old men. Destruction of the innocent is the most incontrovertible proof of power.

Unchecked self-expansion is also consistent with what we know about the Bush administration's efforts to legitimize torture. Many military and intelligence experts claim that torture does not yield reliable information, endangers U.S. prisoners of war, and can serve enemies as a recruitment tool. Other intelligence experts disagree, claiming that torture can yield useful information, and may terrorize opponents, but comes at too high a price: loss of American prestige internationally and corruption of the military. Pragmatic objections to torture are convincing only if national honor and the well-being of our troops and citizens are primary concerns. The administration has had a very different, overriding concern: that the president not be restrained by the Geneva Conventions or the Constitution as traditionally interpreted. We do not need to psychoanalyze George W. Bush or understand the inner life of Dick Cheney to recognize broad patterns in their behavior. Their primary concern is and has been power, irrespective of traditional morality or law.

As every dreamer learns sooner or later, and as the framers of the Constitution, who were hardly sentimental about humankind, knew very well, something in us would sculpt the universe. In itself this is neither good nor bad; it is simply a psychological phenomenon. It informs everything from law to art to child rearing to exploration of the solar system. But it also produces tyranny.

Améry considered torture an essential feature of totalitarian rule. Under German fascism, torture became "the total inversion of the social world . . . in the world of torture man exists only by ruining the other person who stands before him."[11] Améry's insights are relevant to us because although the United States is profoundly unlike Nazi Germany, our society accommodates not only democratic practices but undemocratic ones, including outright totalitarian rule as at Abu Ghraib and Guantánamo Bay. For several decades torture has been a feature of U.S. proxy wars, clandestine campaigns, CIA actions, and partnerships with military regimes and death squads. From the 1970s to the 1990s American involvement in torture, especially in Latin America, surfaced from time to time in the media. Numerous reports focused on the School of the Americas (renamed the Western Hemisphere Institute for Security Cooperation in 2001). In 1996 the Pentagon was forced to release school training manuals that taught torture. However, the mainstream media usually characterized the role of the School of the Americas in torture as indirect, and downplayed instances of direct involvement as aberrations.[12]

Until photographs from Abu Ghraib were aired on national television, most Americans probably did not know that their government sometimes encouraged torture. Or, if they did know, they could tell themselves that it was quite rare—this was what I believed. I believed that torture by Americans existed, but involved very few people and played a very small role in American foreign policy. Relative to other extremely serious problems, such as mass extinctions, global warming, the spread of nuclear weapons, and the population explosion, torture was distinctly less important. I still think that in a very general way this is true, but my failure to comprehend what was happening arose from not wanting to think about torture, from a sense of having no personal connection with torture or the tortured, and from the reports themselves. Arriving intermittently from distant places, the words seemed ghostly and insubstantial in their horror. They needed a catalyst to gain psychological substance. Photographs from Abu Ghraib provided the catalyst.

Writing these notes, I held on to the belief that I had no personal connection to the tortured. I had almost completed my notes (or so I thought) when I began to think about the long-term effects of torture. I began to think about friends who had lost family in the Holocaust—was torture involved? How does torture affect the second and third generations? How does not knowing whether a close relative had been tortured affect a family? I thought about a boy I played with when I was in junior high school. His family was from Armenia. I recalled his mother telling me that the family had arrived in the United States in 1920, but I never learned more. Then there was the doctor from El Salvador who for a short time cleaned house for my mother. What was his story? What was his family's story? I realized that I did not know my degrees of separation from the tortured, or from torturers.

But this too was a trick that I played on myself. Years ago, at a conference in São Paulo, I became acquainted with an amateur scholar of Paracas culture. He was Brazilian, perhaps fifteen years my senior, tall and distinguished-looking, and one evening at dinner he told me in excellent, German-inflected English about his many visits to Nasca to see the ancient earthworks there. The Nasca Lines, which were scraped into the earth some eighteen hundred years ago and stretch for miles across the desert floor, are some of the largest artworks in the world. What they meant to their creators no one knows, but because weaving played a central role in Paracas culture, some authorities believe that the lines diagram the loom of the stars.

I asked him if he had ever seen the lines at night.

"Once," he said. "It was as I imagine the beginning of the universe, and the end. " For me that was the beginning of our friendship.

Over the next twelve years we corresponded, mostly about Paracas art but also about ourselves. His father, I learned, had been involved in the 1944 attempt to assassinate Hitler. But we did not discuss this. He made it clear mat he did not want me to ask questions. "I never think about it," he wrote. I could only begin to imagine his situation. I had read that the plotters were tortured to death after they were captured. His father had sent him to boarding school in Switzerland, which probably saved his life. From there his mother took him to Brazil.

Several years ago, in declining health, he shot himself. He bungled the attempt and took two months to die.

Writing these notes, I turned to novels for relief, a safe haven from the subject of torture, or so I assumed, typically American. The tide character in J. M. Coetzee's *Elizabeth Costello* is a distinguished novelist, navigating the mildly hazardous waters of literary fame. She uses her renown to speak out for animals suffering under industrialism, comparing them with the victims of the Holocaust. Strongly criticized for making this comparison, she reads Paul West's *The Very Rich Hours of Count von Stauffenberg*, a history of the 1944 Plot to assassinate Hitler. West recounts in detail how the plotters were tortured to death, and their agonies were filmed so that the Führer could replay them at his leisure. Elizabeth Costello is so wounded by horror that she publically attacks the author and tells him that he should never have written his book. There is such a thing as too much knowledge.

I found myself arguing with her. The written word, except for a few works of poetry, never provides more than incomplete knowledge. Reading cannot provide too much knowledge, but timing is everything. The art of reading involves intuiting when to read and when not. As readers, we do not enlarge ourselves by taking no risks, but even a masterpiece read at the wrong time is a waste of time, or worse.

If I knew then what I know today, I could have been a better friend. Right now I do not have the heart to read more about what happened to my dead friend's father. But when the time is right I will do the reading.

The outbreak of torture today is different from previous torture by Americans in three significant ways. First, the Bush administration carefully laid the groundwork for torture. In previous wars torture did not result directly from White House planning, even if commanding officers and their civilian superiors were willing to avert their eyes when it occurred. Second, the administration and the Pentagon, for all of their formidable skills in managing imagery, did not take digital cameras and the Internet into account. Third, more information about torture by Americans is available today than ever before.

The election of 2004 was an indirect referendum on torture. Neither George Bush nor John Kerry made torture an election issue, but reports about what had happened at Abu Ghraib and what was happening at Guantánamo Bay and elsewhere appeared intermittently in the major media throughout the campaign. The election confirmed what both candidates apparently knew from the beginning, that torture would bear no political price.

As I write, all that is necessary to practice torture outside the country on noncitizens, and on citizens such as John Lindh, is to maintain a measure of secrecy abroad, and appearances domestically. President Bush has attempted to accomplish the latter by condemning torture as not reflecting American values. "Freedom from torture," he said in a typically hypocritical speech, "is an inalienable right."[13]

On November 4, 2004, the greater part of the electorate became implicated in torture. Nothing like this had happened in any previous American war. The closest parallel to the present situation is, of course, not a previous war but the heyday of lynching. During the half century from the 1880s to the 1930s, most of the American public, along with much of the press and Congress, ignored or downplayed atrocities, and by doing so tacitly endorsed them.

Consider the contrast with the French in the early 1960s, when evidence of torture in Algeria became public. Half the nation rose up in protest. That largely put a stop to torture.

Will new categories of victims emerge, such as foreign nationals living within the boundaries of the United States or citizens suspected of supporting terrorism, ever more broadly defined? Only time will tell, but this much is certain: torture, and the imperial project that favors it, has a price. One part of the price is loss of American innocence.

Improbable as it may seem today, at one time the United States had a genuine claim to innocence. Although the republic was conceived amid genocide and slavery, the sheer daring of the experiment in representative government allowed informed men and women of good faith to believe that even the worst crimes were vestiges of an older order in the process of being outgrown.

Balzac* considered the virgin to be the most terrifying of all figures. This is because we are fallen but she is pure. Her inexperience and spiritual invincibility do not predispose her to be merciful to us for our failings. Throughout the nineteenth century America's virginity made the nation invincible, to itself first of all, as it projected itself onto the world. But such innocence cannot indefinitely survive empire. The rhetoric of the Bush administration mimics the old moral invincibility, but today American innocence, except for those elements that have changed to disillusionment or that we share with all other peoples, has completed its transformation into kitsch.

Kitsch has its own powers, and great ones too—the powers of ignorance and public relations. Kitsch innocence is cartoonlike and amplified, all smiles and snarls and formulaic sincerity, rapt with faith one minute, boundlessly cynical the next, but always tuned to public desires. None of this is new, of course. Europe knows all about it. European history cautions against any leader who talks like a cartoon. And Europe is littered with the remains of empires.

*Balzac: Honoré de Balzac, a nineteenth-century French novelist and playwright.

Many of our leaders, to widespread domestic applause, scorned Old Europe, but amid the cheers America had become like the Europe we read about in books, the Europe of the unro-mantic past, the genuine Old Europe. The spectacles and orgies of self-expansion, the murderous hypocrisy, the denial and religious fanaticism and systemic corruption of language, and above all the tragic waste began to look familiar. They began to look like what centuries of immigrants crossing oceans to begin again dreamed that they had left behind forever.

According to Jean Améry, the source of torture is our innate drive for unchecked self-expansion. If this is true, the possibility of torture will always be with us. How are we to deal with this today?

Machiavelli summarized the relationship of ordinary people to power as a shadow play of deceptions brought by the people on themselves. A prince "should seem to be all mercy, all loyalty, all sincerity, all humanity, all religion. And nothing is more necessary to seem to have than [religion] . . . Everybody sees what you appear to be, few feel what you are, and those few will not dare to oppose themselves to the opinion of the many, who have the majesty of the state to defend them . . . Let a prince therefore conquer and maintain his state: his means will always be judged honourable and praised by everyone, for ordinary people will always be taken by appearances and by the outcome of action."[14] To put this into contemporary language, presidents are encouraged in evil by the people, who are eager to be deceived.

Machiavelli wrote about the nature of power after his political career had ended in disaster. He had been accused of plotting against the Medici, and tortured. The experience of torture may have convinced him that human beings are fundamentally evil. His insights into power are brilliant, but his assessment of human nature is as reductive as the belief that human beings are fundamentally good. Such formulations are alluring. They voice our hopes and fears, but they bring only factitious clarity to experience by ignoring evidence that does not fit. The overwhelming lesson of history and of daily life is that human beings are capable of beautiful behavior and terrible behavior, individually and collectively. What this implies is that aldiough taboos, information, empathy, moral intelligence, uncorrupted law, and democratic practices are crucial lines of defense against torture, the single most important defense is the separation of powers. The more concentrated power becomes, the fewer the obstacles to extremity, including torture. The deeper our society descends into militarism, one-party rule, and rule by a single branch of government, the more embedded the practice of torture will become in American life.

Notes

1 Jennifer K. Harbury, *Truth, Torture, and the American Way* (Boston: Beacon Press, 2005), pp. 2–4.

2 Ibid., pp. 4–5.

3 The memo of August 1, 2002, defines torture as applying only to acts that produce "physical pain . . . equivalent in intensity to the pain accompanying . . . organ failure . . . or even death." The memorandum goes on to say that "even if the defendant knows that severe pain will result from his actions, if causing such pain is not his objective, he lacks the requisite specific intent." What this means is that if extracting information is a torturer's objective, he or she is not legally responsible for causing pain, no matter how intense and no matter how lasting the damage.

   For about two years the memo guided the administration and provided legal protection for torturers and their superiors. After the publication of photographs from Abu Ghraib, the administration revised the guidelines, but in a footnote protected the August 1 memo's extremely limited definition of torture.

4 Human Rights Watch, *Leadership Failure: Firsthand Accounts of Torture of Iraqi Detainees by the U. S. Army's 82nd Airborne Division: Summary.*

5 In February 2006, while this manuscript was being prepared for press, hundreds of additional images were released by the Australian news show *Dateline.*

6 "44 percent of the public thinks that torture is often or sometimes justified to obtain important information . . . a clear majority—58 percent—would support torture to thwart a terrorist attack." Evan Thomas and Michael Hirsch, "The Debate over Torture," *Newsweek,* November 21, 2005, p. 29.

7 Susan Sontag, "Regarding the Torture of Others," *New York Times Magazine,* May 23, 2004.

8 Jean Améry, *At the Mind's Limit,* trans. Sidney Rosenfeld and Stella R Rosenfeld (Bloomington and Indianapolis: Indiana University Press, 1980), p. 25.

9 Elaine Scarry, *The Body in Pain* (New York: Oxford University Press, 1985), P. 45.

10 *Report of the International Committee of the Red Cross (ICRC) on the Treatment by the Coalition Forces of Prisoners of War and Other Protected Persons by the Geneva Conventions in Iraq During Arrest, Internment, and Interrogation,* Section 1.7, February 2004. Brigadier General Janice Karpinski, who oversaw Abu Ghraib at the time that the photographs were taken, provides a slightly different, but substantially similar assessment: "The vast majority of them [prisoners] were [arrested for] minor crimes. They were missing curfew. They were subjected to a random inspection and a weapon was found in their trunks . . . they were minor crimes, nonviolent crimes." Interview with Marjorie Cohn, *Truthout,* August 24, 2005.

11 Jean Améry in ICRC report, p. 35.

12 The School of the Americas' involvement in torture may not always have been indirect. At the school's interrogation classes in Panama, street people may have been used to demonstrate torture techniques. In Uruguay, four homeless people were reportedly used as guinea pigs in an "anatomy class" and tortured to death. Jennifer Harbury in ibid., pp. 95–96.

13 George W. Bush, Reuters, June 26, 2005.

14 Niccolò Machiavelli, *The Prince,* trans. Wayne Rebhorn (New York: Barnes and Noble, 2003), pp. 76–77.

Reflections and Responses

1. Why does Gessert introduce autobiographical elements into an essay about torture, a subject with which he admits he has very little privileged experience? What are the advantages (and disadvantages) of an approach to torture told with a strong personal voice as opposed to a detached, analytical one? How does the opening paragraph fit into the essay as a whole? What about Gessert's story of his friend's suicide?

2. Gessert argues that Americans had trouble believing its government tortured prisoners until it saw the photos from Abu Ghraib. "They needed a catalyst to gain psychological substance," he writes. Why are photographs especially powerful in this instance? Do you agree with Gessert's contention that movies have made ours into a

"visual culture" in which we must see to understand? Or is the power of photography universal?

3. Gessert concludes with a warning: "The deeper our society descends into militarism, one-party-rule, and rule by a single branch of government, the more embedded the practice of torture will become in American life." Gessert was writing in 2006, during the Bush administration. Is his essay obsolete? Now that a new president and a new political agenda are in place, is torture less of a concern? What elements of the essay still resonate?

VICKI HEARNE

What's Wrong with
Animal Rights

*When people argue for the rights of animals, what exactly do they mean by
"rights"? Does their definition of animal rights take into account the "certain unalienable rights" that Thomas Jefferson wrote into the Declaration of
Independenc—the right to "life, liberty and the pursuit of happiness"? In
the following essay, Vicki Hearne skillfully combines personal and professional experience with philosophical reflections on happiness as she builds a
case against the reductive view of animals that typifies the animal-rights
movement. In Hearne's opinion, the problem with animal-rights advocates
is not that they take their position too far; "it's that they've got it all wrong."*

A professional dog trainer and Yale University professor, Hearne published three volumes of poetry, Nervous Horses *(1980),* In the Absence
of Horses *(1983), and* Parts of Light *(1994); three books of essays,*
Adam's Task: Calling Animals by Name *(1986),* Bandit: Dossier of
a Dangerous Dog *(1991), and* Animal Happiness *(1994); and a
novel,* The White German Shepherd *(1988). "What's Wrong with
Animal Rights" originally appeared in* Harper's Magazine *in 1991 and
was selected by Susan Sontag for* The Best American Essays 1992. *Vicki
Hearne died of lung cancer in August 2001.*

Not all happy animals are alike. A Doberman going over a hurdle
after a small wooden dumbbell is sleek, all arcs of harmonious
power. A basset hound cheerfully performing the same exercise
exhibits harmonies of a more lugubrious nature. There are chimpanzees who love precision the way musicians or fanatical

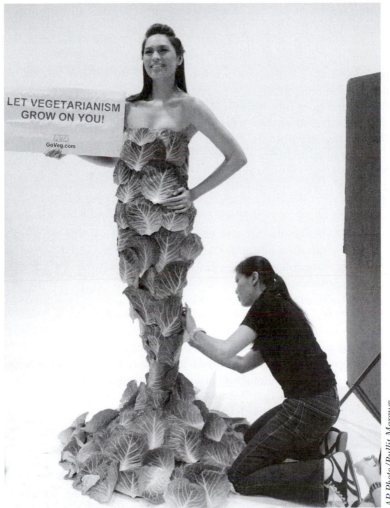

LET VEGETARIANISM
GROW ON YOU!

GoVeg.com

AP Photo/Bullit Marquez

housekeepers or accomplished hypochondriacs do; others for
whom happiness is a matter of invention and variation—chimp
vaudevillians. There is a rhinoceros whose happiness, as near as I
can make out, is in needing to be trained every morning, all over

again, or else he "forgets" his circus routine, and in this you find a clue to the slow, deep, quiet chuckle of his happiness and to the glory of the beast. Happiness for Secretariat is in his ebullient bound, that joyful length of stride. For the draft horse or the weight-pull dog, happiness is of a different shape, more awesome and less obviously intelligent. When the pulling horse is at its most intense, the animal goes into himself, allocating all of the educated power that organizes his desire to dwell in fierce and delicate intimacy with that power, leans into the harness, and MAKES THAT SUCKER MOVE.

If we are speaking of human beings and use the phrase "animal happiness," we tend to mean something like "creature comforts." The emblems of this are the golden retriever rolling in the grass, the horse with his nose deep in the oats, the kitty by the fire. Creature comforts are important to animals—"Grub first, then ethics" is a motto that would describe many a wise Labrador retriever, and I have a pit bull named Annie whose continual quest for the perfect pillow inspires her to awesome feats. But there is something more to animals, a capacity for satisfactions that come from work in the fullest sense—what is known in philosophy and in this country's Declaration of Independence as "happiness." This is a sense of personal achievement, like the satisfaction felt by a good woodcarver or a dancer or a poet or an accomplished dressage horse. It is a happiness that, like the artist's, must come from something within the animal, something trainers call "talent." Hence, it cannot be imposed on the animal. But it is also something that does not come *ex nihilo.*[*] If it had not been a fairly ordinary thing, in one part of the world, to teach young children to play the pianoforte, it is doubtful that Mozart's music would exist.

Happiness is often misunderstood as a synonym for pleasure or as an antonym for suffering. But Aristotle associated happiness with ethics—codes of behavior that urge us toward the sensation of getting it right, a kind of work that yields the "click" of satisfaction upon solving a problem or surmounting an obstacle. In his *Ethics*, Aristotle wrote, "If happiness is activity in accordance with excellence, it is reasonable that it should be in accordance with the highest excellence." Thomas Jefferson identified the capacity

---

[*]*ex nihilo:* Latin, "out of nothing."

for happiness as one of the three fundamental rights on which all others are based: "life, liberty, and the pursuit of happiness."

I bring up this idea of happiness as a form of work because I am an animal trainer, and work is the foundation of the happiness a trainer and an animal discover together. I bring up these words also because they cannot be found in the lexicon of the animal-rights movement. This absence accounts for the uneasiness toward the movement of most people, who sense that rights advocates have a point but take it too far when they liberate snails or charge that goldfish at the county fair are suffering. But the problem with the animal-rights advocates is not that they take it too far; it's that they've got it all wrong.

Animal rights are built upon a misconceived premise that rights were created to prevent us from unnecessary suffering. You can't find an animal-rights book, video, pamphlet, or rock concert in which someone doesn't mention the Great Sentence, written by Jeremy Bentham* in 1789. Arguing in favor of such rights, Bentham wrote: "The question is not, Can they *reason?* nor, can they *talk?* but, can they suffer?"

The logic of the animal-rights movement places suffering at the iconographic center of a skewed value system. The thinking of its proponents—given eerie expression in a virtually sadopornographic sculpture of a tortured monkey that won a prize for its compassionate vision—has collapsed into a perverse conundrum. Today the loudest voices calling for—demanding—the destruction of animals are the humane organizations. This is an inevitable consequence of the apotheosis of the drive to relieve suffering: death is the ultimate release. To compensate for their contradictions, the humane movement has demonized, in this century and the last, those who made animal happiness their business: veterinarians, trainers, and the like. We think of Louis Pasteur as the man whose work saved you and me and your dog and cat from rabies, but antivivisectionists of the time claimed that rabies increased in areas where there were Pasteur Institutes.

An anti-rabies public relations campaign mounted in England in the 1880s by the Royal Society for the Prevention of Cruelty to Animals and other organizations led to orders being issued to club

---

*Jeremy Bentham: British philosopher and social reformer (1748–1832) whose *Introduction to the Principles of Morals and Legislation* appeared in 1789.

any dog found not wearing a muzzle. England still has her cruel and unnecessary law that requires an animal to spend six months in quarantine before being allowed loose in the country. Most of the recent propaganda about pit bulls—the crazy claim that they "take hold with their front teeth while they chew away with their rear teeth" (which would imply, incorrectly, that they have double jaws)—can be traced to literature published by the Humane Society of the United States during the fall of 1987 and earlier. If your neighbors want your dog or horse impounded and destroyed because he is a nuisance—say the dog barks, or the horse attracts flies—it will be the local Humane Society to whom your neighbors turn for action.

In a way, everyone has the opportunity to know that the history of the humane movement is largely a history of miseries, arrests, prosecutions, and death. The Humane Society is the pound, the place with the decompression chamber or the lethal injections. You occasionally find worried letters about this in Ann Landers's column.

Animal-rights publications are illustrated largely with photographs of two kinds of animals — "Helpless Fluff" and "Agonized Fluff," the two conditions in which some people seem to prefer their animals, because any other version of an animal is too complicated for propaganda. In the introduction to his book *Animal Liberation*, Peter Singer says somewhat smugly that he and his wife have no animals and, in fact, don't much care for them. This is offered as evidence of his objectivity and ethical probity. But it strikes me as an odd, perhaps obscene underpinning for an ethical project that encourages university and high school students to cherish their ignorance of, say, great bird dogs as proof of their devotion to animals.

I would like to leave these philosophers behind, for they are inept connoisseurs of suffering who might revere my Airedale for his capacity to scream when subjected to a blowtorch but not for his wit and courage, not for his natural good manners that are a gentle rebuke to ours. I want to celebrate the moment not long ago when, at his first dog show, my Airedale, Drummer, learned that there can be a public place where his work is respected. I want to celebrate his meticulousness, his happiness upon realizing at the dog show that no one would swoop down upon him and swamp him with the goo-goo excesses known as the "teddy-bear complex" but that people actually got out of his way, gave him room to work. I want to say, "There can be a six-and-a-half-month-old puppy who can care about accuracy, who can be fastidious, and whose fastidiousness will be a foundation for courage later." I want to say, "Leave my puppy alone!"

I want to leave the philosophers behind, but I cannot, in part because the philosophical problems that plague academicians of the animal-rights movement are illuminating. They wonder, do animals have rights or do they have interests? Or, if these rightists lead particularly unexamined lives, they dismiss that question as obvious (yes, of course animals have rights, prima facie) and proceed to enumerate them, James Madison style. This leads to the issuance of bills of rights—the right to an environment, the right not to be used in medical experiments—and other forms of trivialization.

The calculus of suffering can be turned against the philosophers of festering flesh, even in the case of food animals, or exotic animals who perform in movies and circuses. It is true that it hurts to be slaughtered by man, but it doesn't hurt nearly as much as some of the cunningly cruel arrangements meted out by "Mother Nature." In Africa, 75 percent of the lions cubbed do not survive to the age of two. For those who make it to two, the average age at death is ten years. Asali, the movie and TV lioness, was still working at age twenty-one. There are fates worse than death, but twenty-one years of a close working relationship with Hubert Wells, Asali's trainer, is not one of them. Dorset sheep and polled Herefords would not exist at all were they not in a symbiotic relationship with human beings.

A human being living in the "wild"—somewhere, say, without the benefits of medicine and advanced social organization—would probably have a life expectancy of from thirty to thirty-five years. A human being living in "captivity"—in, say, a middle-class neighborhood of what the Centers for Disease Control call a Metropolitan Statistical Area—has a life expectancy of seventy or more years. For orangutans in the wild in Borneo and Malaysia, the life expectancy is thirty-five years; in captivity, fifty years. The wild is not a suffering-free zone or all that frolicsome a location.

The questions asked by animal-rights activists are flawed, because they are built on the concept that the origin of rights is in the avoidance of suffering rather than in the pursuit of happiness. The question that needs to be asked—and that will put us in closer proximity to the truth—is not, do they have rights? or, what are those rights? but rather, what is a right?

Rights originate in committed relationships and can be found, both intact and violated, wherever one finds such relationships — in social compacts, within families, between animals, and between people and nonhuman animals. This is as true when the nonhuman animals in question are lions or parakeets as when they are dogs. It is my Airedale whose excellencies have my attention at the moment, so it is with reference to him that I will consider the question, what is a right?

When I imagine situations in which it naturally arises that A defends or honors or respects B's rights, I imagine situations in which the relationship between A and B can be indicated with a possessive pronoun. I might say, "Leave her alone, she's my daughter" or "That's what she wants, and she is my daughter. I think I am bound to honor her wants." Similarly, "Leave her alone, she's my mother." I am more tender of the happiness of my mother, my father, my child, than I am of other people's family members; more tender of my friends' happinesses than your friends' happinesses, unless you and I have a mutual friend.

Possession of a being by another has come into more and more disrepute, so that the common understanding of one person possessing another is slavery. But the important detail about the kind of possessive pronoun that I have in mind is reciprocity: if I have a friend, she has a friend. If I have a daughter, she has a mother. The possessive does not bind one of us while freeing the other; it cannot do that. Moreover, should the mother reject the daughter, the word that applies is "disown." The form of disowning that most often appears in the news is domestic violence. Parents abuse children; husbands batter wives.

Some cases of reciprocal possessives have built-in limitations, such as "my patient/my doctor" or "my student/my teacher" or "my agent/my client." Other possessive relations are extremely limited but still remarkably binding: "my neighbor" and "my country" and "my president."

The responsibilities and the ties signaled by reciprocal possession typically are hard to dissolve. It can be as difficult to give up an enemy as to give up a friend, and often the one becomes the other, as though the logic of the possessive pronoun outlasts the forms it chanced to take at a given moment, as though we were stuck with one another. In these bindings, nearly inextricable, are found the origin of our rights. They imply a possessiveness but also recognize an acknowledgment by each side of the other's existence.

The idea of democracy is dependent on the citizens' having knowledge of the government; that is, realizing that the government exists and knowing how to claim rights against it. I know this much because I get mail from the government and see its "representatives" running about in uniforms. Whether I actually have any rights in relationship to the government is less clear, but the idea that I do is symbolized by the right to vote. I obey the government, and, in theory, it obeys me, by counting my ballot, reading the *Miranda* warning to me, agreeing to be bound by the Constitution. My friend obeys me as I obey her; the government "obeys" me to some extent, and, to a different extent, I obey it.

What kind of thing can my Airedale, Drummer, have knowledge of? He can know that I exist and through that knowledge can claim his happinesses, with varying degrees of success, both with me and against me. Drummer can also know about larger human or dog communities than the one that consists only of him and me. There is my household—the other dogs, the cats, my husband. I have had enough dogs on campuses to know that he can learn that Yale exists as a neighborhood or village. My older dog, Annie, not only knows that Yale exists but can tell Yalies from townies, as I learned while teaching there during labor troubles.

Dogs can have elaborate conceptions of human social structures, and even of something like their rights and responsibilities within them, but these conceptions are never elaborate enough to construct a rights relationship between a dog and the state, or a dog and the Humane Society. Both of these are concepts that depend on writing and memoranda, officers in uniform, plaques and seals of authority. All of these are literary constructs, and all of them are beyond a dog's ken, which is why the mail carrier who doesn't also happen to be a dog's friend is forever an intruder—this is why dogs bark at mailmen.

It is clear enough that natural rights relations can arise between people and animals. Drummer, for example, can insist, "Hey, let's

go outside and do something!" if I have been at my computer several days on end. He can both refuse to accept various of my suggestions and tell me when he fears for his life—such as the time
when the huge, white flapping flag appeared out of nowhere, as it
seemed to him, on the town green one evening when we were
working. I can (and do) say to him either, "Oh, you don't have to
worry about that" or, "Uh oh, you're right, Drum, that guy looks
dangerous." Just as the government and I—two different species
of organism—have developed improvised ways of communicating,
such as the vote, so Drummer and I have worked out a number of
ways to make our expressions known. Largely through obedience,
I have taught him a fair amount about how to get responses from
me. Obedience is reciprocal; you cannot get responses from a dog
to whom you do not respond accurately. I have enfranchised him
in a relationship to me by educating him, creating the conditions
by which he can achieve a certain happiness specific to a dog,
maybe even specific to an Airedale, inasmuch as this same relationship has allowed me to plumb the happiness of being a trainer and
writing this article.

   Instructions in this happiness are given terms that are alien to a
culture in which liver treats, fluffy windup toys, and miniature sweaters are confused with respect and work. Jack Knox, a sheepdog
trainer originally from Scotland, will shake his crook at a novice
handler who makes a promiscuous move to praise a dog, and will
call out in his Scottish accent, "Eh! Eh! Get back, get BACK! Ye'll no
be abusin' the dogs like that in my clinic." America is a nation of
abused animals, Knox says, because we are always swooping at them
with praise, "no gi'ing them their freedom." I am reminded of
Rainer Maria Rilke's* account in which the Prodigal Son leaves—has
to leave—because everyone loves him, even the dogs love him, and
he has no path to the delicate and fierce truth of himself.
Unconditional praise and love, in Rilke's story, disenfranchise us,
distract us from what truly excites our interest.

   In the minds of some trainers and handlers, praise is dishonesty.
Paradoxically, it is a kind of contempt for animals that masquer-
ades as a reverence for helplessness and suffering. The idea of
freedom means that you do not, at least not while Jack Knox is

---

*__Rainer Maria Rilke:__ Austrian lyric poet (1875–1926).

nearby, helpfully guide your dog through the motions of, say, herding over and over—what one trainer calls "explainy-wainy." This is rote learning. It works tolerably well on some handlers, because people have vast unconscious minds and can store complex pre-programmed behaviors. Dogs, on the other hand, have almost no unconscious minds, so they can learn only by thinking. Many children are like this until educated out of it.

If I tell my Airedale to sit and stay on the town green, and someone comes up and burbles, "What a pretty thing you are," he may break his stay to go for a caress. I pull him back and correct him for breaking. Now he holds his stay because I have blocked his way to movement but not because I have punished him. (A correction blocks one path as it opens another for desire to work; punishment blocks desire and opens nothing.) He holds his stay now, and—because the stay opens this possibility of work, new to a heedless young dog—he watches. If the person goes on talking, and isn't going to gush with praise, I may heel Drummer out of his stay and give him an "Okay" to make friends. Sometimes something about the person makes Drummer feel that reserve is in order. He responds to an insincere approach by sitting still, going down into himself, and thinking, "This person has no business pawing me. I'll sit very still, and he will go away." If the person doesn't take the hint from Drummer, I'll give the pup a little backup by saying, "Please don't pet him, he's working," even though he was not under any command.

The pup reads this, and there is a flicker of a working trust now stirring in the dog. Is the pup grateful? When the stranger leaves, does he lick my hand, full of submissive blandishments? This one doesn't. This one says nothing at all, and I say nothing much to him. This is a working trust we are developing, not a mutual congratulation society. My backup is praise enough for him; the use he makes of my support is praise enough for me.

Listening to a dog is often praise enough. Suppose it is just after dark and we are outside. Suddenly there is a shout from the house. The pup and I both look toward the shout and then toward each other: "What do you think?" I don't so much as cock my head, because Drummer is growing up, and I want to know what he thinks. He takes a few steps toward the house, and I follow. He listens again and comprehends that it's just Holly, who at fourteen is much given to alarming cries and shouts. He shrugs at me and goes about his business. I say nothing. To praise him for this performance would make about as much sense as praising a human being for the same thing. Thus:

A. What's that?
B. I don't know. [Listens] Oh, it's just Holly.
A. What a goooooood human being!
B. Huh?

This is one small moment in a series of like moments that will culminate in an Airedale who on a Friday will have the discrimination and confidence required to take down a man who is attacking me with a knife and on Saturday clown and play with the children at the annual Orange Empire Dog Club Christmas party.

People who claim to speak for animal rights are increasingly devoted to the idea that the very keeping of a dog or a horse or a gerbil or a lion is in and of itself an offense. The more loudly they speak, the less likely they are to be in a rights relation to any given animal, because they are spending so much time in airplanes or transmitting fax announcements of the latest Sylvester Stallone anti-fur rally. In a 1988 *Harper's* forum, for example, Ingrid Newkirk, the national director of People for the Ethical Treatment of Animals, urged that domestic pets be spayed and neutered and ultimately phased out. She prefers, it appears, wolves—and wolves someplace else—to Airedales and, by a logic whose interior structure is both emotionally and intellectually forever closed to Drummer, claims thereby to be speaking for "animal rights."

She is wrong. I am the only one who can own up to my Airedale's inalienable rights. Whether or not I do it perfectly at any given moment is no more refutation of this point than whether I am perfectly my husband's mate at any given moment refutes the fact of marriage. Only people who know Drummer, and whom he can know, are capable of this relationship. PETA and the Humane Society and the ASPCA and the Congress and NOW—as institutions—do have the power to affect my ability to grant rights to Drummer but are otherwise incapable of creating conditions or laws or rights that would increase his happiness. Only Drummer's owner has the power to obey him—to obey who he is and what he is capable of—deeply enough to grant him his rights and open up the possibility of happiness.

Reflections and Responses

1. How does Hearne define *happiness?* What is its relation to work? Why, in her opinion, are the interrelated concepts of happiness and work not "in the lexicon of the animal-rights movement"?

2. Why does Hearne bring up the life-expectancy statistics of animals living "in the wild"? In what way do these statistics reinforce her argument? How might an animal-rights advocate respond to her use and interpretation of these statistics?

3. The Declaration of Independence reads: "We hold these truths to be self-evident, that all men are created equal, that they are endowed by their Creator with certain unalienable rights, that among these are life, liberty and the pursuit of happiness." Do you think Hearne legitimately or illegitimately extends Jefferson's words to apply to nonhumans? Explain your position.

GARRET KEIZER

Loaded

*The debate over guns in America has traditionally taken place on estab-
lished lines: In general, liberals argue for tighter gun control laws in the
name of safety, while conservatives argue that the Second Amendment to
the Constitution protects ownership of guns, and that they're necessary to
maintain a free society. In this essay, Garret Keizer, a self-proclaimed progressive, challenges the liberal orthodoxy, asserting that the ownership of
guns should be a right liberals defend as ardently as they do civil rights.
Only an armed population—and more broadly a population willing to
fight back physically against oppression—can withstand tyranny, Keizer
argues. And to the pragmatism of his fellow progressives, who contend that
gun ownership is no longer compatible with modern life, Keizer offers a
stunning rebuke: "If the Second Amendment is a dispensable anachronism
in the era of school shootings, might not the First, Fourth, and Fifth amendments be dispensable anachronisms during a 'war on terror'?"*

*Garret Keizer is a writer in northeastern Vermont, but has also spent time as
an Episcopal priest and a teacher. His books include* No Place But Here: A
Teacher's Vocation in a Rural Community *(1996),* A Dresser of Sycamore Trees: The Finding of a Ministry *(2001),* The Enigma of Anger:
Essays on a Sometimes Deadly Sin *(2004), and* Help: The Original
Human Dilemma *(2005). He is currently working on a book about the politics of noise. He is a frequent contributor to* Harper's, *where "Loaded" first
appeared; it was selected by David Foster Wallace for* The Best American
Essays *2007.*

> "That rifle hanging on the wall of the working-class flat or labourer's cot-
> tage is the symbol of democracy. It is our job to see that it stays there."
>
> —George Orwell

England was not engaged in a war against Islamo-fascists* when Orwell penned the words above, only a war against Nazi fascists—or, as one now feels obliged to say, *fascist* fascists—and the rifle he referred to was in use by the British Home Guard. Still, his reasons for wanting the rifle to stay on the wall obviously had to do with a different sort of homeland security than the War Office had in mind. Otherwise, why specify the gun owner's *class?*

In fact, Orwell was anticipating a time when the rifle might have a revolutionary purpose. His hopes were not altogether in vain, though supporting examples tend to be about as well known as the quotation itself, and for much the same reason.

Here is one from 1947, three years before Orwell's death. In Monroe, North Carolina, a motorcade of Ku Klux Klansmen pulled up to a funeral home to "claim" the body of Bennie Montgomery, a black sharecropper recently tried and executed for killing his white boss. With the help of a skilled mediator and a regimen of trust-building exercises, the night riders might have been persuaded to settle for a limb or a chunk of Bennie's torso, but instead they were met by forty African Americans armed with rifles and shotguns. Among them was a former Army private named Robert Williams (1925–96), whose career as a rogue civil rights activist and NAACP officer, a story he tells in his 1962 book, *Negroes with Guns*, seems to have begun with that (ultimately bloodless) incident.

Although the rifle club he formed in his community had an NRA charter, there is as far as I'm aware no "Rob Williams Armed Citizen Award" offered by that organization, no essay contest bearing his name sponsored in the public schools. Nor does Williams appear in the official narrative of the civil rights movement, where Negroes with guns are seldom permitted to upstage folk singers with guitars.

To talk about guns in America is inevitably to talk about race. Both sides of the so-called gun debate have strange fruit† in their family trees. The Second Amendment speaks of the importance of "a well regulated militia," and although framers like James Madison saw the local militia and the right "to keep and bear arms" as a check to the tyranny of standing armies, some historians have

*Islamo-fascists: A controversial term for Islamic fundamentalists.

†strange fruit: A reference to a poem about southern lynchings made popular by a musical version sung by Billie Holiday.

John Brown (1800–59) captured by Marines at Harper's Ferry, 1859.

noted that one probable function of a well regulated militia was to keep slaves in their place.

Likewise one of the regulatory questions of Colonial times was what, if any, access slaves ought to have to guns; what, if any, role free blacks ought to have in the militias. Neither slavery nor the militias lasted as long as that dilemma. When Robert Williams aimed his gun at a racist mob during a campaign—to integrate a public swimming pool, an old white man burst into tears and cried, "What is this God damn country coming to that the niggers have got guns?" From the beginning, gun control in America has had much to do with that question.

With antecedents like these, one might suppose that adversaries in the ongoing gun debate would have a harder time maintaining their stridency. I happen not to suppose anything of the kind, but then, my suppositions in regard to the limits of human reasonableness are one reason I own a gun.

As with its sister issue abortion, the debate over guns amounts to a clash of absolutes: the right of bodily self-determination versus the right to be born, the right of self-defense versus the right to walk down the street without being shot. In both cases the debate is frequently conducted by pretending that the opponent's concerns hardly deserve mention and by an inevitable transference of opprobrium from the adversary's position to his or her cultural "type." I wonder, for instance, as I read the various pro- and anti-gun polemics, who the actual enemy is supposed to be: the marauding outlaws who might be deterred by an "armed citizen," or the execrable Clintons, who, according to an editorial in the *American Rifleman,* attacked the Second Amendment *every day.* Are we supposed to be more incensed by the shady dealer who sells guns to Murder Incorporated or by the straight-arrow collector who thinks Charlton Heston* could act? Issue-driven politics in red-and-blue America are like a man whose appetite for a steak is greatly enhanced by his contempt for vegetarians.

The gun issue is further complicated by a good deal of silliness, and in this it differs noticeably from the politics of the womb. Guns are either objects of superstition (they will just about *make* you commit suicide, according to some accounts) or pieces of pornographic paraphernalia, the things that get whipped out at the climax of a thousand socially smutty plots, on TV, in our heads, and then, insanely, in an actual event in which real people die. We all know what the Terminator said and the Taxi Driver said, but who recalls, much less ponders, what Thoreau said in his *Plea for Captain John Brown* (1853): "I speak for the slave when I say that I prefer the philanthropy of Captain John Brown to that philanthropy which neither shoots me nor liberates me. . . . I do not wish to kill nor to be killed, but I can foresee circumstances in which both these things would be by me unavoidable."

Unfortunately, a progressive, as someone with my politics has come to be called, does not like to ponder such mortal circumstances. Notice the telling grammatical shift by which the adjective "progressive" becomes a titular noun—comparable to a godly person who begins to speak of himself as a god. As the living embodiment of progress itself, a progressive is beyond rage, beyond "the politics of yesterday," and certainly beyond anything as retro as a

---

*Charlton Heston:** The classic American film actor who later became president of the National Rifle Association.

gun. More than I fear fundamentalists who wish to teach religious myths in place of evolution I fear progressives who wish to teach evolution in place of political science. Or, rather, who forget a central principle of evolutionary thought: that no species completely outgrows its origins.

Like democracy, for example. What is that creature, if not the offspring of literacy and ballistics? Once a peasant can shoot down a knight, the writing is on the wall, including the writing that says, "We hold these truths to be self-evident." Self-evident because Sir Galahad doesn't appear to be moving. *Guns, Germs, and Steel* is a good title for a book about European imperialism; *Guns, Fonts, and Ballots* would serve for a book about the rise of the European democratic state.

There are those who will insist, and many do, that what might have been true in the days of James Madison and Henry David Thoreau—and even in the days of Robert Williams—is no longer true in the days of neo-Nazis and Guantánamo Bay. But that questionable premise gives rise to an even more interesting question: If the Second Amendment is a dispensable anachronism in the era of school shootings, might not the First, Fourth, and Fifth amendments be dispensable anachronisms during a "war on terror"? Small wonder if some of those who readily make the first concession were equally ready to queue up behind the Republican right in ratifying the second.

Historians of weaponry tell us that one effect of the gun was to change the ideal of courage on the battlefield from a willingness to engage in hand-to-hand combat to an ability to stand firm under fire. At this point in our history, I'll take any form of courage I can get, but had Congress the smallest measure of the gunner's kind, the Patriot Act[*] might still be a doodle on Dick Cheney's cocktail napkin.

I grew up with guns and I live in a region where many people have them. They have guns because they hunt for meat, and they have guns for the same reason that many of them also have ponds dug close to their barns and houses. In a community with no fire hydrants, you want water for the fire engine. And in an area where

---

[*]**Patriot Act:** A 2002 law that the Bush administration lobbied heavily for, and that many liberals accused of curtailing civil liberties.

a handful of state police and part-time sheriffs patrol a vast web of back roads spread across three counties, you might want the means to defend yourself. I own a fire extinguisher, a first-aid kit, and a shotgun. Not to own any of these would strike me as an affectation.

I hope that I shall never have to confront anyone with my gun, but owning a gun has forced me to confront myself. Anyone who owns firearms for reasons other than hunting and sport shooting (neither of which I do) has admitted that he or she is willing to kill another human being—as opposed to the more civilized course of allowing human beings to be killed by paid functionaries on his or her behalf. Owning a gun does not enhance my sense of power; it enhances my sense of compromise and contingency—a feeling curiously like that of holding down a job. In other words, it is one more glaring proof that I am not Mahatma Gandhi or even Che Guevara, just another soft-bellied schlimazel trying to keep the lawn mowed and the psychopaths off the lawn.

If the authorities attempted to confiscate my gun in a house-to-house search, I believe I would offer resistance. What I would not offer is a justifying argument; the argument is implicit in the ramifications of a house-to-house search. But all of this is so much fantasy, another example of the disingenuousness that tends to color our discussion of guns. The Day When All the Guns Are Gathered Up— what the paranoids regard as the end of the world and the Pollyannas as the Rapture—it's never going to happen. There are nearly 1.4 million active troops in the US armed forces; there are an estimated 200 million guns in private hands. The war over the proper interpretation of the Second Amendment is effectively over. The most reasonable and decent thing that gun groups could do at this point is to declare victory and negotiate terms with the generosity that is so becoming in a victor. *Five-day waiting periods? Agreed, but our sense of honor compels us to insist on ten.* (Oh, to have been born in a time of so many guns and so little gallantry! Perhaps we ought not to have shot Sir Galahad after all.) *No assault rifles owned by civilians— also agreed, so long as no assault rifles are used on civilians.*

Of course, none of this is going to happen either. It would require a confidence that scarcely exists. One need only peruse the ads and articles in gun magazines to see the evidence of its rarity—to see that poignant, ironic, and insatiable obsession with overwhelming force. That cry of impotence. The *American Rifleman* I recall from my boyhood was closer to *Field & Stream* than to *Soldier of Fortune*, more like *Popular Mechanics than National Review*. My father and my uncles were do-it-yourself guys; their guns were just something else to lube. When I was a kid, I thought a liberal was a person who couldn't fix a car. But the cars aren't so easy to take apart anymore; the "check engine" light comes on and only the dealership has all the codes. As in Detroit, so in Washington: the engineering works the same. I am not the first to point out the sleight of hand that bedevils us: the illusion of power and choice perpetuated to disguise a diminishing sphere of action. A person dry-fires his Ruger in the same reverie of preparedness as another aims her cursor at her favorite blog. What precision, what access, what an array of options! Something's going to happen one of these days, and when it does, man, I'm going to be ready. In the meantime, just listen to that awesome sterile click.

Recreational purposes aside, the problem with guns is that their only conscionable private use is defensive. Even Robert Williams was insistent on this point. Hannah Arendt says as much when, in her book *On Violence*, she writes that "Rage and violence turn irrational only when they are directed against substitutes." Who are you likely to shoot in a modern uprising if not a substitute?

The other trouble with guns is their reductive effect on the question of violent versus nonviolent resistance. They predispose us to think of violence exclusively as gun violence. Arendt herself seems close to this assumption when she defines violence as the forceful use of "implements." Her definition makes sense to me only if the human body also counts as an implement.

In that regard it may be instructive to look at the political history of violent confrontations in America. None has been pretty; perhaps a few led to reform. But of the latter, not all or even many have involved guns. Shootouts always follow a predictable script. They are like bullfights: the matador may get gored but the bull always dies. Red flags wave and perhaps a white flag after that, but with a few exceptions, like Harpers Ferry and Matewan, one finds very little to salute.

The prospect changes when we consider certain mostly unarmed, often spontaneous engagements. They include the worst instances of mass behavior and, if not also the best, at least some of the most defining for their times. One thinks of the Boston Massacre, Haymarket Square, Kent State, Stonewall, Watts*. Some of the participants carried signs and some did not, but in retrospect they all seem to be massing under the same banner: "If you are so afraid of 'the mob' that you would deny us our place at the table, then we will remind you what a real mob looks like." Aeschylus put the Furies under the hill of the Areopagus; that is, under the taming influence of rational persuasion. Under the pretext of taming them further, overweening governments only manage to let them loose.

This is the lesson our leaders seem to have forgotten and that the more comfortable among us would just as soon forget: that when the rules of participatory government are broken, the governed have a tendency, a right, and an obligation to become unruly.

Saul Alinsky† liked to say that a liberal is someone who leaves the room when an argument is about to turn into a fight. We are currently in need of a liberalism that goes back into the room and starts the fight. We are possibly in need of some civil unrest. This is not a conclusion I come to lightly. I have always believed in the superiority of nonviolent non-cooperation. The Hindu sage Sri Ramakrishna is supposed to have said that if a person could weep for a single day because he had not seen God, he would behold his heart's desire; I continue to believe that if the mass of Americans refused to earn or spend a dollar for a single day following a fishy election—no matter whose guy won—by the dawn's early light we would behold our country. But the likelihood of achieving that kind of solidarity brings us back to the subject of weeping.

The harvest is great but the laborers are few. Still, if asked to choose between an urban guerrilla armed with an AK-47 and a protester armed with a song sheet and a map showing how to get to the designated "free speech zone,"†† I would decline on the grounds of insufficient faith and negligible inspiration. Rather, give me some people with very fanatical ideas about the sanctity of

---

*Boston Massacre, Haymarket Square, Kent State, Stonewall, Watts: All riots in which civilians and law enforcement clashed at various points in American history.

†Saul Alinsky: An American political activist known as the founder of local organizing.

††Free speech zone: Areas designated for protest, notably set up during political conventions.

habeas corpus and the length of time an African American or any other American ought to have to wait on line to vote. Give me some people who are not so evolved that they have forgotten what it is to stand firm under fire or even to squat near the fire in a cave. Give me an accountant who can still throw a rock.

Reflections and Responses

1. Although this essay is no doubt an entry into a political argument, it has a personal element as well. Keizer analyzes his own gun ownership and describes his life in Vermont, for instance, as an antidote to the inner-city setting in which liberals often place the gun debate. How does personalizing the argument make it more or less effective for you? In your opinion, should writers making a political case use the first person singular as often as Keizer?

2. Keizer offers, or quotes, several tongue-in-cheek definitions of a liberal: "a person who couldn't fix a car," for instance, or "someone who leaves the room when an argument turns into a fight." How does Keizer ultimately define liberalism in the essay? What is his ideal of liberalism, and what does he think the reality is? Do you agree with his definitions? How do they fit with the specific principles he believes liberals should be defending?

3. Characterize the prevailing tone of the essay. Is it collected and methodical overall? Or does it have a more forceful thrust? Identify points at which Keizer's tone becomes aggressive, angry, or even sardonic. How do these advance the essay? Why is it important to sound especially firm in an essay like this?

JAMAICA KINCAID

On Seeing England for the First Time

One of the most sinister sides of imperialism is the way it promotes the ruling nation's culture and rejects the colony's. The effect of this on an impressionable young person is vividly described in Jamaica Kincaid's sensitive and angry autobiographical essay about growing up in Antigua with the dark shadow of England continually looming over her. England and a reverence for things English invaded every aspect of her daily life and education. Yet it was not until adulthood that she finally journeyed to England and really saw it for the first time. "The space between the idea of something and its reality," Kincaid writes, "is always wide and deep and dark." The real England she finally sees is far different from the other England, whose maps and history she was made to memorize as a schoolgirl in Antigua.

Born in Antigua, Kincaid is the author of At the Bottom of the River *(1983),* Annie John *(1985),* A Small Place *(1988),* Lucy *(1990),* The Autobiography of My Mother *(1996),* My Brother *(1997),* My Garden Book *(1999),* Mr. Potter: A Novel *(2002), and* Among Flowers: A Walk in the Himalaya *(2005). A staff writer for* The New Yorker, *Kincaid has had stories and essays published in* Rolling Stone, Paris Review, *and other literary periodicals. She was the editor of* The Best American Essays 1995 *and is a visiting professor of creative writing at Harvard University. "On Seeing England for the First Time" originally appeared in* Transition *(1991) and was selected by Susan Sontag for* The Best American Essays 1992.

When I saw England for the first time, I was a child in school sitting at a desk. The England I was looking at was laid out on a map gently, beautifully, delicately, a very special jewel; it lay on a bed of sky blue—the background of the map—its yellow form mysterious, because though it looked like a leg of mutton, it could not really look like anything so familiar as a leg of mutton because it was England—with shadings of pink and green, unlike any shadings of pink and green I had seen before, squiggly veins of red running in every direction. England was a special jewel all right, and only special people got to wear it. The people who got to wear England were English people. They wore it well and they wore it everywhere: in jungles, in deserts, on plains, on top of the highest mountains, on all the oceans, on all the seas, in places where they were not welcome, in places they should not have been. When my teacher had pinned this map up on the blackboard, she said, "This is England"—and she said it with authority, seriousness, and adoration, and we all sat up. It was as if she had said, "This is Jerusalem, the place you will go to when you die but only if you have been good." We understood then—we were meant to understand then—that England was to be our source of myth and the source from which we got our sense of reality, our sense of what was meaningful, our sense of what was meaningless—and much about our own lives and much about the very idea of us headed that last list.

At the time I was a child sitting at my desk seeing England for the first time, I was already very familiar with the greatness of it. Each morning before I left for school, I ate a breakfast of half a grapefruit, an egg, bread and butter and a slice of cheese, and a cup of cocoa; or half a grapefruit, a bowl of oat porridge, bread and butter and a slice of cheese, and a cup of cocoa. The can of cocoa was often left on the table in front of me. It had written on it the name of the company, the year the company was established, and the words "Made in England." Those words, "Made in England," were written on the box the oats came in too. They would also have been written on the box the shoes I was wearing came in; a bolt of gray linen cloth lying on the shelf of a store from which my mother had bought three yards to make the uniform that I was wearing had written along its edge those three words. The shoes I wore were made in England; so were my socks and cotton undergarments and the satin ribbons I wore tied at the end of two plaits of my hair. My father, who might have sat next to me at breakfast, was a carpenter and cabinet maker. The shoes he wore to work would have been made in England, as were his khaki shirt and trousers, his underpants and undershirt, his socks and brown felt hat. Felt was not the proper material from which a hat that was expected to provide shade from the hot sun should be made, but my father must have seen and admired a picture of an Englishman wearing such a hat in England, and this picture that he saw must have been so compelling that it caused him to wear the wrong hat for a hot climate most of his long life. And this hat—a brown felt hat—became so central to his character that it was the first thing he put on in the morning as he stepped out of bed and the last thing he took off before he stepped back into bed at night. As we sat at breakfast a car might go by. The car, a Hillman or a Zephyr, was made in England. The very idea of the meal itself, breakfast, and its substantial quality and quantity was an idea from England; we somehow knew that in England they began the day with this meal called breakfast and a proper breakfast was a big breakfast. No one I knew liked eating so much food so early in the day; it made us feel sleepy, tired. But this breakfast business was Made in England like almost everything else that surrounded us, the exceptions being the sea, the sky, and the air we breathed.

At the time I saw this map—seeing England for the first time—I did not say to myself, "Ah, so that's what it looks like," because there was no longing in me to put a shape to those three words that ran through every part of my life, no matter how small; for me to have had such a longing would have meant that I lived in a certain atmosphere, an atmosphere in which those three words were felt as a burden. But I did not live in such an atmosphere. My father's brown felt hat would develop a hole in its crown, the lining would separate from the hat itself, and six weeks before he thought that he could not be seen wearing it—he was a very vain man—he would order another hat from England. And my mother taught me to eat my food in the English way: the knife in the right hand, the fork in the left, my elbows held still close to my side, the food carefully balanced on my fork and then brought up to my mouth. When I had finally mastered it, I overheard her saying to a friend, "Did you see how nicely she can eat?" But I knew then that I enjoyed my food more when I ate it with my bare hands, and I continued to do so when she wasn't looking. And when my teacher showed us the map, she asked us to study it carefully, because no test we would ever take would be complete without this statement: "Draw a map of England."

I did not know then that the statement "Draw a map of England" was something far worse than a declaration of war, for in fact a flat-out declaration of war would have put me on alert, and again in fact, there was no need for war—I had long ago been conquered. I did not know then that this statement was part of a process that would result in my erasure, not my physical erasure, but my erasure all the same. I did not know then that this statement was meant to make me feel in awe and small whenever I heard the word "England": awe at its existence, small because I was not from it. I did not know very much of anything then—certainly not what a blessing it was that I was unable to draw a map of England correctly.

After that there were many times of seeing England for the first time. I saw England in history. I knew the names of all the kings of England. I knew the names of their children, their wives, their disappointments, their triumphs, the names of people who betrayed them, I knew the dates on which they were born and the dates they died. I knew their conquests and was made to feel glad if I figured in them; I knew their defeats. I knew the details of the year 1066 (the Battle of Hastings, the end of the reign of the Anglo-Saxon kings) before I knew the details of the year 1832 (the year slavery was abolished). It wasn't as bad as I make it sound now; it was worse. I did like so much hearing again and again how Alfred the Great, traveling in disguise, had been left to watch cakes, and because he wasn't used to this the cakes got burned, and Alfred burned his hands pulling them out of the fire, and the woman who had left him to watch the cakes screamed at him. I loved King Alfred. My grandfather was named after him; his son, my uncle, was named after King Alfred; my brother is named after King Alfred. And so there are three people in my family named after a man they have never met, a man who died over ten centuries ago. The first view I got of England then was not unlike the first view received by the person who named my grandfather.

This view, though—the naming of the kings, their deeds, their disappointments—was the vivid view, the forceful view. There were other views, subtler ones, softer, almost not there—but these were the ones that made the most lasting impression on me, these were the ones that made me really feel like nothing. "When morning touched the sky" was one phrase, for no morning touched the sky where I lived. The mornings where I lived came on abruptly, with a shock of heat and loud noises. "Evening approaches" was another, but the evenings where I lived did not approach; in fact, I had no evening—I had night and I had day and they came and went in a mechanical way: on, off; on, off. And then there were gentle mountains and low blue skies and moors over which people took walks for nothing but pleasure, when where I lived a walk was an act of labor, a burden, something only death or the automobile could relieve. And there were things that a small turn of a head could convey—entire worlds, whole lives would depend on this thing, a certain turn of a head. Everyday life could be quite tiring, more tiring than anything I was told not to do. I was told not to gossip, but they did that all the time. And they ate so much food, violating another of those rules they taught me: do not indulge in gluttony. And the foods they ate actually: if only sometime I could eat cold cuts after theater, cold cuts of lamb and mint sauce, and Yorkshire pudding and scones, and clotted cream, and sausages that came from upcountry (imagine, "up-country"). And having troubling thoughts at twilight, a good time to have troubling thoughts, apparently; and servants who stole and left in the middle of a crisis, who were born with a limp or some other kind of deformity, not nourished properly in their mother's womb (that last part I figured out for myself; the point was, oh to have an untrustworthy servant); and wonderful cobbled streets onto which solid front doors opened; and people whose eyes were blue and who had fair skins and who smelled only of lavender, or sometimes sweet pea or primrose. And those flowers with those names: delphiniums, foxgloves, tulips, daffodils, floribunda, peonies; in bloom, a striking display, being cut and placed in large glass bowls, crystal, decorating rooms so large twenty families the size of mine could fit in comfortably but used only for passing through. And the weather was so remarkable because the rain fell gently always, only occasionally in deep gusts, and it colored the air various shades of gray, each an appealing shade for a dress to be worn when a portrait was being painted; and when it rained at twilight, wonderful things happened: people bumped into each other unexpectedly and that would lead to all sorts of turns of events—a plot, the mere weather caused plots. I saw that people rushed: they rushed to catch trains, they rushed toward each other and away from each other; they rushed and rushed and rushed. That word: rushed! I did not know what it was to do that. It was too hot to do that, and so I came to envy people who would rush, even though it had no meaning to me to do such a thing. But there they are again. They loved their children; their children were sent to their own rooms as a punishment, rooms larger than my entire house. They were special, everything about them said so, even their clothes; their clothes rustled, swished, soothed. The world was theirs, not mine; everything told me so.

If now as I speak of all this I give the impression of someone on the outside looking in, nose pressed up against a glass window, that is wrong. My nose was pressed up against a glass window all right, but there was an iron vise at the back of my neck forcing my head to stay in place. To avert my gaze was to fall back into something from which I had been rescued, a hole filled with nothing, and that was the word for everything about me, nothing. The reality of my life was conquests, subjugation, humiliation, enforced amnesia. I was forced to forget. Just for instance, this: I lived in a part of St. John's, Antigua, called Ovals. Ovals was made up of five streets, each of them named after a famous English seaman—to be quite frank, an officially sanctioned criminal: Rodney Street (after George Rodney), Nelson Street (after Horatio Nelson), Drake Street (after Francis Drake), Hood Street, and Hawkins Street (after John Hawkins). But John Hawkins was knighted after a trip he made to Africa, opening up a new trade, the slave trade. He was then entitled to wear as his crest a Negro bound with a cord. Every single person living on Hawkins Street was descended from a slave. John Hawkins's ship, the one in which he transported the people he had bought and kidnapped, was called *The Jesus.* He later became the treasurer of the Royal Navy and rear admiral.

Again, the reality of my life, the life I led at the time I was being shown these views of England for the first time, for the second time, for the one-hundred-millionth time, was this: the sun shone with what sometimes seemed to be a deliberate cruelty; we must have done something to deserve that. My dresses did not rustle in the evening air as I strolled to the theater (I had no evening, I had no theater; my dresses were made of a cheap cotton, the weave of which would give way after not too many washings). I got up in the morning, I did my chores (fetched water from the public pipe for my mother, swept the yard), I washed myself, I went to a woman to have my hair combed freshly every day (because before we were allowed into our classroom our teachers would inspect us, and children who had not bathed that day, or had dirt under their fingernails, or whose hair had not been combed anew that day, might not be allowed to attend class). I ate that breakfast. I walked to school. At school we gathered in an auditorium and sang a hymn, "All Things Bright and Beautiful," and looking down on us as we sang were portraits of the Queen of England and her husband; they wore jewels and medals and they smiled. I was a Brownie. At each meeting we would form a little group around a flagpole, and after raising the Union Jack, we would say, "I promise to do my best, to do my duty to God and the Queen, to help other people every day and obey the scouts' law."

Who were these people and why had I never seen them, I mean really seen them, in the place where they lived? I had never been to England. No one I knew had ever been to England, or I should say, no one I knew had ever been and returned to tell me about it. All the people I knew who had gone to England had stayed there. Sometimes they left behind them their small children, never to see them again. England! I had seen England's representatives. I had seen the governor general at the public grounds at a ceremony celebrating the Queen's birthday. I had seen an old princess and I had seen a young princess. They had both been extremely not beautiful, but who of us would have told them that? I had never seen England, really seen it, I had only met a representative, seen a picture, read books, memorized its history. I had never set foot, my own foot, in it.

The space between the idea of something and its reality is always wide and deep and dark. The longer they are kept apart—idea of thing, reality of thing—the wider the width, the deeper the depth, the thicker and darker the darkness. This space starts out empty, there is nothing in it, but it rapidly becomes filled up with obsession or desire or hatred or love—sometimes all of these things, sometimes some of these things, sometimes only one of these things. The existence of the world as I came to know it was a result of this: idea of thing over here, reality of thing way, way over there. There was Christopher Columbus, an unlikable man, an unpleasant man, a liar (and so, of course, a thief) surrounded by maps and schemes and plans, and there was the reality on the other side of that width, that depth, that darkness. He became obsessed, he became filled with desire, the hatred came later, love was never a part of it. Eventually, his idea met the longed-for reality. That the idea of something and its reality are often two completely different things is something no one ever remembers; and so when they meet and find that they are not compatible, the weaker of the two, idea or reality, dies. That idea Christopher Columbus had was more powerful than the reality he met, and so the reality he met died.

And so finally, when I was a grown-up woman, the mother of two children, the wife of someone, a person who resides in a powerful country that takes up more than its fair share of a continent, the owner of a house with many rooms in it and of two automobiles, with the desire and will (which I very much act upon) to take from the world more than I give back to it, more than I deserve, more than I need, finally then, I saw England, the real England, not a picture, not a painting, not through a story in a book, but England, for the first time. In me, the space between the idea of it and its reality had become filled with hatred, and so when at last I saw it I wanted to take it into my hands and tear it into little pieces and then crumble it up as if it were clay, child's clay. That was impossible, and so I could only indulge in not-favorable opinions.

There were monuments everywhere; they commemorated victories, battles fought between them and the people who lived across the sea from them, all vile people, fought over which of them would have dominion over the people who looked like me. The monuments were useless to them now, people sat on them and ate their lunch. They were like markers on an old useless trail, like a piece of old string tied to a finger to jog the memory, like old decoration in an old house, dirty, useless, in the way. Their skins were so pale, it made them look so fragile, so weak, so ugly. What if I had the power to simply banish them from their land, send boat after boatload of them on a voyage that in fact had no destination, force them to live in a place where the sun's presence was a constant? This would rid them of their pale complexion and make them look more like me, make them look more like the people I love and treasure and hold dear, and more like the people who occupy the near and far reaches of my imagination, my history, my geography, and reduce them and everything they have ever known to figurines as evidence that I was in divine favor, what if all this was in my power? Could I resist it? No one ever has.

And they were rude, they were rude to each other. They didn't like each other very much. They didn't like each other in the way they didn't like me, and it occurred to me that their dislike for me was one of the few things they agreed on.

I was on a train in England with a friend, an English woman. Before we were in England she liked me very much. In England she didn't like me at all. She didn't like the claim I said I had on England, she didn't like the views I had of England. I didn't like England, she didn't like England, but she didn't like me not liking it too. She said, "I want to show you my England, I want to show you the England that I know and love." I had told her many times before that I knew England and I didn't want to love it anyway. She no longer lived in England; it was her own country, but it had not been kind to her, so she left. On the train, the conductor was rude to her; she asked something, and he responded in a rude way. She became ashamed. She was ashamed at the way he treated her; she was ashamed at the way he behaved. "This is the new England," she said. But I liked the conductor being rude; his behavior seemed quite appropriate. Earlier this had happened: we had gone to a store to buy a shirt for my husband; it was meant to be a special present, a special shirt to wear on special occasions. This was a store where the Prince of Wales has his shirts made, but the shirts sold in this store are beautiful all the same. I found a shirt I thought my husband would like and I wanted to buy him a tie to go with it. When I couldn't decide which one to choose, the salesman showed me a new set. He was very pleased with these, he said, because they bore the crest of the Prince of Wales, and the Prince of Wales had never allowed his crest to decorate an article of clothing before. There was something in the way he said it; his tone was slavish, reverential, awed. It made me feel angry; I wanted to hit him. I didn't do that. I said, my husband and I hate princes, my husband would never wear anything that had a prince's anything on it. My friend stiffened. The salesman stiffened. They both drew themselves in, away from me. My friend told me that the prince was a symbol of her Englishness, and I could see that I had caused offense. I looked at her. She was an English person, the sort of English person I used to know at home, the sort who was nobody in England but somebody when they came to live among the people like me. There were many people I could have seen England with; that I was seeing it with this particular person, a person who reminded me of the people who showed me England long ago as I sat in church or at my desk, made me feel silent and afraid, for I wondered if, all these years of our friendship, I had had a friend or had been in the thrall of a racial memory.

I went to Bath—we, my friend and I, did this, but though we were together, I was no longer with her. The landscape was almost as familiar as my own hand, but I had never been in this place before, so how could that be again? And the streets of Bath were familiar, too, but I had never walked on them before. It was all those years of reading, starting with Roman Britain. Why did I have to know about Roman Britain? It was of no real use to me, a person living on a hot, drought-ridden island, and it is of no use to me now, and yet my head is filled with this nonsense, Roman Britain. In Bath, I drank tea in a room I had read about in a novel written in the eighteenth century. In this very same room, young women wearing those dresses that rustled and so on danced and flirted and sometimes disgraced themselves with young men, soldiers, sailors, who were on their way to Bristol or someplace like that, so many places like that where so many adventures, the outcome of which was not good for me, began. Bristol, England. A sentence that began "That night the ship sailed from Bristol, England" would end not so good for me. And then I was driving through the countryside in an English motorcar, on narrow winding roads, and they were so familiar, though I had never been on them before; and through little villages the names of which I somehow knew so well though I had never been there before. And the countryside did have all those hedges and hedges, fields hedged in. I was marveling at all the toil of it, the planting of the hedges to begin with and then the care of it, all that clipping, year after year of clipping, and I wondered at the lives of the people who would have to do this, because wherever I see and feel the hands that hold up the world, I see and feel myself and all the people who look like me.

And I said, "Those hedges" and my friend said that someone, a woman named Mrs. Rothchild, worried that the hedges weren't being taken care of properly; the farmers couldn't afford or find the help to keep up the hedges, and often they replaced them with wire fencing. I might have said to that, well if Mrs. Rothchild doesn't like the wire fencing, why doesn't she take care of the hedges herself, but I didn't. And then in those fields that were now hemmed in by wire fencing that a privileged woman didn't like was planted a vile yellow flowering bush that produced an oil, and my friend said that Mrs. Rothchild didn't like this either; it ruined the English countryside, it ruined the traditional look of the English countryside.

It was not at that moment that I wished every sentence, everything I knew, that began with England would end with "and then it all died; we don't know how, it just all died." At that moment, I was thinking, who are these people who forced me to think of them all the time, who forced me to think that the world I knew was incomplete, or without substance, or did not measure up because it was not England; that I was incomplete, or without substance, and did not measure up because I was not English. Who were these people? The person sitting next to me couldn't give me a clue; no one person could. In any case, if I had said to her, I find England ugly, I hate England; the weather is like a jail sentence, the English are a very ugly people, the food in England is like a jail sentence, the hair of English people is so straight, so dead looking, the English have an unbearable smell so different from the smell of people I know, real people of course, she would have said that I was a person full of prejudice. Apart from the fact that it is I—that is, the people who look like me—who made her aware of the unpleasantness of such a thing, the idea of such a thing, prejudice, she would have been only partly right, sort of right: I may be capable of prejudice, but my prejudices have no weight to them, my prejudices have no force behind them, my prejudices remain opinions, my prejudices remain my personal opinion. And a great feeling of rage and disappointment came over me as I looked at England, my head full of personal opinions that could not have public, my public, approval. The people I come from are powerless to do evil on grand scale.

The moment I wished every sentence, everything I knew, that began with England would end with "and then it all died, we don't know how, it just all died" was when I saw the white cliffs of Dover. I had sung hymns and recited poems that were about a longing to see the white cliffs of Dover again. At the time I sang the hymns and recited the poems, I could really long to see them again because I had never seen them at all, nor had anyone around me at the time. But there we were, groups of people longing for something we had never seen. And so there they were, the white cliffs, but they were not that pearly majestic thing I used to sing about, that thing that created such a feeling in these people that when they died in the place where I lived they had themselves buried facing a direction that would allow them to see the white cliffs of Dover when they were resurrected, as surely they would be. The white cliffs of Dover, when finally I saw them, were cliffs, but they were not white; you would only call them that if the word "white" meant something special to you; they were dirty and they were steep; they were so steep, the correct height from which all my views of England, starting with the map before me in my classroom and ending with the trip I had just taken, should jump and die and disappear forever.

Reflections and Responses

1. Note that Kincaid opens her essay with various images of England. What do these images have in common? How do they reflect colonialism? How do they reflect literature? Why do you think Kincaid begins by placing the images in the context of a classroom?

2. Consider Kincaid's account of her father's hat. In what ways does the "brown felt hat" represent England? How does Kincaid view the hat?

3. When Kincaid finally visits England, what aspects of the country does she dislike the most? What does she mean when she says toward the end of her essay, "I may be capable of prejudice, but my prejudices have no weight to them"? Do you find her opinions prejudiced? In your opinion, has she or has she not "prejudged" England?

VERLYN KLINKENBORG

Our Vanishing Night

We're constantly reminded of the dangers pollution poses to our natural landscape—our oceans, our air, and even the world's temperature. In this brief essay, Verlyn Klinkenborg reveals, in a calm and methodical tone, the danger of something apparently innocuous: city lights. Urban light pollution, he argues, poses a serious (and easily reversible) threat to many aspects of the natural environment. While light pollution was once thought of merely as an impediment to astronomers, Klinkenborg expounds, one by one, on its wider effects: "Wherever human light spills into the natural world," he writes, "some aspect of life—migration, reproduction, feeding—is affected."

Verlyn Klinkenborg was born in Colorado and raised in Iowa and California. He graduated from Pomona College and received a PhD in English Literature from Princeton University. He serves on the editorial board of the New York Times, *where he often writes about life in rural New York State; his work has appeared in numerous other publications. His books include* Making Hay *(1986),* The Last Fine Time *(1991),* The Rural Life *(2003), and* Timothy: Or, Notes of an Abject Reptile *(2006). "Our Vanishing Night" originally appeared in* National Georgraphic *and was selected by Mary Oliver for* The Best American Essays 2009.

If humans were truly at home under the light of the moon and stars, we would go in darkness happily, the midnight world as visible to us as it is to the vast number of nocturnal species on this planet. Instead, we are diurnal creatures, with eyes adapted to living in the sun's light. This is a basic evolutionary fact, even though most of us don't think of ourselves as diurnal beings any more than we think of ourselves as primates or mammals or Earthlings. Yet it's the only way to explain what we've done to the night: We've engineered it to receive us by filling it with light.

This kind of engineering is no different than damming a river. Its benefits come with consequences—called light pollution—whose effects scientists are only now beginning to study. Light pollution is largely the result of bad lighting design, which allows artificial light to shine outward and upward into the sky, where it's not wanted, instead of focusing it downward, where it is. Ill-designed lighting washes out the darkness of night and radically alters the light levels—and light rhythms—to which many forms of life, including ourselves, have adapted. Wherever human light spills into the natural world, some aspect of life—migration, reproduction, feeding—is affected.

For most of human history, the phrase "light pollution" would have made no sense. Imagine walking toward London on a moonlit night around 1800, when it was Earth's most populous city. Nearly a million people lived there, making do, as they always had, with candles and rushlights and torches and lanterns. Only a few houses were lit by gas, and there would be no public gaslights in the streets or squares for another seven years. From a few miles away, you would have been as likely to *smell* London as to see its dim collective glow.

Now most of humanity lives under intersecting domes of reflected, refracted light, of scattering rays from overlit cities and suburbs, from light-flooded highways and factories. Nearly all of nighttime Europe is a nebula of light, as is most of the United States and all of Japan. In the south Atlantic the glow from a single fishing fleet—squid fishermen luring their prey with metal halide lamps—can be seen from space, burning brighter, in fact, than Buenos Aires or Rio de Janeiro.

In most cities the sky looks as though it has been emptied of stars, leaving behind a vacant haze that mirrors our fear of the dark and resembles the urban glow of dystopian science fiction. We've grown so used to this pervasive orange haze that the original glory of an unlit night—dark enough for the planet Venus to throw shadows on Earth—is wholly beyond our experience, beyond memory almost. And yet above the city's pale ceiling lies the rest of the universe, utterly undiminished by the light we waste—a bright shoal of stars and planets and galaxies, shining in seemingly infinite darkness.

We've lit up the night as if it were an unoccupied country, when nothing could be further from the truth. Among mammals alone, the number of nocturnal species is astonishing. Light is a powerful biological force, and on many species it acts as a magnet, a process being studied by researchers such as Travis Longcore and Catherine Rich, co-founders of the Los Angeles-based Urban Wildlands Group. The effect is so powerful that scientists speak of songbirds and seabirds being "captured" by searchlights on land or by the light from gas flares on marine oil platforms, circling and circling in the thousands until they drop. Migrating at night, birds are apt to collide with brightly lit tall buildings; immature birds on their first journey suffer disproportionately.

Insects, of course, cluster around streetlights, and feeding at those insect clusters is now ingrained in the lives of many bat species. In some Swiss valleys the European lesser horseshoe bat began to vanish after streetlights were installed, perhaps because those valleys were suddenly filled with light-feeding pipistrelle bats. Other nocturnal mammals—including desert rodents, fruit bats,

opossums, and badgers—forage more cautiously under the permanent full moon of light pollution because they've become easier
targets for predators.

Some birds—blackbirds and nightingales, among others—sing
at unnatural hours in the presence of artificial light. Scientists have
determined that long artificial days—and artificially short nights—
induce early breeding in a wide range of birds. And because a longer day allows for longer feeding, it can also affect migration
schedules. One population of Bewick's swans wintering in England
put on fat more rapidly than usual, priming them to begin their
Siberian migration early. The problem, of course, is that migration, like most other aspects of bird behavior, is a precisely timed
biological behavior. Leaving early may mean arriving too soon for
nesting conditions to be right.

Nesting sea turtles, which show a natural predisposition for dark
beaches, find fewer and fewer of them to nest on. Their hatch-
lings, which gravitate toward the brighter, more reflective sea horizon, find themselves confused by artificial lighting behind the
beach. In Florida alone, hatchling losses number in the hundreds
of thousands every year. Frogs and toads living near brightly lit
highways suffer nocturnal light levels that are as much as a million
times brighter than normal, throwing nearly every aspect of their
behavior out of joint, including their nighttime breeding
choruses.

Of all the pollutions we face, light pollution is perhaps the most
easily remedied. Simple changes in lighting design and installation
yield immediate changes in the amount of light spilled into the
atmosphere and, often, immediate energy savings.

It was once thought that light pollution only affected astronomers, who need to see the night sky in all its glorious clarity.
And, in fact, some of the earliest civic efforts to control light
pollution—in Flagstaff, Arizona, half a century ago—were made
to protect the view from Lowell Observatory, which sits high
above that city. Flagstaff has tightened its regulations since then,
and in 2001 it was declared the first International Dark Sky City.
By now the effort to control light pollution has spread around
the globe. More and more cities and even entire countries, such
as the Czech Republic, have committed themselves to reducing
unwanted glare.

Unlike astronomers, most of us may not need an undiminished view of the night sky for our work, but like most other creatures we do need darkness. Darkness is as essential to our biological welfare, to our internal clockwork, as light itself. The regular oscillation of waking and sleep in our lives—one of our circadian rhythms—is nothing less than a biological expression of the regular oscillation of light on Earth. So fundamental are these rhythms to our being that altering them is like altering gravity.

For the past century or so, we've been performing an open-ended experiment on ourselves, extending the day, shortening the night, and short-circuiting the human body's sensitive response to light. The consequences of our bright new world are more readily perceptible in less adaptable creatures living in the peripheral glow of our prosperity. But for humans, too, light pollution may take a biological toll. At least one new study has suggested a direct correlation between higher rates of breast cancer in women and the nighttime brightness of their neighborhoods.

In the end, humans are no less trapped by light pollution than the frogs in a pond near a brightly lit highway. Living in a glare of our own making, we have cut ourselves off from our evolutionary and cultural patrimony—the light of the stars and the rhythms of day and night. In a very real sense, light pollution causes us to lose sight of our true place in the universe, to forget the scale of our being, which is best measured against the dimensions of a deep night with the Milky Way—the edge of our galaxy—arching overhead.

Reflections and Responses

1. After a series of mostly scientific facts about light pollution, Klinkenborg concludes with a philosophical admonition: "In a very real sense, light pollution causes us to lose sight of our true place in the universe." What does he mean by this? Do you agree that being able to see the stars is an important element of (or limit on) our humanity?

2. Klinkenborg's paragraphs generally put forward one discreet danger of light pollution (to birds, to bats, to our internal clocks,

to the aesthetics of modern cities, etc.) each. Consider the way he organizes these paragraphs. Do you think he offers his strongest arguments first? Or perhaps his most viscerally appealing? Or does he delay these for the end of his essay? Why is the argument structured the way it is? Do you find this structure effective?

3. "Of all the pollutions we face," Klinkenborg writes, "light pollution is perhaps the most easily remedied." What remedy does he offer? Do you consider his solution practicable? Effective? What are some other ways you can think of to reduce light pollution? Or do you disagree fundamentally that it's a problem worthy of our attention at a time when so many other forms of pollution threaten us?

MICHAEL LEWIS

The Mansion: A Subprime Parable

"A man is rich," Henry David Thoreau *wrote in* Walden, *"in proportion to the number of things which he can afford to let alone." Thoreau attempted to reject the material comforts of the world and live as austerely as possible in the woods near his hometown of Concord, Massachusetts. In today's world, in which wealth is exhibited in conspicuous ostentation and often comes at the price of massive debt, journalist Michael Lewis attempts the reverse experiment: He moves into a house he can not afford. In the context of the housing collapse of 2008, which cost millions of Americans their homes, Lewis wonders if our obsession with big houses has led us into financial ruin. Of the crisis he writes: "The money-lending business didn't create the American desire for unaffordable housing. It simply facilitated it." Moreover, though, he discovers the affects that living in an outsize house has on him and his family; like one of the house's previous tenants, Lewis finds that he was never in control of the mansion—in fact, that "the mansion owned him."*

Michael Lewis initially went to work as a bond trader in London, an experience he documented in his first book, Liar's Poker *(1989). He has since written extensively for a wide range of publications on subjects including politics, finance, and baseball. His books include* Trail Fever *(1997),* The New New Thing *(2000),* Next: The Future Just Happened *(2001),* Moneyball *(2003),* Coach: Lessons on the Game of Life *(2005), and* Panic: The Story of Modern Financial Insanity *(2008). After the stint in New Orleans described in "The Mansion," Lewis moved back to California with his wife, former MTV VJ Tabitha Soren, and their children. "The*

Mansion: A Subprime Parable" originally appeared in Portfolio *and was selected by Mary Oliver for The* Best American Essays 2009.

I was looking to return to New Orleans, where I'd grown up, to write a book. The move would uproot my wife and three children from California, and I felt a little bad about that. They needed a place to live, but places to live in New Orleans are hard to find. Ever since Hurricane Katrina, the real estate market there has been in turmoil. Owners want to sell, buyers want to rent, and the result is a forest of for sale signs and an army of workers commuting from great distances.

At the bottom of every real estate ad I saw was the name of the same agent. One woman ruled the market, it seemed, and her name was Eleanor Farnsworth. I called her and threw myself on her mercy. She thought my problem over and then said, "I only know of one place that would work for you." She'd suggested it to Brad Pitt and Angelina Jolie, she said, before selling them their more modest place in the French Quarter.

That shouldn't have been a selling point; it should have been a warning. I should have asked the price. Instead, I asked the address.

As soon as I saw it, I knew it—the mansion. The most conspicuously grand house in New Orleans. As a child, I'd ridden my bike past it 2,000 times and always felt a tiny bit unnerved. It wasn't just a mansion; it seemed like the biggest mansion on the street with all the mansions, St. Charles Avenue, an object of fascination for the tourists on the clanging streetcars. But it was hard to imagine a human being standing beside it, much less living inside it, and as far as I could tell, none ever did. There was never any sign of life around it; it was just this awesome, silent pile of pale stone. The Frick Museum,* but closed.

Inside, it was even more awesome than outside. It was as if the architect had set out to show just how much space he could persuade a rich man to waste. The entryway was a kind of ballroom, which gave way to a curved staircase, a replica of one in the Palace of Versailles.† The living room wasn't a kind of ballroom; it was a

---

*The Frick Museum: A museum in Manhattan, located in the former residence of steel magnate Henry Clay Frick.

†Palace of Versailles: Louis XIV's splendidly opulent palace outside of Paris.

Hisham Ibrahim/Photographer's Choice/Getty Images

An example of the type of oversize house (pejoratively referred to as a McMansion) that many Americans have desired since the 1980s

ballroom, with $80,000 worth of gold on the ceiling. The bedrooms were the size of giant living rooms. The changing rooms and closets and bathrooms were the size of bedrooms. There were two of everything that the rest of the world has one of: two dining rooms, two full kitchens, two half kitchens. Ten bathrooms and seven bedrooms.

I didn't ask the price—I was renting—so I didn't know that the last time it changed hands it had sold for close to $7 million, and was now valued at $10 million. I imagined how it would feel to live in such a place. What it wouldn't feel like, clearly, was anything close to being in the other houses in which I'd lived.

Upper middle class: That's how I've always thought of myself. Upper middle class is the class into which I was born, the class to which I was always told I belonged, and the class with which, until this moment, I'd never had a problem. Upper middle class is a sneaky designation, however. It's a way of saying "I'm well-off" without having to say "I'm rich," even if, by most standards, you are. Upper-middle-classness has allowed me to feel like I'm not only competing in the same financial league as most Americans— I'm winning! Playing in the middle class, I have enjoyed huge success.

In this house, I now glimpsed the problem with upper-middle-classness: It isn't really a class. It's a space between classes. The space may once have been bridgeable, but lately it's become a chasm. Middle-class people fantasize about travel upgrades; upper-class people can't imagine life without a jet. Middle-class people help their children with their homework so they'll have a chance of getting into Princeton; upper-class people buy Princeton a new building. Middle-class people have homes; upper-class people have monuments. A man struggling to hold on to the illusion that he is upper middle class has become like a character in a cartoon earthquake: He looks down and sees his feet being dragged ever farther apart by a quickly widening fissure. His legs stretch, then splay, and finally he plunges into the abyss.

This house, and everything it represents, stands on the more appealing side of the chasm. "It's perfect," I said.

Every few days, I googled the house and stared at it. Then a funny thing happened: It began to shrink. Sure it's big, I told myself, but houses come bigger. The White House, for instance. I told my wife and children only that I'd found a house with a swimming pool and enough bathrooms for everyone to have his or her own. Which is to say, they really had no idea what they were getting into. How could they? It didn't occur to them that not only would they have their own bathrooms, they'd need to decide before dinner which of the two dining rooms to eat in—and afterward, which of the three dishwashers to not put their dishes in. To believe it, and to grasp its full upper-class implications, they'd need to see it.

On the day we move in, we're all stuffed together, Beverly Hill-billies-style, in a rented, dirty, gold Hyundai Sonata. For fun, as I drive up and down St. Charles Avenue, I ask them to guess which of these improbably large houses is ours.

"That one?"

"No."

"That one!"

The exercise turns giddy. Each house is bigger than the last. The girls squeal in the backseat and press their noses against the windows, while their mother, in the front, does her best to remain calm. We pass in front of the mansion and they look right past it. The thing takes up an entire city block, and somehow they can't see it. It's too implausible. It's not a home. It's a mint.

We circle around the block and approach from the rear, the Sonata rolling up the long driveway and coming to a stop beneath the grand stone porte cochere. "This is our new house?" asks Quinn, age eight.

"This is our new house," I say.

She begins to hyperventilate.

"Omigodomigodomigod!"

My small children plunge from the rental car into the driveway. They leap up and down as if they've just won an N.B.A. championship. By the time we get inside, they're gasping. They sprint off to inspect their new home.

"There's another floor!"

"Daddy! There's an elevator!"

My children love me. They have a house with an elevator.

In all the public finger-pointing about the American real estate bust, surprisingly little attention has been paid to its origin. There's obviously a long list of people and ideas that can share in the blame: ratings agencies, mortgage brokers, big Wall Street firms, small Wall Street firms, Angelo Mozilo, Alan Greenspan. Every few weeks, the New York Times runs a piece exposing some new way in which a big Wall Street firm has exploited some poor or middle-class family. The rich people on Wall Street blame their bosses. The brokers at Merrill Lynch blame Stan O'Neal; the traders at Bear Stearns blame Jimmy Cayne. Everyone blames Countrywide. But all of this misses the point: However terrible the sins of the

The Mansion: A Subprime Parable

financial markets, they're merely a reflection of a cultural predisposition. To blame the people who lent the money for the real estate boom is like blaming the crack dealers for creating addicts.

Americans feel a deep urge to live in houses that are bigger than they can afford. This desire cuts so cleanly through the population that it touches just about everyone. It's the acceptable lust.

Consider, for example, the Garcias. On May 30, the *New York Times* ran a story about a couple, Lilia and Jesus Garcia, who were behind on their mortgage payments and in danger of losing their homes. The Garcias had a perfectly nice house near Stockton, California, that they bought in 2003 for 160 grand. Given their joint income of $65,000, they could afford to borrow about $160,000 against a home. But then, in 2006, they stumbled upon their dream house. The new property was in Linden, California, and, judging from its picture, had distinctly mansionlike qualities. Its price, $535,000, was a stretch.

Then, of course, the market turned. The Garcias failed to make their mortgage payments and couldn't sell their original house. They owed the bank about $700,000 and were facing eviction. The mistake supposedly illustrated by the Garcias' predicament was that they held on to their former home in Stockton as an investment. The moral: Americans are in their current bind because too many of them saw houses as moneymaking opportunities.

But the real moral is that when a middle-class couple buys a house they can't afford, defaults on their mortgage, and then sits down to explain it to a reporter from the *New York Times*, they can be confident that he will overlook the reason for their financial distress: the peculiar willingness of Americans to risk it all for a house above their station. People who buy something they cannot afford usually hear a little voice warning them away or prodding them to feel guilty. But when the item in question is a house, all the signals in American life conspire to drown out the little voice. The tax code tells people like the Garcias that while their interest payments are now gargantuan relative to their income, they're deductible. Their friends tell them how impressed they are—and they mean it. Their family tells them that while theirs is indeed a big house, they have worked hard, and Americans who work hard deserve to own a dream house. Their kids love them for it.

Across America, some version of this drama has become a social norm. As of this spring, one in 11 mortgages was either past due—like Ed McMahon's* $4.8 million jumbo loan on his property—or in foreclosure, like Evander Holyfield's† $10 million Georgia estate. It's no good pretending that Americans didn't know they couldn't afford such properties, or that they were seduced into believing they could afford them by mendacious mortgage brokers or Wall Street traders. If they hadn't lusted after the bigger house, they never would have met the mortgage brokers in the first place. The money-lending business didn't create the American desire for unaffordable housing. It simply facilitated it.

It's this desire we must understand. More than any other possession, houses are what people use to say, "Look how well I'm doing!" Given the financial anxieties and indignities suffered by the American middle class, it's hardly surprising that a lower-middle-class child who grows up in a small house feels a burning need to acquire a bigger one. The wonder is how an upper-middle-class child who grew up in a big and perfectly enviable house is inexorably drawn to a mansion.

When you move into a house you cannot afford, the first thing you notice is everything that you suddenly need—things that, before you arrived, you didn't even want. The dressing room was a microcosm of our mansion's ability to instruct. It wasn't a closet, but a room as big as the master bedroom we'd left behind in California. Even after my wife had stored her countless pairs of shoes, there was more than enough space for all of my stuff. Three weeks later, I noticed a door near the master-bedroom suite that I hadn't seen before; it was like a magical door that someone had carved into the wall while I slept. What could it be? I opened it to find. . .another huge dressing room! Inside, I could have fit every stitch of clothing I owned, three times over. It seemed weird to just leave it empty, but I didn't have anything left to put in it, so I closed the door and pretended the room wasn't there. But the thought occurred: Maybe I need more clothes.

---

*__Ed McMahon:__ For years, Johnnie Carson's sidekick on NBC's *The Tonight Show.*

†__Evander Holyfield:__ A former heavyweight boxing champion.

The pool was another example. Because we moved in during the winter, we didn't pay that much attention to it at first. Had we bothered to dip our fingers in, we'd have discovered that it was not merely heated but was saltwater. It was a full six weeks before we really even noticed the pool house. Full bathroom, full kitchen, shiny new Viking range, and a fridge stuffed with 24 bottles of champagne. For a few weeks I felt that all of this was excessive. Then one day I became aware of the inconvenience of having to walk, dripping wet, from the pool back into the main house. This is what you need a pool house for—so you can make the transition from water to dry land without the trouble of walking the whole 15 yards back into the house and climbing a long flight of stairs to the giant dressing room. From that moment on, it seemed to me terribly inconvenient to not have a pool house. How on earth did people with pools, but no special house adjacent to them, cope?

The problems posed by the mansion were different from the problems posed by most other houses. How to locate loved ones, for instance. There's been no room inside any home I'd ever lived in from which, if I yelled at the top of my lungs, I couldn't be heard in every other room. The mansion required a new approach to human communications. Standing inside the mansion and screaming at the top of your lungs, you knew for certain that your voice wasn't reaching at least half the house. If you wanted to find someone, you could run around the house, but that took ages and presupposed that the other person was not similarly wandering in the void. A trek up the Himalayan staircases quickly became the subject of an elaborate cost-benefit analysis. How badly do I really want to find my six-year-old daughter? How much does my one-year-old son's diaper really need to be changed? After a while, it seemed only natural to my wife to begin with the assumption that her husband could not be found. Even when she knew for a fact that I was somewhere in the house, she'd begin her search with a phone call. She'd call my cell when I was two flights up and she'd call my cell when I was a room away. One afternoon she called my cell 20 minutes after I had come home with our three children and had gone looking for her to take them off my hands.

"Where are you?" she asked.

"I'm in the house taking care of the kids," I said, a little indignantly.

"Well, you can't be watching them very closely," she said, "because I'm in the house taking care of the kids."

Even though you couldn't find anybody, all sorts of people could find you. People stumbled into other people's spaces and terrified them. The house was so vast that the sound waves that normally precede the arrival of a living creature got lost. And so while there was, in theory, a great deal of privacy, there was, in practice, none. The mansion came with a gardener, a pool man, a caretaker, and a housekeeper. Any one of these people might turn up anyplace, anytime. The housekeeper, a sweet woman, came twice a week. She developed a habit of turning up over my right shoulder without warning and, as I stared helplessly at my computer screen, booming, "How's that book of yours coming along??!!!"

"Ah!" I'd yell, and leap out of my chair.

"Always writing, writing, writing!" she'd say with a laugh. (Writing in the mansion never ceased to be inherently comical.)

Money was another problem. It was suddenly going out faster than it was coming in. When I'd finally gotten around to asking the real estate agent what the mansion cost to rent, she'd said—in the most offhand tone, as if it were the least important thing about the house—"I'll have to see, but I think it's around 13." Thirteen. The extra digits are just assumed. One reason is that no one can bring themselves to actually utter the sentence: "Your rent will be $13,000 a month."

Thirteen thousand dollars a month is not the rent I was raised to pay. When I let it slip to my mother what I'd be paying, she just said, "Oh, Michael," in exactly the same tone she'd have used if I'd informed her that I'd just run over the neighbor with a truck or been diagnosed with pancreatic cancer. Thirteen thousand dollars a month might be a record rent in New Orleans, but it was really just the ante.

We'd been there only three weeks when the first bills arrived. Utilities were $2,700. That turned out not to include water, which was another $1,000. Think of it: $1,000 a month for water you don't drink. (The drinking water came in truckloads from a spring-water company.) How did we use so much water? you might reasonably ask. The answer is, we didn't. The mansion did. The pool, the fountains, the sprinklers that came on in the wee hours to keep the great lawn lush and green—all were suddenly necessary. So, it turned out, was cable, at $800 a month. Who was I to argue? I wasn't even entirely sure how many televisions we had. Nine, at least. I thought I'd found the last of them when, two months after we'd arrived, I opened a cabinet and found another.

Walking into the mansion after school one day, my younger daughter, Dixie, asked, "Daddy, what's a Daddy Warbucks?" She'd caught a ride with a new friend's babysitter, who didn't know where we lived. Instead of giving the babysitter directions, the friend's mother had just said, "They live in the Daddy Warbucks house."

The first request for money came exactly 11 days after we arrived. A former schoolmate was calling on behalf of our high school; its fundraising department had somehow learned that I'd not only moved back to town but had moved into the mansion. My old school friend had a number in mind, somewhere between $25,000 and $100,000. Two days later, we had another old friend to dinner and—in hopes that she'd spread the word—I spoke of my amazement that anyone thought we could fork over 100 grand on a whim. "It's funny you should say that," she said. She'd just spoken with the director of a New Orleans museum, who had also heard we'd moved into the mansion. "He's trying to figure out the best way to approach you," she said.

We'd become an engineering problem.

Late one night the doorbell rings. There on our great stone porch is a man, obviously down on his luck, doing his best to appear subservient.

"I was just wondering if you have anything," he asks.

"Have anything?" I ask back.

"Some work that might be done, you know."

It's a feudal exchange right out of the 11th century. Vassal calling on lord with the mutual understanding that lord owes vassal employment. The only thing missing is the offer of a freshly slaughtered rabbit.

A couple of months into our stay, we all sit in the formal dining room, under the gilded ceiling and the crystal chandelier, eating packaged tortellini off paper plates. We are Cuban peasants in late 1959 who have just moved into a Havana mansion on the heels of the rich owner, who has fled in terror from the revolution. Dixie, then five, blurts out, "I hate it when people say, 'Oh, I love your house,' because then I have to say, 'It's not my house.'" To which Quinn adds, "Yeah, I hate it when people say, 'You must be rich.'"

This was new. My children had taken to their new splendor like ducks to water. They'd see the St. Charles streetcar rolling past, and the tourists gawking and pointing at their new house, and their first reaction was not to cringe but to perform. They'd throw on their most princesslike dresses and run out front and dance around the malfunctioning marble fountain, pissing water in all the wrong directions, and wave to the commoners. One morning, as Quinn descended the staircases, overdressed for school, she announced, "I need to look good. I'm the girl who lives in the mansion."

But after a few months, the charm of pretending to be something they know they are not is wearing off.

There's a moment in the life of every American child when it dawns on him or her that the divvying up of material spoils is neither arbitrary nor a matter of personal choice, that money is a tool used by grownups to order and rank themselves, and that the easiest way to establish those rankings is through their houses. At first, everyone's house appears more or less the same; at any rate, you don't spend much time dwelling on the differences. But then, one day, someone's house is either so much humbler or so much grander than anything you've ever seen that you realize: A house is not just a house. It's one of the tools people use to rank me.

Children are basically communists. Seeing other children's material prosperity, they follow their first instinct, which isn't to understand it or stew about it. It's to ask for some of it—to get invited to the mansion. As far as I knew, my children had never given much thought to what their house said about them and their place in the world. They'd been friends with rich kids and poor kids, without dwelling on the differences. That had just changed.

I resist the urge to explain how their misery might be good training for grown-up American life; how we are, quite obviously, a nation of financial imposters, poised to seize the first opportunity to live in houses we cannot afford; and how, if they want to fit in, they'll need to learn to handle the stress. They will have to learn these important lessons for themselves.

Instead, I turn my attention to survival. The mansion was not satisfied with making us uneasy. It wanted us out. It preferred us to leave quietly, without a fuss. But if we didn't, it was prepared to get violent.

The first inkling of this came one lazy Sunday afternoon. I was fathering my one-year-old son by teaching him how best to watch an N.B.A. game—which is to say, in high-def with surround sound. Our bliss was disrupted by the cry of a small child. It was muted, as if someone were calling out from inside the walls. It was from inside the walls. Our girls, with their 10-year-old cousin, were trapped inside the elevator, which had mysteriously jolted to a stop. I tried to yank the metal gate off its hinges to get into the shaft, but failed. It wouldn't have mattered anyway, as they were between floors. For a good 20 minutes, I grunted and groaned and sweated and pretended that this wasn't anything I couldn't handle. Then I called the caretaker, who gave me the number of the man who had made the elevator work in the first place. By some miracle, he was around and willing to drive the 20 miles from his home to ours on a Sunday. Two hours later, the girls, sobbing melodramatically, were sprung. The elevator man turned to me and said, "I'm surprised you let them in there."

"Why?"

"She didn't tell you about the cat?"

No one told me about the cat that had been riding up in the elevator with its billionaire owner. As they ascended, the cat had jumped out of the owner's arms and stuck its head out of the metal gate. Its head had been chopped off.

I shut down the elevator.

A few days later, the phone rang. "We want to let you know that we received a message from the equipment-supervision device on your control panel," said the voice on the other end of the line. The what on the what? The mansion, I learned, was equipped with tiny cameras that enabled it, in effect, to watch its inhabitants. One of these, apparently, had malfunctioned. I went into the basement, found the video-control panel, and yanked out as many plugs as I could find.

The next afternoon, the house felt chilly. I hunted down the many thermostats and turned them back up, from the 68 degrees to which they'd somehow plummeted, to 72. The house ignored the request; no matter what I did, it remained at exactly 68 degrees. My skin became the world's most sensitive thermometer, an expert on the state of being 69 degrees, because the moment the house would reach that temperature, all hell would break loose—one, then another, and then a third of the massive air-conditioning units that sat outside would begin to purr. Every now and again, I'd feel a brief tingle of warmth, a premonition of climate change, but that moment was always followed by the roar of engines and a correction.

The day after I tried to change the mansion's temperature, early in the morning, the alarm went off. Then the phone rang: It was the alarm company, wanting to know our password. I gave it to them.

"I'm sorry, we don't have that as a password," said the lady on the other end of the phone, and then, as I begged and pleaded ("No, please, no! Let me try again!"), she quickly hung up.

Moments later, two squad cars with lights flashing sped into our driveway. Four police officers leapt out and banged on the front door. The mansion had phoned the cops at exactly the moment I appeared most shockingly arrestable: wearing only underpants and a T-shirt, hair sticking up in six different directions, and without a trace of evidence that I belonged there. I grabbed Dixie ("Daddy, I don't want to go! What if they arrest me too?") and pulled her close to me, as a kind of human shield.

"Sir, we're responding to an alarm signal."

"It was obviously a mistake. Sorry to trouble you."

Silence.

"We're just renting the place."

The police drove away, more slowly than they'd arrived. But obviously they weren't the problem. The house had a mind of its own, like one of those old horses you find at dude ranches. You begin with the assumption that you are in control of the beast. Then you try to guide it as much as two feet off the assigned path, and it resists and takes control of the steering. You are left feeling ashamed of whatever cowboy pretense you had to begin with.

I investigated the history of our property. It was built in 1912 by an entrepreneur named E.V. Benjamin, whose son, raised in the mansion, became eccentric enough for a small group of interested residents of New Orleans to create a gathering called the Benjamin Club, whose sole purpose was to swap stories about him. The house then moved into the hands of another very rich man, J. Edgar Monroe, who had made the bulk of his fortune from taking over the Canal Bank. When the bank was closed by the federal government during the Great Depression, he had himself appointed the bank's liquidator, repaid its shareholders, and then bought up a huge chunk of the leftover shares for pennies.

Monroe went on to buy not only this house but also Rosecliffe, the Newport mansion used in the filming of *The Great Gatsby*. He was famous for telling anyone who would listen how much money he had given away to charity. After he donated a music building to Loyola University New Orleans, he insisted that the school mount a plaque on one of its walls with an inscription he wrote:

J. Edgar Monroe has donated to construction of this building $1,000,000.00 (one million) in cash. my secretary has strongly urged me to make a plaque of this donation so that the students of the music school and the public will know of this gift. father carter, president of loyola university, acknowledged receipt of four $250,000.00 checks, or $1,000,000.00. mr. monroe has given over one hundred million dollars ($100,000,000.00) to organized charity of which the largest share was given to loyola university.

When Monroe's wife, Louise, died in 1989, the old man wrote her obituary. It opened with a paragraph or two about the deceased, but then quickly moved on to detail her husband's incredible generosity. "Mr. Monroe is still living and is 92 years of age," he wrote. "He has been very generous and has given over one hundred million dollars to organized charity. . ." and so on. He too died in the house a few years later.

Until the mid-1990s, the house had been owned by men who could comfortably afford it. They didn't need the house to prove how rich they were; everyone knew how rich they were. The moment the house became troubled was the moment someone who couldn't afford it moved in—a man who was using it to slake his own thirst for status. He was a lawyer.

Lawyers are upper middle class. But this lawyer grabbed the saddle horn of magnificence and hung on for dear life—until the day in 2004 when he was bucked off. There in the dust he lay, exposed—in the New Orleans Times-Picayune—for defrauding his law partners. His firm defended big companies from class-action suits. To make the kind of money he needed to live in this house, the poor guy had resorted to allegedly cutting secret deals with plaintiffs' lawyers. He reportedly gave up his law license to avoid being formally charged.

The mansion made him do it: That's what I thought when I heard the story. As sordid as his behavior was, I'm incapable of feeling toward him anything but sympathy. He wanted this mansion, he bought this mansion, and then he discovered that the mansion owned him.

The next owner was a woman. She'd grown up middle class in New Orleans, and in her youth had driven past the mansion and fantasized about owning it. Then she'd married an oil-and-gas billionaire who gave her the house as a surprise for her birthday.

The billionaire's wife proceeded to spare no expense in redoing it exactly as she wanted. She spent $250,000 on gold to touch up the gilt fringe of the moldings and the ceiling medallions. I spoke with the interior decorator she hired. It was this man who grasped the inappropriateness of a mere lawyer owning this house. "They tried to shrink it," he said to me one day. "They painted the walls taupe; they had canopies over the beds to make a room within the room. They tried to make it homey." The billionaire's wife succeeded in undoing that. The taupe returned to white, the canopies fell, and the gilding on the ceiling soon gleamed like new. Several million dollars later, she had the mansion looking as she wanted it to look, which was more or less like Versailles. Luckily for her, birthday presents are not community property, because by the time she was finished touching up the house, her husband was divesting himself of her. No matter what the settlement came to, the property belonged to her outright. But she was not happy.

And neither was her mansion. When we moved in, she'd been trying to sell it for the $10 million or so she had put into it. Characteristically, the house was refusing to give her the money back. It resented people trying to sell it, just as it was beginning to resent people who can't afford it.

Now it was expressing that resentment. It committed an act which, for a New Orleans house in summer, is tantamount to eviction. All by itself, with the temperature outside rising into the low 90s, it shut down its air-conditioning. I do not mean that any of its 11 air-conditioning units broke. A broken unit can be repaired. The repairmen came and went, shaking their heads. There was nothing they could see that was wrong with even one of the mansion's massive air compressors. The problem was deep inside the walls, perhaps in the wiring. The ballroom, interestingly, was still 68 degrees, but the bedrooms were now 83. The house not only had microclimates, but also a unifying theme. The grand public spaces continued to be pleasant and comfortable, as if the mansion, in chasing us out, had no interest in sullying its public reputation. Only its putatively private spaces—bedrooms, bathrooms—were uninhabitable. Amazingly, it could be 83 degrees and humid in one room and 68 and dry in another—on the same floor. For the first time inside a house, it occurred to me that it might rain.

And so we fled, back to where we'd come from: the upper middle class. Obviously this presents new problems. Even as my children grew weary of pretending they were richer than they are, they became accustomed to living as the rich do. On the way back to California, my wife drove Quinn, who'd just turned nine, across the Southwest and then up the coast. They came to Hearst Castle* and stopped to take the guided tour. A few minutes into it, as they stood in one of William Randolph Hearst's many bedrooms, the guide asked if anyone had a question. My child raised her hand. The guide smiled indulgently and called on her.

"Why," Quinn asked, "is it so small?"

Responses and Reflections

1. Lewis never explicitly delineates why he wanted to live in the mansion—why his childhood queasiness cycling past it subsided into a desire to own it. Do you detect an answer to this question in the essay's first few paragraphs? Is he chastising himself for his decision later when he describes the impact the house has on him? What is he suggesting about his motives?

2. Lewis characterizes America as a "nation of financial impostors." Do you agree? How does the desire to appear better off than one really is figure into the crises—personal and macroeconomic—Lewis is discussing?

*__Hearst Castle:__ The sprawling, opulent estate of newspaper publisher William Randolph Hearst near San Simeon, California.

3. How does Lewis *personify* the house in his essay, and to what effect? When he writes "The house had a mind of its own, like one of those old horses you find at dude ranches," how is he characterizing the mansion, and why? When he writes of its former felonious tenant that "the mansion made him do it," is he really suggesting that the house has a supernatural effect on its owners? Or that the pretense of wealth it requires does? What is the purpose of this personification?

DANIELLE OFRI

Living Will

"Living Will" is a fine example of the type of essay that follows a narrative arc as the author describes the process of moving from one state of mind to another, usually from a moral or intellectual dilemma to resolution and insight. Such essays often involve an epiphany. *The Irish novelist James Joyce first used this ancient religious term in a modern literary sense to describe the sudden flash of recognition or the unexpected illumination that can transform our understanding. "Living Will" takes us inside today's medical profession—with its awesome technological capability—and confronts one of medicine's major issues: Why are severely ill and depressed patients who have lost the will to live kept alive at such an enormous cost of time, expense, and professional effort?*

Danielle Ofri, MD, PhD, is the author of Singular Intimacies: Becoming a Doctor at Bellevue *(2003) and* Incidental Findings: Lessons from My Patients in the Art of Medicine *(2005). Ofri is editor in chief and cofounder of the* Bellevue Literary Review *and associate chief editor of an award-winning medical textbook,* The Bellevue Guide to Outpatient Medicine. *Her stories have appeared in both literary and medical journals as well as in several anthologies. She is an attending physician at Bellevue Hospital and on the faculty of New York University School of Medicine. "Living Will" originally appeared in* The Missouri Review *and was selected by Susan Orlean for* The Best American Essays 2005.

WILBUR RESTON was already in the intensive care unit of the tiny Florida hospital when I arrived at two-thirty A.M. I had been doing a series of temp jobs after having completed my medical residency at New York City's Bellevue Hospital and now found myself in a small town on the Gulf Coast. The breathing tube in Mr. Reston's throat and his heavy sedation precluded formal introductions. But there was a typewritten summary of his medical history that his wife had left with the nurses; a two-page, single-spaced account that chronicled the rebellion and demise of each organ in this sixty-one-year-old white man. He had survived three heart attacks and seven strokes. One kidney had been removed. He suffered from diabetes, high blood pressure, and congestive heart failure. He had emphysema, glaucoma, severe migraines, and arthritis. His medical history included pancreatitis, diverticulitis, pyelonephritis, sinusitis, cholelithiasis, tinnitus, and ankylosing spondfylitis. The typed paper also mentioned gastroesophageal reflux, vertigo, and depression. I quickly glanced over to the man hooked up to the ventilator to verify that he was indeed alive.

His wife had told the ER physicians that he'd stopped taking his water pills several days ago. Eventually he could no longer breathe. He possessed a living will stating that he did not want any life-sustaining procedures. In the ER, however, he had apparently agreed to be intubated. It had taken an enormous amount of sedation to get the breathing tube in, and then his blood pressure bottomed out. He was now unconscious in the ICU, on multiple pressor medications to support his blood pressure and augment his weak heart. In Bellevue terminology, he was a "train wreck."

Mr. Reston had been admitted to East General Hospital at two A.M. My colleagues in the small private practice where I was working had instructed me *never* to go to the hospital in the middle of the night. "Give your orders over the phone and see the patient in the morning," they advised. But I was still too new at this kind of medicine to be that confident; I had to at least lay eyes on the patient before I could decide on any medical orders.

I couldn't take a history from Mr. Reston, since he was at present unarousable because of all the sedation. My physical exam was brief. Mainly I plowed through the typed medical summary, converting it into a concise admission note. I handed my admitting orders to the nurse, and then there was nothing for me to do. In this small community hospital, the nurses were used to, and entirely comfortable with, working without any doctors around. How unlike Bellevue, where interns and residents roamed the halls twenty-four hours a day, deeply and intricately involved in the minutiae of medical care.

Here the nurses took most of the doctors' orders over the phone and did everything themselves: drew blood, inserted IVs, did EKGs, obtained blood and urine cultures, sent patients for x-rays, followed up on test results, and so on. The doctors, with their busy private practices, usually visited once a day, either very early in the morning or late, after their office hours. The emphasis was on remembering to sign verbal orders within twenty-four hours. Not surprisingly, the head nurse was taken aback and almost alarmed when I showed up in the middle of the night for Mr. Reston's admission.

It was now nearly four A.M. as I drove back to the hotel in my rental car. The main roads of the town were deserted. I rolled down the windows and was quickly enveloped in humid, orange-scented fog. Stretches of flat, boring landscape were broken up periodically by strip malls. Neighborhoods of low-slung, white stucco houses were dotted with pickup trucks and palm trees. The smell of blossoms had not been fully eradicated by the burgeoning construction industry.

Southwest Florida was nothing like West Palm Beath, which I had assumed represented all of Florida. This area was rural, with acres of fields farmed by itinerant workers, mostly from Central America. I had just returned from Guatemala, so I was eager to practice my Spanish, but in the private practice where I worked, I rarely had the opportunity, except for the time when I was called upon to explain to a Honduran fruit picker that we couldn't treat his high blood pressure because he didn't have medical insurance. The hospital emergency room had called me when he'd shown up there needing prescriptions, and I'd said sure, send him over right now. When he arrived at the office, however, the practice manager informed me that we could not treat patients without insurance except for medical emergencies. Since I was the only one in the office who spoke passable Spanish, the duty of telling him fell to me. My verb-conjugating ability floundered, and my pronouns disagreed with their antecedents. My vocabulary in Spanish—and in English for that matter—had never included such phrases as "We cannot take care of you. You must go to a different doctor." I suddenly longed for Bellevue, for the chaos of the emergency room there, with its bubbling tumult of languages, ethnicities, colors, and socioeconomic classes, and its assumption that everybody received medical care regardless of ability to pay.

But aside from that one incident, the office was a pleasant place to work. Three doctors had started this practice several years ago, and they were now extremely successful. They had built an impressive clientele of devoted patients, mainly older but many middle-aged. They had equipped their office with a tiny pharmacy and a stress-test machine, and had arranged for weekly visits from an ultrasound technician, who performed all their sonograms. They'd even opened a small gym next door, in which they sponsored exercise classes for the elderly and rehab classes for their patients with emphysema. The doctors were in their forties, looking for ways to cut down on hours and enter semi-retirement. They were more than happy to hand over a third of the office patients and one hundred percent of the inpatient hospital duties. They gladly acceded to my request for paid prep time so that I could read patients' charts in advance of their appointments, all in a comfortable office with an experienced, full-time nurse to assist me. It was the lap of luxury. Within a week they offered me a permanent, full-time position with a salary that was four times what I'd earned as a resident for half the working hours, plus a share in the practice.

The patients were pleasant and apparently particularly happy to have a woman doctor, something new to that practice. And for the first time in *my* life, medicine was not a struggle: I could practice the best medicine I wanted without having to fight for anything. Coming from the trenches of Bellevue, where medicine felt almost like warfare, I found the case of practicing good medicine almost disconcerting. I couldn't deny that the job offer was tempting.

But I could never leave Manhattan—certainly not to live in such a tiny town.

The town was a speck on the map in southwest Florida that no one I knew had ever heard of. The pace was unhurried, and the locals were unceasingly friendly and helpful, traits that were sometimes unsettling to a native New Yorker. Overly polite strangers made me suspicious, though everyone assured me that this was the normal style in the South. There was no place to get sushi, but the two-room library across the street from my office did stock Spanish-lesson tapes, and I was able to study a semester's worth of grammar on my way to work each day. Much to my dismay and disbelief, the library did not subscribe to the *New York Times*. A very weak consolation was the *Wall Street Journal*—only available, however the following day.

The private practice was affiliated with East General, an eighty-eight-bed community hospital. I'd never seen a hospital that small. Eighty-eight beds was one floor at Bellevue, and Bellevue sported twenty-one floors. East General Hospital reminded me of my elementary school—spread out over two wings, each only two stories high. The elevator seemed redundant. Some of the services that I was used to from Bellevue, like twenty-four-hour-a-day access to cardiac catheterization and hemodialysis, were not available, but there were other advantages. With a maximum census of eighty-eight patients, there was never any waiting time for anything I ordered. Stress tests, sonograms, CT scans, pulmonary consults, social-work requests—I had only to jot a request in the chart and it would be completed by the end of the day. The staff was small, but everyone seemed competent and extremely friendly. Within a week even the housekeepers were greeting me by name, and the phone operators recognized my voice when I called.

The following morning Mr. Reston was awake but extremely uncomfortable. He had tried to pull out his breathing tube several times, so the nurses had tied his arms down. I apologized to him for the wrist restraints and explained that I would try to get the tube out as soon as possible. I was self-conscious about my words because Wilbur Reston's body was sentient. He heard and understood everything I said, but the tube and the restraints prevented him from speaking or even gesturing; my awkward reassurances met with no response. I spent the morning in the ICU weaning Mr. Reston off the ventilator and draining fluid from his lungs. When the nurses were rolling him over to change the sheets, he managed to dislodge his own breathing tube and set himself free.

There is an entire scientific literature on the most appropriate time to extubate a patient, based on pulmonary function tests, blood gas values, and chest x-ray findings. But the Bellevue ICU's wisdom was that a patient was ready to be extubated when he or she reached over and yanked the damn tube out. Mr. Reston proved this to be true, since enough fluid had been removed from his lungs that he was able to breathe, if a bit huskily, without the tube. His condition was still tenuous, though, and he was too exhausted from his ordeal to talk much, I waited a while for his wife to arrive, but she never showed up.

Thirty-six hours after his admission I was finally able to actually "meet" Mr. Reston. He was a burly fellow who looked surprisingly robust for a patient with such a thick medical record. I would have expected a shriveled old man, but he had beefy arms and a hefty belly. There was a tattoo of an alligator on his left biceps. The ICU bed sagged slightly under his weight whenever he shifted or turned.

Mr. Reston's face was pulled low on his neck by meaty jowls, and dark bags weighed his eyes down. He had lived his entire life in this small town on the west coast of Florida. He was a veteran of the Korean War, with a specialty in artillery. After the war he'd worked as a police officer and spent some time training guard dogs.

His voice was surprisingly soft and somewhat morose. In slow, deliberate phrases he described a lifetime of progressively declining health. His arthritic pains and severe headaches seemed to have taken a greater toll on him than his many strokes and heart attacks. He was confined to his house, unable even to walk down the driveway to retrieve his mail.

Did he have any hobbies? He heaved a melancholic sigh. "I fancied myself a carpenter. I built miniature furniture for dollhouses. Always used the best wood."

I imagined this bearlike man hunched over delicate divans and bedroom sets.

"Can't do it anymore. My hands." He threw up his gnarled, arthritic paws for inspection.

"I also collect Civil War memorabilia. Once found a belt buckle from the second battle of Bull Run," he said with a puff of pride. "They had it in the museum for a while." But his recollection of his former glory was brief. "My wife thinks it's a stupid hobby," he said.

What about depression? "I've never *not* been depressed," he sighed ruefully. "Ever since college, I suppose." His records showed that he'd been treated at the VA psychiatric clinic with both psychotherapy and antidepressant medications for more than twenty years. His only daughter had died of a brain tumor the year before. His mother and sister had both died in the past five years, So had his dog.

Had he ever attempted suicide? "I'm handy with guns, you know. I have at least five in the house," he said dryly. "Different models. Always keep a loaded one at my bedside."

Did he ever use it? "Well, I stuck the barrel in my mouth. Didn't pull the trigger, though. Too messy. Just stopped taking my pills."

I had an image of Mr. Reston sitting on the side of his bed, shoulders sagging, cradling the gun in his hand. Perhaps he'd raised the gun to his head several times, each time not able to bring it close enough. But then he'd take a quick, dry swallow and, squinting, slide the gun into his mouth. I imagined that he might be startled at how comforting the gun felt in his mouth. But then that very comfort would make him shudder, and he'd rip the gun out, stuff it back into the nightstand drawer, and slam the drawer shut.

Then he'd be left staring at the pill bottles lined up on that nightstand, loaded with promises of good heath. He'd finger them, recalling what ill each was meant to cure. And cure they did. And then what?

I envisioned him opening that drawer again and, with the crook of his clublike arm, sweeping the bottles in, their hard plastic clattering against the gun as they came to rest at the bottom. He'd sink his head into his hands, forgetting to shut the nightstand drawer.

What about his wife, I asked. "She's busy with that volunteer work. She don't have time for me and all my pills," he said sadly. An uneasy silence settled in. I could see moisture accumulating at the edges of his soulful eyes, "We haven't shared a bed in fifteen years," he whispered.

His voice was plaintive but resigned. "Why should I live this life? I can't walk, my wife don't speak to me, I can't do nothing. What's the point?" He fixed his mournful gaze upon me. "*You* tell *me*."

It was both a plea and a demand. His simple statement had caused the space between us to evaporate, and I suddenly felt naked. Without my clinical armor to shield me, I was just one human facing another, squinting before the raw question. What *was* the point? What were the reasons for him to go on living?

I struggled to come up with one. Mr. Reston's body had withered sufficiently to keep him in perpetual pain but not enough to let him die. He had no friends; his wife was estranged. His daughter, mother, and sister had died and abandoned him. He was too weak to walk out of his house. He could no longer do any of the things that brought him pleasure. Why should he want to live? I could see why he had stopped taking his pills.

I didn't have an answer for him, but the law dictated what I had to do: actively suicidal patients must be prevented from harming themselves.

Like all good emergencies, this one occurred late on a Friday afternoon. Unlike Bellevue, there was no residency program in psychiatry to supply immediate consultations. There were several psychiatrists in the community, but they were busy with their private practices during the day and rarely made after-hours calls. But the staff of this tiny hospital was resourceful and helpful. They got me in touch with the local mental health agency, which was able to dispatch a psychiatric nurse practitioner. She agreed with my concerns and helped the nursing staff arrange a round-the-clock "suicide watch" over Mr. Reston. I could have Mr. Reston transferred to a psychiatric hospital once his medical condition stabilized if I felt he was still in danger of hurting himself. The nurse practitioner explained the procedures to invoke the Baker Act, the state legislation that allowed involuntary psychiatric commitment in such circumstances.

Over that weekend Mr. Reston's medical condition slowly improved, but his mood did not, Why should it? I thought. What did he have to look forward to? As much as I tried, I could not bring myself to utter flimsy platitudes about the value of life and how things would be better tomorrow. They weren't going to get better—he knew it and I knew it. Although he was clearly depressed, Mr. Reston was perfectly lucid. Despite his many strokes, his mind seemed to be working just fine. He could do all the tasks in the mental status exam: spell "world" backward, count down from one hundred by sevens, name the president, interpret the proverb "A rolling stone gathers no moss."

Although Mr. Reston seemed to have a reasonably realistic grasp on his situation, I wasn't so sure I had a grasp on mine. Doctors aren't supposed to agree with their patients who say they want to kill themselves, but I found myself overwhelmed by the utterly dismal facts of Mr. Reston's situation. Whom did Mr. Reston have left to live for? Even his dog had died.

I tried to imagine pacing the blank landscape of an empty life. How could I survive if every source of pleasure was denied? How could I live if the flavors, colors, and textures that made life palatable were flattened into a monochrome gray? If I were Mr. Reston, I might have pulled that trigger.

To complicate matters, he was in a rather unique medical situation. Although he had multitudes of medical problems, he was not yet terminally ill. He had a long list of diseases, but none was close to killing him. He was sick enough to be miserable but not sick enough to die. He was still able to eat, care for himself, and communicate with others. There were plenty of services and options for people on the verge of death, but Mr. Reston was not sick enough to qualify. His body, honed from years in the military and police force, was holding on too tenaciously. It left him stranded, strung too far from the shores of either health or death. Mr. Reston had severe physical pain, apparently unresponsive to various treatments, but more important, he was being eaten away by psychic pain.

The medico-legal issues were clear: a suicidal patient is prevented from committing suicide, even against his will, period. But the shades of gray needled me. My patient didn't want his life, and I wasn't sure it was ethical to force him to continue living it.

These issues plagued me for the remainder of the week. Ashamed to reveal my heresies to anyone, I secretly toyed with my doubts, picking at them as one does a loose tooth, perversely finding pleasure in its pain. What if I let him go home to his household of loaded guns? What if I discharged him, knowing full well that he'd stop taking his life-saving medicines? What if I turned my head and let him kill himself, as he so desperately wanted to do? There are those who say that all suicidal thoughts are products of depression, but Mr. Reston had been assiduously treated with medications and psychotherapy for decades. Perhaps he was being entirely rational. Who was I to stand in his way?

Then the toothache would burrow down to the raw nerve: What kind of evil doctor was I to even *consider* not protecting my patient from his violent tendencies? How could I be so negligent?

As I drove back and forth to work each day, this dilemma nagged at me. Lulled by the bland landscape, my mind would wander from the Spanish vocabulary coming from the car's tape deck to Mr. Reston languishing in his bare hospital room. Could there ever be any happiness for him? What if I found him a new hobby, one that he could manage with his disabilities? Stamp collecting—that wouldn't require much mobility. But probably his fingers couldn't manipulate the fragile paper stamps. Maybe he could take up painting.

Large, easy brushes with hefty tubs of paint—he could manage that. Perhaps there was an artist waiting inside his weary body.

Traffic was stopped as a cumbersome tractor-trailer backed out of a construction site, attempting to turn around. A grove of orange trees had just been plowed, probably for a new strip mall. The trailer was open on top, and I could see the stacks of shimmering steel girders. The driver backed up a few feet, and then the trailer swung in the opposite direction, blocking his turn. The workers on the road waved their hands, shouting contradictory instructions: "Pull back a bit." "Swing to the right." "Turn your wheels on a sharp left." The driver edged forward and back, craning his neck out the window, then up toward his rearview mirror, as he tried to extricate himself from the tight spot. The steel girders flashed in the sunlight each time he changed angles. The smell of fresh, damp earth blended with the intoxicating sweetness of the orange blossoms, something I'd never smelled in New York City.

The metallic clanking and the competing shouts, along with the glare of the sunlight and the overpowering fragrance, made me feel heady and somewhat faint. I leaned my head into the steering wheel, and suddenly I saw the hole in Mr. Reston's armor: he had let himself be intubated. This man, who possessed a living will explicitly refusing all life-sustaining procedures, had *voluntarily* allowed a breathing tube to thrust air into his drowning lungs. He had reached for a life preserver.

I picked my head back up, feeling the murkiness begin to clear. Despite all of Wilbur Reston's misgivings and doubts, a desire to live had somehow percolated through.

As I leaned back in my seat, I wondered how that had come to pass. Was it simply the life-grabbing instinct that springs forward in such moments of near doom? Or was it truly evidence of Mr. Reston's ambivalence, of a desire to be saved and cared for?

Clearly, I had no way to know—I doubted if he himself would even know—but it seemed to me that Mr. Reston had given himself permission for a second chance. Now that he had done so, I had the opportunity, perhaps even the obligation, to allow that chance to flourish. If this second chance wasn't nourished, there probably wouldn't be a third. As if to confirm my realization, the tractor-trailer veered to the left and finally pulled itself out of its trap. The traffic snarl cleared, and I jammed on the accelerator, flying down the road with the breath of orange blossoms sweeping against my face.

When his medical condition stabilized, Mr. Reston was involuntarily committed to a VA psychiatric facility. He didn't protest when I informed him. He just nodded his head, his baggy jowls bobbing. During his entire stay, I'd never once met his wife; her occasional visits never seemed to coincide with mine.

The VA doctors assumed care of Mr. Reston, and I had no more contact. The private practice was busy, and I saw many patients every day. My mind was filled with Shana Elron's brittle diabetes and Henry Shaw's uncontrolled hypertension. There was the couple who lived in Pennsylvania during the summer but spent winters down south, and I was helping them coordinate his prostate cancer treatment between the two locations. I had recommitted myself to Spanish and spent my evenings conjugating verbs. I planned to leave for Mexico as soon as this stint in Florida was over, and I wanted to have the conditional tense under my belt. I had to decide if I wanted to start my trip in Guadalajara and end it in Chiapas, or vice versa. Or maybe just fly straight to Oaxaca and enroll in the Spanish school there. And then there was that shell-beach peninsula set against a tangle of mangroves twenty minutes from my hotel which beckoned me every night after work. I soon forgot about Mr. Reston.

Several weeks later, as my assignment in Florida was drawing to a close, some paperwork concerning Mr. Reston's original hospital admission turned up in my office needing a signature. Wilbur Reston's morose face flickered in my mind, and I thought about his miniature doll furniture. I wished I were still his doctor.

Besides giving himself a second chance, Mr. Reston had granted me the opportunity to tease out some of the more subtle aspects of medicine. He forced me to see beyond his imposing résumé of disease to his simple, hurting human self. The patient is not simply the sum of his illnesses, Wilbur Reston taught me. It is far more—blessedly far more—intricate than that.

After a labyrinth of phone calls through the VA bureaucracy, I finally tracked down his psychiatrist. Mr. Reston had just been discharged a few days ago. The psychiatrist described the long weeks and the laborious effort it had required to get Mr. Reston to take responsibility for simple things like brushing his teeth. By the end, though, he was showing up at the group meetings, even if he rarely spoke. Once in a while he even went to arts and crafts. Mr. Reston did not beome an effusive, energetic person, but according to the psychiatrist he no longer actively expressed the wish to die. That was considered a major success. And once he was continue involuntarily hospitalized. He could go home to his wife and no longer suicidal, there was no justification for keeping him with his regular outpatient therapy.

The psychiatrist commiserated with me over the many painful but immutable realities of Mr. Reston's life. A social worker was trying to help Mr. Reston get a new dog—that was about the only thing they could remedy.

I flew to Mexico the following week. In the end I'd decided to fly directly to Oaxaca for a month of Spanish lessons. Afterward I'd trek to Chiapas to see the Mayan ruins. I plunged into my classes, determined not to speak a word of English for six weeks, if that was possible. I rented a room from a family that spoke no English; I purchased Spanish editions of *Jonathan Livingston Seagull* and *The Little Prince* as my reading material; I tried to minimize my social contacts with the other foreigners in my classes and instead hang out at local cafés.

But I still thought about Wilbur Reston and wondered how he was doing. Those thoughts could only be in English. I imagined that he was sitting alone in his house, his wife at yet another volunteer function, his bones still aching, his weak heart preventing him from even getting the mail. But maybe there was now a puppy yapping at his feet, freely dispensing and demanding love. When the headaches and joint pains became overwhelming, maybe Mr. Reston would again consider ending his life. But then he might stop and think: Who would feed the puppy?

Reflections and Responses

1. Consider Danielle Ofri's title for her essay. What two meanings does it possess simultaneously? How are these two meanings in opposition to each other? How are both of these meanings relevant to the essay as a whole?

2. What dilemma prompts Ofri's "epiphany"—the realization that her patient actually has the will to live? How and where does this sudden realization occur? In what ways is the specific context in which the epiphany occurs appropriate? How does it help to trigger the sudden insight?

3. Note the number of times that Ofri imagines her patient's life and activities. Why do you think she does this? Reexamine the final paragraph, for example. How would you evaluate this conclusion? How would a reader know whether it's at all accurate? Do you find the conclusion satisfying from a narrative point of view? Explain why or why not? How else might the essay have ended?

ROGER SCRUTON

A Carnivore's Credo

The debate over meat has most often taken place between ethically motivated vegetarians, who take the view that eating animals is morally wrong, and carnivores, who see it as morally innocuous. Both sides, moreover, have traditionally embraced a "live and let live" ethos. In this essay, the British moral philosopher Roger Scruton turns up the heat under the pan. Scruton suggests that not only is eating meat morally acceptable—it's morally imperative. Scruton draws a distinction between what he calls "pious" and "vicious" animal eating. We've moved away from piety, he writes, because we're alienated from our sources of food: We no longer think about what we're eating or where it comes from, and hence don't appreciate the way proper, humane animal husbandry fits perfectly into the ecosystem. "Anybody who cares for animals," he writes, "ought to see this kind of husbandry as a complex moral good, to be defended, on the one hand, against those who would forbid the eating of meat altogether and, on the other hand, against those carnivores who prefer the unseen suffering of the battery farm and the factory abattoir."

Roger Scruton is a British philosopher, essayist, novelist, and composer. He has written thirty-five books—some on politics, animal rights, aesthetics, and history— others memoirs and novels. His nonfiction works include On Hunting *(1998),* Gentle Regrets *(2005), and* Animal Rights and Wrongs *(2006). He has also written two operas,* The Minister *(1994) and* Violet *(2005). Scruton is considered a conservative philosopher, and campaigned vigorously (and unsuccessfully) to keep fox hunting legal in England. "A Carnivore's Credo" originally appeared in* Harper's Magazine *and was selected by David Foster Wallace for* The Best American Essays 2007.

The treatment of animals, like much else that was once the prerogative of religion, has become a matter of ordinary morality, with no shortage of sermons directed at hunters, fur wearers, and carni-vores by puritans who cannot abide the sight of sinful pleasure. Eating animals has become a test case for moral theory in Western societies. In confronting opponents of meat eating, we find our-selves exploring the grounds of moral judgments and the nature of the beings who make them.

The moral life, I believe, rests on three pillars: value, virtue, and duty. Some hold that all the weight can be made to rest on only one of them: value, according to utilitarians; duty, according to their deontological* opponents. Whether or not any such reduc-tions can be successfully carried out, we cannot give a coherent account of the moral life without doing justice to all the concep-tions that support it—to value, virtue, and duty—and showing their place, for human beings, in the good life.

I have a strong urge to place at the very center of the subject, especially since the subject is our relation to the natural world, an-other aspect of human nature, often left out by the standard treat-ments of ethics: namely, piety. By this I mean a disposition to acknowledge our weak and dependent state and to face the sur-rounding world with due reverence and humility. It is the residue of religion in us all, whether or not we wish to admit it. It is the at-titude that many people—environmentalists, conservationists, and animal welfare activists included—are attempting to recapture in a world where the results of human presumption are so depressingly apparent.

Unlike other animals, we are self-conscious. We do not live, as they do, only in the "world of perception," to use Schopenhauer's† phrase. Our thoughts and feelings range over the actual and the possible, the probable and the necessary, what will be and what ought to be. Upon these basic facts—traditionally summarized by saying we are rational animals—other and more remarkable facts depend. We have moral, aesthetic, and religious experiences; we pray to things visible and invisible; we laugh, sing, and grieve; are indignant, ap-proving, and dismayed. And we relate to one another in a special

---

*utilitarian . . . deontological: Two major schools of thought in the study of ethics. Utilitarians believe that good deeds provide the greatest good to the greatest num-ber; deontologists believe that acts are inherently good or evil.

†Schopenhauer: Arthur Schopenhauer, a nineteenth-century German philosopher.

way. Human beings are actual or potential members of a moral community, regulated by concepts of right and duty, in which each member enjoys sovereignty over his own affairs, so long as he accords an equal sovereignty to others. With all this comes an immense burden of guilt. Morality and self-consciousness set us in judgment over ourselves, so that we see our actions constantly from outside, judged by ourselves as we are by others. We become cut off from our instincts, and even the spontaneous joy of fellowship is diminished by the screen of judgment through which it first must pass.

Animals rescue us from this predicament. Their mute lack of self-consciousness neutralizes our own possession of it and makes it possible to pour out on them the pent-up store of fellow feeling, without fear of reproach. At the same time, we are acutely aware of their moral incompetence. Their affection, if it can be won at all, is easily won, and based on nothing. However much a man may be loved by his dog, this love brings warmth and security but no release from guilt. It implies no moral approval and leaves the character of its object unassessed and unendorsed. For that very reason, a dog is a far easier companion than a person, and the temptation arises to believe that all animals are really like our pets, with the same moral claims and the same need for consideration that characterizes the animals on whom we depend for companionship. That which distinguishes us from animals—our predicament as self-conscious and judging creatures—leads us constantly to discount the difference, to act as though it were a marginal consideration on which nothing hangs when it comes to the real ethical questions.

But the difference comes immediately to life when we consider the question of eating. Whether or not we think eating people is wrong, we do not think it is on a par with eating other animals. We recoil from the idea that human beings might be on the daily menu along with cabbage, chicken, squirrel, and lentils. This brings to the fore the distinction between our attitude toward the human body, even when dead, and our attitude toward the bodies of other animals. Although elephants and dolphins engage in behavior that shows a partial resemblance to our feelings in the presence of the dead, the emotions with which we approach a corpse are emotions that only a self-conscious being can experience and must be characterized in terms such as "awe," "reverence," and "anxiety." They belong to the philosophically neglected realm of the psyche I have called piety. The corpse is not to be carelessly touched, not to be defiled, not to be abused. Its former occupant surrounds it like an aura, demanding to be mourned.

All this you will find beautifully evoked in the scene between Achilles and Priam in the *Iliad,* when the old king comes to beg for Hector's desecrated body. Not all cultures treat this predicament as the Homeric Greeks did, but in all cultures some form of piety is called forth by the human corpse. This is not some arbitrary or dispensable feature of our condition; it is a nonrational consequence of being rational. We can imagine a perfectly good functional justification for these feelings, but it would disappear if we thought of them in purely functional terms. Piety exists only so long as we don't ask the reason why: that, indeed, is its essence—a sense of duty that does not question what it receives as commands.

So far as I know, people do not eat their pets, even when the pets belong to species that are commonly eaten. Pets are honorary members of the human community and enjoy some imagined version of the nimbus that surrounds the human body—the nimbus Michelangelo presented in his versions of the Pietà*. People bury their dogs and cats, often erecting tombstones over their bodies. And even when this seems absurd, some kind of piety is bestowed on an animal whose companionship has been enjoyed when it is a companion no longer.

Pious feelings survive also in the religious prohibitions that attach to the eating of meat. If God takes an interest in what we eat, it can only be because eating and ingesting are acts not only of the body but also of the soul. Yet dietary codes do not prohibit us from defiling the corpses of other animals. They instruct us not to defile *ourselves* by eating what is forbidden. This is further confirmation of the dramatic way in which animals and people are distinguished in our feelings.

The fact that eating, for us, is not what it is for other animals is related to the fact that we are moral beings. Eating has in every

---

*The Pietà:** Michelangelo's Renaissance masterpiece depicts the Virgin Mary holding and mourning the corpse of the executed Jesus. The name means "pity" in Italian.

traditional society been regarded as a social, often religious, act, embellished by ritual and enjoyed as a primary celebration of membership. Rational beings are nourished on conversation, taste, manners, and hospitality, and to divorce food from these practices is to deprive it of its true significance. Rational beings rejoice less in filling themselves than in the sight of food, table, and guests dressed for a ceremonial offering. Their meals are also sacrifices; some anthropologists have argued that the origin of our carnivorous ways lies in the burnt offerings of ancient ritual. At any rate, the giving of food is the core of hospitality.

In the fast-food culture, on the other hand, food is not given but taken. The solitary stuffing of burgers, pizzas, and "TV dinners"; the disappearance of family meals and domestic cooking; the loss of table manners—all these tend to obscure the distinction between eating and feeding. For many people, vegetarianism is a roundabout way of restoring that distinction. Vegetables are gifts of the earth: by eating them we reestablish contact with our roots. They offer a way of reincorporating food into the moral life, hedging it in with moral scruples and revitalizing the precious sense of shame. Meat eating cannot be vindicated without confronting the deep feelings that prompt our dietary habits. The onus lies on the carnivore to show that there is a way of incorporating meat into a life that does not shame the human race, as it is shamed by the solitary "caveman" gluttony of the burger stuffer.

I have hinted that there might be a distinction between virtuous and vicious eating. Virtuous eating involves behavior that is considerate of others and that permits and facilitates the easy continuation of dialogue. Good manners prevent that sudden and disturbing eclipse of the person by the animal, as the fangs sink themselves into the mess on the plate.

It is also a part of virtue to consider what benefits and harms are promoted by your actions—not, I hasten to add, in the manner of the utilitarian, seeking a comprehensive balance sheet of pleasure and pain, but in the manner of the humane person, who wishes to promote kindness and to oppose cruelty—in other words, to promote virtue over vice. The virtue of kindness cannot be understood without also invoking ideas of responsibility, duty, and right. Kindness means treating with gentleness and consideration all those with whom you have dealings, while also fulfilling your obligations toward them. To speak of it brings us to the fundamental question of deontology: What are our obligations, and do they permit us to eat animals?

Animals bred or kept for our uses are not honorary members of the moral community, as pets are. Nevertheless the use we make of them imposes a reciprocal duty to look after them, which spreads forward from the farmer to the slaughterer and from the slaughterer to the consumer, all of whom benefit from these animals and must therefore assume some part of the duty of care. To criticize battery pig farming as violating a duty of care is surely right and proper. But consider the traditional beef farmer, who fattens his calves for thirty months, keeping them on open pasture in the summer and in warm roomy barns in the winter, feeding them on grass, silage, beans, and maize, attending to their ailments, and sending them for slaughter, when the time comes, to the nearby slaughterhouse, where they are instantly dispatched by a humane killer. Such a farmer treats his cattle as well as cattle can be treated, and such animals are as happy as their nature allows. Anybody who cares for animals ought to see this kind of husbandry as a complex moral good, to be defended, on the one hand, against those who would forbid the eating of meat altogether and, on the other hand, against those carnivores who prefer the unseen suffering of the battery farm and the factory abattoir[*].

The relation between man and animal may not always be as harmonious as it appears in children's books devoted to life on the farm, but it is only one feature of the total ecology of the countryside. Traditional livestock farming involves the maintenance of pastureland, properly enclosed with walls or hedges. Wildlife habitats spring up as the near automatic byproducts of the boundaries and shady places required by cattle. This kind of farming has shaped the English landscape, ensuring it retains its dual character as producer of human food and a complex wildlife habitat with a beauty inextricably connected to its multifarious life. In this way, what is, from the point of view of agribusiness, a wasteful use of land becomes, from the point of view of the rest of us, one of the kindest uses of land yet devised. The animal brought to the table will have enjoyed the protection of the one who nurtured him, and

[*]**Abattoir:** A slaughterhouse.

his death will be like the ritual sacrifices described in the Bible and Homeric literature—a *singling out* of a victim for an important office to which a kind of honor is attached.

The real force of the vegetarian argument stems, I believe, from a revulsion at the vicious carnivore: the meat eater as he has evolved in the solipsistic fast-food culture, with the removal of food from its central place in domestic life and the winning of friends. From Homer to Zola, meat has been seen as the primordial gift to the stranger, the eruption into the world of human conflict of the divine spirit of peace. Reduce meat to an object of solitary greed like chocolate and the question naturally arises: Why should *life* be sacrificed just for this?

The question presents a challenge. It is asking the burger stuffer to *come clean:* to show why it is that his greed should be indulged in this way, why he can presume to kill again and again for the sake of a solitary pleasure that neither creates nor sustains any moral ties. To such a question it is always possible to respond with a shrug of the shoulders. But it is a real question, one of many that people now ask, as the old forms of piety dwindle. Piety is the remedy for religious guilt, and to this emotion we are all witting or unwitting heirs. And I suspect people become vegetarians for precisely that reason: by doing so they overcome the residue of guilt that attaches to every form of hubris, and in particular to the hubris of human freedom.

There is, however, a remedy more in keeping with the Judeo-Christian tradition. We should not abandon our meat-eating habits but *remoralize* them, by reincorporating them into affectionate human relations and using them as instruments of hospitality, conviviality, and peace. That was the remedy practiced by our parents, with their traditional "Sunday roast" coming always at midday, after they had given thanks. Those brought up on fast food are not used to making sacrifices: mealtimes, manners, dinner-table conversation, and the art of cookery itself have all but disappeared from their worldview. But all those things form part of a complex human good, and I cannot help thinking that, when added to the ecological benefits of small-scale livestock farming, they secure for us an honorable place in the scheme of things, and neutralize more effectively than the vegetarian alternative our inherited burden of guilt.

I would suggest that it is not only permissible for those who care about animals to eat meat; they have a duty to do so. If meat eating should ever become confined to those who do not care about animal suffering, then compassionate farming would cease. Where there are conscientious carnivores, there is a motive to raise animals kindly. Moreover, conscientious carnivores show their depraved contemporaries that there is a right and a wrong way to eat. Duty requires us, therefore, to eat our friends.

Responses and Reflections

1. Explore the distinction Scruton draws between farm animals and pets. Does he believe eating pets is morally unacceptable? Or simply taboo? What is the difference, under the moral structure he articulates? Do you agree with Scruton when he writes of household pets that "their affection, if it can be won at all, is easily won, and based on nothing"? Why is this contention important to his argument?

2. Scruton writes that "rational beings are nourished on conversation, taste, manners, and hospitality, and to divorce food from these practices is to deprive it of its true significance." What exactly is it that Scruton feels we've lost in our relationship to food? Do you consider this loss real? Why does Scruton feel that vegetarianism is a "roundabout way of restoring" it?

3. "A Carnivore's Credo" describes the process of raising animals for food in an idyllic way. We find farmers raising happy cows, and finally "sending them for the slaughter, when the time comes, to the nearby slaughterhouse, where they are instantly dispatched by a humane killer." Do you agree that farmers treat their cattle "as well as cattle can be treated"? Or is Scruton creating an idealized description of the food chain? Why is this phrasing critical to the argument he is advancing?

PETER SINGER

The Singer Solution
to World Poverty

Philosophy can sometimes be quite practical: the following essay, which argues for our moral responsibility to behave altruistically, even contains two toll-free telephone numbers the reader can use to make a $200 contribution. Peter Singer, the famous and controversial ethical philosopher, sincerely hopes that his argument will convince you to contribute. He reinforces his argument with several intriguing hypothetical situations that put readers in the driver's seat of a moral dilemma. How will you respond? Would you agree not to buy another hooded Gap sweatshirt or that new Jay-Z CD that you don't really need and instead give the money to UNICEF?

Peter Singer was born in Melbourne, Australia, and studied philosophy there and at the University of Oxford. One of the leading thinkers of the animal-rights movement, Singer has written influential books on ethical issues, including Animal Liberation *(1975)*, Practical Ethics *(1979), and* Rethinking Life and Death *(1995). Among his recent publications are* Writings on an Ethical Life *and* A Darwinian Left: Politics, Evolution, and Cooperation, *both of which appeared in 2000;* One World: Ethics and Globalization *(2002);* The President of Good and Evil *(2004);* The Way We Eat *(with Jim Mason, 2006), and* The Life You Can Save: Acting Now to End World Poverty *(2009). He is currently DeCamp professor of Bioethics in the Center for Human Values, Princeton University. "The Singer Solution to World Poverty" originally appeared in* The New York Times Magazine *and was selected by Alan Lightman for* The Best American Essays 2000.

In the Brazilian film *Central Station*, Dora is a retired schoolteacher who makes ends meet by sitting at the station writing letters for illiterate people. Suddenly she has an opportunity to pocket a thousand dollars. All she has to do is persuade a homeless nine-year-old boy to follow her to an address she has been given. (She is told he will be adopted by wealthy foreigners.) She delivers the boy, gets the money, spends some of it on a television set, and settles down to enjoy her new acquisition. Her neighbor spoils the fun, however, by telling her that the boy was too old to be adopted—he will be killed and his organs sold for transplantation. Perhaps Dora knew this all along, but after her neighbor's plain speaking, she spends a troubled night. In the morning Dora resolves to take the boy back.

Suppose Dora had told her neighbor that it is a tough world, other people have nice new TVs too, and if selling the kid is the only way

ERIC FEFERBERG/AFP/Getty Images

she can get one, well, he was only a street kid. She would then have become, in the eyes of the audience, a monster. She redeems herself only by being prepared to bear considerable risks to save the boy.

At the end of the movie, in cinemas in the affluent nations of the world, people who would have been quick to condemn Dora if she had not rescued the boy go home to places far more comfortable than her apartment. In fact, the average family in the United States spends almost one third of its income on things that are no more necessary to them than Dora's new TV was to her. Going out to nice restaurants, buying new clothes because the old ones are no longer stylish, vacationing at beach resorts—so much of our income is spent on things not essential to the preservation of our lives and health. Donated to one of a number of charitable agencies, that money could mean the difference between life and death for children in need.

All of which raises a question: in the end, what is the ethical distinction between a Brazilian who sells a homeless child to organ peddlers and an American who already has a TV and upgrades to a better one, knowing that the money could be donated to an organization that would use it to save the lives of kids in need?

Of course, there are several differences between the two situations that could support different moral judgments about them. For one thing, to be able to consign a child to death when he is standing right in front of you takes a chilling kind of heartlessness; it is much easier to ignore an appeal for money to help children you will never meet. Yet for a utilitarian philosopher like myself— that is, one who judges whether acts are right or wrong by their consequences—if the upshot of the American's failure to donate the money is that one more kid dies on the streets of a Brazilian city, then it is in some sense just as bad as selling the kid to the organ peddlers. But one doesn't need to embrace my utilitarian ethic to see that at the very least, there is a troubling incongruity in being so quick to condemn Dora for taking the child to the organ peddlers while at the same time not regarding the American consumer's behavior as raising a serious moral issue.

In his 1996 book, *Living High and Letting Die,* the New York University philosopher Peter Unger presented an ingenious series of imaginary examples designed to probe our intuitions about whether it is wrong to live well without giving substantial amounts of money to help people who are hungry, malnourished, or dying from easily treatable illnesses like diarrhea. Here's my paraphrase of one of these examples:

Bob is close to retirement. He has invested most of his savings in a very rare and valuable old car, a Bugatti, which he has not been able to insure. The Bugatti is his pride and joy. In addition to the pleasure he gets from driving and caring for his car, Bob knows that its rising market value means that he will always be able to sell it and live comfortably after retirement. One day when Bob is out for a drive, he parks the Bugatti near the end of a railway siding and goes for a walk up the track. As he does so, he sees that a runaway train, with no one aboard, is running down the railway track. Looking farther down the track, he sees the small figure of a child very likely to be killed by the runaway train. He can't stop the train and the child is too far away to warn of the danger, but he can throw a switch that will divert the train down the siding where his Bugatti is parked. Then nobody will be killed—but the train will destroy his Bugatti. Thinking of his joy in owning the car and the financial security it represents, Bob decides not to throw the switch. The child is killed. For many years to come, Bob enjoys owning his Bugatti and the financial security it represents.

Bob's conduct, most of us will immediately respond, was gravely wrong. Unger agrees. But then he reminds us that we too have opportunities to save the lives of children. We can give to organizations like UNICEF or Oxfam America. How much would we have to give one of these organizations to have a high probability of saving the life of a child threatened by easily preventable diseases? (I do not believe that children are more worth saving than adults, but since no one can argue that children have brought their poverty on themselves, focusing on them simplifies the issues.) Unger called up some experts and used the information they provided to offer some plausible estimates that include the cost of raising money, administrative expenses, and the cost of delivering aid where it is most needed. By his calculation, $200 in donations would help a sickly two-year-old transform into a healthy six-year-old—offering safe passage through childhood's most dangerous years. To show how practical philosophical argument can be, Unger even tells his readers that they can easily donate funds by using their credit card and calling one of these toll-free numbers: (800) 367-5437 for UNICEF; (800) 693-2687 for Oxfam America.

Now you too have the information you need to save a child's life. How should you judge yourself if you don't do it? Think again about Bob and his Bugatti. Unlike Dora, Bob did not have to look into the eyes of the child he was sacrificing for his own material comfort. The child was a complete stranger to him and too far away to relate to in an intimate, personal way. Unlike Dora too, he did not mislead the child or initiate the chain of events imperiling him. In all these respects, Bob's situation resembles that of people able but unwilling to donate to overseas aid and differs from Dora's situation.

If you still think that it was very wrong of Bob not to throw the switch that would have diverted the train and saved the child's life, then it is hard to see how you could deny that it is also very wrong not to send money to one of the organizations listed above. Unless, that is, there is some morally important difference between the two situations that I have overlooked.

Is it the practical uncertainties about whether aid will really reach the people who need it? Nobody who knows the world of overseas aid can doubt that such uncertainties exist. But Unger's figure of $200 to save a child's life was reached after he had made conservative assumptions about the proportion of the money donated that will actually reach its target.

One genuine difference between Bob and those who can afford to donate to overseas aid organizations but don't is that only Bob can save the child on the tracks, whereas there are hundreds of millions of people who can give $200 to overseas aid organizations. The problem is that most of them aren't doing it. Does this mean that it is all right for you not to do it?

Suppose that there were more owners of priceless vintage cars—Carol, Dave, Emma, Fred, and so on, down to Ziggy—all in exactly the same situation as Bob, with their own siding and their own switch, all sacrificing the child in order to preserve their own cherished car. Would that make it all right for Bob to do the same? To answer this question affirmatively is to endorse follow-the-crowd ethics—the kind of ethics that led many Germans to look away when the Nazi atrocities were being committed. We do not excuse them because others were behaving no better.

We seem to lack a sound basis for drawing a clear moral line between Bob's situation and that of any reader of this article with
$200 to spare who does not donate it to an overseas aid agency.
These readers seem to be acting at least as badly as Bob was acting
when he chose to let the runaway train hurtle toward the unsus-
pecting child. In the light of this conclusion, I trust that many
readers will reach for the phone and donate that $200. Perhaps
you should do it before reading further.

Now that you have distinguished yourself morally from people who
put their vintage cars ahead of a child's life, how about treating
yourself and your partner to dinner at your favorite restaurant?
But wait. The money you will spend at the restaurant could also
help save the lives of children overseas! True, you weren't planning to blow $200 tonight, but if you were to give up dining out
just for one month, you would easily save that amount. And what is
one month's dining out compared to a child's life? There's the
rub. Since there are a lot of desperately needy children in the
world, there will always be another child whose life you could save
for another $200. Are you therefore obliged to keep giving until
you have nothing left? At what point can you stop?

Hypothetical examples can easily become farcical. Consider
Bob. How far past losing the Bugatti should he go? Imagine that
Bob had got his foot stuck in the track of the siding, and if he diverted the train, then before it rammed the car it would also amputate his big toe. Should he still throw the switch? What if it would
amputate his foot? His entire leg?

As absurd as the Bugatti scenario gets when pushed to extremes,
the point it raises is a serious one: only when the sacrifices become
very significant indeed would most people be prepared to say that
Bob does nothing wrong when he decides not to throw the switch.
Of course, most people could be wrong; we can't decide moral issues by taking opinion polls. But consider for yourself the level of
sacrifice that you would demand of Bob, and then think about how
much money you would have to give away in order to make a sacrifice that is roughly equal to that. It's almost certainly much, much
more than $200. For most middle-class Americans, it could easily
be more like $200,000.

Isn't it counterproductive to ask people to do so much? Don't we run the risk that many will shrug their shoulders and say that morality, so conceived, is fine for saints but not for them? I accept that we are unlikely to see, in the near or even medium-term future, a world in which it is normal for wealthy Americans to give the bulk of their wealth to strangers. When it comes to praising or blaming people for what they do, we tend to use a standard that is relative to some conception of normal behavior. Comfortably off Americans who give, say, 10 percent of their income to overseas aid organizations are so far ahead of most of their equally comfortable fellow citizens that I wouldn't go out of my way to chastise them for not doing more. Nevertheless, they should be doing much more, and they are in no position to criticize Bob for failing to make the much greater sacrifice of his Bugatti.

At this point various objections may crop up. Someone may say, "If every citizen living in the affluent nations contributed his or her share, I wouldn't have to make such a drastic sacrifice, because long before such levels were reached the resources would have been there to save the lives of all those children dying from lack of food or medical care. So why should I give more than my fair share?" Another, related objection is that the government ought to increase its overseas aid allocations, since that would spread the burden more equitably across all taxpayers.

Yet the question of how much we ought to give is a matter to be decided in the real world—and that, sadly, is a world in which we know that most people do not, and in the immediate future will not, give substantial amounts to overseas aid agencies. We know too that at least in the next year, the United States government is not going to meet even the very modest United Nations—recommended target of 0.7 percent of gross national product; at the moment it lags far below that, at 0.09 percent, not even half of Japan's 0.22 percent or a tenth of Denmark's 0.97 percent. Thus, we know that the money we can give beyond that theoretical "fair share" is still going to save lives that would otherwise be lost. While the idea that no one need do more than his or her fair share is a powerful one, should it prevail if we know that others are not doing their fair share and that children will die preventable deaths unless we do more than our fair share? That would be taking fairness too far.

Thus, this ground for limiting how much we ought to give also fails. In the world as it is now, I can see no escape from the conclusion that each one of us with wealth surplus to his or her essential needs should be giving most of it to help people suffering from poverty so dire as to be life-threatening. That's right: I'm saying that you shouldn't buy that new car, take that cruise, redecorate the house, or get that pricy new suit. After all, a thousand-dollar suit could save five children's lives.

So how does my philosophy break down in dollars and cents? An American household with an income of $50,000 spends around $30,000 annually on necessities, according to the Conference Board, a nonprofit economic research organization. Therefore, for a household bringing in $50,000 a year, donations to help the world's poor should be as close as possible to $20,000. The $30,000 required for necessities holds for higher incomes as well. So a household making $100,000 could cut a yearly check for $70,000. Again, the formula is simple: whatever money you're spending on luxuries, not necessities, should be given away.

Now, evolutionary psychologists tell us that human nature just isn't sufficiently altruistic to make it plausible that many people will sacrifice so much for strangers. On the facts of human nature, they might be right, but they would be wrong to draw a moral conclusion from those facts. If it is the case that we ought to do things that, predictably, most of us won't do, then let's face that fact head-on. Then, if we value the life of a child more than going to fancy restaurants, the next time we dine out we will know that we could have done something better with our money. If that makes living a morally decent life extremely arduous, well, then that is the way things are. If we don't do it, then we should at least know that we are failing to live a morally decent life—not because it is good to wallow in guilt but because knowing where we should be going is the first step toward heading in that direction.

When Bob first grasped the dilemma that faced him as he stood by that railway switch, he must have thought how extraordinarily unlucky he was to be placed in a situation in which he must choose between the life of an innocent child and the sacrifice of most of his savings. But he was not unlucky at all. We are all in that situation.

Reflections and Responses

1. Do you find Singer's hypothetical examples convincing? If you place yourself in the situations he describes, do you reach the same conclusions he does? Can you refute his hypothetical situations?

2. At one point, Singer identifies himself as a "utilitarian philosopher," that is, "one who judges whether acts are right or wrong by their consequences." Do you find any limitations with this manner of evaluating right and wrong? Can you rewrite Singer's hypothetical examples in such a way that the "right" decision would perhaps lead to a bad consequence? Suppose, for example, that Bob pulled the switch and saved the boy's life, but another child hiding in the runaway train was killed in the collision with Bob's fancy automobile. Would that child's death be a direct consequence of Bob's apparently generous act? Would criminal charges be filed against Bob? Consider other variations.

3. Note that throughout the essay Singer argues for just one cause—child poverty. Why do you think he chose this and not a different sort of cause? What if he had selected AIDS research or Amnesty International as likely ways to help human suffering? Would these be just as effective? Why or why not? And if you did give your money to relieve child poverty, would you be making a conscious decision NOT to assist the causes of AIDS or cancer research or the Red Cross or any other legitimate charitable organization?

EDWARD O. WILSON

Apocalypse Now

The rift between science and religion has been at the fore of many of the ethical debates of the recent past: from evolution to stem cells. In this brief, epistolary essay, the renowned scientist Edward O. Wilson frames another crucial debate, over the duty we have to protect the natural environment, in terms of this rift. Wilson, a secular humanist, writes to an imaginary Christian pastor, accusing the evangelical Christian movement of not doing as much as secularists to promote environmental consequences—in fact, in some cases Wilson claims evangelicals interpret scripture as an "excuse to trash the planet." But Wilson argues believers and non-believers should take the issue up in common. After all, he says, Christianity has a long tradition of teaching that we are stewards of our increasingly endangered world. He writes: "Earth is a laboratory wherein nature—God, if you prefer, pastor—has laid before us the results of countless experiments. We damage her at our own peril."

Edward O. Wilson is a biologist and author. Among countless accolades, he was named one of America's 25 *most influential people by* Time *magazine in* 1995, *and has won the National Medal of Science (in* 1976) *and two Pulitzer Prizes (in* 1979 *and* 1991). *Wilson, a native of Alabama, was the Pellegrino University Professor at Harvard and is now a member of the National Academy of Science. His many books include* The Insect Societies *(*1971*),* Sociobiology: The New Synthesis *(*1975*),* The Diversity of Life *(*1992*),* In Search of Nature *(*1996*),* Consilience: The Utility of Knowledge *(*1998*), and most recently* The Creation: An Appeal to Save Life on Earth *(*2006*) and* Nature Revealed: Selected Writings *1949–2006.* "Apocalypse Now" *originally appeared in* The New Republic *and was selected by David Foster Wallace for* The Best American Essays 2007.

Dear Pastor,

We have not met, yet I feel I know you well enough to call you a friend. First of all, we grew up in the same faith. As a boy, I, too, answered the altar call; I went under the water. Although I no longer belong to that faith, I am confident that, if we met and spoke privately of our deepest beliefs, it would be in a spirit of mutual respect and goodwill. I know we share many precepts of moral behavior. Perhaps it also matters that we are both Americans and, insofar as it might still affect civility and good manners, we are both Southerners.

I write to you now for your counsel and help. Of course, in doing so, I see no way to avoid the fundamental differences in our world-views. You are a strict interpreter of Christian Holy Scripture; I am a secular humanist. You believe that each person's soul is immortal, making this planet a waystation to a second, eternal life; I think heaven and hell are what we create for ourselves, on this planet. For you, the belief in God made flesh to save mankind; for me, the belief in Promethean fire seized to set men free. You have found your final truth; I am still searching. You may be wrong; I may be wrong. We both may be partly right.

Do these differences in worldview separate us in all things? They do not. You and I and every other human being strive for the same imperatives of security, freedom of choice, personal dignity, and a cause to believe in that is larger than ourselves. Let us see, then, if we can meet on the near side of metaphysics in order to deal with the real world we share. You have the power to help solve a great problem about which I care deeply. I hope you have the same concern. I suggest that we set aside our differences in order to save the Creation. The defense of living nature is a universal value. It doesn't rise from, nor does it promote, any religious or ideological dogma. Rather, it serves without discrimination the interests of all humanity. Pastor, we need your help. The Creation—living nature—is in deep trouble.

Scientists estimate that, if habitat-conversion and other destructive human activities continue at their present rates, half the species of plants and animals on earth could be either gone or at least fated for early extinction by the end of the century. The ongoing extinction rate is calculated in the most conservative estimates to be about 100 times above that prevailing before humans appeared on earth, and it is expected to rise to at least 1,000 times greater (or more) in the next few decades. If this rise continues unabated, the cost to humanity—in wealth, environmental security, and quality of life—will be catastrophic.

Surely we can agree that each species, however inconspicuous and humble it may seem to us at this moment, is a masterpiece of biology and well worth saving. Each species possesses a unique combination of genetic traits that fits it more or less precisely to a particular part of the environment. Prudence alone dictates that we act quickly to prevent the extinction of species and, with it, the pauperization of earth's ecosystems.

With all the troubles that humanity faces, why should we care about the condition of living nature? Homo sapiens is a species confined to an extremely small niche. True, our minds soar out to the edges of the universe and contract inward to subatomic particles—the two extremes encompassing 30 powers of ten in space. In this respect, our intellects are godlike. But, let's face it, our bodies stay trapped inside a proportionately microscopic envelope of physical constraints. Earth provides a self-regulating bubble that sustains us indefinitely without any thought or contrivance of our own. This protective shield is the biosphere, the totality of life, creator of all air, cleanser of all water, manager of all soil—but is itself a fragile membrane that barely clings to the face of the planet. We depend upon its razor-thin health for every moment of our lives. We belong in the biosphere, we were born here as species, we are closely suited to its exacting conditions—and not all conditions, either, but just those in a few of the climatic regimes that exist upon some of the land. Environmental damage can be defined as any change that alters our surroundings in a direction contrary to humanity's inborn physical and emotional needs. We must be careful with the environment upon which our lives ultimately depend.

In destroying the biosphere, we are destroying unimaginably vast sources of scientific information and biological wealth. Opportunity costs, which will be better understood by our descendants than by ourselves, will be staggering. Gone forever will be undiscovered medicines, crops, timber, fibers, soil-restoring vegetation, petroleum substitutes, and other products and amenities. Critics of environmentalism forget, if they ever knew, how the rosy periwinkle of Madagascar provided the alkaloids that cure most cases of Hodgkin's disease and acute childhood leukemia; how a substance from an obscure Norwegian fungus made possible the organ transplant industry; how a chemical from the saliva of leeches yielded a solvent that prevents blood clots during and after surgery; and so on through the pharmacopoeia that has stretched from the herbal medicines of Stone Age shamans to the magic-bullet cures of present-day biomedical science.

These are just a few examples of what could be lost if Homo sapiens pursue our current course of environmental destruction. Earth is a laboratory wherein nature—God, if you prefer, pastor—has laid before us the results of countless experiments. We damage her at our own peril.

You may well ask at this point, *Why me?* Simply because religion and science are the two most powerful forces in the world today, and especially in the United States. If religion and science could be united on the common ground of biological conservation, the problem might soon be solved.

It may seem far-fetched for a secular scientist to propose an alliance between science and religion. But the fact is that environmental activists cannot succeed without you and your followers as allies. The political process in American democracy, with rare exceptions, does not start at the top and work its way down to the voting masses. It proceeds in the opposite direction. Political leaders are compelled to calculate as precisely as they can what it will take to win the next election. The United States is an intensely religious nation. It is overwhelmingly Judeo-Christian, with a powerful undercurrent of evangelism. We secularists must face reality. The National Association of Evangelicals has 30 million members; the three leading American humanist organizations combined have, at best, a few thousand. Those who, for religious reasons, believe in saving the Creation, have the strength to do so through the political process; acting alone, secular environmentalists do not. An alliance between science and religion, forged in an atmosphere of mutual respect, may be the only way to protect life on earth, including, in the end, our own.

Yes, the gulf separating our worldviews is wide. The Abrahamic religions—Judaism, Christianity, and Islam—believe that the universe was constructed to be relevant to humanity. The discoveries of science, in unintended opposition, have reduced earth to an infinitesimal speck within an immensity of space unrelated to human destiny. The Abrahamic religions envisage a supreme ruler who, while existing outside the material universe, nevertheless oversees an agenda for each and every one of our immortal souls. Science can find no evidence of an agenda other than that fashioned by the complex interaction of genes and environment within parallel evolving cultures. Religious creation stories have a divinely engineered beginning and a divinely ordained ending. According to science, in contrast, humans descended from apish ancestors; our origin was basically no different from that of other animals, played out over geological time through a tortuous route of mutation and environmentally driven natural selection. In addition, all mainstream religious belief, whether fundamentalist or liberal, is predicated upon the assumption that humanity is not alone, and we are here for a life and purpose beyond our earthly existence. Science says that, as far as verifiable evidence tells, we are alone, and what significance we have is therefore of our own making. This is the heart of the agonizing conflict between science and religion that has persisted for the past 500 years.

I do not see how the difference in worldview between these two great productions of human striving can be closed. But, for the purposes of saving the Creation, I am not sure that it needs to be. To make the point in good gospel manner, let me tell the story of a young man, newly trained for the ministry and so fixed in his Christian faith that he referred all questions of morality to readings from the Bible. When he visited the Atlantic rainforest of Brazil, he saw the manifest hand of God, and in his notebook he wrote, "It is not possible to give an adequate idea of the higher feelings of wonder, admiration, and devotion which fill and elevate the mind." That was Charles Darwin in 1832, early into the voyage of the HMS *Beagle*, before he had given any thought to evolution. And here is Darwin, concluding *On the Origin of Species* in 1859, having first abandoned Christian dogma and then, with his newfound intellectual freedom, formulated the theory of evolution by natural selection: "There is grandeur in this view of life, with its several powers, having been originally breathed into a few forms or into one; and that, whilst this planet has gone cycling on according to the fixed law of gravity, from so simple a beginning endless forms most beautiful and most wonderful have been, and are being, evolved." Darwin's reverence for life remained the same as he crossed the seismic divide that separated his religious phase and his scientific one. And so it can be for the divide that, today, separates mainstream religion and scientific humanism. And that separates you and me.

Indeed, despite all that divides science from religion, there is good reason to hope that an alliance on environmental issues is possible. The spiritual reach of evangelical Christianity is nowadays increasingly extended to the environment. While the Old Testament God commands humanity to take dominion over the earth, the decree is not (as one evangelical leader recently affirmed) an excuse to trash the planet. The dominant theme in scripture as interpreted by many evangelicals is instead stewardship. Organizations like the Green Cross and the Evangelical Environmental Network (the latter a coalition of evangelical Christian agencies and institutions) are expanding their magisterium to include conservation—in religious terms, protection of the living Creation.

This evangelical interest in the environment is part of a worldwide trend among religions. In the United States, the umbrella National Religious Partnership for the Environment works with evangelical groups and other prominent organizations, including the U.S. Conference of Catholic Bishops, the National Council of Churches of Christ, and the Coalition on the Environment and Jewish Life. In 2001, the Archbishop of Canterbury urged that "it may not be time to build an Ark like Noah, but it is high time to take better care of God's creation." Three years earlier, Bartholomew I, Patriarch of the Greek Orthodox Church, had gone further: "For humans to cause species to become extinct and to destroy the biological diversity of God's creation . . . these are sins." He and Pope John Paul II later issued a "Common Declaration" that "God has not abandoned the world. It is His will that His Design and our hope for it will be realized through our co-operation in restoring its original harmony. In our own time we are witnessing a growth of an ecological awareness which needs to be encouraged, so that it will lead to practical programs and initiatives." Unfortunately, a corresponding magnitude of engagement has not yet occurred in Islam or the Eastern religions.

Every great religion offers mercy and charity to the poor. The poor of the world, of whom nearly a billion exist in the "poverty trap" of absolute destitution, are concentrated in the developing countries—the home of 80 percent of the world's population and most of Earth's biodiversity. The solution to the problems of both depends on the recognition that each depends on the other. The desperately poor have little chance to improve their lives in a devastated environment. Conversely, natural environments, where most of the Creation hangs on, cannot survive the press of land-hungry people who have nowhere else to go.

To be sure, some leaders of the religious right are reluctant to support biological conservation, an opposition sufficient to create a wedge within the evangelical movement. They may be partly afraid of paganism, by which worship of nature supplants worship of God. More realistically and importantly, opposition rises from the perceived association of environmental activism with the political left. For decades, conservatives have defined environmentalism as a movement bent on strangling the United States with regulations and bureaucratic power. This canard has dogged the U.S. environmental movement and helped keep it off the agenda of the past two presidential campaigns.

Finally, however, opinion may be changing. The mostly evangelical religious right, which, along with big business, has been the decisive source of power in the Republican Party, has begun to move care of the Creation back into the mainstream of conservative discourse. The opportunity exists to make the environment a universal concern and to render it politically nonpartisan.

Still, for all the positive signs, I remain puzzled that so many religious leaders have hesitated to make protection of the Creation an important part of their magisterium. Pastor, help me understand: Do they believe that human-centered ethics and preparation for the afterlife are the only things that matter? Do they believe that the Second Coming* is imminent and that, therefore, the condition of the planet is of little consequence? These and other similar doctrines are not gospels of hope and compassion. They are gospels of cruelty and despair.

You and I are both humanists in the broadest sense: Human welfare is at the center of our thought. So forget our disagreements, I say, and let us meet on common ground. That might not be as difficult as it first seems. When you think about it, our metaphysical differences have remarkably little effect on the conduct of our separate lives. My guess is that you and I are about equally ethical, patriotic, and altruistic. We are products of a civilization that rose from both religion and the science-based Enlightenment. We would gladly serve on the same jury, fight the same wars, and sanctify human life with the same intensity. Surely we also share a love of the Creation— and an understanding that, however the tensions play out between our opposing worldviews, however science and religion wax and wane in the minds of men, there remains the earthborn yet transcendental obligation we are both morally bound to share.

Reflections and Responses

1. The title of Wilson's essay alludes to Francis Ford Coppola's 1979 film about the horrors of the Vietnam War. But it also plays on the Christian notion of the end of the world by an act of God (as described in the New Testament book of Revelations; in Greek *Apokalypsis*) and a secular concept of the end of the world by natural deterioration. Find other points in the essay where Wilson deliberately conflates notions from evangelical Christianity with non-Christian ideas. What purpose does this conflation serve?

2. Wilson strikes an ostensibly conciliatory tone throughout the essay, notionally refusing to attack the religious worldview as such.

*The Second Coming: Many evangelical Christians believe that Jesus Christ will return to earth, ending the world as we know it.

But in advancing the environmentalist argument is Wilson subtly putting forward an argument for secular humanism? Locate a few points in the essay in which Wilson doesn't quite follow his own injunction to "set aside our differences in order to save the Creation." What is the effect of these moments?

3. What is the effect of framing this essay as a letter to an "imaginary" Christian pastor? Why didn't Wilson just write a neutral, third person essay in defense of his environmentalism?

INTERVIEW

THE MIND AT WORK: AN INTERVIEW WITH ROBERT ATWAN
BY KYLE GIACOMOZZI AND MATTHEW KEOGH

Robert Atwan *is the series editor of the prestigious annual anthology* The
Best American Essays, *which he founded in 1985. His essays, reviews, and
critical articles have appeared in the* New York Times, *the* Los Angeles
Times, *the* Atlantic Monthly, *the* Iowa Review, *the* Denver Quarterly, *the*
Kenyon Review, River Teeth, *and many other publications. His edited
books include* The Writer's Presence; Popular Writing in America;
America Now; Ten on Ten: Major Essayists on Recurring Themes;
Our Times; Convergences; *and* Left, Right, and Center: Voices from
Across the Political Spectrum. *He served as* director of The Blue Hills
Writing Institute at Curry College from 2002–2008. In January 2009,
Mr. Atwan *invited* **The Bridge** *editors to his home in Milton, MA to gather
around a roaring fire to discuss the art and craft of the essay. Editors Kyle Giacomozzi and Matthew Keogh were in charge of the questions; other editors
participating in the interview included Laura Bowen, Rachael Dunphy, Jil-
lian Moore, Lauren Rheaume, Shannon Rosenblat, and Tara Sullivan. All
of the editors helped maintain the fire.*

*The Bridge is a journal of literature and fine arts produced and man-
aged entirely by students at Bridgewater State College in Bridgewater, Massachusetts. Each year since its inception in 2004, the journal has received a
Crown Award from the Columbia Scholastic Press Association (CSPA) and
a Gold Medal in the CSPA's Annual Critiques (The CSPA is operated by
Columbia University and its Graduate School of Journalism). The Bridge
has also received the coveted Pacemaker Award—widely regarded as the
"Pulitzer Prize" of student publications—from the Associated Collegiate
Press for both its third and fifth volumes, among many other honors. The
interview below appeared in the 2009 issue of The Bridge.*

*Kyle Giacomozzi is a senior at Bridgewater State College majoring in
English with a concentration in Writing. At BSC he worked as an editor on*

volume six of The Bridge. After graduation he intends to join the Peace Corps and hopes to one day earn an MFA in Creative Writing. Matthew Keogh is a double major in Math and English at Bridgewater State College. He served as an editor for The Bridge from 2008–2009 and is the Literature Editor-In-Chief for its seventh volume.

The Bridge: Could you tell us about what your job as series editor entails?

Atwan: There's a guest editor every year and that guest editor is required to read approximately one hundred essays, and then choose about twenty from that pool for the book. So my job is basically to go through all the national periodicals and screen the hundred that I consider best and submit these to that person. To do that, I probably go through about three hundred, three hundred fifty essays, and pick the ones that I think will have the best chance of being selected. The fact is that there aren't a lot of essays published in a given year that are of really high literary quality. So I actually find, say, perhaps sixty really first-rate essays—but we do one hundred because that's sort of a generous sampling and gives the guest editor a chance to look at a variety of topics and forms. But essentially in any give year I think I see only about fifty to sixty really, really solid literary essays.

The Bridge: So why do you think it's so difficult to be published if the quality isn't very high? And does that mean that these periodicals are publishing primarily works that are average or less?

Atwan: The *New Yorker* isn't. It depends on the periodicals that you're looking at. Many periodicals, such as the *Nation,* the *New Republic,* and *Commentary,* are dealing with the political world and not publishing essays, most likely. They're publishing articles, political commentary. When I'm talking about essays I'm referring mainly to the essay as a work of literature. That's what the series is devoted to. The kinds of things that Emerson wrote, Montaigne wrote, Robert Louis Stevenson, E. B. White, Virginia Woolf, James Baldwin. That's a different animal from the general prose you find in most of the magazines, even the *New Yorker.* I want the series to showcase the kind of literary, reflective, personal essay that is a work of literature. There aren't many periodicals that publish these, nor I should add, even want to publish these. Most periodicals are interested in journalism, up-to-date reporting—not literary essays.

The Bridge: Why do you think that is?

Atwan: First of all, it's not their bread and butter and especially not in this economy. *Atlantic*, for example, a terrific magazine, is really interested in informative articles or articles that have some sort of newsy quality. And it's not looking for what magazine editors once called "navel gazing "or "thumb sucking" pieces. They generally, with a few exceptions, want hard news or information or interview material as opposed to a work that demonstrates a literary effort, a clear literary intention. And I'm going to complicate this by saying that so many people are writing memoirs now and many of these memoiristic essays do not qualify for *Best American*. They often seem to be pieces from a longer work or something in progress. I'm finding that a lot of my guest editors would rather have reflective essays, essays *about* something, than the now common "I-I-I-I-I-I." I don't know how many guest editors have said the equivalent of: , "Bob, please don't send me any more essays in which I see the word "I" fifteen times on the first page."

The Bridge: Should young writers avoid writing essays about themselves?

Atwan: No, I wouldn't go that far, and the liberal usage of "I" doesn't mean the piece is bad. Henry David Thoreau used "I" throughout all of his works, but when experiences are entirely mundane and so particularized to an individual, readers will think: "Well you know, why should I care about your experiences unless they translate into something larger that offers me some substance for thought and reflection and experiences that more people can identify with?" I think a big problem with memoirs today is that the writers seem to take a reader's "identification" for granted. Good writing never does that—it earns the reader's identification. When I select the candidates for the volume, I like to see essays contending with a subject. Virginia Woolf, a great essayist, was referring to the essay when she said that "The art of writing has for backbone some fierce attachment to an idea." I'm always looking for essays with "backbone."

The Bridge: Was starting *Best American Essays* as easy? How did you get that off the ground?

Atwan: I was reviewing books then for the *New York Times Book Review* and they sent me *The O'Henry Stories* to review in 1984, I believe it was. It made me wonder why there wasn't a similar book like that for essays. And so I wrote a proposal and after a few rejections a publisher accepted it. But one day the editor said, "Bob, I've got to bring up a sensitive subject. No one likes to use the word 'essay.' Can we call it something else?" I went back and rethought it. God, what else are you going to call it? *Best American Articles* doesn't sound right. *Best American Nonfiction* doesn't sound right. So I told the editor that we were just going to have to take the plunge and use the word 'essay'." And the publishers said, "Okay, we'll take a chance. We'll give you a contract for two years. If at the end of two years, we don't sell anything, we'll kill the series." So I had two years and I made sure the anthology was literary, one that would attract literary people. The first guest editor was Elizabeth Hardwick, a very talented novelist and essayist herself and very prominent in the New York literary world, and the second year I went to Gay Talese, who was considered a founder of new journalism. It worked. After that, about five, six years later I noticed magazines had begun using the word "essay" in their tables of contents. They'd been avoiding the "E-word" because it reminded people of what they had to write in school. The term was used as a pejorative.

The Bridge: In your 2005 foreword, you disclosed your initial uncertainty about the series' longevity. When exactly did you realize that it was here to stay?

Atwan: I guess after about the fifth year I knew it was going to stick around. But the first year was very sketchy. No one knew about it. It didn't get promoted very well. It was a good idea to get Gay Talese to do the second year because that got more attention due to the popularity of literary journalism. And we got some reviews. Anthologies are not often reviewed.

The Bridge: In the same foreword, 2005, you mentioned that going into the second edition you felt like you had boosted the spirit of the essayists. Do you think that was key in getting the material so that you could continue the series?

Atwan: I believe, and many people have told me this, that the series definitely helped re-establish the essay as a literary form. Back in the eighties, very few people considered it to be such, even though there were plenty of talented essayists at work. You would probably be hard pressed if you went into academia, even in the mid-nineties, to find any dissertations, PhD dissertations, on the essay. Very, very few. And yet, in the twentieth century you had incredible essayists. James Baldwin, one of the greatest American essayists, received at first little attention for his nonfiction. Now, however, he's read primarily as an essayist. The essay was, through almost all the twentieth century, the form in which you wrote criticism about fiction, poetry, drama. You didn't write about other essays. Let's put it this way, the essay had no critical stature. In a literature course, you studied twentieth-century American poetry, or you studied the nineteenth-century Victorian novel, or you studied the history of drama or Shakespeare or Milton. You did not have a course called The History of the Essay.

In my graduate school you read Ralph Waldo Emerson, but you did not read him as an essayist. Nobody even talked about him as an essayist. They talked about him as a great American writer or thinker, as a great influence. They talked about his prose. But they never discussed his genre or his craft. And this neglect of criticism kept the essay in the dark for a long time because it was considered a fourth genre. E. B. White once said that because he wrote essays he was a second-class citizen in the republic of letters. There could be no Nobel Prize for him, since he wasn't a dramatist, a poet, or a novelist. Those are the three genres. In the 1950s, one of the most important books of criticism at the time, *The Theory of Literature,* opened with a statement that implicitly defined literature as poems, plays, and novels. It seems that around that time the essay was no longer being taken seriously as literature.

Yet when Fielding wrote *Tom Jones,* one of the great novels of the eighteenth century, he inserted essays between chapters every now and then throughout the book. And you know why he did that? He did it to prove he was a writer. Because he thought that anybody could write a novel. "I'm going to show you how I can *really* write by including these essays," he seemed to be saying. In the eighteenth century, the essay was considered a serious literary endeavor by many.

The Bridge: Now *The Best American Essays* is regarded as the most important anthology of its kind. But lately, a few others have sprouted up, such as Lee Gutkind's *Best Creative Nonfiction*. What do you think sets BAE apart from all the others?

Atwan: It's really more dedicated to the essay as a work of literature than to nonfiction prose in general. And so the essay—its structures, its various types, the way that the author's mind works inside the essay—these literary matters are all very important to the series. Whereas in creative nonfiction anthologies there are often lots of narrative memoirs, personal narratives, expository narratives, and so on, which years ago would not have been considered essays. So I think the series is distinguished by its dedication to looking at the essay as a craft and as a serious aesthetic form. Still, I try to concentrate on three types of essays: the personal essay, which overlaps with autobiography and memoir; the informative essay, in which you're reading something that's really well written and well done but you're gaining information at the same time; and the polemical essay, which is your argumentative piece, but done in a way that you can still see, in a sense, the mind at work. Each volume of *The Best American Essays* usually consists of a mix of these three types of essays.

The Bridge: Can you elaborate on "the mind at work"?

Atwan: The essayist takes a topic and looks at it the way, say, a cubist painter looks at objects, from all different kinds of angles and perspectives. Good essayists are able to do this, to make you see the mind in process. One of the biggest problems I've found when you teach freshman composition is that students have very little sense of process, so they think that they have to begin a paper with their conclusion, then in the middle part support the conclusion, and then, well . . . conclude. Writing essays isn't necessarily about coming to a conclusion. Few students know how to show a mind reflecting on something and evaluating it as it's in process. Students are rarely taught this nor exposed to appropriate models of writing to gain appreciation for the process. But that's what Montaigne did as an essayist, it's what so many great essayists have done, and so the models are out there, but the models students follow these days are driven by news and commentary. There's one thing you can never say to a talented essayist, and it's "What's your point?" Because a good essayist is going to say: "Wait, there isn't necessarily a single point here. I'm looking at a whole bunch of things." But in freshman composition, the worst way writing can be taught in my opinion is by asking students to write five paragraphs that add up to a single point. Perhaps it has its functional use—writing as utility, so to speak. But the results won't duplicate the literary essay or the way the essayist's mind operates.

The Bridge: How do you define the essay?

Atwan: I've been trying to define it for a long time. The attempt now strikes me as an unsatisfying enterprise. It's like defining anything. If you try to define the novel your definition leaves out seven different kinds of novels. Just try defining poetry. Basically, briefly, the essay to me is a literary form that's marked by a mind in the process of its own unfolding.

The Bridge: How do you define creative nonfiction?

Atwan: I never was sure what that was. It's a term of convenience, I think. The term I first used was "literary journalism." That was the term that everybody used back in the sixties and early seventies. It's an umbrella term that also includes "literary nonfiction," but it isn't necessarily essayistic. Literary journalism or nonfiction could be a long book by Tracy Kidder on how people build houses. John McPhee has written probably twenty-five to thirty books of nonfiction, but he has published only a handful of essays in his entire career, and he would acknowledge that. Literary nonfiction and creative nonfiction are very topic driven. They—and I'll use the terms interchangeably—consist of interviews, profiles, information-gathering. They involve a lot of skillful reporting techniques. But these are done in a much more literary fashion than standard journalism, which is trying hard not to be too literary. John McPhee, for example, might choose salmon as a topic, perhaps seeking to discover why salmon is now a major part of American cuisine, which it didn't used to be. And then he would go research the history of salmon, visit rivers and fishermen, and conduct interviews and then he'd craft all of the information he's gathered into a prose narrative. He called his course at Princeton "The Literature of Fact" and that's not an essayistic method. He's collecting facts and then orchestrating and choreographing them into prose in the best possible way, but his own mind in action isn't a significant part of his writing process as he's doing it. The subjective mental process is largely eliminated. He's giving you this factual, objective, treatment of a subject. Still, he truly cares about the *form* in in*form*ation.

The Bridge: And so the essay and creative nonfiction are not synonymous?

Atwan: Not really. Creative nonfiction could refer to a three hundred page book. That's not an essay. *Walden* is not an essay. *Walden* is a nonfiction book, although you probably could make a case that the basic structures behind it are essays. Creative nonfiction just became a popular term to encompass the literary nonfiction that was coming from the new journalism. Quite a few really good writers back in the sixties and seventies, Tom Wolfe, Gay Talese, Lillian Ross, Hunter Thompson, began developing this form of reporting that was very personalized and impressionistic. It got them in a lot of trouble because the older and more traditional journalists couldn't stand it. And there were some knotty legal problems because most people assume nonfiction is true.

The Bridge: Isn't it?

Atwan: One of the biggest issues when you're writing nonfiction is that you have to think about what it is that we can't know. The New Journalists were doing things that seemed overly impressionistic and subjective, and Tom Wolfe was at the forefront of that. There was steady criticism, but that work really took off because it was so much more entertaining and more fun to read than the standard fare. But people lost jobs along the way, especially newspaper columnists when they began making things up. By the eighties and nineties, there was a lack of tolerance for these kinds of columns as opposed to what had been the case in the past. The essay has been damaged by this, in my opinion, because essayists no longer feel comfortable inventing characters and situations.

The Bridge: Was there a time when they were comfortable doing this?

Atwan: In the eighteenth century, when the essay was considered a solid literary form, Addison and Steele, Samuel Johnson, and Oliver Goldsmith were among the chief practitioners, and they had enormous influence on America's first major literary essayist, Washington Irving. None of these writers had problems with making up stuff, even though they were writing for newspapers. No one said, "You can't say that without documentation or without two witnesses, etc." The audience was sophisticated enough to know there may be made-up characters and situations. We've reached this real problem, I think, with writing essays, and now with memoirs, always demanding to know if something is true or not. If you're writing something that's verifiable, you better be careful. But if it isn't, you have some creative room.

The Bridge: In the wake of the whole James Frey debacle.

Atwan: These liberties with factuality were going on long before he was born. But because Oprah went overboard with that book it created so much more publicity. Now there's a new memoir scandal. Did you see the news about the Holocaust story? [*Angel at the Fence*, by Herman Rosenblat.]

The Bridge: It's about the little girl with the apples. She would bring him apples and then they met in America and they got married.

Atwan: Now, what they said in the *Times* the other day is that they're now not going to publish it as a memoir. It's going to be published as a novel. And you think, "Wait a minute, someone writes a memoir, some parts are discovered untrue and then suddenly the same work can be called a novel?" What happened to art forms? Can you simply say, "I wrote a work of nonfiction but it had some fictional details, so now it's a novel?" What talented writer would imagine that you could do that? The novel is an art form. It's a literary form that is a complex and extremely difficult thing to do. You don't just write a nonfiction narrative and say, "Oops, it's not all true, so now I'll just call it a novel." These stories just show us how little critical judgment the public possesses. It's too bad Americans as a whole aren't better readers.

The Bridge: But if you write a nonfiction piece and it's not one hundred percent true, what would you call it? Does nonfiction equal "not true," and, if it's not true, doesn't "not true" equal fiction?

Atwan: Ah, now you're getting at the heart of the problem, the heart of darkness, actually. It's really tough to get into that. I think we need to return to a notion of the essay that allows for fictive or say semi-fictive characters, situations, and events. Humorous essays do this frequently. I find David Sedaris's autobiographical humor hilariously funny but does anyone think he's not exaggerating and bending facts and situations for comic purposes? One of the greatest essays in American literature is Hawthorne's preface to *The Scarlet Letter*, in which he writes about finding an actual scarlet letter used by Puritan officials in his office drawer, and that's how the famous novel comes into being. Well, that never happened. Now, does that automatically make his essay a short story?

The Bridge: If you are about to go to press with *Best American Essays* and someone called you and said, "I confess, everything in my essay is made up," what would you do?

Atwan: Well, that of course would depend on what's at stake— libel? Hurtful lies? But generally I would encourage my publisher to go with it if I thought it could still be regarded as an essay. To me it's an issue of form and genre, not truthfulness. Why couldn't someone write an essay about intelligent life on Mars even if we don't have proof there is such life on Mars—couldn't there be a speculative essay? Logical inconsistency can also be considered untruthful, but if you found such inconsistency in a political essay would you then conclude it's therefore not an essay but a fiction? That would be nutty, no? But anyway my publisher would most likely get nervous and say no. When I was working with Joseph Epstein on *Best American Essays 1993* I came across an unlabeled piece and I couldn't tell whether it was fiction or nonfiction. I assumed it was fiction, because the author was a prominent short-story writer, but it turned out to be nonfiction. And I remember Joe said something to the effect: "Well, if it were a story it would have been a real good one, but as an essay it stinks." I thought that his remark underscored the importance of artistic criteria. A piece can't just interchangeably move between the two genres.

As I mentioned, Addison and Steele represent the origins of the modern essay. They wrote for a newspaper and they used fictional characters and fictional events. There are responses to fictional letters that would come in from so-called readers who were also fictional. Now, what do we call what they wrote? They have never been known as short story writers. There wasn't even a genre called the "short story" then. When the modern essay began its course in the eighteenth century with the great English periodical essayists and then was carried on into the nineteenth century by some American essayists—there was no short story. The short story evolved long after the essay. Writers like Washington Irving and Nathaniel Hawthorne developed the short story as they experimented with various kinds of essays. Writers at the time often called what they were doing tales and sketches. Hawthorne and Irving referred to their collections as "Tales and Sketches."

The Bridge: I want to follow up on something you said a short while ago, that most readers assume that nonfiction is true. What should writers of nonfiction assume when they start writing in the genre? Should they assume that they are obligated to tell the truth? Or should they understand that maybe truth isn't relevant in nonfiction?

Atwan: Truth is a big, troublesome word. I think if you're looking at what the truth is that you need to think more along the lines of literature than contemporary journalism. But literary truth isn't veracity and accuracy and all the things you're told in J-school or a court of law. What Hawthorne would consider the truth would be the truth of the human heart. If he were writing an essay, he wouldn't be bothered by inventing a character or a composite character he might meet during a leisurely walk. I imagine very few readers at the time were going to say, well, Mr. Hawthorne Liar you never met that person, you're just making that person up. Unless he was referring to a specified and named individual, readers would understand the literary or compositional purpose of the made-up character. Today, we live in a much different literary world. Anyway, I will just come back to this point: I think you can do anything you want to do in nonfiction as long as you don't cross the line and present information as fact that somebody can challenge and establish as false. Then you get into trouble.

The Bridge: So would you say the truth is a lie you can get away with?

Atwan: I'm not saying that's the truth. I'm saying that in writing you can get away with things because who's going to say you aren't telling the exact truth. You may know you aren't but who else knows? And what does it matter? Virginia Woolf's "Death of the Moth" is a wonderful essay, one of her classics. Did she really watch a moth dying on her windowsill that lovely September afternoon? Virginia was there with a moth and that moth was dying all the time? And did it look just like that and was she really watching out this window, or was she thinking that morning, you know "I'd like to write an essay about a moth that sort of dies because I saw one yesterday and now I'm going to set it in my window and . . . "Who can tell? Who knows? So, are we supposed to then say, no that's not an essay because we didn't know it happened, we can't prove it happened? If her husband wrote in his journal: "I was home with Virginia that afternoon, and now and then I peeked into her study and she was writing away. But let me go on record to say that it was a rainy day, not a sunny day, and, second, there was no moth." So if a scholar discovered this testimony tomorrow in a newly found journal of her husband's, would a classic English essay suddenly be eliminated from the history of the essay because the event as she describes it apparently didn't happen? What can we say other than that we don't know whether some of the things we read happened or not.

The Bridge: So a writer of nonfiction should not be constrained by fact?

Atwan: I think a writer of nonfiction is constrained by fact. But verifiable facts. It may be that if no one can verify something it doesn't qualify as a fact. These are muddy waters.

The Bridge: So, if it's not verifiable, then you can get away with lying and no one can say you're lying? But is there any kind of moral obligation to tell the truth, just for your own sake, with your own writing?

Atwan: I'm not someone to dictate moral obligations. Those should be for an individual writer to decide. Yet remember one thing—in a very real sense, just transcribing actual physical events into words entails some degree of falsification—of time sequence, specific details, perspective, and so on. Writers of memoirs seem often to recall what others said to them when they were six years old—do you believe this dialogue is accurate?

The Bridge: Should we say that putting things in nonfiction that did not happen is the equivalent of leaving things out that did?

Atwan: I've got to think that through. That's a very good question. I suppose the answer would involve the old sins of commission as opposed to the sins of omission. But yes, memoirs very often commit sins of omission. My favorite examples have to do with celebrity memoirs where there is so much left out because the celebrity is trying to write a success story. And every celebrity—no matter what field they're in—wants their fans to believe that their success is self-made. They didn't become a success because they had a parental connection that got them into Yale and then that connection helped them get their first job and then one day help them get elected President. Those connections are not going to be a main feature of the autobiography. They're going to be either eliminated or glossed over. The message is: "I made it on my own." That's just one example of omission that I find frequently.

The Bridge: Hopefully we'll get an in-depth answer out of a very simple and our next to last question: What should we write about?

Atwan: Don't always write about what you know. In the first issue of *Best American Essays 1986*, there is a great essay, one of the best in the whole series and I was so happy to have it, by Donald Barthelme—a great short story writer. He died years ago. His essay is called "Not-Knowing," and it's about the importance of seeking rather than having knowledge. Some of the best writing is by people who are struggling with understanding something. That's what the essay is really all about.

Many of us operate under two very questionable principles: (1) we should write about what we know best, and (2) since we know ourselves best we would write best if we write about ourselves. Both of these seem bogus to me.

The Bridge: Final question. Do you have anything else you'd like to share with our readers?"

Atwan: "Oh, no . . ., we covered so much! It was invigorating intellectually. A lot of things I hadn't thought of. Thanks for the opportunity and thanks for keeping the fire going.

The Bridge: Thank you for inviting us.

CREDITS